W9-BLF-229

Harvard Studies in Business History XXIII

EDITED BY RALPH W. HIDY
Isidor Straus Professor of Business History

Graduate School of Business Administration
George F. Baker Foundation
Harvard University

Boston Capitalists and Western Railroads

A Study in the Nineteenth-Century Railroad Investment Process

Arthur M. Johnson and
Barry E. Supple

Harvard University Press
Cambridge, Massachusetts 1967

Distributed in Great Britain by Oxford University Press, London

Library of Congress Catalog Card Number 67-13254

Printed in the United States of America

Foreword

In 1957 when Dean Teele invited me to come to the Harvard Business School, he asked what I considered my most important task in developing the study of business history. I thought that the School should demonstrate, as soon as possible, the potential breadth and depth of the field. To achieve that goal, two courses of action seemed essential: first, to fuse the ideas and contributions of N. S. B. Gras and his associates with those of other historians, notably the group led by Arthur H. Cole in the Center for Research in Entrepreneurial History; second, to show by example of research and publication that business history encompassed more than the histories of individual firms, even though they were in fact the basic units in the business sector of the economy.

From the beginning it was recognized that a generation would probably be required to realize the first objective, but that movement toward the second could be initiated much sooner. Through a fellowship program and other aids the Harvard business historians encouraged young scholars to engage in studies of a significant segment of small business enterprises in New England, of cotton textile trade associations, of factors in the longevity of New England financial institutions, and of changing business morality in the nineteenth and early twentieth centuries. More pertinent to the book at hand, shortly after Arthur Johnson came to the School in 1958 I suggested that he and Barry Supple, then a member of the School faculty, might together produce an example of the possible topics for business historians to tackle. After considering several proposals, the three of us decided that an investigation of a topic that I had suggested and discussed with Dean Teele — "Policies and Practices of Boston Investors in the Development of the Trans-Allegheny West" — would be suitable and would allow Mr. Johnson and Mr. Supple, as joint authors, to use extensive documentary materials in Baker Library and other institutions in the Boston area.

As the present title indicates, the project underwent a metamorphosis over the course of time. After research and discussions, the authors and I gradually narrowed the scope of the inquiry and evolved a conceptualization giving significant meaning, we hope, to this undertaking.

The emphasis of the resulting study is on a continuing process of interaction among different types of men and between them and their environment. The comparative approach, the conception of history as a process shaped by human decisions, and the explicit use of a conceptual framework in dealing with men and events are evidences of the authors' desire to build on, yet advance, the methodology employed in past business history. By applying this approach to such an important topic as nineteenth-century railroad investment, they have shed new light on a dynamic element of American economic development.

I have enjoyed the learning experience afforded by working with these two perceptive scholars, and with confidence I submit the fruits of their labors to historians of the American scene.

Ralph W. Hidy
Editor

Graduate School of Business Administration
Harvard University
September 1966

Preface

IN THIS book we have endeavored to present an interpretation of the investment process in terms of men whose decisions significantly influenced American economic growth in the nineteenth century. By adopting this approach, we have demonstrated our belief that the history of business comes back, in the last analysis, to individuals who see new ways of making their capital, or that of others, productive in a constantly changing environment to which their decisions contribute. We started with the possessors of capital — for the most part obtained from trade — who viewed from Boston the early territorial and industrial expansion of the economy based on the application of new technology to transportation and manufacturing. The bulk of the capital of these Bostonians went into railroads, more particularly into railroads west of the Alleghenies. From this commitment flowed many consequences of importance to the nation as well as to the investors. In the end Boston influence figured significantly in several of the major railroad systems of the American West, but the ways in which this influence was exercised changed markedly with the passage of time. The processes by which these changes came about are a matter of concern to us and, we hope, to the reader seeking insights into the interaction of capitalists and their environment in an era of rapid economic growth.

This study is intended to be suggestive rather than definitive. The fact that we chose Boston as the capital center from which to view the nineteenth-century investment process was mainly related to our own physical location and the consequent availability of primary materials. We did not anticipate the extent to which Bostonians would be found to have engaged in western railroad enterprises. We therefore expect that comparable research on other eastern capital centers would be equally or more rewarding and would reveal patterns of individual involvement and expanding commitment similar to those we have traced for Bostonians. An important purpose of this book is to encourage such endeavors so that we may know more about the processes by which capitalists activated and operated the financial network that underpinned the steam transportation revolution and transformed the economic role of the trans-Allegheny West in the nineteenth century.

Although the quantitative importance of railroads to economic growth in this country has been recently challenged, the argument does not challenge the importance of transportation to the growth of the economy. If anything, it lends additional significance to the task of determining *why* and *how* capitalists identified the course of economic growth and a return to their capital with the railroad sector. These questions are a central concern for this study.

Both authors have participated in the writing of all chapters of this book. To the extent that there has been a division of labor, the first of the undersigned concentrated on the Boston background, the Forbes group of investors, and the Union Pacific. The second covered the China trade background and Boston involvement in the Illinois Central and the Atchison, Topeka & Santa Fe. Professor Ralph W. Hidy played an important role in the conception of the project, in guiding research, and in editing the resulting manuscript. Miss Josepha Perry and Miss Marian Sears made major contributions to the research effort. Miss Perry and Mrs. Nell Strachan did a painstaking job of editorial comment and footnote checking. Miss Ruth Cohen, Miss Janet McMahon, Miss Susan Foley, and Mrs. Joan Parker patiently typed numerous drafts. To them, to the Harvard Business School Divisions of Manuscripts and Research, and to a number of scholars who commented on the manuscript at various stages in its preparation we are deeply grateful. For the errors that remain we are jointly and severally responsible.

Arthur M. Johnson
Barry E. Supple

Graduate School of Business Administration
Harvard University

School of Social Studies
University of Sussex
September 1966

Contents

Tables

Maps

PART I Introduction

Chapter 1

The Problem and Its Setting

THIS STUDY examines the evolution of investment policies, attitudes, and achievements of a small number of nineteenth-century capitalists whose roots and capital, strengths and weaknesses, were tied to Boston's mercantile heritage. In reasonably well-defined groups these individuals became involved with various related ventures, particularly railroads, in the trans-Allegheny West. We seek to analyze, on a comparative basis, the process by which capital, mobilized or controlled in Boston, was allocated to, and managed in, an important sector of the economy over a considerable period of time. Within the limits of the evidence on the activities of a small number of men, this is therefore a study of one aspect of the process of economic development.

THE CONTEXT OF THE STUDY

The spectacular development of the American economy in the nineteenth century took place on many levels. While population multiplied, its geographical distribution underwent a radical shift and new occupational patterns emerged. New sources of natural wealth were opened up, and the structure of economic life was transformed. In 1800 the United States was a land of some 5,300,000 people, still struggling to establish a national identity. One hundred years later the continental United States had more then tripled in area and contained some 76,000,000 people. A trading and frontier nation at the beginning of the century, this country produced 30 per cent of the world's manufactures at the end of it.

These transformations, and the vast increases in the production of goods and services that accompanied them, occurred neither continuously nor uniformly. For example, after 1812 New England underwent a minor but significant Industrial Revolution, and the South in the 1820's and 1830's benefited from a surge in the overseas and domestic demand for cotton. After the setback of the late 1830's, there was a more general spurt of economic activity in the country as a whole, sustained by prior as well as contemporaneous investment in canals, turnpike roads, railroads, banks, insurance companies, western lands, domestic trade, and manufacturing. In the twenty years before 1860 the railroad network grew from 3,000 to over 30,000 miles, the output of wheat and corn more than doubled, that of cotton and pig iron almost tripled, and the production of coal increased almost ninefold.[1] The rate of expansion slowed down in the Civil War, but in the subsequent years another burst of economic development occurred — for all important sectors in the late 1870's and early 1880's, particularly for manufacturing through the 1880's.[2] By the latter decade, although primary production generally boomed, manufacturing industry overtook agriculture in importance.

The opening up and settlement of western lands played an important role in the nineteenth-century development of the United States. One obvious result was the westward shift of the American people: in 1800 the states along the eastern seaboard contained 92.5 per cent of the population; by 1900 they contained only 41.3 per cent of a population that had grown more than fourteenfold. The accompanying changes in regional population distribution are more precisely shown in Table 1. Implicitly, these changes reflect vast increases in the supply of wheat, corn, livestock, and other agricultural products, as well as lumber, lead, iron ore, copper, and other raw materials — in short, the underpinnings of economic growth of the West.

The development and growth of the western primary-producing economy is, in itself, a significant field for historical study, if only because of its size within the national economy. However, it is obvious that the West had far more than a regional importance. The continuing existence of a moving frontier and the maturing of regions rich in natural resources were factors that dominated American growth trends for much of the nineteenth century.

It is not difficult to see why this should have been so. First, by virtue of the West's natural resources, its direct contribution to the nation's material wealth increased. More goods were made available for both the domestic market and for export, which facilitated the purchase of goods and services that other countries were able to produce more efficiently than the United States. Second, these increased supplies were forthcoming at lower real costs. Areas of great

TABLE 1. Percentage distribution of population in the United States by region, 1800–1900 (rounded to nearest percent).

Region[a]	1800	1820	1840	1860	1880	1900
N.E. & Middle Atlantic	50	45	40	34	29	28
South Atlantic	43	32	23	17	15	14
South Central	6	14	18	18	18	19
East North Central	negl	8	17	22	22	21
West North Central	—	negl	2	7	12	14
Mountain & Pacific	—	—	—	2	4	4
Total population (thousands)	5,308	9,638	17,069	31,443	50,156	75,995

[a] The composition of the regions is as follows: N.E. & Middle Atlantic — Connecticut, Maine, Massachusetts, New Hampshire, New Jersey, New York, Pennsylvania, Rhode Island, and Vermont; South Atlantic — Delaware, District of Columbia, Florida, Georgia, Maryland, North Carolina, South Carolina, Virginia, and West Virginia; South Central — Alabama, Arkansas, Kentucky, Louisiana, Mississippi, Oklahoma, Tennessee, and Texas; East North Central — Illinois, Indiana, Michigan, Ohio, and Wisconsin; West North Central — Iowa, Kansas, Minnesota, Missouri, Nebraska, North Dakota, and South Dakota; Mountain & Pacific — Arizona, California, Colorado, Idaho, Montana, Nevada, New Mexico, Oregon, Utah, Washington, and Wyoming.

Source: U.S. Bureau of the Census, *Statistical Abstract of the United States, 1941* (Washington, D.C., 1942), 4–5.

natural wealth were exploited at a time when technological aids to agricultural production were being steadily improved. An increasing proportion of the labor force was therefore freed for manufacturing and service industries,[3] and productivity in the primary industries augmented the supply of cheap food and raw materials available to the growing industrial and urban sectors. Third, the long-run expansion of settlement in the West generated a sustained upward spiral of investment and income.[4] On the one hand, rising western incomes induced waves of local investment in facilities and overhead capital, which in turn generated more income and a demand for further investment. On the other hand, the accelerated growth of income and investment in the West increased the demand for eastern commodities, principally manufactures. This, in its turn, induced a further round of investment and income growth in the older, more industrialized states.

Of course, to understand properly the function of western expansion in national development, it would be necessary to take account of a host of factors: savings, the supply of capital, the actual processes of investment, social institutions and the political environment, entrepreneurial ability, the labor supply and technological innovation, the structure of business and markets, and other factors. However, we shall not undertake the sort of analysis that would involve an extensive discussion of the interrelationship of all such elements in the total process of economic expansion. Instead, we have isolated one aspect of the growth mechanism that we consider to have been of great significance — investment in railroads.

Railroads and Economic Growth

It has been an article of faith with most, if not all, writers on the subject that the railroad was an indispensable element in the economic expansion of this country and particularly of its western regions. Recently, however, the whole question of the relationship between railroads and economic growth has been reopened and extensively discussed. The great significance of these studies is that they have not been content with impressionistic generalizations but have tried systematically to discuss and to measure the various economic consequences of railroad construction and operation.[5]

One of the most important results of these efforts has been the downgrading of the importance of the railroad's *direct* contribution to economic growth in this country — that is, the lowering of railroad costs compared with other means of transportation. For example, with regard to the transportation of agricultural commodities, Robert Fogel has concluded that in 1890* there was an upper limit to the social savings attributable to the railroad of well under $100,000,000 for interregional trade and some $337,000,000 for intraregional trade. These amounts are, respectively, less than 1 per cent and just under 3 per cent of 1890 Gross National Product. Since the contemporary annual growth rate of GNP exceeded these combined percentages, they are not very impressive. Furthermore, for *all* commodities Fogel estimates a saving of under 5 per cent of Gross National Product.

Fogel reaches these conclusions by a meticulous and ingenious measurement of the actual costs of transporting agricultural com-

* On the whole, there is little reason to imagine that the direct social savings attributable to the railroads before 1890 would have exceeded the savings in that year.

modities and of the hypothetical costs of transporting them without the help of railroads — that is, by road, canal, river, and lake. The difference is presumably a rough measure of the direct social saving attributable to the railroad. As Fogel indicates, however, this estimate contains a distinct upward bias, since it assumes that neither the pattern of production nor the network of non-railroad transportation would have been adjusted to the absence of the railroad. Therefore, adjusting for the land that might have gone out of cultivation as a result of the disappearance of the railroad from intraregional trade, he estimates a direct social saving in the intraregional agricultural trade of only $248,000,000, or 2.1 per cent of GNP. In addition, he points out that the problems involved in adapting the transportation network to the hypothetical absence of the railroad by the extension and more intensive use of alternative modes of transport were not intrinsically very great. Therefore, the real social savings might have been significantly below those already quoted.

Albert Fishlow has made an analysis and estimates for an earlier period that is more relevant to our present purposes. In 1859, he concludes, social savings attributable to railroads amounted to about $175,000,000 in the carriage of *all* types of freight and of passengers. This figure represents roughly 4 per cent of the contemporaneous GNP. As he points out, however, the estimate for 1859 is an exaggeration of the true direct benefits of the railroad over the whole prewar period since it ignores both the situation in the decades prior to 1859 and the scale of railroad investment, relative to alternative uses of capital, required to produce this contribution to the National Product. An adjustment in the light of these considerations would scale down his estimate of social savings.

Such findings obviously challenge the argument that American railroads, because of the direct benefits of their low rates, were "indispensable" to nineteenth-century growth.* Even on the most generous assumptions it would seem that the railroads' reduction in transportation charges was not in itself immediately "crucial" to the general pattern and the broad trend of economic development in the West — or, indeed, in the country as a whole.

* Fishlow also points out that since there were abundant unemployed resources in the immediate prewar period, the *real* cost of doing without railroads (of providing alternative transportation or extra production) would have been reduced even further.

But one should not jump to the erroneous conclusion that the railroads were unimportant to American economic growth or that the relevant entrepreneurial and investment processes were insignificant. First, the railroad's primary benefits by no means exhaust its possible economic consequences, some of which are not susceptible to quantitative measurements. Second, despite the existence of alternatives, railroad transportation in fact did make a contribution to, and was an integral part of, the process of American economic development. Third, the application of capital and enterprise to western railroads, even admitting the Fogel and Fishlow qualifications, can still serve as a meaningful example of investment based on the indisputably crucial role of *transportation* in America's development. These points can be briefly dealt with in turn.

Fishlow examines and illuminates the first point in great detail. He points out that besides the direct effects of the lower transport costs attributable to railroads (and these were certainly not negligible), any rounded appraisal must take account of the broad spectrum of indirect effects. Any argument that lower transport costs widened markets and encouraged specialization, capital formation, and growth in other sectors is open to the criticism that this is merely a double-counting of the social savings.* Nevertheless, it is still possible to emphasize the economically beneficial repercussions of the aggregate expenditures involved in railroad construction and operation, and of the demands of the railroads for the products of particular sectors of the economy. Fishlow concludes that the railroad had considerable influence on the pace and shape of American development, as shown by the following: the aggregate incidence of railroad investment, which accounted for over 15 per cent of total capital formation between 1849 and 1858; the effects of this investment on the capital market; the impact of railroads on the dissemination of engineering skills and on the growth of a mineral-fuel-iron industry; and above all, the railroads' broad and sustained effects on agricultural expansion and settlement and also, therefore, on the construction boom that accompanied those developments.

It is nevertheless important to acknowledge Fogel's appraisal of

* Fogel points out that "the social savings includes all of the increase in national income attributable to regional specialization in agriculture induced by the decline in in shipping costs," for if an amount equal to social saving had been spent on the transportation of agricultural goods, "the nation could have reaped all of the benefits of regional agricultural specialization and trade in the absence of the railroads that it obtained with them." (*Railroads and American Economic Growth,* 224–225.)

what he calls the "embodied" derived consequences of the railroads — that is, the consequences "attributable to the specific form in which railroads provided cheap transportation services." * Thus, considering the railroad sector as a consumer of the products of other industries, he arrives at an estimate indicating that railroads did not play the dominant role frequently assigned to them: for the period 1840–1860 they consumed an average of only 17 per cent (admittedly rising in the late 1850's to 25 per cent) of total iron production, and less than 6 per cent of coal production. By the period of peak prewar demand, in 1859, the railroads consumed just under 11 per cent of the total output of the transportation equipment, iron, lumber, and machinery industries.

In the light of recent research, then, it would be wrong to claim that the railroad was indispensable to American economic growth in the sense that without it overall growth would *necessarily* have been catastrophically different. And yet, while discarding grandiose claims, one must guard against an exaggerated underplaying of the role of the railroads.

This raises the second point mentioned above. In the context of nineteenth-century America, to quote Fishlow, "the range of potential solutions to specific problems may be so large that no individual response is ever essential"; nevertheless, it remains true that "from the standpoint of historical fact, it was the railroad that actually brought the lower transportation costs and the induced sequences." [6] Therefore, the economic historian cannot safely ignore a sector which, whatever the hypothetical alternatives, was in point of fact so closely interwoven with the dynamic processes of growth in the period. Although alternative allocations of resources may be imaginable, the *actual* allocation that was made by both private and public decision makers gave a central role to the railroad.

This, in turn, raises the third point. Certainly, the fulfillment of the transportation *function* was indispensable to the type of economic development that actually took place, and railroads were an integral part of the process of growth. Therefore, there is something to be gained by studying the patterns and policies of investment and enterprise that were involved. Accordingly the process and mech-

* By contrast, Fogel classifies as "disembodied" those consequences "that followed from the saving in transportation costs per se and which would have been induced by any innovation that lowered costs by approximately the amount attributable to railroads." (*Ibid.*, 224.)

anisms by which capital and entrepreneurial skills of one eastern center of capital were applied to western railroad transportation in the nineteenth century are the focal points of this study.

The Approach to Investment

As the economic history of the West unfolded, one of its dominant characteristics was very heavy investment in land transportation based upon an interregional and even international flow of capital funds. The growth of fixed capital formation in a booming area, financed by men and institutions located in older regions, raises a number of important questions about the entrepreneurial mechanisms associated with economic expansion. We shall be addressing ourselves primarily to these qualitative questions, rather than to an alternative set of macro-economic problems related to the causes, over-all processes, and consequences of growth. As Joseph Schumpeter pointed out, "The mechanisms of economic change . . . pivot on entrepreneurial activity . . . analysis of which is at the very least a highly important avenue to the investigation of economic changes in the capitalist epoch." [7] This assumption is a necessary starting point for the type of business history envisaged here — an attempt, on the basis of comparative case studies, to distinguish and appraise the policies and processes of western railroad investment and management by selected Boston capitalists and their associates in the nineteenth century.

In a consideration of the character of investment, the simplest, although by no means the least ambiguous, distinction favored by economists is that between *induced* and *autonomous* investment. The former is conceived to be generally responsive to current levels and flows of income and demand, and the latter is generated by broader considerations. Economists appear to agree that rapid and sustained growth is dependent more on the autonomous type.[8] Although this kind of investment clearly cannot be undertaken with a complete disregard for the current situation (which, at the least, may determine the availability of funds and the state of mind of investors), autonomous investment is normally related to such factors as "changes in production methods, the development of new products, growth of population, and the opening up of new areas of settlement." [9] In other words, some long period of expectation is often posited. In one early formulation, for example, D. H. Robertson focused attention on long-run investment decisions which "are . . . very loosely geared to the visible demand for particular types of consumption goods and depend rather on fairly vague estimates of the future progress of whole areas and populations." [10]

To breathe life into these analytical concepts is a difficult task. The lines between induced and autonomous investment, and the operational meaning of the latter, are shadowy at best. Therefore, A. J. Youngson's alternative formulation of the concept of autonomous investment, which distinguishes two different types of capital outlay, is helpful.[11] One, which he calls initiatory investment, is best exemplified by product innovation. It may promote growth by opening up fresh investment opportunities elsewhere, but it need not be undertaken with these factors in mind. The other, which he calls long-period-growth investment, has similar consequences (with possibly even stronger inducements to invest elsewhere) but is undertaken in *conscious* expectation of the development which it itself facilitates. In this type of investment (railroads and public utilities are cited as examples) the possibility of future growth is an integral element in entrepreneurial calculation, and the stimulating consequences of the investment are anticipated before investment takes place.

Investors in nineteenth-century western railroads can be grouped into two categories related to the types of investment identified by Youngson. Some investors committed their capital to land transport in the expectation that this sector might both encourage and benefit from long-run economic development. Others placed their capital in railroads with an eye to existing traffic, or to current levels of potential demand, or to tactical pressure vis-à-vis competition, or to stock manipulation. Differences in expectations and in actual circumstances generated a variety of policies and procedures.

The distinction being drawn here is not intended to be any more precise than the conceptual distinctions normally employed to facilitate research. Its usefulness is not necessarily impaired by the obvious fact that for a given group of men, or a particular situation, expectations (and the policies logically associated with them) might well move along the continuous scale which connects the two conceptual extremes.

In the last resort we are concerned with actual investors and managers faced with the problems and attractions of capital-intensive investment in a developing economy. The contrast is therefore between types of investors, who, admittedly, might rarely exist in a "pure" form. It has proved feasible, however, to distinguish generally between railroad investments made in anticipation of the long-run gains to be derived from sustained economic growth, particularly from the intensive settlement of new regions, and investments made with relatively shorter time horizons, the context of which was not so much future income growth as the securing of profits from available markets — whether for goods, for railroad services, or for stocks and bonds. In actual investment practice, of course, the types of investors with these disparate outlooks shade off into each other. In order to achieve some brevity, we use the terms "developmental investor" and "opportunistic investor" respectively to describe the two contrasting types of personal investors. Similarly, we use the terms "developmental investment" and "opportunistic investment" to describe in general terms the most obvious characteristics of a specific capital commitment at a given time.

This study is concerned with refining these concepts against a broad, evolving historical background and through comparative case-studies extending over a considerable period of time. We are interested in different types of investment policy and their relationship to environment, in contrasting types of entrepreneurial behavior, and in the practical ways in which such behavior, on the part of a limited number of men, evolved and worked itself out. The railroad investment process covered the better part of a century and stretched across an entire continent. Our approach is basically empirical, but we have attempted to wed it to an explicit conceptual framework and to point up uniformity as well as uniqueness in responses to an ever changing investment and business picture.

Although propinquity to sources determined our vantage point, our study has confirmed the importance of Bostonians in the evolution of major western railroad systems. This should not be interpreted, however, as denigrating in any way the role of other capital centers. The sheer scope of our undertaking forced us to limit our investigation, and its results in terms of understanding a process may well have applications to investment capital flows originating in other eastern seaboard cities.

PART II The Era of Preparation

Chapter 2

Boston as a Center of Capital, 1820–1845

RAPID ECONOMIC expansion in undeveloped or underdeveloped areas normally requires a supply of surplus capital from more advanced areas, together with men who have the skills to make such capital productive in both physical and financial terms. Among eastern centers of advanced economic life, Boston was accumulating appropriate human and capital resources in the crucial decades after the American Revolution when the relatively backward trans-Allegheny West was being transformed from a wilderness frontier to a series of settled communities knit more and more closely into the fabric of the nation. Having added to or built fortunes in foreign trade, Massachusetts businessmen after the War of 1812 led a revolution in industry, finance, and transportation which changed the orientation and nature of their state's economic activity. While one generation of foreign merchants turned to canals, railroads, and textile manufacturing, part of the next generation continued to amass capital from trade in far corners of the world. By the mid-1840's, however, even these younger merchants were looking for new opportunities in domestic investment. The West offered them one important outlet for their capital. This chapter outlines the Boston background to these shifting patterns of investment and enterprise.

BOSTON'S FOREIGN TRADE

The commercial orientation of the nation's economy in 1820 was well exemplified in Boston, much of whose wealth came from the sea. Although New York surpassed her as a port, Boston was a center of regional and overseas trade, and Massachusetts was to hold first place in shipowning until 1843.[1] The city had long been a center for trade with Calcutta and with Canton, the only Chinese port open to foreigners. Boston merchants developed a growing business in South American goods, and they also made Boston the central distributing point for Mediterranean fruit and wine, as well as a market for shipbuilding materials from the Baltic. The old trade to the Pacific Northwest was revived after the War of 1812, but its importance gradually decreased in relation to the new trade in California hides.

Although the nation's share in the world's carrying trade declined, Boston's maritime commerce showed a steady increase from 1820 to the 1840's. The average number of annual arrivals there from foreign ports in the first of these decades was 787, but in the years 1835 to 1841 the figure was nearly doubled. Coastwise arrivals mounted from 2,592 in 1825 to 4,406 in 1840. However, while Boston's imports rose, its exports did not, and in both categories New York increasingly improved its lead.[2]

In the course of the rivalry with New Yorkers, Boston merchants slowly but steadily absorbed the foreign trade and shipping of other Massachusetts ports. By 1825, for example, Caleb Cushing could write, "Newburyport has withered under the influence of Boston." [3] The story was the same for other long-established ports of the Massachusetts coast: Beverly, Marblehead, Plymouth, and, most notably, Salem. Salem traders continued to engage in foreign commerce and dominated the East India pepper trade long after the Treaty of Ghent, but when William Gray, pioneer in the Northwest trade, moved to Boston in 1809, this signalized the beginning of the end of Salem's maritime glory.

Gray's migration anticipated a rapid rise in population that enhanced and reflected Boston's growing importance as Massachusetts' principal city. Within the same territorial limits, the population increased from 43,000 persons in 1820 to 61,000 in 1830 and by the early 1840's passed the 100,000 mark.[4]

Although blessed with a harbor as good as New York's, Bostonians had to rely largely on coastal shipping to distribute their imports and to collect products of outlying areas. They had no natural waterway to the interior comparable to the Hudson. For trade purposes their only geographical advantage over New York was the relatively slight one of being closer to Europe, and even this was more than offset by the fact that Boston's hinterland offered few sizable markets, and to reach others a long coastal voyage was necessary.

Hence, despite expanding activities, Boston lagged behind New York Port. Following the Treaty of Ghent, New Yorkers had made a timely and successful effort to improve their position in foreign trade. The establishment of an auction system and state legislation in 1817 to lower the state duty on auction sales of European goods attracted British manufactures. At the same time New York merchants set up the first line of American packets between New York and Liverpool. In addition, New York aggressively encouraged trade with its hinterland, especially through construction of the Erie Canal, begun in 1817 and completed in 1825. Finally, New York's coastwise trade developed so effectively that even the produce of western Massachusetts was carried to that city, via the Connecticut River and Long Island Sound, rather than to Boston.[5]

From New England, New York pulled many successful merchants, among them the Howlands, the Grinnells, and the Griswolds, much as Boston had attracted men from Salem. A far greater number of New Englanders, however, did business through New York commission houses. Of the ninety-one vessels that arrived in New York from Canton and Manila in the period 1839–1842, for example, thirty-six were owned in Massachusetts. In 1841 imports to New York were more than three times those to Boston, but about 74 per cent of the New York imports were on foreign accounts, yielding only commissions instead of owner's profits. By way of contrast, over 80 per cent of Boston imports were on Boston accounts.[6] Boston, whatever its relative disadvantages as a seaport, was still a center of capital and enterprise. In a world of changing technology such enterprising businessmen could not long confine their interest to overseas trade.

Textile Manufacturing

While fortunes were still being made in foreign trade, some old shipowning and merchant families of Massachusetts had turned their attention to another profitable field — textile manufacturing. Up to the War of 1812, Massachusetts' wealth had been derived primarily from trade, and the merchant group, allied by kinship and common interests in foreign voyages, had been fairly homogeneous in their investment patterns as well as in their backgrounds. By closing off overseas trade in some areas, federal trade restrictions and the war had forced merchant capital to look to other employments, especially manufacturing.

With peace came the opportunity to resume foreign trade, to continue in the new lines of investment developed during the war, or to do both. Those who turned to or continued in manufacturing found a profitable employment for their capital, formed ties with a new group of businessmen, and tended to keep their major investments close to home for many decades to come.

Francis Cabot Lowell had shown the way in large-scale textile manufacture. His mercantile career had been nurtured in the web of kinship and social liaison typical of the mercantile aristocracy of Boston and coastal towns north of it. His trading connections included his uncle William Cabot, Nathan Appleton, his brothers-in-law Patrick Tracy Jackson, Charles Jackson, and James Jackson, Uriah Cutting, and the great Boston mercantile firm of J. and T. H. Perkins.* Lowell's spheres of economic activity extended to Europe, Canada, India, and China. In 1810, having earned a fortune at the age of thirty-five, ill health and commercial disturbances prompted him to consider leaving trade. On a visit to the United Kingdom ostensibly for his health, he became sufficiently interested in cotton textiles to spend the bulk of his time there visiting manufacturing establishments and to broach the possibility of such an enterprise to his friend Nathan Appleton when they met in Edinburgh in 1811.

Back in Massachusetts, Lowell initiated the drive that led to the incorporation of the Boston Manufacturing Company early in 1813 and to the development of a practical power loom. As with his commercial ventures, his industrial undertaking blossomed within the kinship and personal framework of the local merchant class. With an authorized capital of $400,000, the company's organizers intended to raise $100,000 for the initial experimental period. Smarting from an earlier unhappy experience with such investment, the Cabots refused financial aid. But Lowell, five of his brothers-in-law, and various other outstanding merchants, some of whom had almost completely ceased their commercial activities during the war, agreed to contribute the necessary capital. Their factory at Waltham, established during the textile shortages of the war, came into full production only after 1814. It prospered greatly as a result not only

* Francis Cabot Lowell was related directly to the Cabots through his mother, to the Higginsons through his father, and to the Jacksons and Tracys through his wife. His wife's sister married Henry Lee, and his brothers-in-law Patrick Tracy Jackson, Charles Jackson, and James Jackson cemented the Jackson–Cabot alliance by marrying Lydia Cabot, Fanny Cabot, and Elizabeth and (a second marriage) Sarah Cabot, respectively. Fanny Cabot was Charles Jackson's second wife — his first was Amelia Lee!

of market conditions but of functional integration and the technological knowledge of Francis Cabot Lowell and Paul Moody, a mechanic by vocation. Patrick Tracy Jackson, whose trading interests had been sharply reduced before the war,[7] assumed full-time management of the new company as agent and treasurer.

Emerging directly from Boston's mercantile background, the Boston Manufacturing Company led the way in profitable textile operations. Its entrepreneurial structure was knit by old, strong ties; its technical strength rested on a pioneer American power loom; and its operations reflected a highly efficient, large-scale, fully integrated, innovative organization. The corporation began paying dividends in 1817, and by 1822 had paid 104½ per cent. Between 1817 and 1826 dividends averaged almost 19 per cent annually.[8]

Such success naturally induced emulation and extension. With Nathan Appleton playing an important role, the moving spirits of the pioneering company looked for a new site with abundant water power and suitable for extensive industrialization. They found it on the Merrimack River at East Chelmsford, incorporated and aptly renamed Lowell in 1824. In 1825 Lowell had a population of 2,500 and its power turned 11,000 spindles; by 1835 the population stood at 15,000 and the number of spindles at 120,000.[9] The profitability of textile manufacturing, carried on by a small group of large companies, was supplemented for the pioneers by their participation in the Proprietors of the Locks and Canals on the Merrimack River, a development corporation which leased water rights to individual mills, and by the activities of machine shops that soon turned out locomotives as well as textile machinery.

The mercantile capital and skill which was created before 1812 was not, of course, suddenly and massively switched into the textile industry. Although some men like Francis Cabot Lowell, Patrick Tracy Jackson, and Kirk Boott turned their full attention to industrial management, others merely channeled some of their capital into manufacturing investment while retaining an active interest in commerce. For example, even though he was much involved in Lowell affairs at the managerial level, William Appleton expanded his mercantile operations in the decades after 1814. On the other hand, his cousin Nathan Appleton maintained his strong commercial interest only until the 1820's.[10]

The men who spanned the worlds of commerce and textiles also participated in the development of financial institutions and, later, of local railroads serving their main interest in manufacturing. To examine the original incorporators of and subscribers to the stock of such institutions as the New England National Bank (1813), the Tremont National Bank (1814), the Suffolk National Bank (1818), and the Massachusetts Hospital Life Insurance Company (1818) is to be reminded once more of the importance of the interlocking groups of merchants and pioneer manufacturing entrepreneurs.[11]

Minor Capitalists

The political and economic power of the merchant-manufacturing group, however, did not go unchallenged in the decades following the War of 1812. A rising group of minor capitalists emerged from more prosaic pursuits than foreign trade and shipowning, their business interests more deeply rooted in the local economy. This group was composed of domestic merchants, small bankers, and small manufacturers, many of whom established themselves in Boston, or centered their business activities there, about the time of the War of 1812. They organized their own financial institutions and sought political power to oppose the ruling group. David Henshaw, who moved to Boston in 1814 from Leicester in Worcester County and entered the wholesale drug business with his brother, was representative of this group both in his connection with banks that challenged those of the old merchant group and in his role as a Democratic politician.

Other important newcomers were Franklin Haven and David A. Neal. Haven became cashier of the Merchants' Bank in 1831 and its president five years later. In this position, which he held for many years, he took an active interest in western railroads. Neal, son of a Salem merchant in foreign trade, started his career at sea. When he came ashore in the 1820's to engage in trade and later in railroad management, he continued to live in Salem.

Essex County, abandoned by the Cabots and Lowells, still produced enterprising small capitalists. From Lynn came Mark Healy, for a short time president of the Merchants' Bank and later associated with Neal in an Ohio railroad. From another Essex County town, Beverly, came Robert Rantoul, Jr. Born in 1805, the son of a druggist, he became a successful lawyer and Democratic politician. He moved to Boston in 1838 and served as a collector of the port and for a brief time in the United States Senate. In 1850 he was to be associated with Neal and Haven, among others, as an incorporator of the Illinois Central Railroad. Still "on the make" when the development of domestic markets and transportation offered risky and challenging fields for enterprise, these men and others like them responded more vigorously and enthusiastically than the older merchant group who had found an earlier challenge close to home and were content with the bountiful fruits of their local endeavors.

The China Trade as a Source of Capital and Entrepreneurial Talent

More important in the development of Boston's western railroad interests after 1840 than either the merchants turned textile manufacturers or the small capitalists of Boston and the North Shore of Massachusetts were the young China traders. The capital accumulated by them and the attitudes and aptitudes they developed were of the kind needed at home. A close-knit group, accustomed to managing far-flung enterprises, they appeared on the domestic scene at a time when the West offered great opportunities to capital and entrepreneurial talent. Experience in the China trade provided them with rare qualifications to meet this challenge.

In terms of capital or goods involved, the China trade would appear to have been relatively unimportant to Boston and the Massachusetts economy in the early nineteenth century. Measured against the lively, extensive trade to other areas, or the burgeoning development of industrial, financial, and railroad enterprise within the Commonwealth, the commerce with Canton would seem to play an insignificant, if romantic, role. But this is an indication of the dangers of purely statistical measurement, for the part which the China trade played in the crucial stimulus which Boston gave to western economic development transcended its statistical position in Boston's own economic activity.

Massachusetts' participation in the China trade began when the *Grand Turk* of Salem, owned by Elias Hasket Derby, docked at Canton in 1786. In Boston and the surrounding ports, the prospects of the trade to China appeared as a glowing attraction for merchants, capital, and seafaring skill. As time passed, commercial men in Massachusetts wholeheartedly joined, and ultimately led, the American trade to Canton: a trade which brought back the crockery, the cottons, the silks, and, above all, the teas so much in demand in America.*

Although American firms trading to China rose to a position of some importance and affluence, they were never fully able to override the British predominance. Therefore, competition at Canton was shaped by the extent and drive of British trade which, until 1834, was divided by the British government between the East India Company and a selective list of merchants. After an intensive campaign in 1831 and 1832, the newly powerful industrial free traders of Britain won the day. The government withdrew the East India Company's privileges and in 1834 declared the trade to China open to all Britishers. One result of this move was that the British residents in Canton rose from 66 in 1833 to 156 in 1837.

Since the aggregate market at Canton (the supply of and demand for western and Chinese goods) did not expand commensurately with the number of middlemen servicing it, the profitability of commercial transactions, although not their extent, was reduced. "The truth is," wrote a British merchant in 1837, "the China trade has been too much run on," and his partner wrote to an American correspondent: "We are sighing almost for a return of the Company's monopoly in preference to the trouble and endless turmoil of free trade." [12]

It now appeared to British interests that the problems posed by the free trade could only be resolved by using pressure to expand the narrow channel by which western goods reached the Chinese market. This pressure and counterpressure, centering particularly on the opium trade and the Chinese government's desire to exclude it, resulted in the Opium War (1839–1842). By the Treaty of Nanking, British commercial interests achieved their aims: Chinese control of trade at Canton was relaxed, four new ports were opened up, tariffs were limited, and various other privileges were afforded to the British.

* By the 1860's tea accounted for well over 50 per cent of total U.S. imports from China, bearing out the verdict of Samuel Shaw, first American consul in Canton, that "The inhabitants of America must have tea, the consumption of which will naturally increase with the increasing population of our country." (Quoted in Justin Winsor [ed.], *The Memorial History of Boston . . . 1630–1880* [Boston, 1883], IV, 205.)

There ensued a disrupting boom in business. Anticipating that the new ports would mean an increased market, American merchants exceeded all previous levels by shipping over 500,000 pieces of domestic cottons to China, while from England came textiles amounting to double any previous year's shipments. The result was a collapse of prices until in October 1843 it was reported that cottons were selling for prices below their cost at Lowell and Manchester.[13]

Thus, a combination of business and governmental pressures during the 1830's and 1840's generated a revolution in the structure and the profitability of the China trade. This was the period when American fortunes made in the port of Canton began to be markedly withdrawn from Asiatic commerce. Although this development coincided with the booming demand for capital in the growing American economy, particularly in the West, the plain fact is that wealth was pushed as well as pulled out of the China trade.

The returns on commercial operations, which had been so munificent in the first four decades of the century, were bound to be reduced by the new climate of enterprise. As John Murray Forbes wrote in the early 1840's, in the course of arguing that the China trade would not yield above 6 per cent, "The truth is that competition is so sharp here [he was writing from Boston] that money must be made either by the most penurious saving in fitting ships or storing goods, etc., etc., or by being constantly on the look-out and giving up body and soul to managing business." [14] And, as good businessmen, the American merchants whose wealth had been accumulated under favorable auspices looked for new outlets for investment when those auspices became less favorable.

Kinship and Enterprise in the China Trade

The pattern of entrepreneurial and personal relationships which had been built up during the China boom remained significant in the new fields of domestic western enterprise. Since investment decisions important to American economic development reflected these relationships, it is necessary to trace briefly their genesis.

When Elias Hasket Derby of Salem dispatched his first ships to Canton, he indirectly helped to establish at least four of the most important Boston mercantile fortunes in the China trade. Thomas Handasyd Perkins (1764–1854), through a connection by marriage with the captain of one of Derby's ships,[15] sailed to China as the Salem merchant's supercargo in 1789. Members of a mercantile family, Thomas Handasyd and his brother James in 1792 organized the Boston firm of J. & T. H. Perkins. This firm established a Canton branch, Perkins & Co., which in turn, at a later date, handed over its commission business to and kept a close liaison with Samuel Russell & Co., later simply Russell & Co.

The influential Perkins brothers had three nephews destined for outstanding roles in Asiatic commerce and later domestic investment. They were William Sturgis, John Perkins Cushing, and John Murray Forbes.* In each case, the boy's father died while the son was still young, and each boy was taken, at different times, into Thomas H. Perkins' counting house and subsequently aided in his start in the China trade.

William Sturgis (1782–1863) was the first of these youths to come under the beneficent influence of Perkins. After two years in the counting houses, first of his uncle, Russell Sturgis, and later of J. & T. H. Perkins, he determined to go to sea, and in the summer of 1798 sailed aboard a Perkins ship bound for Mexico, the Pacific Coast, and China. He quickly established a good reputation as shipmaster and supercargo among New England merchants in the China trade, and in 1810 he formed a co-partnership in Boston with John Bryant under the name of Bryant, Sturgis & Co.

John P. Cushing (1787–1862) went to Canton in 1803 to be clerk in Perkins & Co. Almost immediately the resident manager fell mortally ill and Cushing, not yet seventeen years old, took charge of the firm's operations. In terms of personal wealth and reputation he became the outstanding China merchant of his time in Boston. Except for a visit home in 1807, he remained in China until 1828, and returned there to wind up his business in 1830–1831. Then, at the age of forty-four, he retired to a life of gracious and educated ease and turned over the investment of his money to Bryant, Sturgis & Co.

Thomas H. Perkins' youngest sister married Ralph Bennet Forbes, and their three sons became, in different ways and varying degrees, concerned with the China trade. Thomas T. Forbes (1803–1829)

* William Sturgis seems to have been generally considered as a nephew, although in fact this was not precisely true. William Sturgis' uncle, Russell Sturgis, married T. H. Perkins' sister. In Cushing's and Forbes's cases, the kinship was more direct: both their mothers were sisters of T. H. Perkins.

joined Perkins & Co. in Canton in 1820 and remained there until his death by drowning. Robert Bennet Forbes (1804–1889), after a taste of clerking for a small firm of his Perkins cousins, went to sea at the age of thirteen in one of his uncles' ships and continued as a mariner in trading vessels.[16] In 1830 John Murray Forbes (1813–1898), who had been working for about two years in the J. & T. H. Perkins counting house in Boston, went out to Canton to join the firm of Russell & Co., which under John P. Cushing's supervision had been reorganized to take over the affairs of Perkins & Co. With Forbes went Augustine Heard (1785–1868), who had been active as shipmaster and supercargo in trade with India, China, and South America. Heard was received as a partner in Russell & Co., and young John Forbes, by an agreement then unknown to him, was scheduled for a partnership in 1834. Robert Bennet Forbes, whose love of the sea was greater than his interest in business, was given charge of the company's storeship.*

Some men in the China trade lived in Canton for long periods and other men, particularly the more important ones, stayed there only for short periods. Cushing returned to Boston after Russell & Co. was established, leaving it the most powerful house in Canton. Robert B. Forbes went back to America in 1832 to act as consignee for the company until 1838, when he again sailed out to Canton. In 1833 John Murray Forbes left China for reasons of health, but returned the following year as supercargo for Bryant, Sturgis & Co. and accepted the partnership in Russell & Co. that had been planned for him. Meanwhile Heard had taken into partnership John C. Green, formerly supercargo for the New York firm of N. L. & G. Griswold, and Joseph Coolidge, Jr., of Boston.[17] Green and Coolidge, as well as Forbes, were to move into American railroad investment at a later date.

Apart from his own mercantile aptitudes, John M. Forbes brought to Russell & Co. the commission business of Houqua, the wealthy Hong merchant who had befriended American traders and placed special confidence in the young Bostonian. Cushing, through Perkins & Co., had handled transactions for Houqua on a commission basis and Forbes took over this agency. Houqua's friendship was one

* The "storeship" system was developed after 1821 to circumvent the effort of Chinese authorities to halt the traffic in opium. The drug was sold from a ship anchored downriver from Canton beyond their reach.

of the pillars of Forbes's fortune, for it not only brought him 10 per cent of the profits of the merchant's business, but later gave Forbes the management of large sums of Houqua's capital, which he invested in America's western expansion.

Heard sailed for America in the fall of 1834, and two years later John M. Forbes left Canton for good, although he retained an interest in the company long after he turned his prime attention to domestic investment. In fact, Russell & Co. continued to create relationships and generate capital, both of which were important to American expansion and development. Russell Sturgis, who eventually joined the influential Baring Brothers, merchant-bankers in London, was with the Canton firm for two years in the 1840's. John N. A. Griswold, who later became president of the Illinois Central Railroad and still later an ally of John M. Forbes in the Chicago, Burlington & Quincy, was a partner in Russell & Co. for six years, taking with him the China business of his father's firm, N. L. & G. Griswold, of New York. In the late 1850's, while deeply involved in western railroad development, the Forbes family still dominated the Canton firm, and money from Robert B. and Paul S. Forbes flowed as capital into the western enterprises in which John M. Forbes was prominent.

Other Boston merchants maintained close relationships with the firms and traders already mentioned. Among them was William Appleton, whose business interests embraced textile manufacturing, local railroad financing, and general trade. A member of the older generation, he had close connections with the younger groups who were to be active in western investments. Marriage provided one of the strongest of these links. For example, one of Appleton's daughters became the wife of Amos A. Lawrence; another married Franklin G. Dexter; and a third, T. Jefferson Coolidge, son of Joseph Coolidge, Jr. These men also were to invest in the West when the time was ripe.

The Significance of the China Trade

The China trade proved an important source of men and capital for America's western development. The reasons for its importance can be considered in terms of men, money, and techniques — the influence of all three being interdependent.

There emerges with sharp clarity from any study of the pattern of commercial enterprise in Canton the fact that the leading firms were small in number and close in their relationships with each other. Largely through the intermediacy of such key figures as Thomas H. Perkins and John P. Cushing there were direct connections among the main houses and the outstanding men: Perkins & Co., John P. Cushing, Bryant, Sturgis & Co., the Forbes brothers, Russell & Co., Augustine Heard, Joseph Coolidge, Jr., John N. A. Griswold, William Appleton, and others. More than this, the intimate web of business relationships in the China trade was reinforced by the family relationships which existed between so many China traders. Such kinship ties served to instill confidence and trust into commercial organizations where large areas of authority and decision making had necessarily to be delegated. And these family connections, in their turn, were merely part of the greater kinship network typifying and sustaining the Boston social and business scene. Further, where the ties of blood or marriage were not present, frequently those of friendship evolved to serve the same functions.

The moral character of this generation of Boston businessmen resulted in an honest and upright treatment of associates that could flower into the closest of friendships. For example, even though in the early 1840's Augustine Heard and John M. Forbes had a serious misunderstanding which produced hard words,[18] the friendship that they had established on their initial journey to Canton in 1830 lasted a lifetime and produced complete confidence in matters of business. While it is true that such men's devotion to business was almost superhuman, it is no less true that many of the personal relationships growing out of their economic enterprise exceeded, in warmth, sincerity, and integrity, much that other types of men were able to experience. The trust which these relationships engendered during the trade to the Orient were to be of real significance in business activities at home, for they meant that China traders, when they invested in domestic enterprise, frequently did so as a community knit and strengthened by a mutual confidence. Sociologically speaking, they belonged to a distinct in-group.

Many of the China merchants already mentioned rose to a prominent position with respect to the flow of Boston's capital westward after the 1830's. John M. Forbes, it will later be seen, occupied a strategic role in investment patterns. His capital, as well as the early roots of his influence, derived almost solely from his participation in Asiatic commerce. Part of Forbes's importance rests in the fact that he made crucial decisions on investment for other men, too. In managing, by recommendation and trust, the investments of his brother Robert B. Forbes, his cousin Paul S. Forbes, and his friend Augustine Heard, as well as those of other men in his Boston circle, he was exercising indirect control over capital that had been derived almost entirely from the China trade.

A parallel instance was the relationship between John P. Cushing and William Sturgis. Cushing, perhaps the richest of China merchants, placed his wealth unconditionally in the hands of Bryant, Sturgis & Co., the outstanding Boston-based mercantile house in the 1830's.* Although only a small part of Cushing's or Bryant & Sturgis' capital was ever committed to investment truly designated as "western," a great deal was invested in areas outside Massachusetts and particularly in railroads.[19]

The Griswolds, both father (George) and son (John N. A.), who had been closely concerned with the China trade through their family firm and through Russell & Co., came to be identified with western railroad development, especially in Michigan and Illinois.

As a partner in Baring Brothers, Russell Sturgis' connection with western investment was somewhat less direct but probably not less significant than the others, since his firm supplied capital to Boston-backed enterprises in the West.

The mercantile firm of Samuel Hooper & Co., successor in 1860 to William Appleton & Co., invested heavily in enterprises west of the Alleghenies, and particularly west of the Mississippi. These investments appeared in the names of the partnership and of such individual partners as Samuel Hooper, who had formerly been associated with Bryant, Sturgis & Co., and of his brother-in-law, Franklin G. Dexter.

The story of the personnel of the China trade was essentially one of the succession of relatives and friends to positions of mercantile importance. It was, after all, natural that men should turn to tried friends or trusted relatives when they had to choose clerks and partners to assume positions of responsibility thousands of miles beyond immediate control.

* After 1841, Bryant, Sturgis & Co. became Bryant & Sturgis.

Kinship and friendship as keys to money-making opportunities in the China trade also meant that a fortune could be made while a man was still young, giving him most of a lifetime to apply his money to investments at home. The youth of many China traders is a matter of record. John P. Cushing went to China at sixteen and became a partner in Perkins & Co. at nineteen; Thomas T. Forbes was seventeen when he arrived in Canton and was apparently a partner with Cushing before 1828 when, at twenty-five, he took charge of the business of Cushing, Perkins, and Sturgis at Canton; John M. Forbes sailed to join Russell & Co. at seventeen and some three years later was presented with a partnership; John Heard, after three years in Canton with Augustine Heard & Co., was also made a full partner at twenty and very shortly took complete authority in China; even Robert Bennet Forbes, who had already enjoyed a long seafaring career, was only thirty-four when he arrived in Canton to take over Russell & Co.

While numerous older men engaged in the China trade at Canton, the younger man frequently proved the better representative of a Boston house. With a career yet to be made, his motivation was strong, and it could be expected that his period of residence would be relatively longer. John M. Forbes, offered responsibility, independence, and profit-making opportunities at an age when more domesticated contemporaries were still clerking for a living, managed to span in his lifetime at least two business careers. Before he was twenty-five he had left China for good and was soon to turn most of his attention toward the domestic economy.

The China trade also offered Boston merchants an opportunity to recoup losses from other ventures. Robert B. Forbes, for example, returned to Canton in an attempt to offset his losses in the 1837 panic. His cousin Paul S. Forbes took over Robert's partnership in Russell & Co. in 1844 to try to recover losses he suffered in the importation of South American coffee. John M. Forbes, after what he felt was a successful first stay in Canton, was forced to return to China in 1834, when he discovered that his assets were less than he had thought.[20]

Prior to 1833 American merchants generally considered the China trade a reasonably certain producer of profit. When a young man had ability, and his luck ran well, he could expect to make money earlier, faster, and with less initial capital than in almost any other business. It is impossible to document this in any comprehensive way, but the following examples are suggestive.

As early as 1827, when his partnership with Bryant had been in existence for seventeen years, William Sturgis valued his share in the business at $171,349; in 1830 his credit balance was $201,443 and in 1847, by which time the partnership had not been concerned with active trade for over five years, it was $550,000, in addition to more than $125,000 of assets outside the firm.[21]

There is also some evidence of capital accumulation by other men and firms. In July 1829 Thomas T. Forbes was winding up the affairs of Perkins & Co. in Canton. His figures, which unfortunately are by no means clear, indicate that there had been three partnerships whose accounts still had to be settled. The "property" of the first was valued at $1,598,000, of the second at $1,019,000, and of the third at $277,000. Of the total, Cushing's nominal share was $983,304, but Forbes himself owned a part of this, amounting to some $188,000.[22]

Russell & Co., successor to the Perkins firm, had $90,000 estimated net profits for 1834, and for 1835 and 1836, $310,000. Nominally, Augustine Heard held a one sixteenth interest in the firm for all three years plus an extra sixteenth for 1834, but John M. Forbes held half Heard's share in 1835 and 1836. Of the firm's net profits for 1834–1836, Heard was due $36,250 and Forbes, $19,375.[23] In 1849 Robert B. Forbes returned once more to Canton with an interest in Russell & Co. for 1850 and 1851 of four sixteenths. He gleefully reported to Augustine Heard in May 1850 that the house had made a net profit of some $220,000 in the previous year and that by the spring of 1852 he hoped to have cleared $150,000. In 1849, he claimed, he had invested in several voyages which would net $35,000 to $40,000.[24] In 1854 Russell & Co. cleared $104,000.[25]

Such figures may be deceptive. They perhaps exaggerate the rewards to the successful, and they certainly ignore the undoubted existence of men who lost or failed to make money at Canton. The China trade did not necessarily produce a large return on investment in the long run. Writing in the early 1840's, for example, John M. Forbes claimed that, apart from two lucky speculations, his earnings since he left China in 1837 were not above 6 per cent, and even including those two strokes of fortune were not much above that figure. It was his firm conviction, "that for twenty years past the average interest gained on the whole capital engaged in the China trade has not exceeded six per cent."[26] Nevertheless, this much can perhaps be said: where a man once got a foothold in an established China house, then, other things (luck and ability) being equal, he stood more chance of making big profits quickly than in virtually any other mercantile business.

In any case, by itself the accumulation of capital is not a sufficient explanation of the importance of Asiatic commerce to America's western development. The China trade developed more than a pattern of group relationships and capital; it produced ways of doing business which had important applications once the men and their money turned toward the American West rather than the Far East.

The China trade had provided Boston merchants with world-wide financial connections. America's or Boston's trade with Canton was part of a variable commercial network which could encompass India, South America, the Pacific Northwest, the Mediterranean, Russia, or England. From the present point of view, its outstanding feature was the extent to which the bill on London was used as a means of exchange in Canton by American merchants. In the 1850's Russell & Co., according to Robert B. Forbes, became exchange bankers in every new Chinese port in which it established itself, "by virtue of the currency of its sterling bills in India."[27] Until the English houses began sending their surplus assets from China to the United States, they had been accustomed to taking bills from American houses in China in return for the excess of their inward over their outward trade.[28] That the multilateral nature of such trade could lead to extensive mercantile contacts is illustrated by a partial list of Russell & Co.'s "extensive connections":[29]

London:	Baring Brothers & Co.; Forbes, Forbes & Co.; N. M. Rothschild & Sons
Europe:	Daniel Crommelin & Sons; Berenberg, Gossler & Co
Boston:	J. & T. H. Perkins & Sons; Bryant & Sturgis; W. Appleton & Co.; Robert G. Shaw
New York:	N. L. & G. Griswold; Howland & Aspinwall; Goodhue & Co.; Grinnell, Minturn & Co.
Bombay:	Forbes & Co.; Jamsetjee Jejeebhoy & Sons.

This trade in bills also depended upon friendship and relationships of confidence between American traders and financial houses in Europe, and more particularly in England. By the early 1830's the Barings were extending liberal credits to finance the American trade with Canton, India, and the East Indies,[30] and were in the habit of circulating special reports on the prices of Asiatic goods and British manufactures to such valued friends as John P. Cushing, Bryant & Sturgis, and Thomas H. Perkins.[31] In fact, Baring Brothers & Co. appears to have been the foreign firm closest to the dominant merchants in Boston's commerce with China. For example, in 1843–1844 when the Barings undertook a drastic (and risky) change in policy by granting uncovered credits to American houses in China — a change made necessary by the vacuum created by Houqua's death in 1843[32] — it was Augustine Heard & Co. and Russell & Co. who benefited.

Financial business was enough based on personal experience, trust, and confidence so that men like John M. Forbes, when they went into the business of western railroads, were able to make use of the Barings' financial services.* Earlier, William Sturgis had also called on the Barings for aid in the financing of the Eastern Railroad.[33] The fact that Russell Sturgis joined the Barings in 1849 and became a full partner in 1851 undoubtedly testified to and strengthened the existing connections between that firm and the Boston mercantile aristocracy.

A second aspect of the China trade that made it a good training ground for management of western investments was its extensiveness. Long spans of time and distance had to be overcome by entrepreneurial and managerial techniques. Western investment, as its pattern evolved, was to demand similar techniques. The construction and management of a western railroad system or a speculative land company necessitated reliance on men at points of responsibility a thousand miles or more from Boston. When John M. Forbes in the 1850's had to send out young men to be trained to manage rail-

* As Houqua's confidential secretary and advisor, Forbes managed Houqua's shipments to Europe and America in the early 1830's. He subsequently wrote: "The invoices were made out in my name, and the instructions as to sales and returns given just as if the shipments were my own property, and at one time I had as much as half a million dollars thus afloat, bringing me into very close correspondence with Baring Brothers & Co., and other great houses." (Sarah Forbes Hughes, ed., *Letters and Recollections of John Murray Forbes* [Boston, 1900], I, 63.)

roads in which he was concerned, the considerations relevant to his process of choice were not unlike those regulating the selection of junior clerks and managing partners for Canton. And the difficulties of exercising control from half a continent away were not dissimilar to those involved in managing trade from half the world away.

The importance of the China trade to Boston's investment in the West was related to time and place, as well as to the specific question of its techniques. By the 1840's and 1850's the first influx of commercial capital to domestic investment was already deeply committed to the Massachusetts and New England economy — to the textile industry, local railroads, and financial institutions. Textiles were part of the stable complex of Boston business, and if the investment could not be seen from home or office window, it could at least be visited by a brief and easy journey. Managerial disturbances[34] and a relative decline in profits by the 1840's and, especially, the 1850's, did little to alter the basic situation: industrial growth had engendered a business realignment of Boston's leading families — a realignment which was respectable, remunerative, substantial, and relatively inflexible.

By the time that new capital, acquired by a younger generation, was ready to flow out of the China trade, many important outlets in New England had already been pre-empted by the original mercantile aristocracy. This is not to say that some China traders did not invest heavily in local enterprise — William Sturgis, John P. Cushing, and William Appleton are outstanding examples of those who did — or that there was a sharp cleavage between the older and the younger groups: in fact they were part of the same homogeneous society. But many of the China traders, and particularly those who had spent some time in Canton and made their money after the second decade of the century, did have their own interrelationships and brought their capital to the American market at a time when the West offered great incentives to their particular type of business skill, and when the first heroic period of eastern economic development was already passing.

In contrast to the nature of enterprise and investment in local textiles, the demands of development further West carried elements of speculative risk and insecurity and the problems of extended lines of communication and control. Yet to men bred in the China trade uncertainty and distance were everyday features of business. Consequently, while western enterprises before the Civil War were economic innovations too risky to be very attractive to the settled capital safely ensconced in the textile industry, they were qualitatively comparable to the type of business to which active, long-distance traders were accustomed. In short, prewar western investment demanded a kind of business skill and capital that was becoming increasingly available in eastern commercial centers. While the first wave of mercantile capital had helped to industrialize New England, a second wave, coming from a new direction, helped to stimulate economic development in new regions.

Chapter 3

Moving into Railroad Investment: Experience in the East

THE COMING of the railroad in the 1830's opened new opportunities for investment; it offered potentialities for growth and adaptation in a continent where distances were great and transportation was crucial for settlement and development. The size of the capital requirements of this new mode of transportation, however, combined with the risks that accompany adoption of any innovation, meant that railroad investment was not automatically attractive to private investors. Therefore, to minimize risk, the methods of railroad financing in its early stages were often experimental and exemplified various combinations of public and private resources. The gradual involvement by individuals and groups was more on the basis of their existing interests than a sudden transfer of their allegiance to railroads as a primary field of investment.

The groupings of Boston investors, their methods of finance, and their ventures in railroad construction, operation, and extension on the eastern seaboard provided the alliances and experience on which they and others from the Bay State drew as they moved decisively into railroads west of the Alleghenies. To understand the process of involvement in the West it is first necessary to examine these patterns as they emerged in earlier eastern ventures.

Genesis of Massachusetts Railroads

The movement of Boston capitalists into railroads, first in New England and then further South and West, was a multi-faceted process. Locally, the large textile manufacturers took an active interest in roads that would serve their mills; Boston merchants looked to railroads as a link with the hinterland market and then with the Great Lakes; numerous smaller capitalists like Salem's David A. Neal saw in local steam railroad transportation a promising new field of enterprise which they cultivated assiduously and hopefully.

On the other hand, the China traders generally paid little attention to the early development of New England steam railroads, though John Bryant and William Sturgis were notable exceptions.

Massachusetts had given desultory and occasional attention to internal improvement problems for nine years when, in 1825, the completion of New York's Erie Canal, with its threat to the Bay State's trade with the West, gave a new impetus to the study of Massachusetts' transportation potentialities. By early 1827 state improvement leaders had decided against building a canal to the Hudson in emulation of New York. In March 1828 the legislature created a nine-man Board of Directors of Internal Improvements and this established a rallying point from which agitators for railroads called for state aid.[1]

From the standpoint of furthering railroad development in Massachusetts the most important member of this board was Nathan Hale. More than anyone else he demonstrated to doubting Bostonians that railroads could be profitable investments. As editor of the Boston *Daily Advertiser,* Hale was in a position to influence public opinion, and he became corresponding secretary of the Massachusetts Rail Road Association, organized in 1829 to carry on an educational campaign. In January of that year he was also the principal author of the Board of Directors of Internal Improvements' report — a landmark in Massachusetts railroad development.[2] At a later date Hale had particular importance because he was president of the Boston and Worcester Rail-Road and acted as an intermediary between western roads and Boston investors.

Since at best the investment community was cool toward getting involved in railroads, and certainly so without some guarantee of privilege, the Board of Directors of Internal Improvements was prepared to endorse a state-backed endeavor. In their words: "It is the opinion of the Directors that works of such magnitude, and on which the public accommodation so essentially depends, should be under the control of the government of the State." [3] The conservative, agrarian groups that controlled the legislature, however, opposed any drain on their pocketbooks to aid internal improvements. To induce private investment, therefore, it was necessary for the state to approve favorable charters, even if they included monopoly privileges — a normally unpopular provision.

In 1830 the Massachusetts legislature approved petitions for incorporation of four railroad companies, only one of which, the Boston and Lowell Railroad, was actually organized. That the charters were granted in such a way as to meet the demands of both private investors and the legislature's anti-corporation faction is illustrated by the case of the Boston and Lowell. That road received monopoly rights over a specified route for thirty years, but at the end of twenty the state could take over the franchise and property on payment of the road's cost, expenses, and repairs, plus amounts necessary to give stockholders a dividend of 10 per cent on original investment, if they had not already received it. The Boston and Lowell could set its own tolls, but the legislature could reduce them after four years if during that time net income had exceeded 10 per cent annually on the cost of the road.[4]

Textile manufacturers took the lead in organizing and financing the Boston and Lowell to link their mills on the Merrimack River with Boston and to avoid the uncertainties of transportation via the Middlesex Canal, wagons, and stages. The rights and liabilities of stockholders and directors were specified by the charter. Each investor was entitled to as many votes as he had shares, up to one fourth of the total. Subscribers who did not complete payment of their assessments were personally liable for the difference if the shares failed to bring the amount of the assessment when sold.

Although key figures in the Locks and Canals Company were incorporators, many other names were included "because it was thought proper that the Stock should be offered to the public, generally, and not confined to these Proprietors." [5] In the expectation that substantial interests would take hold of a project adjunct to textile mills,[6] the $500,000 authorized capital for the company was to be represented by 1,000 shares of $500 par value. After the first efforts to sell stock to the public failed, apparently because adequate financial information was not provided, a committee was appointed to investigate. It reported that a single-track road with equipment would cost $600,000.[7] On the basis of estimated annual gross earnings of $58,514 and expenses of $22,424, the committee concluded that the net income would yield a 6 per cent return on the capital investment.

The cautious remarks accompanying this estimate are notable since they indicate contemporary expectations of Bostonians concerning a railroad as an investment. After admitting that 6 per cent was not a return in itself "sufficient to induce capitalists to embark in such a project," the committee declared that its estimates were on the conservative side and ventured an opinion that "a property of this kind, not subject to loss by fire or other like casualties, will be considered good for investment, if an income of five per cent per annum, can be calculated upon with certainty, and the prospect of increase of business on this road is so good, as to render it certain, in the opinion of the Committee, that the income will fully equal the statement in this report." [8] Of course the return on investment was only one factor — the beneficial effects of improved transportation for their textile and other interests were perhaps more important to the railroad's promoters.

As railroad investors were often to find, the cost of the Boston and Lowell exceeded original estimates and capital had to be obtained from several sources. The promoters relied, however, almost entirely on equity financing. The Locks and Canals Company subscribed $250,000 to the railroad enterprise and gradually outside financial backing was acquired.[9] By January 1834 stockholders had met ten assessments, bringing the amount paid in to $450 per share. Since additional funds were still required, the railroad executives successfully petitioned the legislature for permission to increase the capital stock to $1,200,000.[10] By the end of 1835 that sum had been paid in,[11] supplemented by additional receipts from loans and acceptances on iron.

As was the case later in western railroad promotion, the organizers of the road expected to receive corollary benefits from their transportation investment by speculation in land at both ends of the line. At Lowell the land in question was held in the name of the Locks and Canals Company and in Boston under the name of the Boston Mill Pond and Wharf Company. In 1837 the road itself owned land that had cost $51,684, and hoped to sell this property for $28,000 above its cost.[12]

Fortunately, estimates of transportation revenues as well as of expenses proved to be conservative. In 1835, with less than a full year's operation, the Boston and Lowell's gross receipts were $65,000. The following year they rose to $165,000.[13] The net price of a share at the time of the first settlement of accounts, November 30, 1835, amounted to $540.75, and over the next fourteen years dividends averaged 6.87 per cent on this amount. In the words of the directors, "this rate, considering the early uncertainty and continued hazards of railroad investments, can not be considered more than a fair remuneration." [14]

Meanwhile, the railroad fever spread rapidly in Massachusetts. In the period 1831–1835, eleven railroad corporations were chartered. The most important were the Boston and Providence, Boston and Worcester, and the Western.

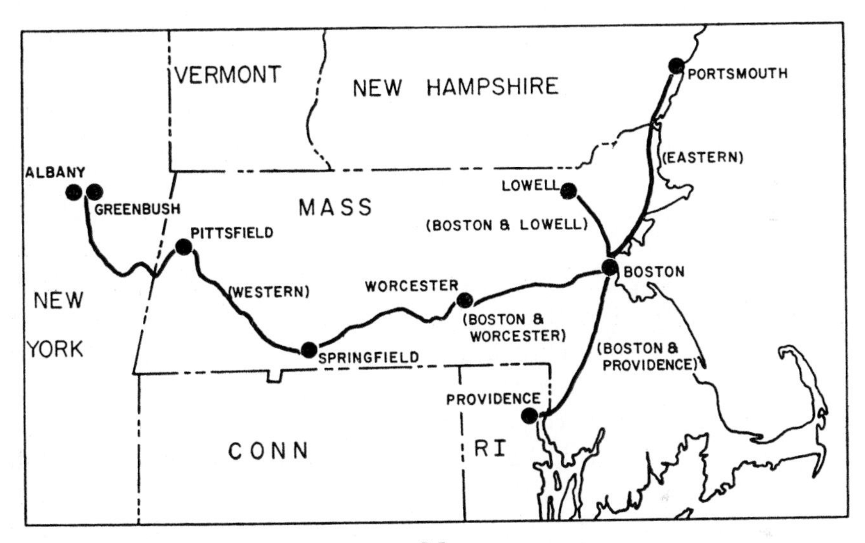

KEY ROUTES OF EARLY MASSACHUSETTS RAILROADS

Financial support for the Boston and Providence was easily obtained and was multi-city in nature. This road was intended to improve Boston's connection not only with Providence, which was the center of another textile complex, but with New York through connection with steamboats on Long Island Sound. Capital was raised through the issuing of stock, but the largest shareholder in 1835 held only seventy-five shares.[15] New Yorkers had substantial holdings and after 1832 were represented on the board of directors.[16] Among the influential Bostonians connected with the Providence road were John Bryant, William Sturgis, and John Bryant, Jr., indicating that the Bryant & Sturgis firm was diversifying its investments, though on a small scale and probably in connection with its commercial interests.

Chartered in 1831, the Providence road was completed in 1835 and was built in a very substantial manner. It proved financially successful from the first, and for a number of years paid dividends averaging over 7 per cent.[17]

The primary objective of Boston merchants, however, was to connect Boston with the Hudson, and the rising textile interests in western Massachusetts naturally added their encouragement. Since a proposal that the state finance such a project had been defeated in 1830, the undertaking became one for private enterprise and was divided into two parts. First, the Boston and Worcester Rail-Road was chartered in 1831 to provide the less expensive link in this route. Second, as a major step toward joining Worcester with Albany, the Western Rail-Road was chartered in 1833 on terms which showed that it was in effect an extension of the B. and W.[18]

As far as the rights of the state were concerned, the B. and W. charter resembled that of the Boston and Lowell. In return for guaranteeing that no other road would be built in the same direction within five miles of the B. and W.'s route for thirty years, the state reserved the right to purchase the road at the end of twenty years and, after ten years, to adjust tolls if they had returned more than 10 per cent on the cost of the road.[19]

Like the Lowell road, the B. and W. was built with equity capital. The initial authorized capital stock of $1,000,000, although fully subcribed by 1832, was not fully assessed until the completion of the road in 1835. The committee offering stock in July 1831 included Nathan Hale but no others so prominent as the textile men connected with the financing of the Boston and Lowell or the investors in the Boston and Providence. Among the early directors, besides Hale, were David and Samuel Henshaw and Thomas Motley, a director of several Lowell textile companies. In 1837, John Bryant of the Bryant & Sturgis house became a director and after serving one year was succeeded by his partner, William Sturgis.[20]

Although a number of influential Bostonians, especially textile men, initially subscribed to Boston and Worcester stock, many of them temporarily lost their enthusiasm. Once the road was opened, however, and the risks therefore reduced, Boston capitalists renewed their interest. Among the late-comers, besides John Bryant and William Sturgis, were such well-known individuals as William Gray, several members of the Hooper family, H. H. Hunnewell, Thomas

W. Ward, and the Robert Rantouls, Senior and Junior. Among the Boston firms represented were the new and important financial house of John E. Thayer & Brother and the Massachusetts Hospital Life Insurance Company. Significant New York firms interested in the road were Prime, Ward & King, Morgan Ketchum & Co., and John Ward & Co.[21]

As with the Boston and Lowell, stockholders in the B. and W. were also apparently involved in land speculation, in this case through the South Cove Corporation. Intending to provide a terminus for the B. and W. at tidewater, this corporation concluded a contract with the railroad in April 1833. By this agreement, the Worcester road, in return for a bonus of about $75,000, partially paid in land, agreed to establish its depot on the reclaimed land owned by the South Cove Corporation.[22] The bonus was paid by 1834, and the terminal was built in 1836.

The South Cove agent's report for the latter year linked the corporation's potential success with western trade. "We may thus hope," Francis Jackson wrote, "for our own enterprise and for this community the immense advantages that must result from a continuous Rail Road to the Lakes, and from a close connection with the stupendous public works which form the pride of the State of New-York, and with the innumerable sources of business to which they lead — works where millions have been invested, and to which millions more will be added." [23]

Indicating that significant amounts of Boston capital had not yet moved west of the Hudson, this report emphasized the benefits to be derived from using the fruits of western internal improvements financed by others. "To these vast advantages," Jackson declared, "the community have been roused at last by the individual exertions of the public-spirited and enterprising among us, through whose successful efforts we may avail ourselves of the immense and constantly accumulating investment of capital in other States, and make that minister to our prosperity as truly as if the great internal improvements of the western country had been effected by capital drawn from our own community." Jackson also concluded that the company's land would "take rank among the most safe and permanent investments of the day." [24]

In August 1838 the directors of the South Cove Corporation voted to divide part of its lands among the stockholders. As a result, 415 lots were marked off and priced at half their estimated current value; each shareholder was entitled to one lot for each two shares of stock ($500 par value per share) that he held.[25] The same procedure was later followed by Boston investors in Illinois, Michigan, and farther west.

The second phase of the effort to link Boston with the Hudson by rail, involving construction from Worcester to the New York border, got under way after the B. and W. reached Westboro in November 1834. The Western Rail-Road's promoters refused a New York offer to subscribe the total amount of capital, on the grounds that Wall Street's control might be contrary to Massachusetts' best interest. Although the promoters still hoped that New York might take as much as 45 per cent of the stock, they were doomed to disappointment. After a ten-day campaign early in 1835 to dispose of 20,000 shares of Western stock in Boston, New York City, Worcester, Springfield, Pittsfield, and Albany, only 13,000 shares were taken. Of this amount Bostonians had subscribed for 8,500 shares, Springfield and Albany investors the rest. New York City capitalists refused to support the stock at all; their negative attitude was quickly explained away as the result of fear that the Western would make it possible for Boston to compete with New York for the Erie trade.[26] Still, in the very region to be served by the road, there was no enthusiasm for investing in it. The practical difficulties of building a route through the Berkshires, Worcester's dislike of being replaced as a terminus, and the seemingly large element of risk in the enterprise combined to discourage the taking of stock.

A major effort in Boston to complete the subscriptions made slow progress at first. Josiah Quincy, Jr. found many excuses offered by potential investors during his round of solicitations in November 1835. Some thought Boston large enough and that there was no need to increase it through new rail connections. Others thought that little reliance — at least in dollars-and-cents commitments — could be placed on legislative grants of railroad privilege, but few came out and forthrightly declined to subscribe.[27]

The pattern of subscription makes it obvious that uncertainty about the Western's future still bulked large in the minds of many Boston capitalists. The largest subscription was for only 200 shares, and many wealthy Bostonians were reluctant to risk more than $500 or $1,000 in the project.* [28] Nevertheless, by early December the thorough canvassing was rewarded and the books were closed. By January 1836, the corporation was organized.**

The purchase of Western Rail-Road stock was regarded in some quarters more as a patriotic gesture than as an investment. The directors of the railroad pointed out in 1840 that "no one subscribed to it for investment, merely, but in order to promote a great public improvement . . ." [29] Some wealthy Bostonians like Harrison Gray Otis and David Sears even decided it would be more prudent to give money to the road than to assume any liabilities by subscribing to the stock. Their contributions were applied to assessments on defaulted stock and permitted new subscriptions at a 10 per cent discount.

The reluctance of private capitalists to invest in the Western Rail-Road turned the attention of its friends to state aid. Clever legislative maneuvering resulted in a law increasing the authorized capital by $1,000,000. The state treasurer was empowered to subscribe this amount, but he was to pay no assessment until private stockholders had met 75 per cent of their obligations. The interests of the state were to be further protected by having three of the nine directors chosen by the legislature. The men so chosen were Isaac C. Bates, William Jackson, and Robert Rantoul, Jr.[30] This same type of public-private cooperation, involving larger public commitments and fewer safeguards, was prominent in many transportation ventures in mid-Atlantic and southern states.[31] Later it characterized many western roads in which Boston capitalists took an interest.

Among the Western's private directors, Thomas B. Wales, retired merchant and president of the road, and George Bliss of Springfield, later a key figure in the Michigan Southern, were the most impor-

* The following list of stockholders, though incomplete, indicates the small size of individual holdings: James K. Mills & Co., 200 shares; A. & A. Lawrence & Co. and Whitwell, Bond & Co., 150 shares each; Nathan Appleton, Lawrence & Stone, Palmer Co., T. H. Perkins, T. R. Sewell, R. G. Shaw, Israel Thorndike, Waterston, Pray & Co., J. D. Williams, 100 shares each; W. Raymond Lee, Samuel Appleton, William Appleton, J. C. Gray, F. C. Gray, Horace Gray, G. W. Lyman, G. W. Pratt, William Pratt, William Sturgis, T. B. Wales, 50 shares each; Edward Everett, John E. Thayer, 20 shares each; W. F. Weld, 10 shares.

** Among the first Boston directors were: Thomas B. Wales, William Lawrence, Edmund Dwight, Henry Rice, John Henshaw, Francis Jackson, and Josiah Quincy, Jr.

tant. Bliss succeeded Wales as president in 1842 and served, with the exception of one year, until 1846.

William H. Swift, a West Point graduate, was resident engineer for the Western. He later became an adviser on American railroads to Baring Brothers of London and was closely associated with a number of Boston-sponsored projects in the West.

The Panic of 1837 hit the Western hard. A corporation report submitted to the Massachusetts legislature early in 1838 reflected the unfortunate results of enforced reliance on small stockholders. According to this report, many stockholders had "lost either their entire means of payment, or at least, the surplus that they had thus appropriated." [32] One group of directors and stockholders favored suspension of all work on the road pending an improvement in economic conditions; another group, in which P. P. F. DeGrand was apparently the leading figure, sought a loan from the state. The second group won out. Looking back on this event, Charles Francis Adams, Jr. saw in it a major defeat for the principle of private enterprise and with it the beginning of Boston capitalists' estrangement from local railroad investment.[33]

On February 21, 1838, the Massachusetts legislature created $2,100,000 of 5 per cent sterling bonds and assigned them to the Western Rail-Road. The railroad assumed responsibility for protecting the Commonwealth against loss and executed a mortgage in its favor covering the franchise, income, and property of the road. To complete the loan, the Western's treasurer first had to collect six assessments on privately subscribed stock. To retire the debt, a sinking fund was to be created.[34] Baring Brothers engaged to sell the securities on commission within one year from April 1, 1838.

The bond issue of 1838 was but the first of several state loans, which by 1841 amounted to about $4,000,000. A total of $1,838,912 was sold in England and $2,168,731 in the United States.[35] A correspondent of *Hunt's Merchants' Magazine* pointed out in September 1845 that Massachusetts 5 per cents were selling above par in London. He suggested that the eastern capitalists could sell securities to foreigners and invest the proceeds in "railroad shares of a far higher intrinsic value. In this way," he continued, "the superior knowledge possessed by our eastern capitalists, of the rapidly developing resources of the west, will enable them to profit largely by the introduction of European capital; and all the parties to the arrangement will participate in its benefits." [36]

The statistics on private ownership of the Western Rail-Road as reported to the legislature in February 1841 indicate the importance of Boston's interest and also confirm the small size of the average holding. Of 1,949 stockholders, 1,095 were located in Boston. However, only seventeen persons owned 100 shares or more, whereas 1,652 owned one to ten shares. Of the total number of stockholders, only 183 were not among the original subscribers.[37]

The Western's Massachusetts charter authorized building to the state border, but the final leg to Albany was provided by the Albany and West Stockbridge Railroad Company, chartered in New York in 1836. To finance its construction, the city of Albany subscribed $1,000,000, the entire capital stock, paying for it in city bonds. On payment of principal and interest, the Western was to come into complete control of the road.[38] Thus the Western, estimated to cost $3,000,000, in the end cost about $7,000,000, and of this amount some $5,000,000 was advanced by state and local government.

Trains first traversed the whole route on October 9, 1841. On December 27, Bostonians journeyed to Albany, and the next day the New Yorkers repaid the visit. For their dinner that evening there was bread made from flour brought from Albany, symbolic of the major source of the Western's anticipated traffic.

Hopes that the Western would give Boston a decisive advantage over rival Atlantic coast ports were not realized. It was still cheaper to ship flour down the Hudson than over the rails to Boston. In part this disappointing situation could be traced to Troy's jealousy of Albany which had kept a bridge from being constructed to give the Western Rail-Road direct access to Albany, and to the fact that the Boston and Worcester's South Cove terminal did not prove suitable for directly loading ocean-going ships.

Quite aside from these difficulties, a rift developed between B. and W. directors and those of the Western over rates and their division. The two roads operated as independent entities, and the best chance of union — in 1846 — was lost as the result of unfortunate criticism of the Western by B. and W. president Nathan Hale.

In the fifties New York forged far ahead of Boston in both imports and exports, and trade with the West by rail was decisively drawn to this center rather than over the Berkshires to Boston.[39] Nevertheless, both the B. and W. and the Western proved profitable. The former had little difficulty in making the annual 10 per cent profit permitted by its charter. From 1845 on, the Western paid dividends and eventually paid off the state loan. However, the bickering between the managements of the two roads during the period when Boston had excess capital available for investment apparently helped to turn the interest of new Boston railroad investors toward areas outside the state.

The decline of Salem as a port — though it remained the home of numerous merchants — and the rising importance of Boston, enhanced by its proposed rail connections with the West, influenced the incorporation of the Eastern Railroad Company in 1836. Three years earlier a legislative committee had found no public necessity for a road from East Boston to Salem, had concluded that such a railroad would be unprofitable, and had noted with disapproval the connection between the proposed route and the real estate interests of the petitioners. This attitude was changed, however, by a flood of new petitions asking for the road. In 1836 a charter was granted, on condition that the road extend to the New Hampshire line instead of ending at Salem.

The Eastern's initial authorized capital was $1,300,000, which could be increased to $2,000,000. By April 1836 George Peabody, the Salem merchant who actively promoted the road, reported subscriptions for 8,300 shares.[40] The directors of the East Boston Company, which held lands in that part of the city, had been disappointed in their own application for a railroad charter to serve Salem, but they subscribed generously to the new road once it was established that the route would pass through their property.[41] Residents of towns along the way, like Lynn, were also eager subscribers. Receipts from stock assessments, however, proved inadequate to complete the road to Salem, much less to the state border.

When the Eastern turned to the state for aid, the legislature responded generously. In April 1837 it authorized a loan to the road of $500,000 in state scrip, bearing 5 per cent interest and repayable in twenty years. Again capital came from abroad, with Baring Brothers purchasing this scrip. A year later the state authorized an additional loan of $90,000, contingent on the sale of stock.[42]

In August 1838 the road was opened to Salem. In his address on this occasion, the company's president, George Peabody, observed: "The aid which has been latterly bestowed on projects of internal improvement will go far to maintain that rank which she [Massachusetts] has always held among the States of the Union." And he predicted, "The future growth and prosperity of our country must be powerfully influenced by the introduction of Rail Roads." [43]

Peabody's optimism was soon justified by the progress of his road. Good business between Salem and Boston encouraged the sale of additional stock, which in 1839, when the first dividend was paid, almost reached par. In addition the state in that same year extended $100,000 more in aid, still without insisting that a representative of the Commonwealth be seated on the Eastern's board. With these resources the line was pushed to the Merrimack River at Newburyport by June 1840, and reached Portsmouth, New Hampshire, the following December. Within two years the Eastern helped link Portland, Maine, and Boston by connections with the Portland, Saco and Portsmouth Rail Road.

Whereas about one fourth the net capital used in construction of the Eastern Railroad depended on credit provided by the state, construction of the Portland, Saco and Portsmouth, organized in December 1840, was financed for the most part by Boston stockholders. Three of the road's seven directors came from the Eastern. One of them, David A. Neal, who became a director of the Eastern in 1840 and its president in 1842, was chosen president of the affiliated road.*

From 1847 on the Eastern ran into increasing financial difficulties, which led the management to seek new loans. Dividends were made a first charge against net income. To maintain the 8 per cent payments, the directors in 1848 began dipping into accumulated surplus. Dividends finally were cut back, but only slightly. Indebtedness mounted and the total accumulated surplus melted away from $156,851 in 1849 to a deficit of $465 at the end of 1852.[44] To meet this crisis the directors authorized ten-year 5 per cent convertible bonds to an amount of $750,000. The Barings took $650,000, and

* Other members of the Eastern's board, like Neal, were later important investors in western railroads. Among them were John E. Thayer, William Sturgis, and John Bryant. Benjamin P. Chamberlain of Salem, later influential in Ohio's Mad River and Lake Erie Railroad, was also active in the Eastern.

the remainder was placed by William Sturgis and other New Englanders.[45]

The Eastern's difficulties were the result of errors of both commission and omission. First, the directors maintained an attractive dividend rate regardless of earnings. Second, in its competition with the rival Boston & Maine, the road acquired branches and attendant obligations without sufficient investigation and without the approval of stockholders. Third, authority was divided between Neal, the president; the treasurer, William S. Tuckerman, who abused the trust placed in him; and a superintendent who reported directly to the board rather than to the president.

It should be remembered, however, that the problems of attracting and holding good men and capital, of meeting competition, and of insuring sound management and accounting practices were perennial ones. Several of the key figures in the Eastern faced precisely the same difficulties in connection with their later investments in western railroads.

In the two decades after the chartering of the Boston and Lowell in 1830, and especially during the forties, Boston's resources grew and its influence expanded. The establishment of semi-monthly steamship service between Boston and Europe and the growth of a railroad network centering on Boston were partially responsible for this growth. Manufacturing also played an important part. Whereas New York had seized the lead in trade after the War of 1812, the industrial and transportation revolutions had placed Massachusetts in a commanding position as a center of capital during a crucial decade of western development. To illustrate, between 1840 and 1850 the population of Boston and its surrounding towns increased from about 159,000 to about 270,000, while assessed valuation of property rose from slightly above $120,100,000, to more than $266,600,000, or an average of more than 12 per cent per year.[46] In foreign commerce, however, Boston had not kept pace with its population growth; its high point in exports had been reached in 1832, in imports in 1836.[47]

The rate of expansion of Massachusetts' wealth was more rapid after the Panic of 1837 than before. The *American Railroad Journal* attributed this growth, centered in Boston, mostly to the railroads.[48] E. Hasket Derby, son of the great Salem merchant and one of the most ardent advocates of Massachusetts railroads, made a more balanced appraisal when he wrote: "It would not be just, however, to ascribe all this [growth] to the railroad system; a part is doubtless due to commerce, manufactures, and the fisheries; but the improved system of communications has given to them a vast impulse, and they have exerted a powerful influence on the system itself." [49]

Manufacturing, of course, competed with railroads for capital. Statistics on Boston's manufacturing capital of this era are of dubious validity, and sometimes contradictory.[50] One source indicates that total manufacturing capital, after a sharp decline in the wake of the Panic of 1837, almost doubled between 1840 and 1845, though it still fell far short of the 1837 figure.[51] An incomplete estimate of capital invested in manufacturing in the Bay State as revealed by assessors' reports for 1845 placed the figure at over $59,000,000.[52] By way of contrast, the seven principal railroads serving Boston reportedly had, with branches, a capital of $22,202,700 and represented expenditures of almost $27,000,000.[53]

At the beginning of 1845 Bostonians' railroad interests apparently were primarily local — a conclusion which seems to be confirmed from available records of individual investors. The general success of their experience encouraged additional railroad investment, some of it outside Massachusetts.

Boston Railroad Investment Outside New England Prior to 1845

Before the mid-forties, some Boston capitalists had broadened their experience by investment in eastern rail lines outside New England. Among these capitalists, on a cautious basis, were China traders, following the advice of trusted friends like Bryant & Sturgis, who invested for themselves and John P. Cushing, and of John E. Thayer & Brother. These Bostonians moved primarily into New York and Pennsylvania railroads.

All the New York railroad stocks and bonds owned by Cushing and purchased by Bryant & Sturgis were (with one minor exception) those of roads that were eventually merged into the New York Central line. The two partners themselves were heavy investors; Sturgis claimed in 1849 that, while taking more interest in the Attica and Buffalo than in any other road between Albany and Buffalo, he had a pecuniary interest in all of them beyond Schenectady.[54] There is no need to trace the yearly changes here, but it is relevant that Cushing, who held some $35,000 worth of New York railroad securities in 1840, held $177,000 in 1850, and almost $250,000 after the formation of the New York Central. His bond holdings, which only became significant with the 1853 consolidation, were $123,500 in 1855.

To judge by the Cushing data, Bryant & Sturgis had an investment interest in New York roads as early as 1839 — by which time Cushing already owned 300 shares in the Utica & Schenectady, valued at cost at $31,962.[55] Over the years, as was in part indicated above, Bryant, Sturgis, and Cushing built up their portfolios of New York railroad stocks, especially as the strategic and economic value of the lines became apparent. By 1843 Sturgis was a director of the Attica and Buffalo, and by 1850 was on the board of the Auburn & Syracuse.

William Sturgis' relationship with the leading promoter and manager of the New York Central, Erastus Corning, was strong and friendly. Corning, a resident of Albany and a businessman of diverse interests (including the manufacture and merchandising of iron ware), was an orginal subscriber to and commissioner of the Utica & Schenectady (1833) and president and virtual dictator of the road. But his interest in this line, as in such others as the Mohawk & Hudson, was primarily, it seems, based on their suitability as customers for iron — and because control of them gave him a secure, gilt-edged market.[56]

By the summer of 1843 it was apparent that the Attica and Buffalo badly needed funds. Sturgis preferred a loan to selling stock at a discount. Accordingly he wrote the road's treasurer: "I would *not* advise selling any stock belonging to Company at less than par at the present time, because I have little doubt that it can be run off at that rate, or near it, in course of a few months, provided you can appropriate the net earnings . . . to making a dividend as soon as a sufficient amount shall have been earned." Meantime, he offered to negotiate a short-term loan, using the stock as collateral.[57] Sturgis urged the road's president, Oliver Lee, to maintain secrecy about the prospective loan lest the company find that it could not continue to buy up debts at favorable terms from current creditors.[58]

Sturgis' close ties with the Attica and Buffalo led other Bostonians to take a limited interest in it and he raised $50,000 for the company by August 7, 1843, from this source.* This appears to be the first time the Forbes family became involved in railroad financing. The money was apparently used principally to pay some of the outstanding obligations of the company.[59]

As spokesman for Boston stockholders, Sturgis stood between management and important owners. He used this position to give advice to management freely. In view of the policies adopted by China traders when they turned to ownership in western railroads, Sturgis' view that a railroad should be judged purely as a transportation agency is worth noting. A quotation from an 1849 letter to the president of the Attica and Buffalo illustrates the point: "Rail Road Corporations should never purchase land nor any thing else that they do not absolutely require . . . merely because it is *cheap,* and if you still hold land, purchased when you contemplated going to the Creek in another direction, I recommend a prompt sale of it. Let others speculate on the rise of land, it is not judicious for Rail Road Companies to do so beyond their certain wants." [60]

A letter written by Sturgis in December 1842 to a committee of directors of the Syracuse & Utica exemplifies the same financial conservatism which was evident in his discussion of the affairs of the Attica and Buffalo: "You ask our opinion as to the expediency of reducing dividends, to conform to diminished receipts. Upon this subject *we have not the shadow of a doubt.* Our rule of action for ourselves, & our advice to others, always is, to *earn* money before dividing it, & to let corporations *get out of debt, & keep out of debt,* so far as the nature of their business will permit." [61]

Even more important than Sturgis in drawing Boston capital into railroads outside New England in the mid-1840's was the partnership of John E. Thayer & Brother. This financial house was in touch with railroad developments throughout the United States. Like Bryant & Sturgis, it was especially interested in the railroads of west-

* Among the Boston stockholders were the following, with the amount of their subscription:

Name	*Amount*
Dana & Henshaw	$15,000
William F. Weld	10,000
Bryant & Sturgis	13,000
Henry Timmins	3,500
E. Loring	3,500
R. B. & J. M. Forbes (Trustees of Margaret Forbes)	3,700
J. M. Forbes (Guardian to M. C. Hartt, Jr.)	1,300

ern New York state, but the Thayers actively sought and promoted railroad investment wherever a profitable opportunity arose.

One such opportunity was provided by the Philadelphia and Reading Railroad. Incorporated in 1833 with the purpose of transporting coal, the railroad had had various financial difficulties which forced it to resort to debt financing.[62] In these operations the road had the assistance of the United States Bank and of John Gihon & Company of New York, a correspondent of McCalmont & Company of London. The strength of the Gihon connection was shown in 1844 when John Tucker of that firm became president of the Reading.

Tucker faced a debt-laden situation but one in which potential earnings were excellent. The Reading was in a favorable position to dominate the coal-carrying trade and its physical facilities had been steadily improved and expanded. On the other hand, the book cost of the road had risen by December 1, 1844 to slightly under $9,500,000, of which only $2,010,000 was represented by capital stock. Bonds, which had been sold at a discount, accounted for more than $6,600,000 of the total, and floating debt made up the remainder.[63] The heavy debt-equity ratio was of the type that ex-China trader Sturgis deplored and in sharp contrast to early New England practice.

The business affairs of the Reading were of some concern to Bostonians, who by this time had a significant interest in that road. One group of substantial Boston capitalists was drawn into its affairs because the road had purchased coal cars and locomotives from the Proprietors of the Locks and Canals at Lowell on credit. Although 6 per cent bonds, due in 1845, were issued by the Reading to cover this purchase,[64] Patrick Tracy Jackson of the Proprietors was pressing Tucker in February 1844 to pay the road's obligations. In his laconic words, "Our debt is due, and we suppose that we have in our hands the means of obtaining payment . . ." [65]

John E. Thayer & Brother was also connected with the Reading, possibly because, like Gihon & Company, the Boston house was a correspondent of McCalmont & Company. John E. Thayer was a mortgage trustee of the 1843 issue of 6 per cent bonds to finance double-tracking of the road, and his brother Nathaniel performed a similar function for an issue of 6 per cent convertibles in 1844.[66]

The Thayers also assumed responsibility for insuring New England participation in Tucker's effort to end the burden of the floating debt by selling $400,000 worth of bonds and notes in 1845 and 22,000 shares of stock in 1846.[67] John Thayer agreed to take $150,000 of the bonds at 80 to 75, but he had difficulty in disposing of them.[68] He found Bostonians like John M. Forbes, William Sturgis, John Bryant, Thomas Motley, and David Neal interested in the road but hesitant to invest in it.

It was well known that the Reading had incurred a large debt but Thayer had not provided information on the nature of these obligations and the road's prospects. At Neal's suggestion a committee was appointed to investigate the situation,[69] with Dr. Amos Binney and W. Raymond Lee representing Boston interests. The investigating committee submitted its report in December 1845. It concluded that there was no evidence of fraudulent practices but expressed concern about the floating debt. If this problem could be solved and additional equipment provided so that 1,500,000 tons of coal could be transported annually, the members of the committee predicted that a 6 per cent return on investment could be paid.[70]

These recommendations were more easily made than implemented. The Reading's managers tried to meet the situation on the basis of expediency, approving a 10 per cent stock dividend in 1846 and one of 12 per cent in 1847. The policy was frankly designed to placate stockholders, but the managers argued that bondholders should also be satisfied since the cash conserved by this device could be applied to reduction of debt with a corresponding increase in the bondholders' security.[71]

Boston's expanding investment in railroads during the 1840's was evident in the Reading's ownership. In February 1847 it was reported that about one third of the Reading's stock was owned in Boston, another third in Europe, and the remainder in Philadelphia and elsewhere.[72] It was in this year that David A. Neal, according to his account book, first purchased stock in the road. About this time E. H. Derby also took an interest, as did John M. Forbes. But the Reading in March of that year found Boston unable to increase its holdings. "Every channel for money seems dried up," Tucker was informed.[73]

Despite efforts to reorganize the capital structure, the Reading's financial problems became worse in 1848. The road lacked working capital; credit had been extended too liberally to shippers; subscribers to the $1,400,000 bond issue of 1847 had not paid up but the directors had already committed the money. Moreover, the London money market, which had provided the answer to similar problems in the past, was prostrate. Still worse, the rival Schuylkill Navigation Company cut its rates, forcing the Reading to follow suit.[74]

To meet this emergency, the road's managers borrowed heavily, using as collateral bonds held in the company's treasury. In addition, conversion of all debts maturing before 1857 into 7 per cent preferred stock, with a bonus of 30 per cent, was authorized. These securities were sold at a 40 per cent discount, which vastly inflated the book cost of the company's property. Of $2,151,685 added to the balance sheet item of property investment in seven months, only $9,343 represented actual purchases of new property.[75]

Such developments did not escape the notice of the Boston press, which began to urge local investors to dispose of Reading securities. A new Boston committee was formed and in April 1848 queried Tucker on the proposed funding of debt into preferred stock. On May 10 President Tucker addressed a frank letter to the committee pointing out the advantages of the plan in the light of past experience and potential earnings and held forth the "diminution of debt and early cash dividends" as the promised rewards of approval. The Reading managers also invited New England investors to send a representative to Philadelphia to examine the company's financial condition. At a public meeting late in 1848 David A. Neal, president of the Eastern Railroad, was selected to act in this capacity.[76]

Neal investigated the Reading's tangled financial affairs in detail. His report of September 1849 was critical of the road's management for selling bonds below par and for issuing misleading annual reports, but he found excuses for them and concluded that Reading securities were more than speculative playthings. His remedies for the financial problem as put forth in September 1849 and January 1850, were: (1) to refund the maturing debt by extending the date of payments; (2) to create a sinking fund of three cents for every 100 ton-miles of freight transported; (3) to close the capital account at $16,325,032 for the existing plant, although about 50 per cent of it was "water." He also advocated a tightening of managerial controls and structures.[77] In short, his solution was to make adjustments in the existing situation, accept capitalization of future earnings or "good will," and avoid drastic changes. The problem and the "solution" were to become familiar ones to Boston investors in western railroads, although the results were seldom as good as those achieved on the Reading.

The acceptance of Neal's plan, plus an insistence on cash payment by shippers and a pool of the coal traffic with the Schuylkill Navigation Company, resulted in a rapid recovery for the Reading. Freight tonnage increased and unit costs dropped, permitting resumption of dividend payments in 1850. The improved situation led to an appreciation in stock prices, and convertible bonds were increasingly exchanged for equity. As a result the stock portion of total capitalization rose from 28 per cent in 1846 to 61 per cent by 1856.[78]

In fact, the situation worked out much as Neal had predicted. In his 1849 report he had been so confident that the road could earn a return on common stock after paying all fixed charges, that he had offered to take over the road for a period of ten years and, with the aid of five others whom he promised to find, guarantee annual earnings of about 4.75 per cent on the $4,218,117 of common stock.[79]

Boston investors in the Reading displayed distinctive investment principles that later differentiated their attitudes toward western railroads. Conservative John M. Forbes sold his Reading stock in early 1849 after learning of the road's condition. He disapproved of the management's short-run perspective and policies but lacked means of influencing them. Therefore, he withdrew his money. Neal, on the other hand, with judgment based, partially at least, on "inside" knowledge, saw in the Reading an opportunity for a speculative venture. In February 1850, he had a one third interest in the purchase of Reading stock with Horatio H. Hunnewell, a rising Boston financier.[80] By June 1 he had 1,950 shares of the stock, worth $18.59 per share. By mid-October his holdings had been increased to 2,742 shares. Although he began to sell in December, he ended the year with 1,592 shares of common on which his books showed a better than $50,000 paper gain. In March 1851, he formally left his position with the road, and received $2,750 for fifteen months of service. For unknown reasons, he presented $1,000 of this amount to the officers of the company.[81]

Neal's operations in Reading stock with Hunnewell continued but on the whole with decreasing success.[82] Reportedly, Hunnewell reaped $100,000 profit from his investment in the Reading.[83] Part of their holdings were liquidated in December 1853, and applied to bonds of the nation's first federal land-grant railroad, the Illinois Central.

The Neal-Hunnewell alliance is significant in that it exemplified one process by which Boston capital moved increasingly into western railroads and corollary investments. One successful opportunistic adventure led to another — in this instance, from Pennsylvania to Illinois. After his stint on the Reading, Neal became an officer of the newly organized Illinois Central, as will be described in a subsequent chapter. Hunnewell subscribed to $20,000 of Illinois Central bonds, and the stock associated with this purchase was held for him by the Neal firm.[84] Together, David Neal and Hunnewell in December 1852 purchased 480 acres of Illinois land from John C. Dodge of Chicago. Both investors were also interested in the Cumberland Coal Company.[85]

While Neal eventually moved from railroads into land speculation, Hunnewell became more closely allied with the western railroads in which John M. Forbes played a leading role. In following Forbes, Hunnewell became a director of the Hannibal and St. Joseph (1854–1871), a director of the Michigan Central for twenty years, and a mortgage trustee for it in 1857 and for the Chicago, Burlington & Quincy in 1858. Later he also became a director of the Illinois Central (1863–1871) and other western roads. He was one of the incorporators of the Webster Bank of Boston (1853) and served as a director until 1902.[86]

Besides the Reading, another middle Atlantic railroad attracted the attention of Bostonians during the 1840's. The Philadelphia, Wilmington and Baltimore Rail Road, unlike the Reading, was a passenger rather than a freight road. Formed by the union of three separate companies in 1838, it connected Philadelphia with Maryland's largest port and formed the central portion of the heavily traveled north-south route between New York and Washington.

Central to the financing of the Philadelphia, Wilmington and Baltimore were Nicholas Biddle and the Bank of the United States of Pennsylvania, which also aided the Reading. In a letter of 1841, Biddle explained his role in these words: "A large portion of the funds was borrowed from the Bank, and with a view to ensure its completion, I became personally the guarantee to the Bank for the safety of about 400,000 dollars of the loan." [87] In November 1840 the road owed the Bank $232,000 secured by hypothecation of stock and due in April 1841. To meet this obligation the company issued 6 per cent sterling bonds, payable in London in 1850. Heavy debts, including a convertible loan payable in 1842 and other bonds falling due in that and the succeeding year, forced the mortgaging of the road's property and major refunding operations.[88]

By 1846 the P. W. and B.'s problems had become acute. Interest charges were consuming $200,000 a year, and debts coming due remained unpaid. At this point New Englanders, scenting a promising opportunity for profit, moved into the picture. According to *Hunt's Merchants' Magazine,* they purchased four-fifths of the existing common stock of the road and took over the floating debt, which they converted into new shares. Capital stock was thereby increased $1,000,000. Stockholders agreed to subscribe to further new stock at par to the amount of $350,000 for improvement of the road. Second-mortgage bondholders converted their holdings to stock, and first-mortgage bondholders agreed to consolidate their loans under a new mortgage payable in 1860.[89] As a result, debt was reduced from 57 per cent to 34 per cent of the whole investment, and funded.

Among the New Englanders involved in these steps was John M. Forbes, who was instrumental in getting William H. Swift out of the army to take over the presidency of P. W. and B. in 1848.[90] Another was Edmund Dwight, a textile manufacturer and an active promoter and long-time director of the Western Rail-Road of Massachusetts (1836–1839, 1842–1849), where Swift had been resident engineer. Dwight, who was active in western investment, was elected a director of the P. W. and B. in 1849, but died in the same year. John C. Lee of Boston succeeded to his post. David A. Neal apparently had some small interest in the road as early as 1846,[91] and in the fifties John P. Cushing and Augustine Heard also held P. W. and B. securities. New England influence remained strong well into the post-Civil War period.[92]

These two Middle Atlantic roads, the Philadelphia and Reading and the Philadelphia, Wilmington and Baltimore, indicate Boston's pre-eminent position as a center of railroad capital in the 1840's. The fact that these roads turned to the Bay State for financial aid shows that the collapse of the United States Bank in 1841 had ended Philadelphia's role as the nation's financial center. New York was rising rapidly to claim this title, but for a few short years — and especially those that were critical in the early development of trans-Allegheny railroads — Boston held sway.

An analyst of the contemporary scene wrote to president John Tucker of the Reading in June 1845: "The Boston people are certainly the only Community who understand Rail Roads. At the present time they have more money than they know what to do with." [93] Six months earlier the *American Railroad Journal* had noted the influence of Bostonians when it declared that "the opinions of half a dozen eminent Boston merchants — if decidedly unfavorable — will be quite sufficient to deter foreign capitalists from investing in the securities of the Western States, be the advantages offered ever so great." [94]

Patterns of Involvement: A Summary

The era from 1830 to the mid-1840's marked an increasing commitment of Boston capital to railroads. The first step was taken to give the time, reliability, and cost-saving advantages of steam transportation to the Massachusetts textile complex. The next step was to improve the connections of the Bay State with outlying regions, more especially with trade routes from the trans-Allegheny West. These efforts were largely designed to revitalize and protect existing mercantile and manufacturing interests, but as investments *per se* they initially had small appeal to the mercantile aristocracy. Therefore, what private capital failed to provide, the state contributed. Once the process of private involvement had started, however, it gathered momentum. Increasingly, local roads attracted capital because of the return that could be earned on investment, and one investment led to another in an ever-widening geographical area.

Specific patterns of involvement by individuals and the changes wrought in their investment portfolios and vocations differed markedly. The most complete transformation can be seen in David A. Neal. From a seafaring and mercantile career, he turned to railroad management and investment, which carried him from tidewater Salem, the source of his initial capital, to land speculation in Illinois. In the process he apparently attracted investors who relied on his professional and "inside" railroad knowledge to help them identify and take advantage of comparatively short-run profit opportunities.

A different pattern is exemplified by John Bryant and William Sturgis. Turning from the China trade earlier than their contemporaries, they became professional investment managers for themselves and, most notably, for John P. Cushing. In this capacity Bryant & Sturgis took an interest in the major roads radiating from Boston but were careful not to concentrate their risks in any one of them or even in the railroad industry. Their involvement gradually became deeper and carried them into connecting roads in New York state. Never active in day-to-day management, they exerted a conservative influence on the policies of roads with which they were associated, stressing that profitability lay in the long-run development of the railroad as a transportation facility and not in short-run speculative operations.

This was a principle and an approach shared by John M. Forbes, another China trader, whose involvement in railroads came later and more spectacularly than that of Bryant & Sturgis. Naturally such men tended to attract a following that shared their beliefs and formed a more or less cohesive group which moved with few defections or additions from one enterprise to another.

Promotional activity by dealers in securities like P. P. F. DeGrand and John E. Thayer & Brother also encouraged railroad investment. The latter firm had close connections with roads outside New England and acted primarily as a promoter and distributor of their securities. John E. Thayer, for example, was attacked for using pressure tactics in disposing of Reading securities, as well as for a lack of frankness about the condition and prospects of the road. The Thayers had a more speculative approach to investment than Forbes, but they became his close and important allies through several decades of western railroad building.

Investment in eastern railroads brought major Boston capitalists closer together and at the same time differentiated them on the basis of size of resources, past business experience, and time perspectives used in assessing investment "payouts." These differences were reflected in part by the degree of emphasis each type of investor placed on controlling the management of railroads in which he invested and the purposes for which he used his influence. In the case of the Reading, liaison with the management was not initially so close nor so continuous as it might have been. It was not until David A. Neal was invited to investigate the road's affairs in 1848 that the deficiencies of management became fully known to New England investors. Lacking control, Forbes terminated his investment while Neal remained to profit from his position. On the other hand, in the P. W. and B., Bostonians of the Forbes persuasion assured themselves of responsive and responsible management by putting William H. Swift, in whom they had confidence based on experience, at the head of the road.

If the initial Boston involvement in railroads implied a cumulative geographical extension even before tidewater capitalists came to be interested in the Midwest, the types of problems they encountered, given the differences in roads and localities, were not always directly comparable. Nevertheless, there was some significant unity in diversity. For example, as might be expected with new and highly capitalized ventures, difficulties centering upon securing capital and problems of financial management generally predominated.

Managerial policies toward railroad finance, and investors' attitudes toward managerial policies, established a framework which fitted the varieties of experience in the East and yet were applicable to later railroad problems in the West. Some Boston investors, like Forbes, while not averse to speculative gains, showed themselves reluctant to participate in highly uncertain ventures — particularly if the investors lacked direct influence on the managerial side. Others, with shorter time-horizons like Neal's, were perfectly willing to plunge into speculative waters if they could exercise managerial influence to reap short-run profits from inside knowledge. Still others, like William Sturgis, looked for "solid" investments, with managerial responsibility *and* conservatism, and were averse to an intermingling of functions such as transportation enterprise and land speculation. Presumably one reason why Sturgis never participated very extensively in trans-Allegheny railroads was precisely because they so often had the characteristics to which he objected even when they occurred to a relatively minor degree in railroads nearer home, where he centered his railroad investment.

The Bostonians who carried their capital and entrepreneurial skills into the West in the 1840's were principally those who were prepared to assume greater risks than Sturgis, but they did not comprise a homogeneous group. The patterns of management and investment they exemplified had, as will be seen, significant differences, and in many cases such patterns can be detected, at least in embryo, in their earlier eastern railroad ventures.

This was the situation on the eve of major Boston involvement in trans-Allegheny railroads. The new form of transportation had gained an important foothold in Massachusetts and had drawn Boston capital in limited amounts beyond the boundaries of New England. A fund of technical, entrepreneurial, and financial experience had been acquired. Distinctions had appeared between small investors hoping for large, quick returns, financial intermediaries who sought a profit from mobilizing capital wherever it was to be found, and a few large capitalists who approached the field of railroading with caution. But while the men and policies were to some extent constant, a new wave of capital, largely from the China trade, carried these varied interests over the Alleghenies and into a new era of railroad investment destined to dwarf the earlier experience in magnitude and significance.

PART III The Era of Involvement

Chapter 4

The West: Experiment and Opportunity, 1830–1850

THE AMERICAN West was developed by successive waves of capital and of people with many skills who conquered and developed a continent in record time. One such wave occurred in the Old Northwest during the 1840's, bringing a new generation's capital and entrepreneurial skills from the shores of Massachusetts Bay to an area settled by an earlier generation of New Englanders. For each generation, involvement in the West, old or new, was an experiment and an opportunity — an experiment in adapting attitudes and practices to a new environment, and an opportunity, first, to gain subsistence and then to prosper by reaching and developing a market for the wealth that lay on and under the soil of the trans-Allegheny West.

Transforming a geographical frontier into an integral and productive part of the national economy was painful and expensive, as well as rewarding. It was fraught with obstacles and difficulties that challenged familiar techniques of raising capital, organizing enterprises, exploiting and developing natural resources, and relating the results effectively to the existing flows of economic activity.

Within this context, the characteristics of economic development in the West reflected the choices of decision-making individuals. Some invested their lives in the development of the West and helped to channel the capital of others, as well as their own, into the endeavor. Many were possessors of capital who lived far from the frontier but saw profitable investment opportunities in newly settled regions. The resulting process was continuous and partially self-sustaining. Capital was drawn as well as pushed into the West. In this chapter, therefore, we shall examine the western scene that confronted Boston capitalists looking for new investment opportunities as the nation shook off the last consequences of the Panic of 1837.

The West

Precisely where "the West" was located depends on the period with which one is concerned. In economic terms the West in colonial days extended no farther than western New York and Pennsylvania. Even in the 1770's the frontier still ran through eastern Kentucky and Tennessee, and the lands across the Mississippi and Missouri Rivers did not become economically significant until after 1860. In the period 1830–1850, however, the "economic" West lay largely north of the Ohio and east of the Mississippi, encompassing the old Northwest Territory and extending beyond it. Although it had some settlers in the early days of the Republic, the region's real economic development came only after the Anglo-American struggle of 1812–1814, which finally established exclusive American sovereignty over the Northwest and the upper Mississippi River Valley.

Population increase is one measure of economic development in a frontier region. By this yardstick the area west of the Alleghenies and north of the Ohio River grew rapidly in the early decades of the nineteenth century. Because absolute numbers were small, the percentage of increase was greatest between 1790 and 1820. However, in absolute terms population rose from about 1,500,000 in 1820 to nearly 4,600,000 in 1840.[1] The southern part of the region, penetrated by natural waterways, was the first to be occupied, followed more and more rapidly after 1830 by northern Illinois and Indiana and southern Michigan. Thenceforth the Old Northwest developed into the agricultural heartland of the United States, and in economic terms the western country was in the process of a transformation which both invited and depended upon increasing applications of capital and entrepreneurial talent.

Economic Incentives to Develop the West

Men and capital flowed to the trans-Allegheny West in response to a variety of motivations and expectations. Alexis de Tocqueville minimized this diversity of human drives when he wrote in the 1830's: "Millions of men are marching at once towards the same horizon; their language, their religion, their manners differ; their object is the same. Fortune has been promised to them somewhere in the West, and to the West they go to find it." [2] In oversimplifying, however, de Tocqueville also clarified, for he stressed the pull that the West exerted on those who had fortunes to make or increase. Some of these same individuals were pushed West by their inability to find a niche in eastern society or an older economy, or had exhausted or depleted some resource that had given them a livelihood, but such failure was less important than the opportunity to start anew in a virgin land. Primarily it was the land and what lay under it, or grew or could be grown on it, that drew men and money westward.

To the settler and to the absentee investor the availability of rich, untilled agricultural land was one of the West's most enticing attractions. With a liberal federal land policy, which after 1820 made the rapid occupation of the land a primary objective, the settler was able to take up good acreage with a minimum capital outlay and turn it to the production of foodstuffs. For the land speculator there was profit to be gained by acquiring land at government prices as low as $1.25 per acre (after 1820) and holding it for a rise in value which required little or no expenditure on his part. The area of cultivation was greatly enlarged; farms were established where none had existed before; land was tilled which had never known the plow; and whole regions were settled which in their virgin states were more fertile than the farmland from which settlers came. This extension of the agricultural lands distinguished the American experience in the nineteenth century from agricultural revolutions in western Europe, which principally involved changes in organization and techniques.

For agricultural purposes the region north of the Ohio had significant advantages over what many settlers had known east of the mountains. Most of the soil was rich and its lack of stones made tillage easier than on the hard-scrabble farms of New England. Broad plateaus sloped gently to the Mississippi and the Great Lakes, intersected by well-forested river valleys and treeless meadows. Until the 1840's, however, most settlers created farms in wooded areas — first, because this had been the familiar procedure since colonial days and had gained such a hold that the fertility of the soil was judged by its forest cover; and, second, because wood not only provided many of the settler's necessities, but was found close to water-courses that also provided means of transportation. Finally, less capital equipment was required initially for woodland farming than for breaking the hard prairie soil.[3]

As land along waterways became scarcer, the prairies began to receive attention. Covered with a thick grass sward, the prairie soil was not easily broken, but once this was done, it was very workable and productive. John Deere, a Vermont blacksmith who settled at Grand Detour, Illinois, in 1837, produced a plow that was crude but effective in these conditions. A decade later he introduced an all-steel plow which became standard as the farming frontier moved westward. This implement and others, like the reaper, aided extensive agriculture which, in view of the shortage and cost of labor, emphasized the cultivation of a maximum number of acres with a minimum amount of manpower.

Thus, the gifts of nature, an expansionist public land policy, and technological progress combined to make settlement of western agricultural lands attractive. These factors, stimulating an increased supply of products of the soil, were supplemented by the growing demands of the eastern and southern United States and of western Europe for foodstuffs. The western agriculturalist was the agent and beneficiary, or victim, of this mutually reinforcing alignment of supply and demand.

The supply could only become actual and the demand effective, however, with the provision of intermediate facilities which were themselves heavy users of capital: boats, docks, grain elevators, warehouses, canals, roads, railroads, locomotives, and freight cars. Distribution and transportation networks were strategic prerequisites of any co-ordination between potential supply and potential demand. In this sense, low-cost transportation was just as important as cheap plows or fertile prairies, steamboats, canal, and railroad enterprises just as stimulating as eastern manufacturing companies, in establishing the framework within which the West could expand economically. But before considering the importance of transportation in some detail it will be well to examine the increasing availability of natural resources in the West during the early nineteenth century, particularly with reference to New Englanders' attitudes toward these resources

NEW ENGLAND INTEREST IN THE "WEST"

Historically, New Englanders had opposed the disposal of public lands on easy terms or for the benefit of western states alone.[4] The manufacturing interest of the region had able representatives in Congress, and they reflected the New Englanders' primary concern with a protective tariff and cheap labor supply. Abbott Lawrence, for example, told his constituents in March 1837 that those seeking to lower the tariff and the price of western lands did so "from a desire to drain the [Bay] state of its population and wealth." [5] Senator Daniel Webster opposed Thomas H. Benton's bill for selling public lands on a graduated basis, and in his famous debate with Robert Hayne took the position that the public lands belonged to all the states and Congress had no right to give them away.[6] By the 1840's, however, Webster himself had investments in central Illinois, which may have influenced him to take a more favorable view of internal improvements and railroad land grants.[7]

With capital generated by textile enterprise, the Lawrences were also active investors in western land. By the mid-1840's Amos Lawrence, Abbott's brother and business partner, owned nearly 5,000 acres of land on the Fox River in Wisconsin. Land in this area, purchased for $1.25 an acre from the government in 1849, was estimated to be worth $10.00 an acre in 1860, though still unplatted and unimproved.[8] Abbott Lawrence held Illinois state securities.[9] In short, the political spokesmen for New England manufacturers came to have a personal financial stake in western development, though such a stake did not mean their objectives became identical with those of westerners.

From the early days of the Republic, settlers and capital from New England had moved westward, and the pace accelerated in the 1830's. Boston's interest in western lands for investment purposes was indicated by the organization in that decade of land companies which pooled the resources of small investors.* The Boston and

* Paul W. Gates estimates that of the 38,000,000 acres of public land sold in 1837, 29,000,000 were acquired for speculation. A profitable business also developed in lending eastern capital to squatters. William B. Ogden, later president of the Chicago and North Western, found he could lend funds at 28 per cent net before deduction of commissions. Eastern financiers used institutions like the state bank of Illinois for similar purposes. (Paul W. Gates, "The Role of the Land Speculator in Western Development," *The Pennsylvania Magazine of History and Biography*, LXVI (July 1942), 321–324.

Western Land Company, for instance, was organized in 1835 by forty-three small New England capitalists and acquired extensive holdings in Illinois, Missouri, and Wisconsin. The trustees were Bostonians William J. Hubbard, Nathan Rice, and Benjamin Sewall. The problems encountered by this concern were to become familiar to later Boston investors in western lands: communication with and control from Boston, hostility of local people to absentee landowners, protection of resources on and under the land, the pressure of taxes, sale of lands to settlers who lacked cash to pay for them, and the innumerable exigencies of town promotion.[10] A direct connection between this company of small capitalists and the later land operations of the influential Forbes group of Boston investors was provided by Cyrus Woodman, a Harvard Law School graduate, who became the company's chief agent in July 1840.

Individuals and families later associated with Boston-backed western railroad development also invested in western lands during the 1830's. For example, Joseph Nickerson, a successful merchant and later president of the Atchison, Topeka & Santa Fe, bought land at Alton, Illinois, in 1836.[11] Franklin Dexter, Erastus Corning, and Franklin Haven were associated in the American Land Company, whose first report in 1836 showed holdings of 130,000 acres in nine states.[12]

This kind of investment anticipated economic development and, if the tracts had been well chosen, primarily required patience and time to give the investment validity. As the annual report of the New York & Boston Illinois Land Company, the largest landowner in the Illinois Military Tract, observed in 1837: "It ought to be borne in mind, that this company is, in every sense of the word, a Land Company, and as such, requires time and deliberation in all its movements . . . "[13]

During the 1840's some efforts were made to stimulate interest in and development of lands held as an investment, but they were relatively small compared to land-grant railroad programs a decade later. Typically the earlier endeavors were the work of a promoter who, backed by eastern capital, sought to develop his land and attract settlers to it.

In much of the upper Mississippi Valley the lumber frontier was interposed between fur trader and farmer. Timber was the most obvious resource to be taken from the land. The breakthrough of the agricultural frontier to the treeless plains was creating a demand for lumber, and by the 1840's the limited timber stands of the middle Mississippi Valley had largely disappeared. Nature, however, had provided bountifully elsewhere; the vast forest that touched the coast in New England and eastern Canada stretched westward across Michigan, Wisconsin, and northern Minnesota, where waterways radiated to points of lumber consumption in both the Midwest and the East. The light, easily worked white pine of this region was well suited to a multitude of building purposes and could be readily transported by water. Thus by 1840, the lumber industry, still concentrating on white pine as it had in the East, was finding new, rich timber resources strategically located in the Lake states.

By 1836 a beginning had been made in extinguishing Indian titles to the pine forests of the Great Lakes region. Hundreds of thousands of acres had passed into the hands of settlers and speculators. Investors, spurred by profits being made in eastern timber, sought western timberland. Such notable Massachusetts figures as Daniel Webster, Edward Everett, Ralph Waldo Emerson, and Caleb Cushing were caught up in the speculative furor over Wisconsin timber and real estate.[14]

Typical of absentee timberland owners, Caleb Cushing of Newburyport, Robert Rantoul, Jr. of Beverly, and their associates invested in timber and land operations in Wisconsin during the 1840's. Their property at the Falls of St. Croix in Wisconsin, for example, was valued at $250,000 in 1852.[15] One hundred and fifty miles away at the Falls of St. Anthony, on the Mississippi, the same group financed a local lumberman who had extensive pineland holdings. The tools and techniques of lumbering were brought from the East by men like Daniel Stanchfield of Maine, who acted as superintendent of these operations.[16] Under such guidance and spurred by soaring demand, lumber production mounted rapidly. In the St. Croix district alone, 8,000,000 feet were produced in 1843; four years later the amount dropped to 7,750,000 feet, but in 1855 the figure reached 160,000,000 feet.[17]

If timber induced considerable investment in the West during the 1840's, there was at least as much uncritical investor enthusiasm for copper, which had been found in upper Michigan and along the shores of Lake Superior. *Hunt's Merchants' Magazine* reported in July 1848, for example: "So far, many of the companies, whose name is Legion, have been mere experiments upon the gullibility of the ever gullible public, destined to result not even in successful gambling on the part of their authors." [18] In this light, the Lake Superior Copper Company, in which David Henshaw of Boston was a leading figure, was not apparently atypical. Its stock sold for $500 a share when only $35.00 had been assessed on it.[19] Almost predictably, however, this company, organized in 1843, failed three years later.

By 1851 the promotional phase of copper mining was passing. The *American Railroad Journal* was able to observe: "The whirlwind of speculation and fraud has now passed over, and there are no 'fancy' operations; and every company organized has got a real location, and is doing an actual business in getting out copper." [20] Still, of ninety-four copper companies organized between 1845 and 1865 in the Lake Superior region, only eight managed to pay dividends; only six paid their stockholders more than they had invested.[21] From these early days of Lake states copper, Boston became a center for copper stocks and contributed significant amounts of capital to the development of mining properties in the Lake Superior and Michigan Peninsular regions.

Other types of mineral lands also drew entrepreneurs, speculators, and capital. For example, the Boston Association for Purchasing Mineral Property in Missouri and Illinois sent an agent west in 1840. He purchased iron ore lands in Missouri, coal lands on the Big Muddy River and its tributaries in Illinois, and chose a site for an iron works on the Mississippi River.[22] Although the outcome of this venture is not clear, it appears that James Boyd of Boston was mining coal in 1844 on both the Kentucky and Indiana sides of the Ohio River and shipping it by boat to Boston.[23]

Whether the attraction was farmland, timberland, coal, iron, or copper deposits, or any of the other natural resources that could be raised, dug, or cut from the soil, immigrants in growing numbers and capital in mounting quantities were drawn into the trans-Allegheny West during the 1840's. Processing the resulting flow of grain, livestock, minerals, timber, and other products gave a livelihood to many, while others found their place in the interstices of an expanding and increasingly complex network of business relationships.

THE IMPORTANCE OF TRANSPORTATION

After the early concentration of settlers on self-sufficient agriculture, transportation played a key role in the commercial development of the trans-Allegheny West. Integration of the new primary producing regions with the national and international economies depended on low-cost movement of bulk commodities. In the pioneering stages of western development, various expedients served to meet the transportation problem. The first settlements were situated close to navigable water which could be used for exporting the products of the soil. Other early approaches were to concentrate on products which, like cattle or hogs, could — although inefficiently at best — transport themselves, or which could be processed before shipment to raise their value while reducing their bulk — corn into whiskey, for example. But over time, finding more satisfactory ways of reducing the costs of transportation was essential.

Fortunately, there were natural all-water routes to and within the interior of the country. From the center of the pre-1860 West, the Mississippi River and its tributaries (most importantly the Ohio) stretched to the Gulf of Mexico, offering the great cost-saving advantages of water transportation.* This basically north-south route was supplemented by the chain of Great Lakes, facilitating movements of goods and people east and west. Without these great natural waterways, the pace and direction of the nation's economic development would have necessarily been quite different.

Only a small capital investment was required for versatile water transportation, and the mid-continental river system soon achieved significance as an outlet for the food and raw materials of the developing West. While keelboats and flatboats were important even after the application of steam to water transportation, it was the introduction of the steamboat in the second decade of the century which stimulated and developed internal trade all the way from Pittsburgh

* In 1853 the average costs (in cents per ton-mile) of freight were: 15.00 on turnpikes; between 2.30 and 3.50 by railroad; 1.10 on the Erie Canal; 0.80 on the Ohio River; 0.70 on the Hudson; and between 0.05 and 1.10 on the Lakes. (George R. Taylor, *The Transportation Revolution*, 1815–1860 [New York, 1951], 442.) It should be remembered, however, that these figures do not reflect the time, trans-shipment and incidental expense involved in water as against rail transportation.

in the Northeast and Galena in the Northwest to New Orleans. By 1830 the Louisiana port annually registered nearly one thousand steamboat arrivals, and the steamboat tonnage on the western rivers, while increasing in speed and carrying-power, also grew sixfold between 1820 and 1840 and almost doubled again in the next twenty years.[24] The western produce which came down from the Ohio Valley was in part trans-shipped to the northeastern states, in part exported, and in part consumed on those southern plantations which found it profitable to specialize in raising cotton and to buy foods.

While the Mississippi route led directly to the sea, the Great Lakes system had no such natural outlet for shipping. Therefore, the channels of east-west trade had to be created artificially under pressure from the commercial (and political) interests of the seaboard states. In New York state, the Hudson River came near enough to the Great Lakes, with a suitably flat terrain between, to promise a relatively cheap connection by canal. This favorable geography encouraged development of an all-water route from New York City to the Lakes.

Rebuffed by other states and by the federal government in its search for cooperative action, New York itself undertook the construction and operation of the Erie Canal.* The 363-mile waterway was completed in 1825. New York's confidence in it was well placed, for in terms of both corporate profit and regional impact the venture was a resounding success.

The canal's influence was strongly felt from the 1830's. The first grain shipment from Lake Michigan to Buffalo arrived in 1836, and two years later the flour and wheat received there exceeded the receipts at New Orleans. But the canal's widest influence came only after extensive settlement and transportation developments within the West; not until 1839 did grain and flour shipments from western states on the canal exceed those originating within New York, total tonnage not until 1847.[25] As a measure of the canal's impact, Buffalo's receipts of flour and grain between 1836 and 1856 rose from 1,200,000 to 25,800,000 bushels.[26]

* Construction of the canal was financed by the sale of state securities, initially subscribed by New Yorkers in modest amounts. Gradually large investors in New York City and London took hold. By 1829, when the success of the venture was beyond doubt, more than half of the canal debt was owned abroad. (Carter L. Goodrich, *Government Promotion of American Canals and Railroads, 1800–1890* [New York, 1960], 53–54.)

The threat which accompanied the opening of the Erie Canal and the success which marked its operation were not lost on the other commercial centers of the East Coast — although, as they all found, nowhere else did geography allow effective trans-mountain competition by canal with the Erie. Businessmen of seaboard cities did not hesitate to call upon and use the power and credit of public authorities (whether state or municipalities) in their efforts to construct trunk routes as feeders to their cities. One example was the state-owned Pennsylvania Main Line between Philadelphia and Pittsburgh, another was the public-private enterprise of the Baltimore & Ohio Railroad. Completion of the Erie Canal, as noted elsewhere, also stimulated Massachusetts interest in rail connections with the Hudson. Actually, apart from the Erie Canal, effective trunk-line connections between East and West awaited the railroad, and the principal portions of these trunk railroads (the New York Central, the New York & Erie, the Pennsylvania, and the Baltimore & Ohio) were not completed until the 1850's. Indeed, in 1860 the four lines still carried less through tonnage than the Erie Canal.[27] But the trunk lines had secured some two thirds of the shipments of flour, together with almost all merchandise and livestock, leaving the Erie Canal's dominance to be exercised in low-value, high-bulk forest products and grains.

The construction of interregional railroads accelerated a process which was already under way: the inexorable encroachment of the shorter, direct east-west connections on the traffic of the north-south river route. Climatic factors in the case of perishable goods, speed, the superior commercial and financial services of the eastern cities, the growing urban and industrial demand of the eastern seaboard, and declining freight charges — all favored a shift in the main axis of trade. Although the decade of the 1850's was the golden age of the steamboat, the river route suffered a great *relative* fall in its participation in the western trade. The 1860 census reported the change and concluded that, "As an outlet to the ocean for the grain trade of the West, the Mississippi River has almost ceased to be depended upon by merchants." [28]

In contrast to the Mississippi River route, the east-west trunk routes involved unusually heavy outlays of capital. Risks of financial loss were increased because capital put into an uncompleted transportation facility would bring little immediate return, if any: a canal or railroad which *crossed* the mountains was more useful (and profitable) than one which only got up one side!

However they were constructed and managed, the east-west transportation routes implied the sinking of quantities of capital in fixed uses as a prerequisite of their influence on production, and their strategic function meant that they helped shape the path and set the pace of regional economic growth. As a consequence of their existence, the differential between western and eastern prices steadily narrowed. And, since western products were bulkier and stood to gain more from cheap transportation than more highly valued shipments from the East, the terms of trade between East and West increasingly favored the latter.[29] From situations like these there emerged the dynamic of western settlement and western economic growth.

The problem of inexpensive transportation of bulky commodities was as much in need of solution *within* the West — to get produce from farm to primary market or shipment point — as it was among the different regions of the economy. Indeed, since there were only a handful of strategically placed interregional transfer points, while farms were scattered over wide areas, the extensive settlement of the western states created pressing demands for intraregional transportation facilities.

Like the easterners who were planning trunk routes across the Appalachians, men in the western states turned their minds to the possibilities of constructing artificial transportation networks. With the exception of the federally-sponsored National Road, the early settlers had relied almost completely on private enterprise, individual or partnership. This applied to the occupation of the land, early transportation companies, the processing of agricultural products, and lumbering operations. The amount of capital involved in improving transportation facilities forced a departure from this pattern. The next step was toward combined public-private enterprise. In states like Ohio, Michigan, Indiana, and Illinois, state initiative, participation, and sometimes ownership and management, were frequent, and at times inevitable, conditions of transportation development.

Intraregional canals and railroads needed interregional flows of capital from more advanced areas. This was a logical consequence of the fact that costly projects had to be undertaken before the areas to be served developed sufficiently to enable the projects to be locally financed. "A great and extensive country like this," declared Senator William H. Seward in 1850, "has need of roads and canals earlier than there is an accumulation of private capital within the state to construct them." [30] The obvious result of this difficulty was that, even when state governments were attempting to perform an entrepreneurial role, or act as guarantors of private investment, the actual capital needed for transportation projects came largely from the East and Europe.

The first significant moves in the direction of state-aided transportation in the West came in the 1820's at a time when railroads were still untried. As in Pennsylvania and Maryland, the completion of New York's Erie Canal provided a strong stimulus to western action. The most important plans were in fact directed toward establishing further connection with the two principal long-distance routes: the Mississippi and Ohio river system, and the Great Lakes. In 1825 Ohio commenced work on two canals, one to extend northward from the river port of Cincinnati, and the other to cross the state from Cleveland on Lake Erie to Portsmouth on the Ohio River. The first one was completed in 1829 and was subsequently pushed to Lake Erie. The second was opened in 1833. By that date the state had some four hundred miles of canal costing just over $5,000,000.[31]

Meanwhile, more slowly and less successfully, Indiana also undertook internal improvements. In 1832, with the help of an earlier federal land grant, work was begun on the Wabash and Erie Canal to connect the Ohio and Wabash Rivers with Lake Erie. It was nineteen years before the 450-mile waterway, the longest in the country, was completed at a cost of almost $6,500,000.

Illinois showed a similar pattern. In 1827 it received a federal land grant for the comparatively simple task of constructing a canal between the Illinois River and Lake Michigan. But difficulties in raising money delayed the beginning of construction until 1836 and the completion of the canal (under a board of trustees representing bondholders as well as the state) until 1848. Although the Illinois and Michigan Canal cost about $6,500,000, land sales and tolls easily paid off the debt, and the economic effects of the canal, interacting with the spectacular growth of Chicago, more than justified the efforts to join the two water routes.

The handful of canals just described, which, together with some other minor projects, typified the direct economic activities of western states before the mid-1830's, were only a small foretaste of a far more ambitious series of projects which materialized after 1835. The Ohio legislature in 1836 authorized the construction of four canals (two completing links between the Ohio River and Lake Erie, and two feeding the original cross-state canal), a river improvement, and an extensive road. The next year, in a burst of enthusiasm, the same state offered generous financial aid to any transportation enterprise which met certain ludicrously easy conditions. In Indiana the "Mammoth Internal Improvement Bill," as it was known at the time, was passed in 1836, and authorized the public borrowing of $10,500,000 for canals, a railroad, and a main road, besides other smaller projects.

In Illinois a substantial program was undertaken in 1837. It envisaged improvements to five rivers, the construction of one great central and three lateral railroads, and a variety of minor transportation schemes and improvements — at a total authorized cost of $10,500,000, subsequently raised to $11,500,000.

Michigan was also full of good intentions. It became a state in 1837, and its constitution stipulated "that internal improvements shall be encouraged by the government of the state." In the same year, therefore, the legislature instructed the administration to borrow up to $5,000,000 to finance a program of public works — principally three railroads across the state from east to west.

These extensive commitments to grandiose schemes of public enterprise can best be viewed as integral parts of the economic and speculative upsurge culminating in 1836 and 1837. In the middle 1830's the economy in general and the West in particular experienced one of those spurts of investment and frenzied activity that characterized and stimulated economic development in the nineteenth century. But when crisis and recession followed boom, internal improvement schemes proved as vulnerable as they had once seemed glorious.

The failure of most state-backed internal improvement projects can be attributed to two principal groups of interrelated factors. The first was obviously the timing of the programs in relation to a downturn in the economy. The other was the poor planning and implementation of the programs themselves.

Enacted in 1836 and 1837, internal improvement schemes were

hardly put in hand before they encountered the crisis that marked the end of the boom and made the raising of large amounts of capital impossible. In the spring of 1837 a financial panic reduced prices, shrank domestic credit, and led to widespread suspensions of specie payments. After a brief revival, a deep and severe depression settled on the economy in 1839. With capital unobtainable and the environment for investment gloomy in the extreme, the earlier optimism for state projects, as well as the economic basis for the projects themselves, was soon dissipated.

The second group of factors which helped nullify state plans related to the political and more local aspects of contemporary planning. In some cases the state was not yet ready for any advanced degree of capital construction: very large expenditures would have been difficult to justify in rational terms, and wisdom should have dictated more modest aims. For example, Illinois planned to assume a debt of $10,500,000 (in 1837 dollars) when its population was only some 300,000.* Frequently, too, the level of administrative competence or political morality left much to be desired. Inefficiency, waste, and corruption tended to eat into even those resources which *were* available. In any case the parasitic influence of political pork-barreling was too much in evidence. To satisfy different electoral interests, some internal improvement programs assumed a grotesque portmanteau appearance, with expenditures earmarked to benefit far too many communities. In addition, to avoid offending any group, there was often an attempt to begin several projects at the same time — a crippling burden on already sparse resources.

With a combination of deep business depression, poor planning, and worse execution, most internal improvement schemes ground relatively quickly to an abysmal stop. Ohio's experience, like the level of development it had already attained in the mid-1830's, was exceptional. The basic projects of 1836 were pushed through to the bitter end at great cost; the last canal was opened in 1845, by which time the state owned some 731 miles of canal, the revenues of which

* The *American Railroad Journal* (XXIII [1850], 553) commented — with the wisdom of hindsight — on the rashness of the Illinois undertaking in these words: "When the public works of Illinois were projected and commenced all the conditions of success were wanting. Time was necessary to create them. She had no trade, no accumulated property, and only a very scattered population . . . It is very easy now to see that failure then was inevitable."

exceeded operating costs but failed to cover interest charges. Indiana, however, with no provision for taxes to back its projects, ceased all construction in 1839 and by 1841 had defaulted on a debt of more than $13,000,000, of which over $9,000,000 related to internal improvements. In Illinois most projects were abandoned by 1840, and the next year the state found itself unable or unwilling to pay interest on $5,600,000 of bonds. Other than the Illinois and Michigan Canal, the fragments of particular enterprises which remained were virtually useless. Michigan, where the problem was somewhat mitigated by a fortuitously late start, abandoned its program in 1840 and two semi-built railroads were sold in 1846, the state being left with a net debt of just under $2,000,000.

The record of these states after 1835 was taken very much to heart by both creditors and debtors. English investors, for example, were most reluctant to lend to American state governments for a decade or more. The electorates of debtor states forced their representatives to take steps to prevent the wholesale commitment of their credit in the future. Constitutional provisions to this end were enacted in Illinois in 1848; Michigan, 1850; Indiana, 1851; and Ohio, 1851. Even Wisconsin, profiting from the experience of its neighbors, inserted similar clauses in its constitution on entering the Union in 1848.*

Nevertheless, the revulsion was not complete either in ideological or in practical terms. By no means did all states dispose of their public works. Even when they did, they sometimes continued indirect forms of subsidies by selling partially completed transportation enterprises at low prices or by giving other forms of less explicit aid. In any case, at least in most states, it was still quite legal and feasible for town and county authorities to provide help to private corporations. In Ohio, for example, "Almost every one of the railroads projected and being built between 1836 and 1850 asked and received subscriptions or loans from the counties and cities which it was to serve." [32]

Private investors benefited from contrasting aspects of the internal improvement episode. On the one hand, ideological preference, com-

* This new attitude, as with the enthusiastic plans which had indirectly produced it, was not confined to the Midwest: particularly significant repudiations also occurred in Mississippi, Louisiana, Maryland, and Pennsylvania. These states together with Maine, New York, Iowa, and Kentucky, also adopted constitutional provisions against various forms of state aid in the 1840's and 1850's.

bined with the chastening experience of the late 1830's, prevented any renewal of the state governments' direct efforts to build railroads. On the other hand, some ventures were already under way and could be turned over to private corporations, which continued to receive help in many ways from the various levels of government.

The relative withdrawal of the state from the center of the entrepreneurial stage did not really alter the fundamental character of the problem facing the West. Economic production needed transportation networks; transportation networks of a satisfactory sort (i.e., including extensive railroad systems) necessitated heavy capital investment; and sufficiently large supplies of capital could only be obtained from more developed regions.

The prime mover in the transfer of capital was the profit motive. The existence of the market and the potentialities of western production were sufficient to excite the imagination of many promoters and capitalists, who recognized the role of steam transportation in linking the two. The collapse of state experiments of the 1830's had left behind an ideological and physical residue which was conducive to an entry on the part of eastern capital on easy terms; the general recognition of the need for transportation created a favorable climate for the further extension of government help; and, stimulated by an expanding demand and new outlets, the regional export of agricultural products attained new heights.

Accordingly the recovery from the 1837 collapse engendered new interest in western investment. The depression that terminated the boom of the 1830's reached a low point in 1841–1843. Economic trends then turned upward again, with a minor boom in the mid-1840's and a major one in the mid-1850's. And it was this pattern of recovery, stemming from economic decisions made with a new optimism, which established the setting for the large-scale investment of Boston capital in western railroads.

Commitment to western investment was specifically encouraged by an increased demand for western foodstuffs. For example, wheat, corn, and hogs and their products comprised 25 per cent of total United States exports in 1846–1850, and maintained a proportion of 16 or 17 per cent in the booming years of the 1850's.[33] In addition, American farmers reaped considerable short-run benefits from the repeal of the English Corn Laws and European harvest failures in the mid-1840's, and from the inflated European demand during the

Crimean War ten years later. In 1847, as the external demand for grain induced a domestic demand for railroads, John Murray Forbes exulted: "Boston is become the focus of all the Union for capital, & if breadstuffs keep up the U[nited] States will be the Fountain head of wealth instead of England." [34]

The influence of the overseas market, while undoubtedly very important, should not be exaggerated. The other significant pressure of increased demand came from the New England and Middle Atlantic states, where the processes of industrialization and urbanization were proceeding apace. By 1860 this region contained 36 per cent of the nation's population, received 50 per cent of its income,[35] yet produced 20 per cent or less of its wheat. The best available measure of industrial growth* (which was heavily concentrated in the East) yields decennial rates of 152 per cent for 1840–1849; 133 per cent for 1845–1854; and 76 per cent for 1850–1859.[36] In sum, the stimulus to western agricultural expansion was a response to industrialization both abroad and at home.

Given this situation, the actual timing of the flow of eastern capital to the western economy comes into perspective. The existing and potential demand for food from the Midwest created there a need and an opportunity for labor, capital, and transportation. This was particularly felt in the period of quickened growth in the 1840's and 1850's. Clearly, one period of experimentation had been concluded and another was about to begin. This was the opportunity that attracted Boston investors to deep commitments west of the Alleghenies.

* Rates of change of value added (in 1879 prices) in manufacturing.

Chapter 5

Western Railroad Promoters and Boston Capitalists, 1845–1848

IN THE mid-1840's Boston was the center of railroad capital in the United States; as such it played a dominant role in eastern financing of new western lines. Perhaps more than any other financial center, Boston knew railroads from local experience. The potential of a change from sail to steam at sea had made an impression on the China merchants of the Boston area, as had the application of steam to cotton manufacture. Interest in steam locomotives on rails was a natural transition. The Reverend R. C. Waterston summed it all up in a poem delivered before the Boston Mercantile Library Association at its twenty-fifth anniversary meeting, October 18, 1845:

Here magic Art her mighty power reveals,
Moves the slow beam, and plies her thousand wheels;
Through ponderous looms the rapid shuttle flies,
And weaves the web which shines with varied dyes;
Here, gliding cars, like shooting meteors run,
The mighty shuttle binding States in one! [1]

George Peabody, president of the Eastern Railroad, had made a similar point in his address at the opening of the railroad, in August 1838. "The application of steam to the purposes of navigation followed by its adoption as a motive power on land," he said, "has introduced a new and distinct era in the history of the world. The results which have already arisen and which are likely to succeed are of a magnitude that cannot be estimated." He predicted future railroad developments, declaring: "One great advantage of Rail Roads is found in the fact that they are often favorably located where common roads are most difficult of construction. The great alluvial plains of the South and West, extending sometimes for hundreds of miles in an unbroken surface, seem formed by nature to receive them." [2]

With the collapse of state-sponsored internal improvement schemes, promoters of western railroads looked to the East, and particularly Boston, for private sponsorship and private capital to make true such visions as the one held forth by Peabody. The response of Bostonians to these investment opportunities in the West differed. Much depended on the background of the potential investors. The amount of capital they possessed, the way in which they had acquired it, the breadth of their time horizons, the depth of their commitments, and their reactions in the face of adversity or opportunity were as important ingredients of railroad development as were the external factors that conditioned specific investment moves.

Boston Investors, 1845

By the mid-forties, when western railroads caught their imagination, Bostonians were already in the van of railroad investors. On June 1, 1845 an analyst of the Boston scene attempted a summary of the capital situation there for the benefit of president John Tucker of the Philadelphia and Reading. "Money is very abundant," he wrote. "Factory stocks though extremely profitable — are almost too high even for their [Bostonians'] full pockets & Rail Road Stocks — at a great advance — ." [3] Six months before the *American Railroad Journal* had emphasized the extent to which Boston capital had already found its way into railroads, estimating that it represented some $30,000,000 out of a national total of $130,000,000.[4] As noted elsewhere, the bulk of the Bostonians' railroad investment was in the growing network centered on Boston itself and the remainder, with few exceptions, in connecting roads outside the Bay State. Boston did indeed know railroads.

There can be no doubt of the fact that a number of Bostonians also had significant amounts of capital to invest and that investment management, as contrasted with management of trade or manufacturing, was becoming a primary vocation. "Our First Men," a pamphlet apparently inspired by the city census of 1845, listed Boston citizens "credibly reported to be worth One Hundred Thousand Dollars." [5] The objectives of this publication were to satisfy popular curiosity and to remind rich men of their humble origin and the "toil and labor, and close shaving, and tight economy" that had brought them money. The author pointed out: "It is no derogation, then, to the Boston aristocracy, that it rests upon money. Money is something substantial. Everybody knows that and feels it. Birth is a mere idea, which grows every day more and more intangible." [6]

Prominent among the men of this aristocracy who were subsequent or contemporary investors in railroads outside New England were: Nathan Appleton, Amos Binney, John Bryant, John P. Cushing, E. Hasket Derby, Franklin Dexter, John M. Forbes, Franklin Haven, Samuel Hooper, Patrick T. Jackson, Samuel May, Thomas H. Perkins, Thomas H. Perkins, Jr., Josiah Quincy, Jr., William Sturgis, John E. Thayer, Samuel H. Walley, Thomas W. Ward, and William F. Weld.

Although each of these men took an interest in railroad investment against a background of comparative wealth, their attitudes and behavior were not homogeneous. For some, railroad investment became a major preoccupation; for others, it remained merely a profitable sideline. The ties of kinship and common mercantile experience created still other distinctions within the group; for example, newcomers to the ranks of wealth like Samuel May and Samuel Walley were clearly "outsiders." Further distinctions can also be drawn on the basis of speculative temperaments, age, and so on. These different individual and group characteristics were to have a significant effect on the role that Boston's "First Men" played in western development.

Other, less substantial, investors in pioneering western railroads do not appear in the list of "Our First Men" for 1845. These included men like David A. Neal, the Salem sea captain who had turned to local railroads; Samuel Henshaw, a director of the Greenfield and Northampton (Mass.) Railroad; Mark Healy, a Lynn leather merchant who became involved in copper speculation; and similar small capitalists alert to the "main chance," with which they soon identified western railroads.

When western railroad promoters, scenting an opportunity to profit from the holocaust that had wrecked state-backed internal improvement programs, appeared in Boston to raise capital, they came in contact with members of both these groups. As a result, Boston capital began to flow westward through various channels and in different directions.

Boston Capital Moves into Ohio Railroads

Boston capitalists turned their attention to Ohio in 1845. Like other western states, Ohio had undertaken an extensive program of internal improvements in the previous decade, but with more success than most. One project was to connect Lake Erie with the Ohio River by rail. The plan called for the Mad River and Lake Erie Railroad to connect Sandusky on the lake with Springfield, and for the Little Miami Railroad to connect that city with Cincinnati on the river.

At first these roads were financed by local stock subscriptions and state aid. The companies availed themselves of an Ohio act of March 24, 1837, which offered the loan of state credit to the extent of one third the cost of a road when the remainder had been met by subscriptions to capital stock. By 1843 the Little Miami had received $115,000 par value of Ohio bonds, $200,000 in bonds of the city of Cincinnati, and $18,000 cash from Greene County. All three levels of government were also represented in subscriptions to capital stock.[7] The road sold some of the Ohio bonds at a discount to Baring Brothers in London, using the proceeds to buy railroad iron in 1841. But the loans were soon exhausted, contractors' claims mounted, and subscribers to the stock proved reluctant or unable to fulfill their commitments.[8] Meanwhile, the Mad River road had experienced even greater financial difficulties. When the state suspended aid in 1842, the Mad River had had the loan of credit on more than $279,000 of state bonds, and the road was still unfinished.[9]

Bogged down for lack of capital, officers of both the Ohio roads turned to Boston for help in 1845. In reporting their need for $500,000, the *American Railroad Journal* observed: "Private enterprise has now to construct all the really important works in the State, and, in addition to the difficulties inseparable from such vast undertakings, has to clear away the odium with which the state has clothed the very name of Internal Improvements." [10]

The directors of the Little Miami approached Boston capitalists through William Mills. A leading citizen of Yellow Springs, Ohio, Mills had offered to raise money in the East if the road was routed through his town. His effort to sell stock of the company in eastern centers failed, but Mills discovered that Bostonians would take

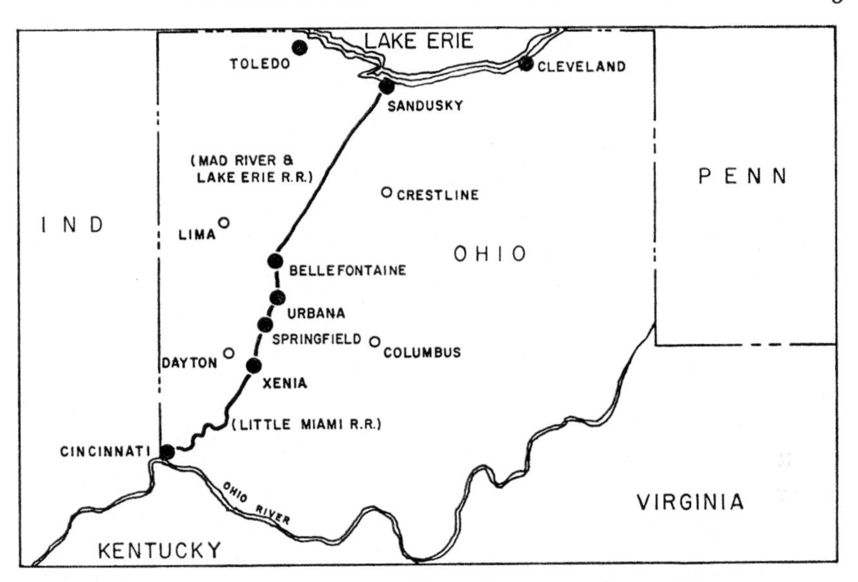

PROJECTED ROUTE FROM THE OHIO RIVER TO LAKE ERIE THAT ATTRACTED BOSTON CAPITAL TO OHIO RAILROADS IN 1845.

bonds.[11] With the aid of Nathan Hale, local railroad booster and editor of the Boston *Daily Advertiser,* Mills succeeded in disposing of $200,000 of the Little Miami's 7 per cent bonds, dated May 1, 1845.

Mills approached investors already familiar with railroad finance in the East. For example, the Boston mortgage trustees of this bond issue were William Sturgis and Josiah Quincy, Jr. The former took $10,000 for John P. Cushing's account, and this fact probably explains Sturgis' role as a trustee of the issue. Quincy was at this time treasurer of the Western Rail-Road of Massachusetts, and his trusteeship function may have reflected connections with Hale in the latter's capacity as president of the Boston and Worcester.

The terms of the bond issue were not happy ones for the directors of the Little Miami, who had no alternative but to accept them or see their road remain unfinished. Under these terms, the bonds, due in ten years, could be converted to stock within five years; on the other hand, the railroad could also retire them in five.[12] Bostonians apparently liked the idea of employing their capital and reducing their risks by loaning at 7 per cent on security, but they also wanted to share in the profits if the enterprise succeeded. The convertible bond offered both possibilities. Although the Bostonians had taken advantage of the most favorable terms available under the Ohio legislature's authorization for the issue, they seated no members on the board of the road or in its principal managerial positions.*

Directors of the Mad River and Lake Erie also turned to Boston. Again Nathan Hale proved helpful, but the most active work was apparently done by Samuel Henshaw and William Ward, Boston securities dealers. The company issued ten-year first-mortgage bonds totaling $300,000 and bearing 7 per cent interest from May 1, 1845. These were followed with $200,000 more in July 1846.[13] The Boston trustees of the first issue were again Sturgis and Quincy. In this instance, Sturgis purchased $20,000 of the road's bonds for Cushing's account.[14] Boston trustees of the 1846 issue were Matthias Sawyer, who had made a fortune in eastern land speculation, and Samuel May, a dealer in metals.[15] Of the total $500,000 in bonds issued in 1845 and 1846, $178,000 was reportedly sold by October 1847, plus $300,000 worth of stock. To protect their investment, Bostonians took places on the board of the Mad River. In addition to Samuel Henshaw, they included David Neal, Matthias Sawyer, and Henry Timmins.[16]

The need for more capital to complete and improve the Mad River road conflicted with the desirability of giving stockholders evidence of its profitability. That the Boston stockholders were impatient for a cash dividend is made clear in a letter from Samuel Henshaw to Benjamin Porter Chamberlain, a Salem man who kept close liaison with the Ohio road. In May 1849, Henshaw wrote, "Nothing short of a Cash div.[d] will satisfy the Stockholders here and induce them to invest in any extension we may desire." Accordingly, he felt a 5 per cent cash dividend in August was essential.[17] Instead, a 12½ per cent stock dividend was declared.[18]

In September 1848, when the Mad River finally made its connection with the Little Miami, which had already been completed to Springfield, the patience and hope of its owners seemed about to be rewarded. The *American Railroad Journal* predicted a rapid increase in traffic, "by which those who have invested their money and

* There was, in addition to Boston money and state aid, $553,300 in capital stock outstanding (not all paid in) and a $100,000 loan from the city of Cincinnati. (Little Miami Railroad, *Annual Report,* 1845, 38.)

waited years for its completion, without return, will now reap their reward, as it must become a good paying stock." [19]

However, more disappointment lay ahead. A cholera epidemic and a short wheat crop in the summer of 1849 affected the road adversely. Although Neal, who continued active in Mad River affairs, tended to discount the importance of through traffic,* it was a sufficiently attractive business to encourage the construction of rival lines against which the Mad River struggled in vain. Moreover, in the rush to begin revenue-producing operations, the directors had constructed the road cheaply, planning to upgrade it later by reinvesting earnings, the common practice on western lines. By early 1851 the directors were seeking to place in New York $800,000 of second-mortgage bonds to finance relaying the track.[20]

While the Mad River was still trying to complete its line from Sandusky to Springfield, the Little Miami was making other alliances that would bring through traffic to it. It aided the completion of the Columbus & Xenia to Columbus, where in 1851 the Cleveland, Columbus & Cincinnati forged a link with Cleveland, Sandusky's rival on Lake Erie.[21] Meanwhile, local traffic had increased rapidly, sometimes beyond the road's capacity to handle it.

The Little Miami's earlier completion, its aggressive seeking of ties with other roads, and its more conservative financing contrasted sharply with the halting progress of the Mad River. Part of the Mad River's troubles may have stemmed from the fact that it had attracted eastern capitalists of limited means and speculative temperaments. For example, the firm of Henshaw & Ward, which had helped to float the 1845 bond issue in Boston, failed to survive the financial crisis of 1848,[22] though Samuel Henshaw continued active in the Mad River. Other speculative investors were David Neal, Mark Healy, and Dr. Estes Howe, all relatively small capitalists from Boston's suburbs. Howe apparently had some influence

* Writing to Dan S. Miller of New York, July 20, 1850, Neal declared: "Up to this time, not only has the mass of travel between East and West been restricted very much to one or two routes, but in proportion to the local business been much larger than it is likely to be hereafter. In other words, the domestic travel of the Western States is more rapidly increasing, than that between them and the Atlantic. Both immigration and natural increase are filling in, around every avenue which facilitates transportation. Wherever there is good soil, a railroad or canal will find support. Hence the security of western railroads, and their increase in number and extent." (Quoted, *Americen Railroad Journal,* XXIV [April 19, 1851], 243.)

with John M. Forbes, whom he induced to invest for the account of Paul S. Forbes. With Forbes we can assume this venture was a minor speculation, but for Howe it was disastrous. When the Mad River finally collapsed in 1857, Forbes wrote to his cousin that the event "ruined poor Dr. Howe," but he merely marked off his own loss as a poor investment.[23]

Quite aside from the nature of its financial backing and cheap construction, the north-south geographical orientation of the Mad River road made it vulnerable. Built athwart instead of in the path of the predominantly east-west movement of traffic, its route was crossed or tapped by seven other roads in 1859.[24]

These first significant commitments of Boston capital in railroads west of the Alleghenies did not deeply involve major Boston investors. However, the path opened by smaller investors for the flow of Boston capital into the Midwest was soon followed by members of the mercantile aristocracy, led by those seeking new outlets for funds generated in the China trade. They found the first of these outlets in Michigan.

Boston and the Michigan Central

Like its neighboring states of Illinois and Indiana, Michigan had also undertaken an unsuccessful internal improvements program, and in its wreckage local promoters and eastern capitalists found promising investment opportunities. Here began a major long-term commitment of Boston capital to western railroad development.

An internal improvement act in 1837, supplemented by a $5,000,000 loan act of the same date, was the cornerstone of the projected state-aided railroad and canal system of Michigan. Under these statutes, public authority undertook to build three railroads across the state — the Michigan Central (whose construction had already been started by a private corporation chartered in 1832 as the Detroit & St. Joseph), the Michigan Southern, and the Michigan Northern. Almost from the start, the roads gave rise to controversy as to route, management, and financing.

It was in financing that the entire state-backed railroad program received a mortal blow. Michigan had counted on attracting capital from the East and from abroad. The first setback to these expectations occurred when Baring Brothers of London refused to handle the Michigan bonds.[25] The picture brightened when the Bank of the United States of Pennsylvania and its allied Morris Canal and Banking Company agreed to take the entire loan at par. They in turn hypothecated a majority of the securities abroad, chiefly with Denison & Company, Hope & Company, Morris & Sons, and with the Rothschilds. The remainder came into possession of the Farmers Loan and Trust Company of New York, some small banks in up-state New York, and individuals like George Griswold, the China trader. Three thousand dollars' worth was held by the United States War Department, whose engineers had surveyed the central route in 1834–1835.

Unfortunately for Michigan's plans, both the Pennsylvania banking concerns encountered financial difficulties and eventually became bankrupt. The state of Michigan received only about $1,500,000 as proceeds from the $5,200,000 worth of bonds issued for internal improvements.[26] Default on interest payments was followed by repudiation of unpaid bonds.

Efforts to give Michigan the benefits of a railroad network built under public auspices were doomed. The only questions that remained to be answered were how and when these abortive endeavors would be liquidated. Before the answers were finally given, there were unsuccessful attempts both to authorize sale of the roads (1844) and to extend them (1845). The firm decision to sell was finally reached in 1846, reflecting the exigencies of Michigan's finances and the governor's view that the business of transporting passengers and freight by railroad was "clearly not within the ordinary designs of a state government . . ." [27]

The likelihood that the Michigan roads, and more especially the Central, then built from Detroit as far as Kalamazoo, would become available to private investors activated a complicated network of personal and financial relationships. On the ground in Michigan was James F. Joy, a native of New Hampshire and a leading Detroit lawyer. Closely associated with him was George F. Porter, his law partner and the Michigan commissioner of internal improvements. Their local political contacts and knowledge were to prove invaluable to the eastern investors who became interested in the Central. This group initially included Erastus Corning, the Albany iron merchant already deep in New York railroads; George Griswold, who, like Corning, held Michigan internal improvement bonds;

Griswold's son-in-law, John C. Green, formerly senior partner in Russell & Co. in Canton; D. D. Williamson, president of the Farmers Loan & Trust Company of New York, another major holder of Michigan bonds; and John E. Thayer & Brother of Boston. Close ties between these men and leading members of Boston's financial, textile, and mercantile communities had been developed in the China trade or in domestic investment. There was a fund of mutual respect and confidence on which to base an expanding alliance of investors interested in purchasing the Michigan Central Railroad.

A key figure in the sequence of decisions and events that brought about this purchase was John W. Brooks. Born at Stow, Massachusetts in 1819, Brooks had learned civil engineering under Loammi Baldwin and on the Boston and Maine Railroad. In 1844 he became superintendent of the Auburn and Rochester.[28] Ambitious and able, Brooks quickly became aware of the importance of western trade to his railroad and he also noted the growing belief, in part fostered by Joy's letters to newspapers, that Michigan would never finish the Central.[29]

Apparently the Boston Thayers and Albany's Erastus Corning encouraged Brooks. At least he was armed with letters of introduction from them when he visited Detroit in 1845 to examine the prospects for purchasing the Central.[30] Finding the situation promising, Brooks, who had some conditional or partial promises of support from Bostonians,[31] entered into close collaboration with Joy, and presumably Porter, men who knew Michigan and its legislature. Together they worked out legislative strategy.

The proposed charter of a privately-owned Michigan Central contained a list of incorporators that, for the most part, might have come directly from the roster of Boston's "First Men." It included such familiar names as William Sturgis, John E. Thayer, David A. Neal, John Bryant, Thomas H. Perkins, Thomas H. Perkins, Jr., John M. Forbes, Robert B. Forbes, William F. Weld, and Josiah Quincy, Jr. The list also included George Griswold, Erastus Corning, and John W. Brooks.[32] The proposed board of directors was initially composed entirely of Bostonians. However, on the suggestion of a partner of Corning's who went to Michigan to see the railroad purchase through the legislature, the Albany merchant's name was substituted for that of Thomas H. Perkins, Jr.[33]

The Michigan legislature, which met in December 1845, did not act quickly on the sale of the Central. There was opposition on the grounds that such action would create a monopoly and cripple or destroy the other state-owned roads.[34] One member wanted to call the legislation "a bill to transfer the sovereignty of the State of Michigan to a company of Yankee speculators." [35] On the other hand, the sale was defended on the grounds that only favorable terms would attract eastern capital and prevent construction of a rival route from Cleveland and Toledo westward through Indiana.[36] The legislative struggle continued to almost the last day of the session, but finally on March 5, 1846, the sale was approved.

Those who had fought the sale on grounds of its anticipated impact on the Michigan Southern learned quickly from their defeat and obtained approval for purchase of that road by private parties. Elisha C. Litchfield of Detroit and John Stryker of Rome, New York, took the lead in organizing the Michigan Southern, whose extension was to prove a powerful spur to the activities of the new owners of the Michigan Central.

The terms of the Michigan Central's sale were set forth in the legislation authorizing it. The purchase price of $2,000,000 was about the amount the state had spent on the project. One fourth of it had to be paid in six months and the remainder within eighteen months. Payment could be made in evidences of state indebtedness, as well as cash. This provision gave the state an opportunity to retire some of its outstanding obligations while the purchasers of the railroad, using depreciated bonds, obtained a 30 per cent discount in the process.[37] Following the early Massachusetts example, the state retained the option to repurchase the road after January 1, 1867, at the market value of its shares plus 10 per cent. Meanwhile, the company could be taxed on the basis of its paid-in capital. The purchasers had to guarantee to complete the road to Lake Michigan within three years and to equip it with rails weighing sixty pounds to the yard.

The charter contained specific provisions as to tariffs. The basic rate for passengers was set at three cents per mile. Rates on flour and grain, mainstays of the state's economy, were not to exceed 75 per cent of those in effect on the road on January 1, 1845. New England influence was again shown in the additional provision that rates on these commodities were not to exceed the average of those charged on the Boston and Lowell, Boston and Providence, and

Boston and Worcester during September and October 1845. Various provisions were made for review and flexibility in these tariffs.[38]

Clearing the legislative hurdle was only the first step in acquiring the road, for $500,000 had to be raised in the next six months. The Boston leaders in this campaign were the Thayers and John M. Forbes. The Thayers had a substantial interest in New York railroads, which could be expected to benefit directly from acquisition of the Michigan Central. Furthermore, they were leading dealers in railroad securities in Boston and had wide contacts with the investment community. Promotion of the purchase of the Michigan Central meant income for the firm.

Forbes, however, was a newcomer to railroad investment. Since returning from China to devote himself to the Boston end of his trading business, he had gradually diversified his investments. At least as early as 1843, as a trustee and guardian, he had subscribed to $5,000 of a $50,000 loan for the Attica and Buffalo — a step probably encouraged by the fact that the loan was sponsored by the reliable ex-China trader, William Sturgis. The following year Forbes had joined with one of the Thayers to buy a hotel in Buffalo. The 1845 financial failure of the steamer *Iron Witch,* in which his brother Robert and one of the Thayers were interested,[39] severely tried Robert Forbes's resources and put John on the alert for a remunerative position for his seafaring brother.[40] In the case of the Michigan Central there was this and other interesting possibilities: the opportunity to purchase the road with depreciated state securities, Brooks's report that revenues had increased in the past year and that the road should yield at least a 7 per cent return,[41] plus the challenge and rewards of completing and operating a potentially important road.

Forbes at this time was definitely in a speculative mood, but he measured long-run returns by a familiar yardstick. As far as trade was concerned, he considered an average long-term return of 6 per cent on investment as typical and satisfactory, and this figure reflected his own experience in the China trade.[42] Coincidentally this was the same percentage that William H. Swift, the experienced engineer and railroad manager, advised Baring Brothers was about the maximum permissible for a road that did not want to invite competition.[43] It was also the return being gained by cautious capitalists of the Boston area who kept their investments close to home.

Numerous references in letters to Paul S. Forbes indicate that while John M. Forbes considered a 6 per cent rate of return quite consonant with the security of capital, it was the minimum acceptable return. With money abundant in 1845, Forbes had been willing to humor his cousin Paul S. Forbes, then in China, in his desire for speculation. Accordingly he had subscribed for 100 to 125 shares of the 8 per cent preferred stock which the Housatonic Railroad issued to raise money for relaying its rails. Forbes reported at the end of November 1845 that the stock, issued at 80, was already worth 95, and said, "there is no reason why it should not go up to 120 or 130$ as it will be a six per cent investment at 133$ pr share." He considered its prospects so good that he took about 250 shares for the American Stock Investment (A.S.I.), the name for Houqua's portfolio under Forbes's care.* [44]

Forbes believed it possible to make 7 or 8 per cent or better without unduly increasing risks. Whether to take such a step with Houqua's funds troubled him. He wrote to his cousin in China in October 1846: "I often have considerable doubts as [to] the proper mode of administering the American S.I. Account — Whether to put it into places where it will draw a small interest very safely, or to do with it as my own placing it where there is more risk & more chance of profit. I have in general chosen the later mode and have got it placed very much to my satisfaction and I hope when my stewardship ends to show a very handsome result — ." [45] Forbes's confidence that a more audacious course was both practical and desirable was reflected in his proposal to take over the American Stock Investment at cost plus 6 per cent — if Houqua desired to sell out. As an alternative, to quiet any fears that the Hong merchant might have had, Forbes offered to be considered as personally interested in half of every investment that he made for the A.S.I.

Meantime, Bostonians had finally taken control of the Michigan Central, although the process had been neither swift nor smooth. Boston capitalists, including Forbes, had taken the lead in chartering the road, but their interest in completing the purchase appeared lukewarm in mid-summer 1846. Fifty thousand shares of stock, $100 par value, were authorized initially, and they could be increased to 80,000. The company could begin business when $2,000,000 worth

* Houqua died in 1843, but Forbes continued to manage American investments for the Hong merchant's son.

of stock was subscribed.[46] However, vigorous steps had to be taken to find purchasers. Forbes had apparently promised Thayer to take $150,000 in stock, but early in August 1846 he put the banker off and his action was expected to influence others. James K. Mills, partner of Edmund Dwight in a textile commission house, was reported good for $100,000 but seemed unlikely to use his influence with other potential investors. Edmund Dwight, whose family had invested to various western banks and who apparently also had an important personal following, had not yet made a move, nor had William Sturgis.[47]

Several weeks later the picture had improved, much to the relief of Joy and his associate, George Porter. In the interim it had been reported that the road would clear $10,000 for the year; Brooks, George Griswold, and D. D. Williamson were convinced that a 10 per cent dividend would be possible from the start and they saw purchase of the road bringing its stock to par.

Forbes had moved cautiously. He wanted assurance that New York's money would be forthcoming, as well as Boston's. For that purpose Brooks was dispatched to New York City with letters of introduction to John C. Green, formerly senior partner of Russell & Co. in Canton and latterly a New York banker. Actually, New Yorkers responded more favorably than New Englanders. The Farmers Loan and Trust Company, which had bought more than $900,000 of Michigan's internal improvement loan,[48] proved eager to exchange the greatly depreciated bonds for railroad securities. Green and his father-in-law, George Griswold, were among the subscribers, and, upstate, Erastus Corning used his influence to good advantage.[49] With money available in New York at 6 per cent, Forbes made a definite commitment to the Michigan Central for $100,000.[50]

By August 20 Edmund Dwight was becoming more interested in the promotion of the Michigan Central and was intent on seeing that the road was properly organized and managed. He wrote on that date to William Dwight: "Should the Stock be taken up, it seems, as matter of course, that the *organization* of the Company will fall naturally into our hands, simply because we know more of Michigan, & Michigan people than any other persons in Massts. On a *proper organization,* the whole success of the enterprise, depends — & much thought, & knowledge of character is necessary." [51]

Edmund Dwight had Forbes in mind for the presidency of the road, provided William could not "think of a better man." He also suggested that James K. Mills's opinion on Forbes's qualifications would carry weight. However, despite Edmund Dwight's large claims in private correspondence, the two Dwights, a week later, had committed themselves for only $50,000, while Forbes increased his subscription to $125,000.[52]

By this time Forbes was working vigorously to insure success of the purchase. He had, for example, taken the initiative in suggesting to D. D. Williamson that depreciated Michigan bonds be exchanged for 7 per cent bonds to be issued by the railroad company.[53] However, important Bostonians like William Sturgis and Thomas Perkins, incorporators of the Michigan Central, still resisted pleas for a financial commitment. Sturgis had declined to use his influence in support of the project, but indicated that he might aid in a last emergency. Perkins, who had lumber interests in Michigan, was being wooed by parties promoting the purchase of the other state-owned road, the Michigan Southern. David Neal was undecided as to what he should do, but late in September — just as the purchase was being completed — invested $1,250.[54]

Early in that month Edmund Dwight and James K. Mills, who had access to the textile group, still had not become active.[55] Thayer talked of getting subscriptions but had little luck in producing them. When Brooks confronted Mills in the banker's office and asked him to make a definite commitment, Mills replied "I will not." This exchange led George Porter to observe: "This is Boston courtesy, which I am inclined to think like Boston piety and Boston enterprise, is much talked of, and hard to find! — George Griswold says Boston is great at *bragging*." [56]

Porter complained that Boston capitalists were as "inapproachable as the Chinese Emperors." When he finally wangled an introduction to one of the Lawrences, he was rebuffed with the textile man's comment that he and his associates "had as much as they could do to care for their own matters these times." [57] Others, like H. Gray, indicated they might subscribe if assured that the Michigan Central would throw business — such as iron purchases — their way.

Under the original scheme of promotion, New England was assigned only 7,000 out of 20,000 shares; yet cautious Boston capitalists insisted that managerial control and a majority of the directors be centered in Boston.[58] Progress had been so slow in the Bay State that Porter was convinced that Thayer was "playing us false" and the Michigan promoter was favorably disposed toward a new subscription suggested by Griswold.[59] But suddenly, the crisis passed. A few days later over 15,000 shares had been subscribed. Salem men had taken 1,000 shares, Springfield 500, Boston 4,000, Albany 800, Canandaigua 800, New York City 8,000, and Syracuse and Buffalo were in the process of completing their subscriptions.[60]

One factor in the improved situation was apparently John M. Forbes's decision to take the presidency of the road. Although it had not be his intention to become involved in railroad management, he found that capitalists had more confidence in him than in the enterprise. Therefore, to gain their support he had acceded to their request that he take the top post in the road, which he thought was largely a formal one that could soon be turned over to his sea-captain brother, Robert. Writing in 1884, Forbes declared: "Little did I dream of the load I was taking when I accepted the office of president." [61] That decision had launched him on a career in railroading which lasted the rest of his life and was to have important consequences for the development of the American West.

In his new search for funds, Forbes had not confined himself to Boston; he also turned to New Bedford, where he had important connections through his wife's family. On September 1, 1846, he reported that the whaling port had been assigned 500 shares and more might be available for sale there.[62] Gradually his own commitment climbed upward until it reached $200,000,[63] most of which was apparently covered by the purchase of Michigan state bonds and warrants which were accepted at 70 per cent of par in payment for stock.[64]

On September 15, 1846, after a hectic scramble, the worst was over. The first assessment on the stock — 25 per cent — came due.[65] On the same date the Michigan Central directors voted an issue of 7 per cent bonds which, by June 1, 1848, yielded $273,500.[66] On September 23 the purchasers completed the down payment of $500,000 and took possession of the road. Recalling the effort involved, Forbes wrote: "I shall, I hope, have cause to look back upon this September as one of the best spent months of my life." [67] It was a hope that was to be well fulfilled.

Once the Michigan Central was in the hands of its new owners, it became clear that the Boston group, although holding a minority interest, intended to exert firm control on favorable financial terms. A Bostonian, George B. Upton, was installed as treasurer. Joy and Porter were appointed Michigan representatives of the company and efforts were made by Forbes and the Dwights to see that the Detroit promoters and other influential Michigan people remained friendly and interested in the Michigan Central.[68]

Brooks was made superintendent but soon collided with Upton on questions of authority and with Forbes on questions of finance. On Christmas Day, 1846, Brooks wrote Corning, "I assure you that your interest as a stockholder is not in any degree promoted by an attempt on the part of Mr. Upton to build the road in or from Boston . . ." In Brooks's view, responsibility for construction and running expenses should be centralized in his own office. "Any other system," he said, "seems to me to scatter responsibility so much that no one is responsible for anything." [69]

Corning replied that Brooks had taken the proper stand. "Your position is correct —," he wrote, "it is useless for one moment to suppose that Mr. Forbes and Mr. Upton can direct matters at Detroit, sitting in their office at Boston." In conclusion, the Albany iron-merchant urged Brooks to "take a stand in this matter and insist on having everything relating to the construction of the road pass through your Books. I repeat you are the party responsible to the Company." [70] Brooks did win a relatively free hand and, as Forbes later agreed, discharged his duties in an exemplary manner.

Corning, of course, was an influential figure in the Michigan Central from the start. His loan on promissory notes of the road had helped to raise the purchase money, and he served on the board of the road until his death in 1872. However, Forbes, who himself acted as a commission agent in the purchase of iron, considered the Central's purchase of iron through Erastus Corning & Company in the early 1850's so large that he suspected the Albany iron-merchant of profiting unduly at the expense of the railroad.[71]

The fact that Brooks turned to Corning in his first tussle with the Boston treasurer also suggests that there was some friction between the Boston and New York interests in the Michigan Central. Further evidence of it appeared in the question of issuing convertible bonds, following the final payment for the road in September 1847. A small issue of 8 per cent bonds in April of that year was followed by one of $1,100,000 in October.[72] Brooks had favored a straight 7 per cent bond for the latter, but Forbes had disagreed. In September he wrote the young superintendent: "I think your notions are wild, there are too many good things offering to make a 7% interest in Rail Road bonds any temptation to people who are likely to touch such securities at all. There is a class of cautious capitalists who go for 5 or 6% interest with security which they can see and know all about and you cannot touch them at all, at any rate of interest. The next class of people who want a large interest for their money is precisely the class that owns all the Rail Road stock, and to these, greater inducements than 7% are held out in all directions." [73]

The discord between Forbes and Corning came to the surface in this connection. Corning disapproved of making bonds convertible, writing: "I fear our friends in Boston desire to make a large operation out of the Central rail road, to the injury of share holders who have not the means to protect themselves." [74] But he overlooked the acute stringency of the money market. In January 1848, for example, the best business paper in Boston was negotiable only at 18 per cent interest, and in Philadelphia and New York at 15 per cent.[75] Under a March 20 dateline, the *Bankers' Magazine* reported: "There has been a continued stricture in the money market at Boston, since December last, and but little relief is yet experienced. This scarcity arises from large investments in heavy undertakings out of the state by Boston capitalists." [76] As noted, the firm of Henshaw & Ward, which had tied itself to the Mad River & Lake Erie, failed to survive.

If additional funds were to be raised for the Michigan Central, the terms had to be attractive. Careful estimates of the road's requirements as determined by Brooks showed a need for at least another million dollars. However, since the Bostonians insisted that bonds should not only bear a high rate of interest but should also be convertible, the directors decided to keep the size of the new loan to an absolute minimum, hoping to raise any additional money on less onerous terms in an easier market. As a result, they authorized an $800,000 issue of 8 per cent convertible bonds which were offered in March 1848. It proved sufficiently attractive to be fully subscribed by the following June.[77] This approach once again illustrated the effort to combine attractive equity possibilities with as much security as possible — seemingly a prerequisite for attracting "risk" capital, at least in Boston.

Patterns of Boston Railroad Investment in the West, 1840's

The initial financing of the Michigan Central showed that Forbes, the China trader, was more venturesome than the Boston manufacturing aristocracy. His most important support, once he had decided to back the road, came from friends and relatives whose capital and business ties with Forbes derived primarily from commerce. On the other hand, such an influential member of that group as William Sturgis added no Michigan Central securities to John P. Cushing's portfolio until 1850.

At this time Forbes himself fitted the pattern of the opportunistic investor, seeking to exploit opportunities as they presented themselves and evaluating them from a comparatively short-run standpoint. In June 1847 he was lyrical about the success of his railroad ventures. The opportunities for short-run profits in them made the once-exciting China trade seem almost dull. In a quite untypical way he wrote Paul Forbes: "I think before the summer is out I shall show you some results that beat the China trade. These Reading Bonds which cost 57 — got interest regularly for years on 100 & then brought 100$ were not bad, neither were the 7% Mohawks — bought at 80. with a 3½% Dis due making them 76½ which paid 7% on par — & have been sold at par lately or paid I am not sure which. The Michigan issued at 76 is now worth par, & some others equally promising. Sanguine people think the Mich. R. R. will be worth 150$ and it would not surprise me." [78]

It seemed that Boston's prominence as a center of capital in the mid-1840's had generated an enthusiasm that almost swept the usually level-headed Forbes off his feet. In October 1847 he was jubilant about Boston's prospects. "Whenever any coal mines are to be made accessible," he wrote, "or ill managed Rail Roads made available, or indeed any scheme that requires Capital & intelligence they come to Boston for help & those that take hold do it on such terms that they play with sure cards." [79]

Such unrestrained optimism lured some Bostonians, including

Forbes, to overextend themselves, By September 1848 he admitted that he had been too deeply infected by the speculative virus. Though he shipped to China for Russell & Co. credits amounting to £20,000 sterling, he emphasized that it should be used only if teas were "very low." "I have had so much trouble from being too much extended," he wrote, "that I shall not make the mistake again." He now revoked his offer to buy out Houqua's American Stock Investment, telling Paul S. Forbes, "I have got speculation so much worked out of me that I would not have you buy in for me now — nor would I advise you to just now for who can see how this Free trade Tariff and war in Europe may complicate things here!" [80]

On the other hand, Forbes was as enthusiastic as ever about the prospects of the Michigan Central. Although he had accepted the president's chair only "to get the thing going and keep it *warm* for Bennet," John Forbes found himself increasingly involved in the company's affairs. In June 1848 he reported to the stockholders: "The business of the road has been more profitable than we had any right to expect from it in its unfinished state."

His confidence in the road was reflected in his investment advice. Since the tightness of the money market had caused the directors to hold the March 1848 convertible bond issue to $200,000 less than the company's estimated requirements,[81] the need for additional capital to complete and improve the road was becoming pressing by the fall of that year. Forbes called the attention of his cousin to the anticipated call for new funds. While stating that he did not know whether this sum would be raised through stock or 8 per cent convertible bonds, he expressed a favorable view: ". . . you couldn't do better than to send me 100,000 to 200,000 to be salted down in this way." [82]

In the meantime, Forbes, Neal, and Thayer were providing money and credit to the Michigan Central on a short-term basis. Forbes reported in November 1848 that he was lending money to the road at 12 per cent interest on notes that could be paid in 8 per cent convertible bonds or extended at 14½ per cent interest.[83] In October, Neal had received a commission of $275 for endorsing, on his account and Neal & Company's, four notes of the Michigan Central. In December, again acting for himself and for Neal & Company, Neal was first endorser on a Michigan Central note for $27,800 and second endorser on one for a similar amount.[84]

By calling on the credit of its backers, for the most part men of substance, the Michigan Central came through the financial crisis of 1848 without, as Forbes put it in his 1849 report, "injury to our credit." He stated that the road could meet its floating debt as it came due, placing primary reliance on an issue of new stock to meet these demands. Additional bonds would only be issued "in case we find it impossible to sell our stock at par at the time when our liabilities mature." [85] Commitment had seemingly induced confidence.

To keep money in 5 per cent investments when Michigan Central 8 per cent convertible bonds were available seemed folly to Forbes. By the fall of 1849 he had placed $20,000 to $25,000 of Houqua's money in the 8 per cents and $39,000 in Michigan Central stock. At this time he indicated his expectations in a letter to Paul S. Forbes: "The time will come within ten years when European Capital will find its way to this country freely & all these things will be sought, & I should not be surprised if it should be soon! Who that knew *any thing* would hold English, French or German funds when they can get Boston 6% stock at under par, & various *sure* 8% stocks — railway shares & Bonds at par & under?" [86]

There were significant differences between large Boston investors like Forbes, who was increasingly committed to the Michigan Central, and smaller Boston capitalists who had varied interests in western railroads. Of the latter group, perhaps Neal was typical. His ledger shows the transition from state and municipal securities to increasingly speculative private ventures. His trial balance as of the end of 1846 indicates that he had over $8,000 of 6 per cent bonds of the state of Illinois and only 25 shares of Michigan Central stock.* By the end of the following year he had increased his holdings of Central stock to 50 shares, had acquired one of its bonds, and held 400 shares in the Mad River & Lake Erie. The Illinois 6 per cents were sold along with New York City 5's, and the proceeds invested in stock of the Worcester & Norwich and of the Philadelphia and Reading. At the same time he converted Auburn and Rochester bonds to stock.

Obviously in these transactions Neal was seeking to increase his equity holdings. He was aided by stock dividends, for the New York

* Apparently Abbott Lawrence and William Sturgis had also invested in Illinois bonds. At least, they, along with Thomas W. Ward, had been appointed a committee to represent foreign bondholders in 1843. (Reginald C. McGrane, *Foreign Bondholders and American State Debts* [New York, 1935], 120.)

road paid a 10 per cent dividend in this form in February 1848, and the Pennsylvania road paid 12 per cent. In July and August 1848 Neal bought several of the newly issued Michigan Central 8 per cent convertible bonds for Neal & Company and for a trust fund. In September he acquired $12,000 more for a trust fund. Meantime, he increased his own holdings of Mad River stock until by the end of the year they stood on his books at $16,000.[87]

It seems then that Neal, who was still president of the Eastern Railroad (and would remain so until 1851), was a relatively opportunistic investor. Clearly the Salem man was not a member of the "cautious capitalists" described by Forbes, but fitted rather well the mold of the railroad investor who looked for situations that he expected to produce large, short-run returns. For his personal account Neal showed a decided preference for stocks as opposed to bonds. As a trustee, however, he was more cautious, confining himself more generally to the senior securities.

Neal's ledger shows that he personally continued to be heavily committed to stocks. The only bonds in his portfolio at the end of 1850 were two Michigan Central 8 per cents and two Mad River 6 per cents. The difference between the performance and therefore the return on his equity investment in the Michigan and Ohio roads is revealed in his ledger. On 87 shares of Michigan Central stock he showed a gain of $987 at the end of 1850. On 486 shares of Mad River stock he showed a loss of $253.80.[88]

Reviewing Bostonians' initial investments in western railroads, several points become clear. Though the main Boston investing groups overlapped, investors even within the same group did not move in unison. The wealthiest group, most of whom had accumulated capital in the China trade, was represented by men like John M. Forbes and William Sturgis. Once convinced that an enterprise was promising, they were prepared to make heavy commitments under certain conditions. One condition was that the financial risks be spread; Forbes for example insisted on New York participation before committing himself to the purchase of the Michigan Central. Second, and related to his attitude toward risk-bearing, he wanted an effective voice in management. Accordingly, control of the Michigan Central was exercised from Boston, a fact of some significance since there was more New York money than Boston money in the enterprise.

The importance of the personal element in financing early western railroads, as well as the varying attitudes toward performing this role, were exemplified by Forbes and Sturgis. Forbes entered the Michigan Central cautiously, but its financial needs and his personal influence with capitalists soon forced him to take a leading role in the road to win and keep their support. Almost involuntarily he was forced to make a personal commitment that continued to deepen contrary to his initial expectations. He continued, however, to have other sizable investment interests besides the Michigan Central, where for the most part he confined himself to major policy decisions. Managerial and operational responsibilities were delegated to specialists like Brooks.

While Forbes became increasingly bullish about the prospects of railroads in the West, William Sturgis, who had gone into New York railroads earlier, seemed content during this period to confine his investments to them. In short, membership in the same elite group and close ties based on business as well as social relationships were not guarantees that new investment opportunities would be viewed in the same way. Although they were members of the same group, Forbes and Sturgis represented different generations, and it was the younger generation that found its main challenge in the trans-Allegheny West.

Another group of Bostonians clustered around Neal, who devoted himself increasingly to railroad management, a development growing out of his experience in the Eastern Railroad. As individuals, the members of this group had smaller resources than the Forbes group. As a result, they were seemingly forced to be more speculative, to accept more risks, and to place more reliance on short-run rather than long-run returns.

The link between the major groups of Boston investors was provided by John E. Thayer & Brother, who increasingly specialized in railroad securities. For example, Neal acted as endorser of Michigan Central paper along with John E. Thayer, and Thayer lent his credit to Neal for the latter's purposes. At the same time the Thayers were allied with Forbes and Corning in various ventures.

It is apparent that from 1845 to 1847 Bostonians had surplus capital from which they sought a better than 6 per cent return. One of the major outlets became the railroads of the West, which by 1845 needed rejuvenating doses of private capital. But other outlets for Bostonians' capital could be found in iron works and in trade, as well as in copper mining and manufacturing stocks. As a result, by 1848, Bostonians' commitments were widely extended, and they were for the time being "frozen" in their existing investments.

PART IV The Era of Commitment

Chapter 6

Emerging Investment Patterns: The Forbes Group, 1850–1860

As noted in the preceding chapter, involvement of Boston capital in railroads west of the Alleghenies in the latter half of the 1840's was primarily opportunistic in character, even on the part of such substantial investors as John M. Forbes. A good return on capital invested, plus the possibility of disposing of capital assets at an advance over their cost — though the time period involved does not seem to have been clearly visualized — appears to have been uppermost in the minds of early Boston investors in trans-Allegheny railroads.

Once involved, investors began to be differentiated by more than the size of their resources. Some clung to opportunism in investment, moving into new fields as railroads, begun as promotions, began to call for increased, longer-term commitments and managerial rather than promotional skills. Others accepted the challenges implicit in railroad development, increased their commitments to meet the new needs, and consciously sought to use their transportation investment as a means of fostering economic growth to give their investment increased value. Neither group shied away from opportunities that complemented or followed from transportation investment.

There were many variations and combinations of these basic approaches, each contributing to the economic transformation of the West. In this chapter we shall trace the pattern of decisions that involved Forbes and his Michigan Central group ever more deeply in western affairs.

From Opportunistic to Developmental Investment: The Michigan Central

Three significant factors contributed to change investment in the Michigan Central from opportunistic to developmental. The first concerned the railroad's location. Extension westward was possible because of the east-west orientation of the road, and necessary because of the conditions of sale by the state and the nature of emerging competition; extension eastward was necessary to give an outlet to the seaboard and thus make the Michigan Central more than a truncated road dependent on connecting carriers.

Second, the timing of Boston involvement in the road's fortunes was propitious. The trans-Allegheny West was beginning a dramatic spurt of growth, evidenced in Michigan alone by an increase in population of nearly one third in the years 1840–1845. The Michigan Central was in a position to encourage and share in that growth. "The Michigan Central Railroad, running westerly from Detroit," *Hunt's Merchants' Magazine* observed in March 1849, "brings to that city nearly all the business of the central portion of the State; and when it shall have been completed to Lake Michigan, a few months hence, it will secure to the city nearly all the trade and forwarding business of the western part of the peninsula."

Finally, the nature and extent of Bostonians' commitments contributed to a change in their attitude toward the Michigan Central investment. Forbes, for example, had taken a position in the management as a temporary expedient, but with a large stake in the road's success, which hinged on sound operational policies and expansion, he was forced to continue in an active role. In performing this role, Forbes believed that true prudence required a certain amount of daring. Therefore, he became an ardent and successful advocate of extension and, necessarily, of greater financial commitments. On the other hand, New Bedford investors and David A. Neal, with a far smaller interest, opposed increasing the debt of the road, regardless of what the additional money would buy.[1]

For the actual management of the Central, the owners were fortunate to have a man of John W. Brooks's capacity. Forbes's evaluation of him, written in 1852, is revealing. "The more I see of the difficulty of getting good managers for other roads and other large things, the more am I satisfied with Brooks. He doubtless has his faults, and one of them is to want to do too much himself, instead of throwing off details upon a subordinate, and thus giving him more time for the general management; but he makes up for it by his industry and *decision,* and certainly combines all the qualities we want, more nearly than anybody else in this country. In fact, if we could have the best railroad president and the best superintendent, — *each* picked out among all the railroad companies here, I think Brooks would be worth the *two*." [2]

Moreover, Brooks early in his career with the Central reflected the long-run view of which his Boston backers became the strongest advocates in western railroading. In his 1848 report the young railroad manager laid down this policy of enlightened self-interest: "Having so large a property here, it may perhaps be our duty, as a portion of the public, and it is certainly for our interest, to do what we can in a proper and legitimate way, to promote the welfare and prosperity of that people, upon whose very prosperity rests the whole value of our enterprise." [3]

Brooks was writing in the language of developmental investment, emphasizing that the railroad's proper function, and in the long run its profitability, rested on serving the public as a transportation agency. In this view, sound economic development, fostered by capably managed railroads, was the surest road to private profit as well as to public welfare. It was a view with which the Boston backers of the Michigan Central became increasingly identified as they pushed rails farther west.

Extension of the Michigan Central

The conditions of Bostonians' initial commitment to the Michigan Central gradually both forced and led them to take an increasingly long-run view of its possibilities. One of the requirements of the agreement with the state was that the road be completed to Lake Michigan. With Chicago, on the other side of the lake, becoming an increasingly important entrepôt of midwestern trade, and with the Michigan Southern, now also in private hands, pushing toward that city, Michigan Central owners and managers had the path of expansion outlined for them by commercial as well as legal incentives. Thus statutory and competitive requirements reinforced any visions of extension that they may have had.

On April 23, 1849, the Michigan Central was completed to New Buffalo, Michigan, on Lake Michigan, 218.5 miles from its origin at Detroit.[4] As compared with the earlier trip of three days by lake boats alone,[5] it was now possible to carry passengers from Detroit to Chicago by rail and ship in fourteen to fifteen hours. With the aid of the new company-owned *Mayflower* on Lake Erie, the entire trip from Buffalo to Chicago could be made in thirty-three to thirty-six hours.

Hunt's Merchants' Magazine predicted the next step. "In a few years we may expect a railroad to be made from New Buffalo, around the head of the lake, to Chicago, and from thence to the Mississippi river, at Galena," wrote the editor, "thus completing the iron chain of communication between Detroit and the Mississippi river." [6] Clearly, the territorial goals of the Michigan Central's extension could be easily visualized by anyone with a map.

In the summer of 1849 the Michigan Central managers decided to make their first westward move from New Buffalo. Their decision called for extension of the line to Michigan City, nine and a half miles away on the Indiana line. It was this entirely logical step that conservative New Bedford investors and David A. Neal had opposed because of its cost. Nevertheless, with the written consent of two thirds of the stockholders, work was commenced.[7] In the words of the president, John M. Forbes: "We think the local business from this point [Michigan City] will give a good return upon our outlay, while it is obviously expedient to have our Western terminus upon a line where we can avail of the Railroads which will eventually be built around the head of Lake Michigan to Chicago, and South through Indiana towards the Ohio . . ." [8]

While the development of through traffic was one of the primary aims of the Central's management, local business was regarded as a mainstay of the road's success. Systematic efforts were made to encourage it. Superintendent Brooks reported in 1850 on the "increasing variety, promising permanency and a rapid growth" of this source of revenue. "I cannot but regard the local business as but just budding into a growth quite certain to more than meet the most sanguine expectations of its friends," he declared.[9] To reduce the road's dependence on a single crop, wheat, he had encouraged farmers to produce others by initiating a policy of reduced rates on coarse grains and some bulk commodities.[10]

By 1850, notwithstanding the significance of local business, there was no question in Forbes's mind that long-haul, through traffic was essential to the Michigan Central's welfare. Otherwise, regardless of what steps were taken, the road would be at the mercy of crop shortages in a single state, or other adverse local conditions. Forbes's strategic goal was clearly stated. "We are bound to use every exertion," he wrote, "to make our road a link in the great chain of communication between the East and the West." [11]

Apparently this goal had not been grounded in any prophetic vision about the magnitude of potential western development. If we may believe James F. Joy, Forbes and his associates were, as late as 1848, singularly blind to the range of these possibilities. Joy and Brooks in that year had negotiated for the purchase of the charter of the Northern Indiana Railroad, whose right of way would have carried the Michigan Central through the Hoosier state toward Chicago. When they laid this proposition, involving $50,000, before Forbes and the other directors, Brooks forecast that Chicago's population would reach 200,000 in twenty years. Although actual events more than justified his optimism, the easterners were so skeptical at the time that, according to Joy, they questioned Brooks's judgment and rejected the purchase.[12]

Despite such limitations of Forbes's vision, a more strategic view was in part forced on him by the Michigan Southern Railroad, purchased from the state of Michigan by New York interests and now headed by George Bliss of Springfield, Massachusetts. The group interested in this road acquired the charter of the Northern Indiana Railroad after Forbes had rejected it, and by the spring of 1851 had found a possible answer to the problem of entering Chicago — by using the route of the yet-to-be-built Chicago & Rock Island. Originally planned to connect Rock Island on the Mississippi River with the Illinois and Michigan Canal, the route and charter of his railroad were changed to include Chicago. These changes were made in accordance with the suggestion of Henry Farnam of New Haven, Connecticut, a contractor connected with the Michigan Southern; his partner, Joseph E. Sheffield, promised to obtain eastern capital for the project. As a result, in April 1851, the Rock Island board was enlarged to admit directors who represented this capital and also the Michigan Southern interest.* A contract between the Rock Island and the Northern Indiana Railroad (Michigan Southern) followed and gave the latter the right to purchase a right of way into Chicago in the name of the Rock Island.[13]

Having missed this opportunity because of the Bostonians' cau-

* John Stryker of Rome, New York, and E. C. Litchfield of Detroit were on the board of the Michigan Southern when elected to the Rock Island's board.

tiousness, Joy had to use his political skills to remedy the mistake. He failed in his first effort to obtain an Indiana charter, but found an alternative solution through aiding the New Albany & Salem Railroad to obtain an amendment to its charter that would permit that road to build anywhere in Indiana.* In October 1851 the Michigan Central concluded a formal agreement with the Indiana company, thereby gaining a route to the Indiana-Illinois state line. In return, the Michigan company promised to subscribe to $500,000 of the Indiana road's stock. When Joy twitted Forbes about paying this amount to secure a route that had been offered to him for $50,000, the Bostonian characteristically replied that he could now pay $500,000 more easily than he could have paid the $50,000 when the proposal originally came up.[14]

The Michigan Southern now sought to frustrate the Central's plans in various ways. In the spring of 1851 its management had offered to let the rival road send its cars over the Southern's proposed line into Chicago for "a reasonable compensation." The Central's management declined this offer, suggesting that it was inspired by a desire to maintain "a *monopoly*" in Indiana.[15] After the Central obtained its route across Indiana, the Southern sought an injunction against the proposed construction. This move was thwarted in the Supreme Court of Indiana, and that decision was sustained by the United States Supreme Court.[16] Commenting on this continuing harassment in his 1852 report, President Forbes of the Central declared there had been no doubt about the outcome. "We consulted the highest counsel both at the east and the west,"** he wrote, "and every step which has since been taken by our opponents or by the Legal Tribunals before which they have called us, has strengthened the conviction which we have always had of the soundness of the advice under which we have acted. . . ."[17]

In Illinois, as in Indiana, the Michigan Central was blocked from obtaining a charter. Early in 1851, however, George Griswold, a key figure in the newly organized Illinois Central Railroad and also a Michigan Central stockholder, had suggested a mutually ad-

* Brooks was impressed by "the acknowledged credit and strength" of the New Albany & Salem. (Brooks to Forbes, April 1, 1851, in Thomas Cochran, *Railroad Leaders, 1845–1890* [Cambridge, Massachusets, 1953], 268.)

** In connection with the New Albany & Salem charter, for example, Forbes employed the services of Benjamin R. Curtis of Massachusetts, who later served on the United States Supreme Court.

vantageous move for the two roads. The Illinois Central had access rights to Chicago but lacked funds. The exchange of participation in this access privilege for sorely needed capital was an obvious possibility. Accordingly, an agreement was signed in May 1851 whereby the Michigan Central agreed to build a line from the Indiana border to Chicago in the name of the Illinois Central and to furnish "certain aid." [18]

No construction took place under this particular agreement, principally because of two factors beyond the control of the Michigan Central management. There was, first, the opposition of Chicago. City leaders feared that a direct connection between the Illinois Central and Michigan Central railroads, anywhere but in the city itself, would divert from Chicago large amounts of through traffic between downstate Illinois (and other connected areas) and the East. This hostility to the rumored plan culminated in two conventions, called to protest the plan in the summer of 1851.[19] Moreover, Chicago held the trump card, for her Common Council had the power to block the I. C.'s entrance to the city.

The second obstacle lay in the procrastination of the Illinois company's managers. The Michigan Central was caught in its own web, for under the May agreements it had given up the right to use any charters other than the I. C.'s to gain its goal.

To force action, Forbes in October 1851 reluctantly agreed to Joy's and Brooks's recommendation that the M. C. build a line six and a half miles into Illinois on its own responsibility,[20] hoping the I. C. would later take it over. Seeing an answer to Chicago's fears that a connection at the state line would mean an alteration of the I. C.'s proposed route and thereby create a through route to Detroit and deflect traffic from Chicago, the I. C. interpreted the Central's offer to mean that it could effect a connection west of the Indiana line rather than at the line as agreed in May. On this basis the mayor of Chicago and Senator Stephen Douglas gave their consent to the plan.[21] Forbes, under pressure to beat the Southern into Chicago, was too far committed to force the I. C. to honor the original May agreements. He had to take the risk of building into Illinois without a charter or see the Chicago connection postponed for a dangerously long time.

The new agreements were confirmed in a contract of February 7, 1852. Its salient features were: (1) the Illinois Central would build the Chicago branch, connecting with the Michigan Central *inside* Illinois; and (2) the Michigan Central would take $2,000,000 of Illinois Central 7 per cent bonds to aid construction of 127 miles of I. C. road south of Chicago.* [22]

Construction went ahead on this basis, and the Michigan Central ran its first train into Chicago over Illinois Central tracks on May 21, 1852. The very next day the Southern reached the city over tracks of the Northern Indiana and the Rock Island.[23]

In the race with the Southern, the key men of the Michigan Central had barred no holds nor had they kept stockholders fully informed about their commitments. Forbes deplored the risks of illegal construction through even a quarter-section in Illinois,[24] but he was accustomed to taking risks and this one at least produced action where time was of the essence. While the Illinois legislature legitimatized the deed after the fact,[25] no mention of the financial arrangements with the Illinois Central was made by Forbes in his annual reports until June 1854. Finally, in 1855, J. W. Brooks gave a public account of the major phases of strategy and said: ". . . to secure very valuable permanent running and ticketing arrangements with them [I. C.], required large advances to be made to that Company. These advances, though collaterally well secured, had to be carried through the late money pressure at a large sacrifice to this Company. We believe, however, the fruits of this sacrifice will be an ample reward." [26]

Both John C. Green and Forbes claimed that secrecy about the agreement between the roads was maintained at the request of the Illinois road. Forbes noted that this concealment, involving a large, unexplained floating debt, "was diametrically opposed to the interests of the Michigan Central but was supposed to be necessary for the interest of the Illinois Central." [27] Although the Michigan Central's treasurer carried the I. C. bonds on the books at $800,000 in 1855 and $200,000 the following year, they disappeared after that. In 1860 the president of the I. C. stated that with the last payment in September 1856 his road had received a total of $1,214,000 in advances from the Michigan Central.[28]

* Bostonians had confidence in other Bostonians. Thus, in declining the terms of a loan to the I. C. shortly before this contract, Forbes wrote Corning that what confidence he had in the Illinois road was based on the prospect that David A. Neal would be put in charge of construction. (Forbes to Corning, February 2, 1852, in Cochran, *Railroad Leaders,* 328.) Neal was concerned with the Illinois railroad but largely in the Land Department.

In securing a route to Chicago for the Michigan Central, Forbes had seemingly made some costly errors because of his financial conservatism and skepticism about the rate of growth of the West. On the other hand, a series of successful tactical maneuvers, engineered by Joy, eventually more than compensated for the initial strategic error. Having afforded the Michigan Southern an advantage by declining to use the Northern Indiana's charter, the Forbes group suddenly found itself on the defensive. Blocked in both the Indiana and Illinois legislatures, the Bostonians sought other means of accomplishing their objectives. They handled the connection with the New Albany & Salem in Indiana deftly but at a high cost. In Illinois the strategy was marred by Forbes's promise to the Illinois Central to use no other charters to reach Chicago. This agreement transferred the initiative to the I. C. and seemingly bound Forbes's fortunes to that road. To rectify this situation, the Michigan Central was forced to build illegally into Illinois. In agreeing to take $2,000,000 of the I. C.'s bonds without the knowledge of his board or stockholders, Forbes again took a risk. Samuel G. Ward, the Barings' agent in Boston, certainly regarded it as a mistake,[29] although the I. C. guaranteed the Michigan Central against any loss on the $800,000 worth of bonds taken by 1855. In the end, the desired results were obtained.

Faced with a difficult situation, Forbes did not shrink from accepting great responsibility, a burden for which the China trade had prepared him well. The entire episode undoubtedly gave him a new perspective on western development, and it certainly left him more deeply committed in that area of investment.

The Michigan Central and the Great Western of Canada

While the efforts to reach Chicago were in progress, others were directed to improving the Michigan Central's connections with the East. Detroit's link with the eastern roads via steamer across Lake Erie left much to be desired, especially in the months of bad or freezing weather. It was for this reason that the Forbes group turned their attention to the Great Western Railroad of Canada. Again the geographical location of the Bostonians' initial capital commitment demanded, if it did not dictate, a particular course of action.

The Great Western, planned to connect Lake Ontario and the

Niagara River on the east with Lake Huron and Windsor (opposite Detroit) on the west, was originally chartered in 1834, but its name, capital, and powers were changed by amendment in 1845.[30] Construction began by 1847, but until 1851 relatively little progress was made. However, the possibility of establishing a fast through route to the East by the Michigan Central's connection with the Great Western had a definite attraction for Forbes. Erastus Corning saw benefits for his New York roads, as well as the Central, in such an arrangement.

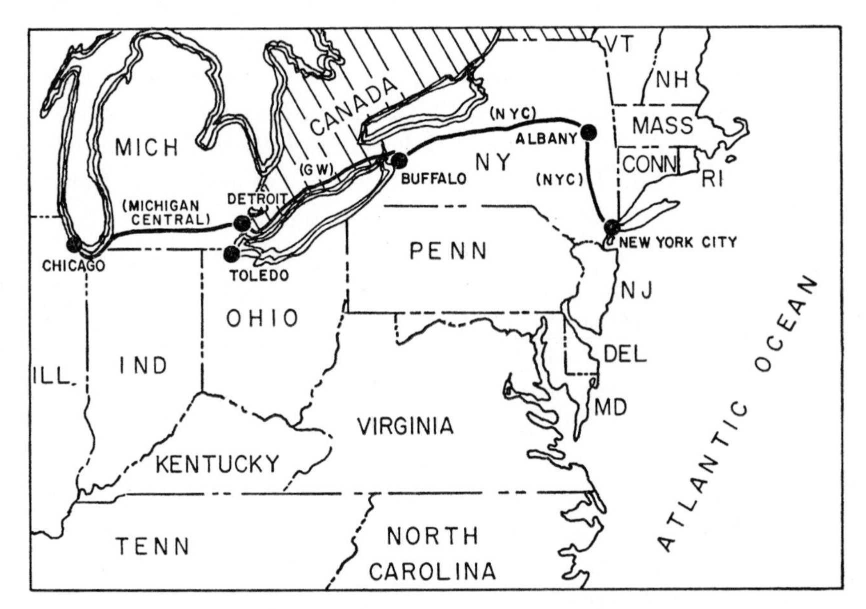

THE MICHIGAN CENTRAL AS PART OF A THROUGH ROUTE FROM CHICAGO TO NEW YORK CITY, 1856.

The committee appointed in May 1851 to obtain subscriptions to the Great Western's stock in the United States was headed by Forbes and included Corning, John E. Thayer, D. D. Williamson, John C. Green, Edward L. Baker of New Bedford, and John W. Brooks.[31] The committee sought to raise $1,000,000 to supplement the provincial government's guarantee of $2,650,000 in 6 per cent bonds. These resources, with private Canadian and American subscriptions and contractors' stock, were to constitute the $6,300,000 capital of the road.[32]

Once again the Michigan Central's rivalry with the Michigan Southern influenced the course of events. A correspondent of the *American Railroad Journal* reported in September 1851 that the Canadian directors of the Great Western were considering turning to both the Erie Railroad and the Michigan Southern, unless the Michigan Central and Corning's New York roads (soon to be combined as the New York Central Railroad) could produce the requisite million dollars.[33]

Forbes was under pressure in this connection since the Michigan legislature had declined to authorize the Michigan Central to subscribe to the Great Western's stock. In his 1851 report, therefore, Forbes urged individual stockholders to do so. "We have entire confidence in the extensive capabilities of the Great Western Railroad, and by taking hold of it now, we believe you may not only improve the permanent value of your own property but obtain a very profitable investment," Forbes wrote.[34]

Corning, a director of the Great Western, had a more direct solution. Through his influence, the New York legislature permitted railroads in that state to subscribe up to 5 per cent of their capital to the Great Western's stock if two thirds of their stockholders concurred.[35] Under Corning's guidance the necessary consent was obtained and, the road were authorized to subscribe as follows:

Albany and Schenectady	$ 25,000
Utica and Schenectady	200,000
Syracuse and Utica	75,000
Syracuse and Rochester	125,000
Niagara Falls Company	75,000[36]
(Rochester, Lockport and Niagara Falls)	

Immediately thereafter the Utica and Schenectady issued a circular asking stockholders' consent to its allocated subscription. William Sturgis, Boston's veteran railroad investor, studied the matter, conferred with Forbes, and then answered in the negative. Although the estimated cost of construction was $5,000,000, he predicted it would go higher, especially if, as planned, the contractors were to be paid in stock. Sturgis, therefore, saw this call on stockholders in the New York roads as but the first of a series. He scoffed at the threat that the Erie might take a hand if the New York Central lines did not. He conceded the importance of the Great Western to the Michigan Central, but not to the New York road soliciting his approval. Bryant and Cushing concurred in Sturgis' position.[37]

Sturgis was an extremely influential stockholder whose opposition it was essential to overcome. This is made clear by a letter he received from Henry R. Gibson of the Syracuse and Rochester on the subject of subscribing to Great Western stock. As Sturgis reported the contents, Gibson declared that his road would fail in its subscription if the Bostonian and his followers continued to oppose the move. Sturgis yielded to Gibson's plea, though in forwarding his consent and that of John Bryant and J. P. Cushing he made it clear that he was acting against his better judgment and hoped that the Michigan Central interests would be required to contribute in proportion to the obvious benefits they would receive from a connection with the Great Western.[38]

In addition to these railroad subscriptions, individual investors in the United States, including Michigan Central stockholders and residents of Detroit, took $300,000 worth.[39] According to the Great Western's annual report for 1852, the Americans subscribed for 8,000 shares in all, while £210,000 sterling from convertible bonds had been raised in England. Forbes in his report to Michigan Central stockholders for that year exulted over the prospects of the connection, which would leave the Central road "shut up but one more winter" as a result of its dependence on ice-bound Lake Erie steamers.

Work did not proceed as rapidly as anticipated, and, as Sturgis had predicted, costs quickly outstripped initial estimates.* However, the Great Western was opened from Windsor to Niagara Falls in late January 1854. Forbes reported in June that despite the obstacles of winter operation and the incomplete bridge at Niagara Falls, receipts showed a very decided benefit from the new connection.[40]

The gauge of the Great Western posed special problems as to its usefulness in a through route. A railway committee appointed by a royal commission had studied this matter, and, on the basis of its evidence, the Canadian government decreed in July 1851 that the

* The directors placed much blame on Chief Engineer Benedict. (Great Western Railway of Canada, *Annual Report,* 1853, 7–9). Benedict attributed his removal to the hostility of American directors, especially Forbes, because he had refused to "accommodate" the Michigan Central. (*American Railroad Journal,* XVI [July 30, 1853], 485–486.)

national gauge should be five feet six inches.[41] This decree was a blow to the Great Western, for its connecting American roads, the New York Central and the Michigan Central, had a gauge of four feet eight and a half inches.* The management of the Michigan Central, seeing the advantages of a third rail that would permit the use of American rolling stock on the Great Western, in 1864 solicited contributions from the Boston and Worcester Railroad for this purpose.[42] Shortly thereafter, the third rail was laid.[43]

By 1856 four through passenger trains per day were running over the Michigan Central and Great Western. It was possible to leave Chicago at 5:15 A.M., arrive in Detroit at 2:45 P.M. and at the suspension bridge at Niagara Falls at 11:15 P.M.[44] At Niagara Falls there was a choice between using the New York Central roads to reach Albany and thence to the seaboard, or taking a steamer to Ogdensburg and proceeding from there by train to Boston through Vermont.

Meanwhile, the doubts of canny William Sturgis had been confirmed. Canadian stockholders in the Great Western proved to have different interests from those south of the border, and they found support for their position among English stockholders. In June 1854 Corning was writing to Henry Gibson that he wished he were rid of his Great Western stock. Early in the fall, Corning resigned from the board of the road, as did Forbes and Brooks.[45] The departure of the Forbes group from the Great Western, however, did not end its usefulness as a connecting link for the Michigan Central.**

The involvement of Forbes and his colleagues in the Great Western indicated that a deliberate design for perpetuating and increasing their railroad investment in the light of western economic growth was definitely established. Expressing the developmental attitude, Forbes wrote in the Michigan Central's 1853 report: "When, a few months hence, our Road becomes a part of the continuous

* The desire of Portland, Maine, to exclude Boston from business with Montreal via the Atlantic and St. Lawrence road may have lent some support to the adoption of the five feet six inches gauge. (W. M. Spriggs, "Great Western Railway of Canada," Railway and Locomotive Historical Society, *Bulletin,* LI [February, 1940], 8.).

** In 1857 the Great Western reported that "the greater part" of its through traffic between United States points came over the Central. However, the existence of alternate routes eastward from Chicago (via Michigan Southern and the Erie; and the Chicago, Fort Wayne & Pittsburg) prompted the Canadian road's interest in making Milwaukee a focal point and for this purpose extending aid to the Detroit and Milwaukee. (*American Railroad Journal,* XXX [August 15, 1857], 513.)

line of Railroads, connecting the seaboard with the Ohio, the Mississippi and the far West, we mean that it shall be in a condition *to do its share of the business well.* And we have not the slightest doubt that our Stockholders will then reap the full benefit of an enterprise, which from the start, has been conducted with an eye to the comprehensive system that is about being realized, rather than with short sighted views of temporary expediency.

"While we have been aware that a different course might have led to more profitable results at the moment, we believe that the true policy has been pursued for securing permanent success to our Company, and promoting the convenience and welfare of the section of country with which it has become identified." [46]

Statistics from the road's annual reports show that the Forbes policy was soundly based. With few exceptions — in most instances due to crop failures and competition from the Michigan Southern[47] — freight and passenger traffic of the Michigan Central showed a strong upward trend through 1854. Net earnings rose from $169,423 for the year ending May 31, 1848, to $674,651 for fiscal year 1854. In June 1852 Forbes described it as "the true policy of the Company to make only such Dividends as will leave a reasonable surplus on hand for contingencies." [48] Apparently 8 per cent dividends were typical, though 14 per cent was declared in December 1851. Meanwhile the track, roadbed, and rolling stock had been improved. In the 1852 report Forbes could state with satisfaction that "the manifest economy in working the Road, which has grown out of its gradual improvement and our increased experience, indicates an advance that is independent of accident." [49]

Unquestionably the timing and nature of their commitment to the Michigan Central had given the Boston investors led by Forbes good reason to consider it an investment worthy of continuing attention and careful development. Forbes brought to this work a combination of prudence and daring, and an increasing insistence on a long-run, broad approach that served well his followers, the road, and the region it occupied. Prodded by an expanding vision of economic growth in the West and pushed by competitive pressures, the Forbes group was to apply lessons learned in the Michigan Central to other roads reaching further west toward the farming frontier. A short-run, opportunistic investment of 1846 had become a long-run, developmental one whose success generated enthusiasm for placing more Boston capital in the West.

Complementary Investment: The Mount Savage Iron Company

When John M. Forbes had turned his attention to domestic investment in the mid-forties, he was definitely in a speculative frame of mind. Far more risky than the Michigan Central venture was the plunge that he took into iron manufacture. While the growing needs of the nation's railroads for iron made such an investment a logical complement to railroad investment, the domestic product up to that time had been no match for the imported material. And, as a matter of fact, Forbes was more pushed than pulled into his first major iron works investment.

The rolling mills of the Maryland & New York Coal & Iron Company, located near Cumberland, Maryland, in 1844 had produced the first heavy iron rails in America.[50] By 1847 this concern had been merged into the Mount Savage Iron Company. The combined property, including 5,000 acres of land, furnaces, and a rolling mill that could produce 9,000 tons of rails a year, represented an investment of well over one million dollars. Forbes had advanced the Mount Savage firm $130,000, apparently through his connection with one of the founders. In 1847 the company was in financial trouble, and Forbes feared he would have to buy it to protect his interest. However, he succeeded in interesting others, including Erastus Corning and the ex-China trader Warren Delano, Jr., of New York. They purchased the property for something over $200,000. Forbes immediately disposed of most of his interest, retaining only about $40,000 worth. In succeeding months he blew hot and cold on this investment, which he described to Paul Forbes in November 1847 as a "ticket in the lottery." [51]

In the long run, the ticket failed to pay off. By December 1859 Forbes thought the Mount Savage investment would not bring half what had been spent on it. In fact, he declared, "I would rather put money into 5% U.S. stocks than into the best Iron Company in this country at ½ cost." [52] However, his disillusionment was not quite that complete. For the interest held by Forbes and his associates in the North Chicago Rolling Mills, a pioneer manufacturer of steel rails, proved a profitable, long-run investment.

Consequential Investment: The St. Mary's Companies

Investment in western land or other natural resources could lead to investment in transportation, or, as in the case of the Forbes group, the process could be reversed. Such investment in turn could be a consequence of existing involvement in the area and situational opportunity, or it could be part of a developmental pattern to give the major investment additional validity. Forbes's connection with the St. Mary's Falls Ship Canal Company's history is a case of consequential investment.

The copper boom on Lake Superior had generated a demand for transportation services and more particularly for a means of passing from the lower lakes to Lake Superior. This route could be provided if the falls of the St. Mary's River, between Lake Superior and Lake Huron, could be circumvented. To provide an incentive for construction of a canal for this purpose, Congress granted the state of Michigan 750,000 acres of land. This grant was an obvious invitation to promotional activity, and it did not escape the eyes of James F. Joy and his partner, George Porter. The Boston investors who had backed these men in the Michigan Central purchase, however, showed little interest in the canal project until Joy early in 1853 got a bill, with appropriate provisions, through the Michigan legislature. Under it, investors were promised the 750,000 acres of land, which they could select, in return for constructing a mile-long waterway with two locks, to be completed in two years.[53]

The pattern of promotion and the key figures of the St. Mary's Falls Ship Canal Company all tended to duplicate those of the railroad. The initial objective of Boston investors in the Ship Canal Company, however, seems to have been a relatively quick recapture of their capital and return on their investment from sale of the lands — not from developing them, or processing their resources, or using them directly to generate traffic for the Michigan Central. Five of the incorporators were active in the Michigan Central: Corning, Forbes, Joy, Brooks, and George Griswold. The first four were also members of the Ship Canal Company's first board of directors.[54] There was an expectation that the requisite capital could be raised without fully assessing the stock, but by November 1854 the full par value had been called. It was also possible to issue bonds, and this too was done.[55]

As soon as the company completed the canal in 1855, the state transferred to the corporation the 750,000 acres granted by the federal government.[56] Since selection of the acreage was the prerogative of the company, attention was given to picking out the most saleable and potentially profitable types of land. Possible mineral lands were selected without precise examination but on the basis of their location in the mineral range of Michigan's upper peninsula. Timber and farm lands in the lower peninsula were selected with more care. The company's 1863 catalog, for example, pointed out: "In all cases two, and in many cases several distinct examinations were made by different parties unknown to each other . . . and with rare exceptions the selections were well made."[57] The 1858 director's report revealed the following types of land selected and the approximate acreage:

Pine and farm lands in the lower peninsula	488,000 acres
Pine and other woodlands in the upper peninsula	76,000
Iron lands, near Marquette	39,000
Copper lands on the mineral range	147,000
Total	750,000 acres[58]

When the expected sale of the mineral lands to European investors fell through, the company decided to withhold these lands for further examination. To acquire and hold this property, Canal Company stockholders formed the St. Mary's Canal Mineral Land Company, chartered in April 1858 and organized the following December.[59] Thus, the investors segregated the potentially more valuable property from the remainder of their acquisition and vested ownership in a separate entity. This was an important decision, for it led to a long-term involvement that apparently was not contemplated in their initial investment decision.

The Ship Canal Company tried to dispose of pine and farm lands as quickly as possible, but progress was slow. In 1862 the managers appointed Cyrus Woodman as land agent in the hope that he could speed the marketing operation. His initial attempt to sell 100,000 acres on the Saginaw and Muskegon Rivers, however, was almost a complete failure. With company expenses running about $50,000 a year, action was imperative. There were two possibilities: either the stockholders could add to their investment, or the lands held by the company could be divided up among the stockholders.[60] The former course would involve an additional capital outlay; the latter could be made less painful by having the company accept its own stock and bonds, as well as cash, in payment for the land. The large stockholders favored division of the lands, while the smaller ones favored holding the lands as long as possible in hope of sale. In this instance, the relative weight given to prospects of long-run gain suggests that the large stockholders were interested in recovering their capital as quickly as possible and at the least cost. Continued management of such peripheral investment was apparently neither sought nor desired, but it turned out to be unavoidable.

Having made the decision to divide up the lands, the directors entrusted Woodman with the execution of the plan. Drawing on his experience in a similar operation for the Boston and Western Land Company in the early 1840's, Woodman prepared 744 parcels from the 525,000 acres of unsold company land. Identified in some detail and valued according to timber stands and their distance from water, the land went on public sale September 2, 1863. Stockholders could use Canal Company stock or bonds combined with relatively small amounts of cash to pay for their purchases.[61] About $900,000 worth of land changed hands at the sale, with major stockholders taking a significant share.[62]

The objective of the large stockholders who had converted their investment from securities into land was to realize on their holdings with a minimum outlay. Accordingly they banded together under the name of the Michigan Pinelands Association. Woodman as agent, and John M. Forbes, John W. Brooks, and R. S. Watson as trustees, were empowered to buy and sell land, lease and erect lumber mills, and otherwise conduct business as though there was a single owner. Although the market was slow during the Civil War, Woodman had some success. In March 1864, for example, he sold nearly 50,000 acres on the Pere Marquette River for $200,000, or an advance of almost 80 per cent over the purchase price. Since the association paid Woodman in land as well as in cash commissions, out-of-pocket costs of marketing were relatively small. In addition, the compensation device was turned into a sales argument. The fact that the land agent accepted his payment in the same type of land that he was selling was presumably proof to buyers of its value. By 1869, only 900 acres of land remained on the Association's books, and they were finally sold in 1874.[63] However, what was expected to be a quick turnover of capital had taken, in fact, almost twenty years.

In the process of disposing of the mineral lands, the owners of the Mineral Land Company became even more deeply involved. The iron lands that they held on Lake Superior were increased in value by the opening of the Sault Canal, and in 1864 the bulk of them were sold for $500,000, netting the sellers a considerable profit.[64] The company disposed of copper lands on Michigan's mineral range more slowly, and often in exchange for stock in new mining companies. In some, the Mineral Land Company kept a controlling interest; in others, the stock was distributed as dividends to the company's stockholders. In this way, the principal figures of the Michigan Central became involved in copper mining activities. John M. Forbes, for example, was a director of the Mineral Land Company from 1860 until his death, and in the interim became the director of several copper companies. A supposedly short-term, consequential investment led to a long-term interest in activities which were incidental to the investor's initial objective, and, indeed, peripheral to his main investment interest.

By the mid-1850's the Forbes group was involved in the West on a continuing basis. They were being pushed westward in response to competitive pressure as well as pulled by an increased appreciation of the West's potential. Such expansion also focused attention on the advantages of a far-flung, unified transportation network. Logically, therefore, the concept of a railroad system, as opposed to a railroad line, was beginning to emerge, and the economic growth of the system's territory was increasingly linked in the investors' minds with the profitability of their investment. For Forbes, western railroad transportation had become a major interest. He regarded his ventures in other fields, primarily opportunistic in character, as less important, even though some of them proved to be far more long-lived and developmental than he had anticipated. Yet, like the burgeoning railroad network, Forbes's complementary and consequential investments, whatever the motives behind them, added to the underpinnings of western economic development.

Chapter 7

Emerging Investment Patterns: Bostonians and the Illinois Central, 1850–1860

THE ILLINOIS Central Railroad occupies a crucial place in the history of American transportation not only because it became the largest railroad in the world in the 1850's but also because it was the pioneering federal land-grant road. Here for the first time federal lands were used directly as an incentive to large-scale private railroad investment, setting a precedent of great significance for future railroad building in the West.

From the standpoint of the investment process, the Illinois Central also provides a significant case study. Boston capitalists, for the most part different ones from those we have so far traced, and acting in cooperation with men from other eastern centers, took part in the enterprise at three levels: as promoters, investors, and managers. Furthermore, the changing scope and character of this involvement became a dynamic process, for the expectations that had characterized the attitudes of the original promoters had to be severely modified as the venture encountered unforeseen circumstances. As a consequence, new policies emerged to fit the new shape of events.

The pattern of investment by Boston investors and their role in this changing picture provide an interesting comparison with those of their contemporaries in the Michigan Central. Put in a somewhat oversimplified way, the original undertaking of the Illinois Central was viewed by the participants as almost purely opportunistic — one in which the future economic development of Illinois was considered the basis of the value of the speculation, and not as the end to be worked for by the original investors. But as time passed and economic difficulties mounted, it became apparent that the men who controlled the enterprise would have to invest far more capital in it and manage it with specific regard to its long-run potentialities. In other words, the pressure of changing circumstances obliged the promoters to choose between withdrawing their investment and taking a financial loss, or transforming their role from an opportunistic to a developmental one. They chose the second alternative, and the land grant was central to their decision. The resulting interaction between expectations and a changing reality gives relevance to the story of the Illinois Central in this study.

Launching the Illinois Central

During the 1850's, a decade of remarkable economic change for the country as a whole, the American railroad network increased from some nine thousand to over thirty thousand miles. In this expansion the Midwest's share increased from a fifth or less to almost one third of the national total. The state of Illinois underwent a burst of economic development. Its population rose from 851,000 to 1,712,000. Agriculturists created some 67,000 new farms and brought over 8,000,000 acres of new land into cultivation. By 1860, with an output of almost 29,000,000 bushels of wheat and just over 115,000,000 bushels of corn, Illinois farmers led the nation in the production of both these grains. Of the enormous amount of capital investment associated with this phase of economic growth, railroad construction, including the seven hundred miles of Illinois Central, represented a strategic portion. And construction of this magnitude, in an area like Illinois of the 1850's, necessitated a heavy inflow of outside capital.

Although Illinois is almost bounded by navigable waterways, and although the Illinois and Michigan Canal finally linked the Illinois River (and therefore the Mississippi system) with Lake Michigan in 1848, there was still a need for inexpensive land transportation to invigorate agricultural production on the fertile and extensive prairie lying within the state. Yet, as was the case in most areas of the West, the demand for additional transportation facilities antedated the accumulation of enough local wealth to finance their construction. This contrast between desire and adequate funds provided an obvious incentive to capitalists outside the state to bridge the gap.

Discussing these problems in 1852, the *American Railroad Journal* touched on the central issue: "We would not convey the idea . . . that any portion of our country is really poor. Far from it . . .

What we mean is, that our capital bears no proportion to our opportunities for profitable investment. Take Illinois for instance . . . in 1850 . . . she produced . . . a surplus [above local needs] of more than 40,000,000 bushels of [corn and wheat] . . . In New York this surplus would have been worth $40,000,000. In Illinois it did not net the producers more than $12,000,00. This difference is due to the charges for transportation alone. Illinois turns her vast resources to small account, for the want of more and better avenues to market . . . Now her people ask capitalists to construct these avenues, and share with them the amount to be saved." [1]

It is not surprising, therefore, that to eastern capitalists like David A. Neal a railroad through central Illinois appeared as an "engine of prosperity," certain to "develope [*sic*] resources that must otherwise have remained hidden from human sight, and beyond the grasp of human hands." [2]

Among the fifteen projects marked for state aid in the notorious Illinois Internal Improvement Act of 1837 had been a railroad from Cairo at the junction of the Mississippi and Ohio Rivers in the south, to Galena, the center of the lead-mining district, in the north. By 1839, however, under the pressure of a recession and an orgy of peculation and inefficiency, all work on internal improvements ceased. This action left only a hundred miles of grading and a few thousand tons of old iron as reminders of the public plan for a north-south railroad through the center of Illinois.

Although little had been achieved by the end of the 1840's, various abortive plans had pointed in the right economic direction: namely, a cross-state railroad which would open up the central prairies to settlement and agricultural production. To obtain the necessary capital for such an expensive project it was essential to have powerful incentives. These had been absent in the 1830's but by 1850 they began to appear. The region had undergone some development, and population growth (from around 300,000 in 1837 to 851,000 in 1850) provided a more feasible economic basis for a railroad. Political pressures also heightened the possibility of securing an abundant land grant as a subsidy to the project. This last factor was associated with another development, the appearance of a determined and qualified group of eastern capitalists, experienced in the ways of finance and railroads and well aware of the opportunity held out by changed circumstances. Taking hold of a scheme that had already existed in various forms for almost twenty years, they drove it through to a successful conclusion.

Of the men who became directors of the Illinois Central early in 1851, a handful played the dominant role in the actual promotion. They were Morris Ketchum, George Griswold, and Jonathan Sturges, all of New York, and David A. Neal of Salem.* There were, in addition, such other men of importance as Joseph W. Alsop and Robert Schuyler of New York and Franklin Haven of Boston. Neal's background and earlier activities have already been sketched. Ketchum was a prosperous financier and locomotive manufacturer; Griswold was an ex-China trader and an important investor in the Michigan Central; Sturges and Alsop were successful merchants; Schuyler was a well-known railroad entrepreneur; and Haven was an established and respectable Boston banker. Although the specific occasion and means by which these men came together are not known, their general relationships through the commercial and railroad worlds are obvious.

The key to the Illinois Central promotion was the federal land grant. There is no need here to follow the intricate developments involved in the congressional bargaining for the grant, in which Senator Stephen A. Douglas was deeply concerned.[3] By a variety of compromises, including an extension of the scope of the proposed grant southwards to the Gulf of Mexico at Mobile, an act was engineered providing for a generous donation of public land, through state authorities, to qualifying railroad companies.**

Eastern investors were politically influential in helping to push

* These were the men credited with the "successful carrying out of this great object" by Governor William H. Bissell (himself a former associate) in a speech in Illinois in 1857. (Carlton J. Corliss, *Main-Line of Mid-America* [New York, 1950], 23.) William K. Ackerman, a former executive of the railroad, named Sturges, Griswold, Neal, Alsop, and John F. A. Sanford as the most important promoters. (*Historical Sketch of the Illinois Central Railroad* [Chicago, 1890], 79.)

** In the case of Illinois the state was given the right of way through public lands from the Illinois and Michigan Canal to the junction of the Ohio and Mississippi Rivers, with branches to Chicago and Dubuque (via Galena). The act also granted alternate sections, six miles deep on each side of the road; the sections remaining in the possession of the United States were to be sold for at least double the minimum for public lands ($1.25). The railroad was to be completed within ten years. Alabama and Mississippi received similar grants for the line from the Ohio River to the Gulf; as it turned out, the Illinois Central was to receive 2.595 million acres of public lands. (Paul W. Gates, *The Illinois Central Railroad and Its Colonization Work* [Cambridge, Massachusetts, 1934], 41–42, 107–108.)

through the grant. Among these were, for example, owners of Illinois internal improvement bonds, now greatly depreciated. In this category were men and firms later important in or to the Illinois Central management: Sturges, Morris and Hiram Ketchum, Franklin Haven, Rogers Bement, Thomas Wren Ward, Abbott Lawrence, and two English firms, Baring Brothers & Company and Magniac, Jardine & Company. Added to these elements were the extensive New York, Boston, and Philadelphia interests involved in Illinois land speculation, especially in the bounty lands of the Military Tract granted to veterans of the War of 1812.[4] Finally, there were the investors and officials of the Michigan Central, which was building its way to Chicago and would ultimately need extensive rail connections there.

The group of men who hoped to promote the railroad were extremely active behind the Washington scenes. They had obtained the services of George W. Billings, a former agent of the Cairo City and Canal Company,[5] a town-promotion corporation that had proposed an earlier plan for a central railroad. Billings' assistant in the delicate art of lobbying was Robert Rantoul, Jr., of Boston. During the summer and fall of 1850 the two maintained a correspondence on the steady progress of the land-grant bill, the consequent fluctuations in Illinois securities, and the possibility of the promoters profiting from these fluctuations or even controlling the market.[6]

Even before the grant was confirmed, Billings and the promoters, with some advice from Douglas, were mapping out a campaign of direct action and newspaper publicity to obtain from the Illinois legislature a charter that would control the disposition of the land. This campaign got under way in the winter of 1851–1852 at the Seventeenth General Assembly of Illinois in Springfield. Adverse publicity and lack of enthusiasm defeated a plan for the owners of internal improvement bonds to follow the earlier example of the Illinois and Michigan Canal by building the railroad to pay off relevant state obligations. Darius Holbrook, promoter of Cairo, Illinois, controller of the Cairo City and Canal Company, and possessor of a charter for a cross-state railroad, was brought off with 1,000 Illinois Central shares and a promise that the new company would undertake extensive improvements and developments at Cairo.[7]

On February 10, 1851, after extensive "wirepulling and back-scratching," the Act of Incorporation for the Illinois Central railroad was passed. Formally, it was a response to a memorial of January 15 presented on behalf of Robert Schuyler, George Griswold, Gouverneur Morris, Jonathan Sturges, Thomas W. Ludlow, John F. A. Sanford, David A. Neal, Franklin Haven, and Robert Rantoul, Jr. By the terms of the act these men, together with Leroy M. Wiley, Henry Grinnell, Joseph W. Alsop, and William H. Aspinwall, all of New York, were incorporators. Significantly, the act provided that the road must be built in a manner equal in all respects to the "Great Western Railway" of Massachusetts, the lines from Boston to Albany.

Other conditions worth noting here were the financial stipulations. Authorized bond interest was limited to 7 per cent. The land grant was to be held in trust and land sales could only proceed *pari passu* with construction; the returns from them were to be used to retire bond issues. Seven per cent of gross income was to be paid to the state.

The Illinois Central Railroad Company was soon organized. The charter's financial conditions were accepted. The incorporators mentioned above, with the exception of Aspinwall and with the addition of Governor French of Illinois, were elected directors on February 10, and Morris Ketchum joined the board two months later. On March 22 Schuyler, now president, formally accepted the act by depositing $200,000 with the state treasurer. According to the president's account, the cost of securing the charter was less than $52,000.[8]

By the business criteria of their day, the promoters and incorporators of the Illinois Central had apparently brought off a considerable coup. From one, and perhaps the most important, viewpoint these men were opportunistic investors. For them the railroad was a speculative prize for an astute piece of business strategy; they hoped to secure outright ownership of a valuable piece of property in return for a very small capital outlay and in the expectation of its not needing much positive or creative work on their part.

In terms of their experience in the field of railroads and transportation these men had impressive qualifications.[9] Sturges was promoter and director of the New York and New Haven; Wiley, Griswold, and Morris were directors of the Great Western of Illinois (later the Toledo, Wabash & Western). Morris was also associated with the New York and Harlem and the Vermont Valley. Alsop, Aspinwall, and Ludlow were involved with the Pacific Mail Steamship Company and the Panama Railroad, and Alsop was the first president of the Ohio & Mississippi. Ketchum had a close interest in the New York and New Haven. Neal was president of the Eastern Railroad and influential in the Reading Railroad, besides investing in Ohio roads and the Michigan Central. And Schuyler, to whom Neal referred as "a gentleman more conversant with and more largely interested in Rail Roads than any other person on the Western continent," [10] besides having been involved with the Philadelphia and Reading at the same time as Neal, was president of four other lines; the New York and New Haven; the Harlem; the Rensselaer & Saratoga; and the Sangamon & Morgan.

More than an interest in railroads, however, bound the members of this group together. Both Neal and Griswold, for example, were linked with the Michigan Central ownership and were closely related to the Boston mercantile community — Neal through his geographical background and commercial career and Griswold through the activities of the New York firm of N. L. & G. Griswold in the China trade. As in other western roads, the interests of trade were strongly represented in the Illinois Central. At least seven of the original group (Sturges, Griswold, Wiley, Sanford, Alsop, Neal, and Aspinwall) were actively involved in commercial enterprise. A close-knit mesh of trading relationships, the type first noted as operative in the China trade, was strongly in evidence in this instance. Of the four New York mercantile houses with which Russell & Co. of Canton was closely involved,[11] three, N. L. & G. Griswold, Howland & Aspinwall, and Grinnell, Minturn & Company supplied personnel to the Illinois Central.

Since the railroad promotion was a cooperative venture, it is not possible to determine the precise importance of Bostonians as a separate element. In letters of 1850, however, Billings clearly considered that their approval was necessary for the whole project, and the evidence suggests that Neal and Haven were both of considerable importance in the road's affairs. Of the Illinois Central promoters closely connected with Boston business circles, at least seven were directors of the railroad in its first two decades: George Griswold (1851–1855), Haven (1851–1862), Neal (1851–1856), Rantoul (1851–

1852),* John F. A. Sanford (1854–1856), James F. Joy (1855–1867), and H. H. Hunnewell (1862–1871). The Illinois Central was certainly not a Boston road in the sense that the Michigan Central was, but there can be no question that it offered an important opportunity for Boston enterprise. And, although relationships between the Illinois Company and the Michigan Central were far from smooth,** they involved some common interests. James F. Joy of the latter road, for example, became a director of the former and acted as its solicitor from 1852 to 1857.

Financial Promotion

The incorporators' plan for financing the Illinois Central was simple and, to insiders, most attractive. They anticipated using the land grant as security for a bond issue, the proceeds of which would pay for construction. In turn, the bonds would be paid off with the proceeds of the sale of lands made more valuable by the finished road. They also anticipated that the original stockholders would hold all the equity, that the management would call only a fraction of the share capital, and this procedure would leave the stockholders in undisputed possession of a railroad and some surplus lands worth

* Contrary to nineteenth-century beliefs, Robert Rantoul, Jr., apparently did not play any significant entrepreneurial role in the flotation. As a well-known lawyer and Democratic politician he was called upon to help with lobbying and to impress (on behalf of Whig businessmen) a predominantly Democratic Illinois legislature. He fulfilled these functions admirably, but far from subscribing to the company, he received a $3,000 fee for his services together with rights to subscribe. In attempting to take them up he fell into severe financial difficulties, a condition which his widow and children inherited upon his death in 1852 and from which the Illinois Central management attempted honorably to rescue them. (See Illinois Land Agency MSS., Vol. 20, typescript on Rantoul, letter by David A. Neal, August 14, 1852 and Vol. 19, letters by George Griswold of October and November, 1852.)

** John Murray Forbes and his brother bought 1,000 shares of Illinois Central stock, but were at no point closely concerned with its management and in the mid-1850's had a deep suspicion of its real value other than as a speculation. The Michigan Central's principal interest in the Illinois road lay in the opportunity it provided for the former to run its trains into Chicago when it was racing with the Michigan Southern. The difficulties led James F. Joy of the Michigan Central to write to J. W. Brooks in January 1852: "I have many misgivings about the Illinois Central Company and am afraid that our connection with them [the Illinois Central] will prove unfortunate to us . . . I am somewhat fearful that the Illinois Central Railroad Company will be an entire failure . . . I hope and pray that all things may result well though [the Illinois Central] has always been like a clog upon our heels." (For the episode of trackage rights, and specifically for this letter, see *Statements and Replies in Reference to the . . . Use of the Road of the Illinois Central . . . by the Michigan Central* [Boston, 1860], 195–196.)

many millions. In their private capacity, too, they probably looked forward to the rich rewards of land speculation near a railroad whose route, within wide limits, they were at liberty to choose.*

The basic plan of promotion was outlined in a letter of June 1851 from one of the incorporators, Joseph W. Alsop, to his old friend and business associate Augustine Heard, the Boston sea captain and outstanding China trader, who was then in retirement. Alsop urged Heard to buy Illinois Central as an insider: "The fact is that it is expected to pay for the whole Road by the sale of lands — the money required to be raised by the Bonds which are secured by the lands — It would be rather a singular thing if it should turn out that this Company should own a Road about 670 miles long and cost the stockholders (the present ones) nothing or not over $4 or 500,000 [i.e. 20 or 25% calls on a planned $2 million of stock] and would be worth 12 or 13 millions — wouldn't it? Come . . . see for yourself — all depends upon the selling of the Bonds. Please keep this to yourself."

Heard did purchase some stock and in April 1852 was urged by Alsop to buy more. Alsop anticipated no more than a 20 per cent call. "But this," he added presciently, "you must take the risk of — Many a fine scheme on paper has proved disastrous in reality." [12] In fact the project, which was "a fine scheme on paper," would turn out to be, if not disastrous, then at least far more risky than had been envisaged.

To promote the road, its backers in 1851 issued two pamphlets publicizing the fertility of Illinois and the potentialities of the Illinois Central. These tracts were written by Robert Rantoul, Jr. and David A. Neal of the Boston circle. It is quite possible that they were chosen as spokesmen in large part because of the weight their opinions might carry in the Boston capital market. Rantoul's paper was an essay in economic development and propaganda; it concluded an ingeniously assembled argument on Illinois' growth potential with the not-unexpected estimate of "an average value of from ten to twelve dollars an acre, to be reached in twelve or fourteen years." [13] Neal concentrated far more on the prospects of the railroad, al-

* In addition, the promoters provided services at a profit. Morris Ketchum, for example, was a partner in the locomotive manufacturing firm of Rogers, Ketchum & Grosvener, which supplied the first locomotives to the railroad. (Ackerman, *Historical Sketch*, 73.)

though his account was no less glowing and his conclusions no less sanguine.[14] Indeed, he argued that the railroad alone would provide ample security for the bond issue, even without the lands whose value had to be judged in terms of the future Illinois of 1860 or 1870. "It is a region dotted with flourishing farms and covered with an enterprising and industrious population, that we offer for sale," wrote the Salem man, who had visited the Midwest only twice.

All this was not merely an exercise in hollow public relations. The promoters' private as well as public attitudes were extremely optimistic. We have already mentioned Alsop's outlook, and it was not atypical. The thirteen original subscribers appear to have taken up 770 shares each in March 1851. The next month Neal, who had sold 100 shares each to John Murray Forbes, J. E. Thayer & Brother, and his close business associate, H. H. Hunnewell, advanced the Company $7,500, which entitled him not only to 6 per cent interest but to a further 750 shares. By the end of 1852 he had also added 24 bonds.[15]

As did their counterparts in the Michigan Central, the Illinois Central promoters wanted to play with "sure" cards, but their methods of financing could hardly be termed conservative by any criterion — and certainly not by New England standards. Although there are no grounds for suspicion of the promoters' intention to build and run the railroad as successfully as possible, nor of the sincerity of their optimism concerning its prospects, their expressed views and actions indicate that the speculative element was uppermost in their minds in the course of 1851–1852. In a *Report to the Directors,* dated September 12, 1851, President Schuyler estimated that the company would only need some $17,000,000 to cover construction costs and that this could be raised entirely by bond issues backed by the mortgage of 2,000,000 acres of the land grant.

As the campaign to raise capital got under way, however, the promoters encountered a series of unanticipated obstacles. They found that they could not market the bonds as easily as they had expected, that a select group could not retain all of the stock, that financial difficulties engendered more than minimal calls on stock, and that the initial estimate of construction costs had been too low.

The first large-scale attempt to sell bonds was directed at Europe, presumably because the promoters felt that only European capital markets were equipped to absorb such large amounts. To negotiate the loan, Neal, now vice president, went to Holland, and Robert J. Walker, a former secretary of the Treasury, went to England. Neither met with any success.

The investing public, domestic as well as foreign, was obviously reluctant to lend money to promoters who appeared unwilling either to commit their own resources extensively or to share their profits with others who would. This fact was perceived by the *American Railroad Journal.* In December 1851 the *Journal* pointed to the fact that the promoters "wish the *public* to furnish the means necessary to build the road, while *they* pocket the profits." It doubted if English investors would be enthusiastic about this prospect, particularly since construction had not yet been started — "if those immediately interested are willing to risk nothing, but little can be expected from those that are not." [16] Later, on the news of the European mission's failure, the *Journal* gave a reverse twist to its earlier argument. It now pointed out that the more the potential investors were convinced of the profitability of the project, the more resentful they would be of any attempt to monopolize the proceeds: "The great mistake that the company committed was in making out too strong a case. There is a way of overdoing things, which often creates greater distrust than a lock of proof. So with the Central Railroad. If all were true that was claimed for it, there was certainly no necessity to go abroad for money . . ." [17]

In England both the Rothschilds and the Barings had refused to cooperate. The latter, although they did not reject the idea outright, lacked confidence in Illinois and in Schuyler. The London merchant-bankers felt that the incorporators should both put up more of their own money and spread the stock over a greater number of capitalists.[18] These views were undoubtedly influenced by pessimistic reports from their American railroad advisor, William H. Swift, who was close to John Murray Forbes and helped both the Michigan Central and later the Chicago, Burlington & Quincy by passing on warm recommendations to the London banking house.

Learning from their initial failure in the London capital market, the Illinois Central promoters readjusted their tactics to fit the real situation. Negotiations were turned over to a resident team, including George W. Billings.[19]

In America, there was more progress. As described in the preceding chapter, the Michigan Central promised to advance up to

$2,000,000 against construction bonds in return for trackage rights into Chicago; the Illinois road covenanted to raise an equal amount of money in stocks, bonds, "or in some other permanent form." Under these agreements, which were not made public, the Michigan Central actually advanced $1,214,000, but a public announcement in February 1852 stated that $4,000,000 of bonds had been sold to "capitalists of New York and Boston at par." [20]

This statement the *American Railroad Journal* immediately attacked. It thought that "not one bond has been sold to a person not immediately interested in the road," for the bonds were not as good as many then selling at 85. "What is more," said the writer, "we do not believe they could be *sold* in this market at all, at the present time." [21] And to a large extent, he was right. In fact, the first breach in the original plan shortly had to be made. In the spring of 1852, $2,000,000 of bonds were allotted to the stockholders, each bond carrying rights to ten shares.[22] The promoters, even though they thereby obtained more equity, had been forced to undertake a reasonably heavy investment. They had started to put their reluctant shoulders to the wheel.

This new financial strategy proved sound; other negotiations on the same basis also proved successful. In March 1852 Neal had returned to England and within two months reached an agreement with an English syndicate which undertook to raise a loan of $5,000,000 in 6 per cent bonds, each one to carry the right to subscribe to five shares of stock.[23] A similar device was later employed at home in the summer of 1853.

The Illinois Central's financial policy had by then been adjusted to the adverse initial reaction of the investing public. The consequent augmentation and wider distribution of equity capital was undertaken primarily in order to stimulate bond sales. At the same time the promoters themselves began to put more money into the venture. By the end of 1853, for example, and no doubt tempted by the stock rights, Neal owned 219 bonds as well as 8,550 shares with rights to a further 240.[24] Nevertheless, the reorientation of financial policy had not gone very far. As late as November 1853 the management still felt that total construction costs would be $17,000,000, or even "very considerably less." [25] And the promoters still anticipated that calls on the new stock would be nominal. Both these expectations, and the presumption that additional bonds could be satisfactorily marketed, were disappointed by the events of the years after 1853 — years which witnessed a further dramatic shift in entrepreneurial attitudes and policies.

Financial Management and Crisis

Despite the changes made in the financial plan, the company encountered difficulties in raising capital as a result of the cyclical downturn of 1854, and to this setback was added the sharp inflation of construction costs relative to the original estimates. By the end of 1854, when only some 480 miles of track had been laid, total costs (including coupon payments and stock dividends) had exceeded $18,000,000: two years later, when mileage stood at 704 and the road was essentially completed, $26,000,000 had been spent.[26]

It is difficult to judge how far the first construction estimates were based on a misjudgment of the engineering situation* and how far they misjudged the future trend of prices and wages. Certainly the second error proved to be significant. It was subsequently estimated, for example, that the inflation which followed the California settlement increased costs by some 30 per cent. Price series also indicate a severe inflation. Between 1851 and 1857 the data available in *Historical Statistics* show the following price increases: all commodities: (national index) +34%; metals and metal products: +23%; food: +46%; Cincinnati (all commodities): +42%.[27] As a result of the financial pressures induced by the rise in wages and prices and the decline in the market value of Illinois Central bonds, contractors were no longer satisfied with the original contracted rates or with the payment to them of bonds at par.[28] Therefore, changes in entrepreneurial attitudes and policies in the Illinois Central can best be appraised in the context of unexpected difficulties in the general capital market, specific factors that reduced the credit of the company and the price at which its bonds could be sold, and a construction cost some 50 per cent greater than originally anticipated.

* The company subsequently placed great emphasis upon the erroneous prediction of construction costs: "The Railway of this Company was almost the first which was carried over a level prairie . . . [extra work, the provisioning of laborers, cholera, and inflation all raised the cost]. It is, therefore, no cause of surprise that such mistakes as the Directors have committed should have been made during the progress of this work, and that every calculation of theirs, founded on former experience, should be overtaken and exceeded by this steady increase of cost." (Lane, *Report,* 7–8.)

Initial financial problems were also aggravated by the discovery in the summer of 1854 that Schuyler, who had resigned the presidency in 1853 but was still a director, had issued large amounts of fraudulent stock as president of the New York and New Haven. Even though it was firmly denied that his bad character touched the Illinois Central in any way, the credit of the road sagged.* This, together with the general weakening of the capital market, meant that the company's bonds, which seem to have been at par in May 1853, declined to 62 per cent of their face value by August 1854. At that price they were bought up by European investors, who held $12,000,0000 of them by September 1856.[29]

The check imposed by the tightening capital market was underscored in mid-1854 by *Hunt's Merchants' Magazine.* It observed: "A few of the most desperate class of borrowers for railroad companies are pressing their bonds upon the public; but most of the projected roads, not approaching completion, will be obliged to postpone their operations to a period when the money market will be more compliant." [30]

With the 1854 crisis, important changes in top-level personnel were a prelude to even more marked policy changes for the Illinois Central. In August 1854, W. H. Osborn was elected to the board, and four months later John N. A. Griswold joined him.** Osborn, who had had a successful youthful career in the Pacific trade, became Jonathan Sturges' son-in-law in 1853. The following year he was sent west to speed up construction work. John N. A. Griswold was George Griswold's son and was, of course, an active participant in the China trade as an agent of his father's firm, N. L. & G. Griswold, and as a partner in Russell & Co. (1848–1854). In January 1855 Griswold became president of the Illinois Central. In December of the same year Osborn succeeded him in that post, and remained there for ten years. As will be seen, both men were highly

* See *American Railroad Journal,* XXVII (August 5, 1854), 482–483, which by this time viewed the road as a mere speculation, and claimed that Schuyler had been driven to issue the fraudulent stock by his original overoptimism concerning the Illinois Central, combined with the depreciation of its securities.

** On December 5, 1854, John Murray Forbes, after reporting the decline of Illinois Central stock, had written to his cousin that "Mr. Griswold is talking of taking hold of Illinois Central as managing director!" (John M. Forbes to Paul S. Forbes, December 5, 1854, typescript, Forbes MSS., Baker Library.) It can be assumed that he was referring to the younger Griswold (John N. A.).

critical of Neal's land policies, and early in 1855 Neal resigned his vice presidency and position as land manager.

In general, Osborn and Griswold were strong additions to the Illinois Central management. Indeed, their advent must be interpreted as evidence of the realization that the financial and entrepreneurial problems of the railroad were both different and more severe than originally envisaged. And this fact was reflected in important changes in financial policy.

By March 1854 arrangements had been made for the marketing of the authorized issue of $17,000,000 of bonds. Various negotiations and allotments also accounted for the entire potential equity of 170,000 shares (nominal value of $17,000,000) — although only about 120,000 had been issued, and a mere $809,050 had actually been called. Thenceforth, as already intimated, the financial scene darkened as securities fell and capital costs mounted. In August and December, $5.00 calls on stock had been made. But this was still meager, and the equity situation remained anomalous. To an acute and responsible observer like John Murray Forbes, who held strong ideas on the great importance of equity investment by railroad entrepreneurs, it seemed scandalous that the company continued to borrow money rather than make serious calls on shares. At the end of 1854, for example, in a burst of emotion normally uncharacteristic of a stockholder, he threatened to sell out, even at a loss, "if they don't assess soon." [31]

In 1855 the new managers turned to fresh expedients. Land previously held back for long-run gains was mortgaged to support a further issue of $3,000,000 of bonds. It is symptomatic of the low ebb of confidence that rights to subscribe to seven shares for every $1,000 bond purchased had to be extended, and that the bonds themselves could only be sold at a 30 per cent discount.[32] In the fall of 1855 another call on capital was made in an attempt to bring all assessments up to $20.00 per share.[33]

When the *Report* to stockholders was made in March 1856, the situation was still precarious, with a net floating liability of some $1,340,000. To help meet this debt, the company issued certificates of indebtedness, secured by prospective receipts from the future taking up of optional rights to shares.[34] Nevertheless, by January 1, 1857, net floating liabilities had increased to over $2,100,000. To reduce this threatening burden the company was relying on the optional rights; if they were taken up, then cash would flow in to meet the debt. But, obviously, possessors of the rights would be reluctant to exercise them if the stock fell below par.

The Illinois Central was basing its financial position on the possibility of the continuance of a good market for its shares. And early in 1857 the company gave even more hostages to fortune by a plan to meet construction costs and debt repayments by an increase in its equity capital from a nominal $17,000,000 to $25,500,000. The new shares were to be distributed to stockholders, who would be expected to pay assessments of $30.00 on the first third of the issue by July 1, 1857.[35]

Initially, the plan went well. Illinois Central shares were at a premium in the first half of 1857 (their average price in June was about $135); the first third of the new issue was taken up, and the assessments paid, by July.[36] But market conditions did not remain favorable for long. By mid-summer 1857, the financial panic and crisis which gripped the country was taking its toll of the Illinois Central. The company's securities held up well in the flurries of June, were steady at lower rates in July and early August, and thenceforth collapsed in the general panic. As the money market tightened to the point of absolute rigidity,[37] Illinois Central stock tumbled: it reached 72½ in mid-October. Bonds fell to 51 by the same date.

As options were not taken up, and a further call of $10.00 on outstanding shares secured only partial payment, it was clear that the market had made a shambles of the company's financial plans. In the words of the *Report* for 1857: "The financial crisis . . . deranged the business of the whole country, rendering it impossible for the Directors to carry the Floating Debt until the Options should mature; and . . . reducing the market value of the Stock below par, so that the entering of the Optional Rights could no longer be relied upon to replenish the exhausted treasury of the Company." [38] Nevertheless, the situation could not be entirely blamed upon market forces; a weak initial policy had made the company especially vulnerable to downturns in the economy.

Faced with a large floating debt of $3,700,000 as of August 1, 1857, but unable to secure liquid funds, the company, although far from bankrupt, was forced to make a formal assignment of its property.

On October 9 it suspended payment in order to keep its property out of the hands of insistent creditors (who might attach it and sell it at ruinous prices) until a sound plan could be formulated.[39]

The new situation demanded some hard rethinking of financial structure. Already, in the course of 1857, calls of up to $30.00 had been made on outstanding shares; even so, the leading stockholders had really persisted in financing the road not by equity sales but by the issue of bonds and short-term obligations. Now, faced with the panic and its implications for the road's finances, an ingenious plan was put forward.[40] While offering incentives to take up a new convertible bond issue of $3,200,000, it proposed to make up any financial shortfall by extensive calls on stock. This latest device carried forward the revolution in financial policy which had grown out of disappointed expectations that bondholders would pay for a railroad whose profits would inure to a small group of insiders.

The new policy inaugurated at the end of 1857 was successful in meeting the post-panic crisis. By the end of 1858 all but a well-covered $400,000 of the floating debt had been retired and all construction costs and interest charges had been paid.[41] In essence, the company had to rely on its share capital to get out of trouble. Thus, in June 1858 a $20.00 call was made, and by the end of 1860 holders of 79,333 shares out of the 178,854 issued had paid $100 on each, the remainder $80.00. The stockholders had provided over $15,900,000 towards the railroad, a very far cry from the earlier estimates.[42]

While the cumulative expansion of the equity base exceeded anything dreamed of in the innocent days of 1851, a greater and greater burden was placed squarely on the shoulders of the legal owners, the stockholders. Two thirds of these, it was estimated in 1858, were English.[43] Clearly, the vicissitudes of creating a railroad and the enforced shifts of financial policy had divorced the Illinois Central from its original close connection with New York and Boston ownership. Significantly, however, control and management *did* remain in New York and, to a lesser extent, Boston hands throughout this period.

What had commenced as a purely speculative venture with few apparent risks had turned into something quite different. The key men concerned, under the pressure of finding new solutions for new problems, had increasingly to recognize the conflict between the opportunism of short-run asset ownership and the more onerous tasks of developmental management over the long run. Matching the concentration of ownership in Europe was a decline in the influence of the Boston element: Haven's directorship terminated in 1862, Joy's in 1867, and Hunnewell's (which had commenced in 1862) in 1871. Accordingly, the Illinois Central's early history is of primary interest for this study; central to it was the land grant.

The Disposition of the Land Grant

The Illinois Central differed from the Michigan Central in its financial policies and tribulations partly because it was a land company as well as a transportation agency. In addition, its north-south geographical orientation, transverse to the main currents of east-west trade routes, denied it the possibilities of open-ended growth such as the Michigan road enjoyed. This combination naturally turned entrepreneurial attention inwards, where it was soon apparent that to profit directly from the Illinois Central road it was necessary to examine the possibility of expansion.

Some of the original promoters followed this logic and turned the railroad into a developmental agency. Others, notably David A. Neal, withdrew from the railroad in order to concentrate on other speculations. In this and the following sections we shall consider these two courses of action in the context of the sale of lands.

The entrepreneurial policy of the promoters of the Illinois Central was related at almost every point to the question of the land grant and its disposal. The financing of the road's construction, the profitability of its traffic operations, and total income to the owners were all to some degree linked with the land policy. Even to outsiders the appeal of the venture seemed to lie in the federal subsidy. "It is not as a railroad investment that I regard so favorably this undertaking," wrote the English free-trader Richard Cobden in 1857, "but its value in my eyes depends on the landed estate." [44]

The promoters, however, were bound to be ambivalent in this regard. If maximum income from land were considered, then it might be better to retain as much land as possible until the railroad had engendered a surge of agricultural activity which would push real estate prices up. If, on the other hand, it was desired to develop freight traffic and maximize current income to reduce the burden of debt, then there would be a good reason to sell land as rapidly as possible in competition with the federal government and other landholders. After some hesitation, the latter policy was the one actually adopted.

Early planning envisaged a division of the land grant into different economic categories. In the fall of 1851, 2,000,000 acres were set aside as security for the construction bonds.[45] In addition, 250,000 acres were reserved as security for the Interest Fund, and the remainder, almost 350,000 acres, was denominated "Free Lands." The Free Lands were originally intended as an unencumbered asset to be retained by the stockholders, but they had to be mortgaged in 1855 to raise more money.

The disposition of these lands was initially placed in the hands of David A. Neal. As one of the original incorporators, he had been associated with the Illinois road from its commencement. Before going to England in the fall of 1851 he had assumed the vice presidency of the company.[46] After bringing the English loan negotiation to a successful conclusion in the spring of 1852, Neal devoted the bulk of his time for the next three years to the management of the Illinois Central's lands.

In many ways the choice of Neal for the all-important task of overseeing the disposal of the land grant was a curious move on the part of the directors. Whatever his experience in handling land sales, it was indeed remote from the western situation. He had visited the Midwest in 1847 and 1850,[47] but two visits do not make an expert. His appointment to a key position in the Illinois Central must have reflected confidence in his general business talent and his experience with Michigan and Ohio railroads, rather than any idea of his acquaintance with the problems of western land. Presumably, also, Neal's vice presidency was an indication of the important part which men from the Boston circle had won for themselves in the Illinois Central promotion.

Naturally, land sales could not proceed immediately with the formation of the railroad company. For one thing, time was needed to locate the road (and therefore the general site of the land) and to make final selection of the land to be used. For another, the charter provided that land sales could not be made to a greater amount than the actual expenditure on the road. In addition, there was a desire to retain certain parts of the land grant until real estate prices had risen as a result of the railroad's construction.

In March 1854 Neal submitted his first annual report to the directors.[48] He described the process of locating and selecting the lands, indicating that after various difficulties the corrected lists had just been received from the General Land Office in Washington and were in every respect to be used as the origin of title. About 2,594,000 acres had been certified, of which 44,000 acres had already been sold at $2.50 an acre to pre-emption claimants. Neal proposed to follow the plan of September 1851 and select 50,000 acres from the lands of highest valuation to be sold at not less than $20.00 per acre, 350,000 to be sold at a minimum of $15.00 an acre, 1,300,000 at a minimum of $8.00, and the balance (300,000 acres) at a minimum of $5.00. Prices of these 2,000,000 acres, mortgaged by the construction bonds, were to be set partly by "the value for agricultural purposes," and partly by their distance from a railroad station.

It was this pricing policy which demonstrated Neal's somewhat ingenuous attitude toward western lands and ultimately provoked much dissatisfaction among his fellow executives. He largely ignored factors of timber, water, and speculative competition. One critic accused Neal of being "a domineering old sea captain and extremely bigoted," claiming that the whole scheduled plan would soon be overhauled.[49]

Neal's report dealt not only with pricing of land but also the terms of sale. The original charter had stipulated that land was to be sold for cash or bonds at par. Now, it was widely appreciated that such conditions would markedly retard sales and the immigration of desirable settlers, especially since other western lands were selling at lower prices. Therefore an amendment to the charter was obtained in February 1854, and Neal suggested that lands be sold on long credits and at low rates of interest. The very liberal credit terms were not to apply to timber lands, which could, of course, be too quickly plundered.

In his 1854 report Neal stated that the company's land was at last ready to be put on the market.* By December agents had been ap-

* In the sale of land the Illinois Central was by no means a monopolist. It had to look to potential competition, although by the mid-1850's this came from private rather than public lands. Between 1830 and 1850 some 14,500,000 acres in Illinois had been sold by the federal government. As of January 1852 just over 9,500,000 acres remained unsold. Deducting the grant to the railroad, just over 7,000,000 acres was available for possible sales by United States land offices. But by 1854 only a negligible amount of government land was on the market in Illinois, and the bulk of unsettled

pointed at nine towns, with two more planned for, and offices had been opened in Chicago and New York.[50] Neal was able to report that up to the end of the year just over 47,000 acres of "Free" and "Mortgaged" land had been sold with a yield of $481,000.[51]

Neal's suggestions showed some awareness of the prerequisites for economic growth. At some length he recommended that the company encourage the building of plank roads, finance a geological survey to publicize the state's mineral wealth, stimulate the erection of steam and water mills, advertise the agricultural potentialities of Illinois, and establish agencies in the East and in Europe to expedite and organize immigration to the company's lands.

While New England investors in western lands had followed a relatively passive policy in the pre-railroad era, the coming of steam transportation demanded active steps not only to raise money but to generate traffic. Virtually from the outset Neal and his associates realized that to benefit from the possession of more than 2,500,000 acres demanded far more than merely waiting for eager settlers to come along and snap up lands which were automatically appreciating in value. Potential settlers had to be coaxed, encouraged, and helped. Positive policies were needed to guide and facilitate the course of immigration and agricultural development. What some people might have considered at the start as a purely speculative venture in the ownership of sound assets was rapidly turning into a complex enterprise — a land and mortgage company, an immigration and development agency.

As the responsible official, Neal was forced to discuss the alternatives of immediate sales to encourage rapid settlement and the postponement of sales to await the higher prices which long-term expansion would bring. His conclusion was that quick sales, by speeding settlement and, therefore, the business of the road, had advantages which outweighed the potentially higher prices that would result from holding on. In any case, he pointed out, prices actually paid had been at least 20 per cent higher than those stipulated in the mortgage as necessary to secure the bonds. His recommendations on reasonably speedy sale were followed, and almost half the land grant was sold by 1857.

---

land, not surprisingly, was in the hands of speculators, who were to hold 15,000,000 acres in 1856. (*Hunt's Merchants' Magazine,* XXVII [December, 1852], 660; Gates, *Illinois Central,* 105–116.)

Neal's policies, which had been generally criticized from the beginning, came under particularly heavy fire from W. H. Osborn and John N. A. Griswold. During their presidential terms they focused on three main points: Neal's policy of pricing land largely by distance from a depot was considered ludicrously unrealistic; his credit terms, although proceeding in the right direction, were held to go too far; and the agency system was judged expensive, irresponsible, confusing, and wasteful, since it hinged on fast sales of the best land.

The new top management also felt that Neal's energetic speculative activity in a private capacity produced an unhealthy conflict of interest. And, in fact, this last was true, for it appears that Neal had used his knowledge of (and authority over) the choice of depot locations in 1852 not only to purchase land near where or on which stations were to be built, but also to do so with funds of the company, which were disbursed by the chief engineer under the impression that the land was being bought on behalf of the company itself.[52]

The result of this criticism was a virtual managerial revolution.[53] In January 1855 the local agencies and the New York office were abolished, and sales were concentrated at Chicago. Neal resigned, under pressure, as vice president and land manager, and the next year he refused re-election as a director. In 1855 the land department was reorganized under the surveillance of Osborn, Griswold, and Charles M. Dupuy, who was made head of the Chicago office. John Wilson, formerly commissioner of the federal General Land Office in Chicago, was brought in as the company's land commissioner. Neal's pricing policies were dispensed with and meticulous surveys were undertaken by land examiners to reprice the company's land on more realistic principles.[54] In addition, an extra 1 per cent interest for each of the first two years was charged on new credit sales.

The underlying aims of land policy had not, however, been changed drastically: the company continued to concentrate on the tasks of encouraging settlement. But the means to this end had been overhauled and, it was felt, made more efficient.

With these reorganizations achieved, the Illinois Central undertook a sustained promotional campaign to dispose of the lands and help settle the state and expand its production. The story of this colonization effort has been expertly delineated and needs no repetition here.[55] By 1860 far more than a million acres had been sold, with the period of heaviest sales in 1855–1857.

As happened with financial policy, the difficulties of the land department consequent upon the Panic of 1857 proved hardly more long-lasting than the recession itself. The railroad's policy was proved fundamentally quite sound and, particularly with the Civil War and the prosperity of the 1860's, the situation of the company was considerably improved. Even in 1860 Neal was able to write that the lands of the Illinois Central had justified the promoters' original enthusiasm: "These have brought more money, and have sold more rapidly than any one ventured to predict." [56] By 1870 the railroad had disposed of all except 500,000 acres (mostly poor) of its land grant. By that time, of course, the company was on its way to a new policy of expansion which would eventually take it south to New Orleans and the sea.

Private Land Speculation

The financial benefits which promoters hoped to derive from the organization of the Illinois Central Railroad Company were not confined to the direct profit from investment in the enterprise. Like the promoters of the Boston and Lowell or the Boston and Worcester before them, they recognized that the road, when constructed, would raise the value of lands through which it ran. Therefore, early investment in such real estate promised a handsome return after a few years. The situation in the West was only a little different. A favored position within the circle of original promoters could secure prior knowledge as to the route which the railroad would adopt and therefore as to the lands which were likely to be most valuable; and this was particularly true with reference to town lots where the company decided to establish a station. Most of the leading Illinois Central directors were involved in such speculation, quite apart from George W. Billings, whose lobbying services were recompensed by advance knowledge of the route which enabled him to set up an extensive system of well-organized speculation.

It is clear from his accounts that David Neal was strongly committed to land speculation in Illinois. His principal associates were H. H. Hunnewell, who was concerned as an investor with Neal, first in the Reading and then in the Illinois Central, and three of the outstanding promoters of the Illinois Central: Jonathan Sturges, George Griswold, and Morris Ketchum. In addition, R. B. Mason, superintendent of the line, participated in the speculation, while John C. Dodge, who became head of the land department under Neal, handled much of the relevant land purchase. As already noted, some of these speculations were actually effected with company funds, although it subsequently appeared that this illicit procedure had been undertaken by Neal and Morris Ketchum without the knowledge of their co-purchasers of land, Griswold and Sturges.[57]

The largest part of the land speculation was managed by Neal in the name of the Associates Land Company, or Associates. This was a reorganization of a plan originating with Billings for an Illinois Land Association to buy up 250,000 acres within six miles of the route of the Illinois Central. The original project, which envisaged raising $600,000 capital, mainly in Europe, fell through and was considerably reduced in scope in the reorganization. For the group, Dodge purchased 19,235 acres at government land offices for $52,965. The efficacy of working through a third party was demonstrated by the fact that the purchase price averaged some $2.75 — only $0.25 above the official minimum.[58] In 1853 Neal held a quarter share in this venture, together with Ketchum, Griswold, and Sturges (the same three men, it should be noted, who had originally hired Billings to secure the Illinois charter). By December 31, 1853 Neal conservatively valued the 19,235 acres at $3.00 per acre, i.e. $57,705. Two years later he placed a cash value on them of $12.50 per acre, or $240,437.50 for the entire holding.[59] This gave him a share worth an estimated $60,109 for an investment of $13,241!

Besides the Associates' venture, Neal was also concerned with five other property investments in the state, all contiguous to the line of the Illinois Central. In 1852, on joint account with Hunnewell, he purchased 960 acres for $2,524, using Dodge as his agent. On December 31, 1855, he valued this land at $10.00 per acre with an intimation that it was probably worth $15.00.[60] By the end of 1853 he also shared, with Griswold, Sturges, Ketchum, and Mason, ownership in two other separate ventures: 960 acres in the Bourbonnais property on the Kankakee River, and a block of land at Amboy. In addition, he owned shares, purchased in 1852 or 1853, in the Kankakee Bridge Company; by the end of 1855 he held 24 out of the total 120 issued, with a par value of $30.00 each. Finally, together with Ketchum, Sturges, Griswold, John F. A. Sanford, George W. Jones (the Iowa senator who had proposed the extension of the federal land grant to Dunleith), and Charles Gregoire, he purchased land and a ferry at Dunleith,* where the Illinois Central terminated on the Mississippi, opposite Dubuque, Iowa.[61] The syndicates involved with the lands at Amboy and Bourbonnais became known as the Proprietors of Amboy and the Proprietors of Bourbonnais, respectively.

The Associates Land Company, as it became in 1860, was as profitable as it was long-lived. The lands owned by the Associates, who included some of the leading directors of the railroad, were extensively used as sites for Illinois Central stations.[62] As such, they enjoyed a marked appreciation in value. After considerable sales had been effected, the original Associates were credited with over $40,000 in notes due and $200,000 paid by the new company for their property in 1860.[63] In May 1883 the company issued its twenty-fourth annual report, showing sales over the previous year of 120 acres (for $1,580) and 107 town lots (for $5,876). The report indicated that of the original (*corporate*) purchase of 13,614.66 acres and 1,738 town lots, a total of 13,030.10 acres and 1,715 lots had been sold. These sales yielded almost $360,000 on an original cost in the vicinity of $190,000.[64]

After his resignation from the vice presidency of the Illinois Central in 1855, accompanied by the liquidation of most of his holdings in the road, David Neal appears to have devoted the bulk of his time to the management of these various land speculations. In 1858, although the old sea captain did not withdraw entirely, his son, Theodore A. Neal, directed the nominal administration of the lands of the Associates and of the Proprietors of Bourbonnais and of Amboy,[65] as well as concerning himself with the Dunleith and Kankakee affairs. When Neal died in 1861, his son took over complete management.

The incorporation of the Associates Land Company in 1860 had apparently been largely a move to simplify the granting of deeds

* Ketchum, Sturges, Griswold, and Sanford obtained a five sixths interest in the Jordan Ferry and the town of Dunleith from Charles Gregoire and were subsequently joined by George W. Jones and David Neal. (Memorandum of Agreement, July 9, 1856. Illinois Land Agency MSS., vol. 20.) It later appears (T. A. Neal to Edward Bement, October 10, 1860. *Ibid.*, vol. 4) that Neal held one fifth of the original investors' interest.

and to provide for continuity in the event of Neal's death.[66] But it is significant that with the incorporation, the equity base was extended: 8,000 shares were created and in May 1861 the stockholders numbered sixteen, including Sturges, John N. A. Griswold, Ketchum, the two Neals, and two members of the Haven family.[67]

The opportunism of the Illinois Central's promoters was not entirely confined to land speculation. Dunleith, for example, was at the terminus of the Illinois Central facing the unbridged Mississippi River. This meant that there were profitable investments to be made in service and transportation facilities. Such investments were clearly consequential in character. The Dunleith investment ultimately involved the original lands, improvements, a hotel, and the ferry. The proprietors sold the ferry and held the notes for its sale (including two boats): $20,833.33. In 1861 the "Illinois Central" interest moved to organize its share of the property into a joint-stock company.[68] When the Dunleith Land Company was organized soon afterwards, Theodore Neal was president and the shares were divided among nineteen people, most of them also involved in the Associates Land Company.*

Neal and his partners appreciated that some conscious and positive policy was a continuous prerequisite of profit-making in their land speculations, but it would be ludicrous to deny that the bulk of their gains stemmed from their favored position as possessors of inside knowledge, capital, and a modicum of foresight. Their ventures were, in fact, successful speculations. Although the Neal group sometimes took active steps to promote economic and social development, the opportunities which they grasped lay primarily in buying well placed land and holding for the rise. These private land operations, unlike the railroads, were more the beneficiaries than the stimulants of economic growth.

Opportunistic Entrepreneurship and the Changing West

In 1856, when David A. Neal left the Illinois Central board and concentrated on private land speculation and the management of his

* Among the holders of the 2,000 shares were such familiar names as Jonathan Sturges (240), Edward Bement, Ketchum's partner and first treasurer of the Illinois Central, (320), George Griswold (274), Theodore A. Neal (240), Morris Ketchum (80), J. W. Haven, Guardian (34), Cornelia W. Haven (34), and John N. A. Griswold (34). (Stockbook, Illinois Land Agency MSS., vol. 13.)

varied securities, it was not only his age of sixty-two that explained the move. His unsatisfactory relationships with others on the railroad's board and his resignation seem quite consistent with much of his previous career as a railroad investor and entrepreneur. Earlier, in the case of the Philadelphia and Reading, his policy seems to have been based largely on the possibility of quick profit from certain types of opportunity. With some exceptions, these opportunities existed where exploitation of the *existing situation* promised high rewards, where profits might accumulate by the judicious disposition and management of capital rather than the more continuous administration of institutions or larger-scale tasks of policy formulation. In the circumstances, then, it was quite logical that in the mid-1850's, when it had become painfully apparent that the Illinois Central presented a much more difficult, and more sustained, task than had been originally imagined, Neal should withdraw from the affairs of the railroad and concentrate on his investments and the land which he and his associates owned.

When it became clear that the Illinois Central was in for the long pull, other significant changes in top management took place. Two new men, William H. Osborn and John N. A. Griswold, assumed, or began to share, the real executive power. Each in his own way was suited to the demands of long-run policy formulation.

Osborn could be suspected by no one of being a speculator. It is probably not entirely coincidental that his career echoes others with which we have been concerned. His initial business ventures were in the far eastern trade, where he made a considerable fortune and from which he retired at an early age to become president of the Illinois Central at thirty-five. As with Forbes and other railroad leaders, family ties were quite important in Osborn's case, for he came into the Illinois Central under the patronage of his father-in-law, Jonathan Sturges.

The other new manager, John N. A. Griswold, whose place was also partially a product of his parentage, was linked with John Murray Forbes by friendship, by investments in the Michigan Central and the St. Mary's Canal project, and by a successful career in the China trade. Griswold, in addition, had an ability, which he shared with Forbes, to distinguish between outright speculation and the running of a railroad, and to devote his undoubted business talents to the latter task when necessary.

Thus, the mid-1850's were to some extent a parting of the ways for the promoters and managers of the Illinois Central. In place of Neal and Morris Ketchum, new executives with different aptitudes came in to face new tasks. Others of the original group (Haven, Alsop, and Sturges, for example) stayed on the board and adapted their entrepreneurial outlook and expectations to fit the new circumstances — conditions which demanded the commitment of further investment funds to the project and the assumption of the long-run responsibility of developmental management. However, even with the new alignments, the groups were not mutually exclusive. Men like John Griswold, Haven, and Sturges could still speculate in land in cooperation with Neal — even when, as happened with Griswold and Neal, there had been a strong disagreement over the management of the Illinois Central.

Neal, who had played important roles in railroad development from the Atlantic to the Mississippi, sank into relative, if profitable, obscurity in the late 1850's, quietly and assiduously managing land ventures. On June 8, 1861, his sixty-eighth and last birthday, he added a postscript to his manuscript autobiography. With a calmness worthy of his training, although not entirely justified by his handling of land purchases when vice president of the Illinois Central, he wrote: "I am all ready. It is only taking a longer nap than usual . . . I am not conscious of ever having wronged a single individual, or of having now an enemy in the world . . . In regard to my business, it is reduced to the simplest form. I owe nothing, nobody owes me." [69]

Looking back, Neal viewed his participation in the Illinois Central venture with mixed feelings. "The road has been built," he wrote reflectively, "but it has cost a much larger sum than was estimated. The original projectors have all lost money instead of making it." [70] Neal's own reaction had been to manipulate and shift investments, to respond to entrepreneurial adversity by reducing his commitment to the Illinois Central. The contrast between this behaviour and that of his contemporaries in comparable situations is instructive. In the case of both the Michigan Central and the Illinois Central some investor-entrepreneurs, having had their original "opportunistic" expectations disappointed, reacted not by getting out or by pulling in their horns, but by staying with their area of initial commitment and, frequently, bolstering it with even more capital.

The prejudice against using railroads primarily as devices for land speculation was a conservative Boston tradition. "Let others speculate on the rise of land," the venerable William Sturgis had written to the president of the Attica and Buffalo in 1849, "it is not judicious for Rail Road Companies to do so." [71] The backers of the Michigan Central seem largely to have had the same policy, perhaps from lack of opportunity. In later years the land agent of the Burlington and Missouri River Railroad in Iowa, which had much the same owners, was to preclude corporate speculation: "We are a *railroad* company and not a *land* company," he wrote, "settlers are more important to us than a high price for our land." While the same investors speculated privately in land, they did not confuse such speculation — whether on a small scale or, like the Sault Ste. Marie Canal, on a giant one — with their principal railroad ventures. Such men, and with them may be included the banker Franklin Haven and Neal's friend Hunnewell, were opportunistic when possible and developmental when necessary. For them, the Illinois Central and its backers showed the way both in corporate land sales and development and in private land speculation. It was a pioneering pattern that others soon followed.

Chapter 8

Prewar Strategic Investment: The Genesis and Expansion of the C. B. & Q.

A SIGNIFICANT share of the pre-Civil War railroad development culminating in the 1850's took place in the area where Bostonians had been led by their railroad investment in the last half of the preceding decade. Between 1850 and 1860 the net addition of new line to the nation's railroad network totaled nearly 22,000 miles, compared with only a quarter of that amount during the previous decade. Much of the new mileage was in the area between the Ohio and Missouri Rivers,[1] where John M. Forbes and his associates centered their interests. Their efforts and capital contributed to this impressive increase in steam transportation and the economic expansion that it both reflected and stimulated.

Central to their expanding investment horizons was the concept of a railroad system. From it emerged a new combination of roads stretching west from Chicago.

THE BACKGROUND OF INVESTMENT

The decade of the 1850's was not one of uninterrupted western economic growth. A land boom that lasted from 1853 to 1855 encouraged railroad construction to serve new areas of crop production, but the bountiful flood of food supplies proved more than the market could absorb, and the prosperity of railroads built to carry them was temporarily undercut by the impact of plummeting prices. These developments contributed to the Panic of 1857, which tested the resources and resourcefulness of investors in western railroads and temporarily curtailed the flow of foreign capital which had supported the preceding boom.

In the slightly longer run, wheat production, which was ideally suited to the virgin territory being brought under the plow in these years, met a strong European demand in the 1850's, followed by wartime domestic demand in the 1860's. The dramatic shift in the location of wheat-growing was a manifestation of the changes wrought by the transportation facilities created in these years. Prior to 1860, three of the ten leading wheat states were east of the Alleghenies and only one, Iowa, was west of the Mississippi. By 1870, four of the leading ten were west of the great river and only one was east of the Alleghenies.[2]

While other factors besides actual and potential wheat production lay behind the strategic decisions of Boston investors in western railroads, extension of the farming frontier was a primary consideration in their developing vision of economic growth during the 1850's. As John Murray Forbes wrote to Russell Sturgis in London in September 1851 concerning railroad building prospects in Illinois, "Imagine a deep black soil, almost every acre of which can be entered at once with the plough, and an enormous crop secured the first season, but where the very fertility and depth of the soil make transportation on common roads almost impracticable at the season when produce ought to be sent to market, and this region now for the first time opened to a market by railroad." [3]

Lured by such pleasing prospects but also pushed by competitors who wanted to share in the rewards, the Forbes group was seeking opportunities west of Chicago even before the Michigan Central had entered that city. Their quest carried them to the Mississippi in a logical extension of their earlier investment and into Iowa and Missouri on a tentative basis. Federal land grants began to figure in the group's investment decisions for the first time, and its members began to combine private land speculation with corporate developmental policies. The foundations of a major western railroad system were being laid.

Genesis of the Chicago, Burlington & Quincy

Relatively early in his relations with the Michigan Central, Forbes had visualized that road as part of an east-west transportation system. If such it was to become, steps had to be taken to connect the Michigan Central at Chicago with lines reaching the Mississippi River. While the ultimate result may have been preordained by geography, and the course of development foreseen by the leading investors in the Michigan road, the process of extension itself had opportunistic and fortuitous characteristics.

The hinge on which extension west of Chicago turned was the so-called Aurora Branch Railroad. This short line occupied a strategic position between the Galena & Chicago Union Railroad, which entered Chicago, and the Illinois Central and other roads in western Illinois tapping the Mississippi River traffic. Representatives of the Forbes group — John W. Brooks and Corning's partner, Gilbert C. Davidson — were elected to the board of the Aurora in February 1852,[4] and thenceforth its new importance was slowly revealed.

The Boston interests moved cautiously and quietly for fear of a misstep that would alert rivals to their strategy. Brooks, for example, wrote to Corning in April 1852 to this effect.[5] Since the interests of local Illinois roads coincided with the Bostonians' over-all strategy, it was deemed tactically wise to allow the initiative in forming new alliances to come from local interests. This procedure became virtually a standardized one in the Forbes group's moves west of Chicago to the Missouri.

In the spring of 1852 representatives of the Aurora Branch, the Peoria and Oquawka, and the Central Military Tract Railroads of Illinois "happened" to meet at the American House in Boston, where they were all seeking funds. According to his own account, Chauncey S. Colton of the Aurora proposed concerted action: "by uniting all our influences we could together build a railroad from *Burlington to Chicago,* via Galesburg: Further, . . . we should endeavor to engage the Michigan Central R.R. Co., which was composed of wealthy people, in our united project . . ."[6]

When these men approached Forbes,* he reportedly followed the same procedure as when John Brooks first called the Michigan Central to his attention; he referred his visitors to John C. Green and George Griswold in New York. They in turn suggested approaching Brooks, who was understandably agreeable to the proposal for forming a through route from Burlington on the Mississippi River to Chicago.

The resulting plan involved amending the charter of the Central Military Tract Railroad to permit its connection with any road from the south. Once again James F. Joy's political skills were em-

* Gates thinks Forbes and Joy were promoting a union of roads as early as June 1851. In 1886 Joy claimed credit for it. See Richard C. Overton, *Burlington West: Colonization History of the Burlington Railroad* (Cambridge, Massachusetts, 1941), 36–37.

ployed to good advantage. The charter changes, plus those changing the name of the Aurora Branch Railroad to the Chicago and Aurora Railroad Company, were approved in June 1852 by the Illinois legislature.[7]

Forbes again assumed his familiar role of capital-mobilizer. In doing so he was careful to point out to potential investors that his opinion of the Chicago and Aurora was based on that of Brooks, Corning, and of "other men who ought to know and who will have a large interest in looking after it." Many of the same sources that had provided funds for the Michigan Central aided the new project. Forbes reported that $90,000 of stock had been reserved for New York and Boston, and said further, "I suppose N. Bedford can have five or ten thousand dollars if you speak quick." His report of subscriptions credited Brooks with $25,000, Corning $30,000, and Joy and Porter $10,000 or $12,000.[8] Brooks obtained subscriptions for 2,003 shares ($100 par) in Detroit and the East, and the final list, approved July 16, 1852, showed 52 persons had taken 4,313 shares ($431,300).[9]

If the Chicago and Aurora was intended to be part of a major new system west of Chicago, that fact was not emphasized by the Bostonians in the summer of 1852. In recommending the Aurora to his New Bedford friends, for example, Forbes talked about it in terms of a feeder line. The form of the stock subscription approved at the July 16 board meeting indicated that the immediate aim of the company was only to reach the Illinois Central at Mendota. Furthermore, the amendment to the charter of the Central Military Tract Railroad, which was to connect Mendota and Galesburg, was purposely ambiguous. It permitted a connection with the Chicago & Rock Island or *"any other railroad or railroads"* extending to or connecting with Chicago.[10] Brooks summarized the situation when he wrote in March 1853: "I have been the cause of commencing several railroads in Illinois, intended for feeders to the Michigan Central, and I must see them through." [11] However, the feeders were integrally related to one another in terms of a system of roads stretching to the Mississippi. In the construction of this system, the Forbes group took one step at a time, trying to make each step self-supporting and as profitable as possible.

The first step was to extend the Aurora to Mendota. At a meeting on July 6, 1852, this 58-mile extension was authorized. A committee was appointed to obtain the necessary iron and Erastus Corning, an iron merchant himself, was a member. As a result, the Forbes-backed Mount Savage Iron Company, in which Corning was also interested, received orders for 2,000 tons of rails.[12] Bond and stock

THE ILLINOIS CENTRAL AND COMPONENTS OF THE EVOLVING C. B. & Q. SYSTEM IN ILLINOIS, 1857. DOTTED LINE INDICATES RUNNING RIGHTS OVER THE GALENA AND CHICAGO UNION.

issues were voted to pay for the extension, and stock sold so successfully that in September 1852 the authorized total was raised from $640,000 to $680,000.[13]

The strategy of extension was now clearly revealed. In October 1852 the Chicago and Aurora authorized James F. Joy to request the legislature's permission for the company to subscribe up to 10 per cent of its own capital stock to that of the Northern Cross (Quincy & Chicago Railroad). This road was to connect the Galesburg terminus of the Central Military Tract road, of which Brooks was now president, with the Mississippi River at Quincy, Illinois. By the time the Chicago and Aurora's route to Mendota was completed in November 1853, the requisite legislative action had been obtained and Bostonians were well entrenched in both the Northern Cross and the Central Military Tract.

Promotional strategy for these roads involved initial financial demands on the communities to be served. James F. Joy, for example, agreed to raise money for the Military Tract road only if local sources pledged $300,000. Once this requirement was met, the remainder was obtained with the help of Forbes, Corning, and Erastus Fairbanks of St. Johnsbury, Vermont. Authorized stock of the company was increased to $600,000, and Forbes and William Amory agreed to float an $800,000 bond issue.[14] Meanwhile, Forbes was using his personal credit with Baring Brothers for the purchase of iron when Central Military Tract and Chicago and Aurora bonds proved unacceptable for that purpose.[15]

The Peoria and Oquawka Railroad completed the strategic design, of which Galesburg was the pivot. It was to run from Burlington on the Mississippi River, north of Quincy, to Galesburg, which the Central Military Tract road reached in December 1854, and thence east to Peoria on the Illinois River. When the Peoria and Oquawka ran out of funds, the Military Tract road purchased it, and completed the tracks to Galesburg in March 1855. The Peoria segment was finished two years later. In January 1856 the Northern Cross linked Quincy and Galesburg. A system of roads under common ownership then stretched from Chicago to two separate termini on the Mississippi River.

Corporate recognition of the growing system of Forbes roads west of Chicago came in 1855–1856. As a result, the Chicago and Aurora Railroad was renamed the Chicago, Burlington & Quincy Railroad. This road became the cornerstone of an expanding network over which the Forbes group exercised control, and it gradually took over the individual roads just discussed. By 1857 Colton and two others were the only westerners on the C. B. & Q. board, while John Murray Forbes, his brother Robert Bennet Forbes, the New Bedford banker Edward L. Baker, Nathaniel Thayer, Stephen

H. Perkins, John W. Brooks, and Erastus Corning represented the eastern interest.* [16]

Forbes was now deeply committed to the concept of an east-west system, and he backed it with his capital and credit even at the cost of short-run losses. In promoting the connections with Burlington and Quincy, he reportedly had to sell $100,000 worth of stock in manufacturing enterprises at a 30 per cent discount to raise money for his director's share in one of the loans.[17]

His confidence was rewarded. A profitable system of roads was created between Chicago and the Mississippi. The Central Military Tract, for example, paid 15 per cent in cash and stock on six months operations in 1856, just before it was merged into the C. B. & Q. The latter company itself fared so well that Forbes feared that a distribution of accumulated earnings would precipitate a demand by shippers for lower rates.[18]

Initial Investment Across the Mississippi

Having identified the future of railroading with the westward movement of population and agriculture, the Forbes group did not confine itself to strictly sequential construction and investment of the type just described. They concurrently demonstrated an interest in proposed or partially completed roads across the Mississippi River, extending from termini which were the immediate objectives of the developing C. B. & Q. system. One such road was the Hannibal and St. Joseph Railroad in Missouri; the other was the Burlington and Missouri River Railroad in Iowa.

As in the case of the Michigan Central and the Illinois components of the C. B. & Q., both these roads had been initiated and organized by local promoters before Bostonians took an interest in them. They were but two of many such undertakings projected to create a hinterland for trade with Mississippi River towns. For the Forbes group, however, involvement in the affairs of trans-Mississippi roads was initially a form of strategically opportunistic investment which could, if circumstances warranted, be fitted into an

* At a meeting in 1858 Sidney Bartlett, a Boston lawyer, was added to the board. At this time it was agreed that no construction work exceeding in amount 1 per cent of the capital stock would be undertaken in any one year without the specific approval of stockholders. (*American Railroad Journal,* XXXI [July 10, 1858], 437.)

over-all developmental framework of which the C. B. & Q. was emerging as the keystone. The timing and location of their moves suggests an early recognition of the possibilities. Meantime, the burgeoning system east of the great river was self-sustaining.

The Hannibal and St. Joseph Railroad

The Hannibal and St. Joseph Railroad Company was chartered in 1847 to provide a route through northern Missouri between the Mississippi and Missouri Rivers, an overland connection between watercourses that followed a well developed pattern in railroad building. The prospects of this road had languished from its incorporation until 1852, when Congress authorized a land grant of over 600,000 acres for the Hannibal,[19] and about this time Forbes and his associates became interested in it.

The Boston capitalist regarded land-grant stimulants to railroad construction with suspicion. For example, in a letter to Charles Sumner, in February 1853, Forbes condemned the federal land-grant policy. His main argument was that the lure of federal aid would spur construction of roads that were not justified by other considerations. He feared that the inevitable collapse of such roads would discredit railroad-building and retard the development of roads which were needed. However, he admitted a subjective element in that his views might "be influenced by my connection with western roads that have been built by dint of hard work in hard times, when it was a word of reproach to be concerned in western enterprises . . ."[20] As he became involved in the trans-Mississippi area, Forbes changed his attitude toward the federal land-grant policy.

The Hannibal and St. Joseph at this time badly needed funds. It had not taken possession of its lands, nor were local subscriptions being paid to the extent necessary to qualify for a loan of $1,500,000 in state bonds, which the Missouri legislature had made contingent on *bona fide* subscriptions of the railroad's securities to the amount of $500,000. As a result, the directors turned in late 1853 and early 1854 to Boston and New York. There they were able to dispose of $1,000,000 of capital stock — enough to pay off existing liabilities and continue work.[21]

The resulting Boston influence was clearly demonstrated in the

Hannibal's roster of directors for 1854. The list read: Robert B. Forbes, John E. Thayer, H. H. Hunnewell, Thomas B. Curtis,* and John M. Forbes. The last was also named as fiscal agent. In addition to the Boston directors, there were three Missourians.[22]

The new board moved as vigorously as the times permitted. By the end of 1854 the lands allotted to the Hannibal and St. Joseph under the Act of June 10, 1852, had been formally certified to the road by the Secretary of the Interior. E. B. Talcott, who had gained valuable experience in land sales while connected with the Illinois and Michigan Canal had been appointed land agent; and, under Forbes's direction, "a plan for mortgaging the lands and the road itself, on such terms as would be likely to command the confidence of capitalists," had been completed.

Forbes was pleased that the road had husbanded its resources in the midst of a slow market for railroad securities. As he put it in his first report as fiscal agent, October 28, 1854: "Until the necessary money is secured, we cannot doubt that the same prudent policy ought to be pursued which has thus far kept you in an independent position." [23]

Since Forbes envisioned the Hannibal as part of a through route, he felt that vigorous action to push construction would only be justified if the line could be completed from the Mississippi River to the Missouri. In October 1854 he expressed a willingness to wait until "substantial people" could take hold of the road. On the other hand, he thought its prospects were so good that, if enough money to complete it could be obtained it would justify paying "the most liberal price for money." [24]

Despite the contemporary slump, which was affecting the Illinois Central so adversely, Forbes was optimistic about the future.** In a letter to his cousin Paul, he conveyed this optimism more lyrically and specifically than elsewhere in his writings or correspondence: "The Rail Way in our Western prairies is the most economical labor saving machine over invented, for it doubles and often trebles the

* Curtis made his money in trade with Russia. He had served in the navy and was aboard the *Chesapeake* during her famous encounter with the *Shannon*. (*Rich Men of Massachusetts* . . . [2d ed., Boston, 1852], 23.)

** Forbes pointed out that the railroad panic prevailing in 1854 made it easier to buy depot lands in St. Joseph and Hannibal and also lowered the cost of labor, a major construction cost.

value to the farmers, of the coarser grains, by bringing them within reach of water carriage & by bringing customers to their doors . . . The richness & depth of the soil . . . furnishes business for the R. Road, and renders it impossible to transport the rich products of the soil to the market by any *other* mode." [25]

Such views are important because they suggest what a major railroad investor thought he was doing in committing capital in the West. Even if, as has recently been contended, railroads were not essential keys to western economic development, their backers often thought that they were, and supported this belief with capital. Moreover, even where railroad investment might not have been viewed as an indispensable factor in regional growth, it was appreciated that it was frequently superior to any conceivable alternative.[26]

In view of the 1854 recession, Forbes saw little likelihood of raising capital to complete the Hannibal unless foreigners could be interested. Ideally, he would have liked to make one negotiation in Europe for bonds and iron to the amount of at least $2,000,000. Under such circumstances, he was confident that another $1,000,000 could be raised in Boston by the sale of bonds. Short of that, he was prepared to consider a smaller negotiation if it would permit building and equipping at least twenty-five miles of track at each end of the line.[27]

Construction on the Hannibal was at a standstill from January 1854 until May 1855,[28] while Forbes and the company's officers sought ways of raising funds. In the relatively unpopulated territory west of the Mississippi, Forbes found that the reliance on developing traffic rapidly, a concept that had underlain private railroad investment east of the river, had to be modified. Therefore he put increasing emphasis on the importance of the Hannibal's land, on foreign capital, and on state aid.

Finally, sufficient private subscriptions were obtained for the railroad to qualify for the loan of $1,500,000 in state credit, which involved a first lien on the entire road.* In February 1855 Forbes

* The faith and credit of the state were pledged to payment of principal and interest of the bonds. Receipts above running expenses and repairs had to be pledged to the payment of interest. If a company defaulted on either interest or principal payments, the governor — with six months' notice — could sell the road to the highest bidder or purchase it for the state. Surplus proceeds from lands or other securities of

predicted that if the state would exchange this mortgage claim for $1,500,000 in stock, leaving the road and land free to secure a new bond issue to complete construction, the land would rise in value to $10.00 an acre before the bonds came due. Then, he said, private capitalists who had loaned $4,000,000 would have first lien on a road worth $6,000,000 and land worth $6,000,000 more![29]

President R. M. Stewart pointed out in his report for 1855 that foreign capitalists could not be expected to step in unless further inducements were "held out by the legislature to insure the construction of the road." [30] In making his point he cited Massachusetts as an example. Noting that the Bay State had provided two dollars of credit for every dollar of private investment in her early railroads, he suggested that Missouri do likewise.[31]

Just as Stewart looked to Massachusetts for an example of public aid, he looked to Boston for private financial advice and support. John M. Forbes reported to his cousin Paul in December 1855 that the Hannibal "*leans* on me for direction & counsel." Although he now hoped for the loan of an additional $1,500,000 in state bonds, many problems would still remain, and the Hannibal, he said, "needs more of my personal attention than I like to give to any thing now." [32]

Forbes's emerging plan for aiding the Hannibal was a highly leveraged one, dangerously akin to the scheme that had intrigued Illinois Central promoters under similar circumstances. His hope was that bonds secured by the railroad's lands and issued at 75 or less, sold abroad and payable 4 per cent per month until the road was completed, would, with state aid, finance construction to the western terminus. On this basis the land could be made to pay for the construction, and stockholders with a $600,000 equity investment would "own the Road clear." The Bostonian suggested that Paul S. Forbes's 500 shares, or 2.5 per cent of the total, would be worth $150,000, although they had cost only $13,000! "The only contingency in my opinion," he wrote, "is on getting the Loan carried thro so that we can build the Road *at once* — and also on *decent management.*" [33]

Forbes pointed out that if a new state loan failed to materialize,

---

the Hannibal, once it was in operation, were to be placed with the state treasurer to help redeem the state bonds granted the road. (*American Railroad Journal,* XXXI [May 1, 1858], 273–274.)

it would be necessary to assess the stock. Although he had condemned the Illinois Central for failing to take this action in a similar situation, he was reluctant to see the Hannibal do so. He preferred, of course, that a sufficient amount be paid in on land bonds to leave the stock unassessed. Thus shareholders, with little or no cash outlay, would reap the rewards of a road completed with borrowed money, a large part of it obtained through use of the state's credit. Even before Paul Forbes received his letter on this strategy, the first condition of the plan had been met: the state legislature voted to loan the Hannibal an additional $1,500,000 in state bonds.[34]

With this encouragement, the railroad prepared its own $5,000,000 bond issue. Forbes now believed that the 7 per cent bonds, secured by land, could be issued at 80 plus a 10 per cent commission.* When the land was sold, the proceeds would be applied to retiring the railroad's bonds acquired from those who desired to sell at par. "With these lands behind as security," Forbes declared, "& the kind of R. Road *whereon* the money will have been expended — the security will be very good if our plans are carried out." The fact that the legality of the new Missouri loan was being contested in court did not bother him. If the Hannibal did not receive the state's aid then no other roads could, and the Hannibal, being in a better financial position than its rivals, would probably get their business.[35]

About $4,000,000 of the Hannibal's new bonds were sold without difficulty at home and abroad. Baring Brothers, although cool to American railroad investments, had enough confidence in Forbes to take $250,000 worth of the issue.[36] The initial enthusiasm was such that by the end of 1856 almost half the subscriptions had reportedly been paid, much of it even before the company had called for the money.[37] Control of the road was now firmly in the hands of Bostonians.

Meanwhile construction was pushed from both ends of the proposed route. By November 1856 the road was completed twenty-five miles west of Hannibal and tracks were being laid eastward from St. Joseph. Early in 1857 the *American Railroad Journal* predicted: "This road will be first to tap the waters of the Missouri, and will

* The issue, dated April 1, 1856, was for $5,000,000 in denominations of $1,500 each. (*The Hannibal and St. Joseph Railroad Co.* v. *Sidney Bartlett and others.* U.S. Circuit Court, District of Massachusetts [1876], 27).

open to market a section of country 200 miles in length, with a healthy and inviting climate, well timbered and watered, and with soil unsurpassed by any portion of the Union." [38] The Grand River *Chronicle* reported that "They [the company] know full well that their road is bound to be the great iron thoroughfare of the West, and being directly interested, as owners of a large quantity of the richest land in the State, this fact alone induces us to believe that they will build us a first-class road." [39]

As a speculative venture, however, the Hannibal was the victim of its inheritance. The construction agreement, made before the Forbes group became active, gave the contractor, John Duff, very favorable terms, including the right to operate the road for his own benefit. Duff was apparently anxious to build a "cheap contractor's road to sell," while Forbes, as in his other roads, wanted to build for permanency, although hoping to do so at minimum cost and risk for himself and his associates. As a result, Forbes struggled for some months to curb the contractor's powers before he finally succeeded.[40]

The Panic of 1857 affected all the Forbes roads adversely, including the Hannibal, but John M. Forbes was prepared to back his existing investment with all the resources at his command. As he wrote Paul Forbes, "by acting boldly & thus carrying capitalists with us we shall really act prudently." [41] This philosophy was reflected in his approach to the Hannibal's continuing financial problems. By June 1858 the bonds issued in 1856 had fallen as low as 60. Forbes, however, was certain that if he and his friends did act boldly and a new loan was made, the old bonds would rise to 70 or better. Once the road was done, he believed that the Hannibal would take a large share of business from the steamboats on the Missouri River, and he was also sure that in a few years Missouri would throw off the last vestiges of slavery with a resulting increase in population that would greatly aid local traffic. For these reasons, and anticipating a rise in stock values for a completed road, he was willing to go heavily into a new Hannibal bond issue, dated July 1, 1858.[42]

In appealing for support to William H. Swift, the Barings' American railroad adviser, Forbes stressed the Hannibal's assets in land as well as its strategic location. Reporting on the anticipated position of the road on July 1, 1859, and placing particular emphasis on the value of the lands, Forbes estimated a net cost of only $4,210,000.* [43]

To emphasize the favorable transportation outlook Forbes argued that the Hannibal could compete for the passenger and freight business between the Missouri River and St. Louis on favorable terms. "I am satisfied," he said on the basis of first-hand observation of the route, "that no road in the country occupies *as good* a place for through business." [44] However, he foresaw a possible need to issue more convertible bonds and to sell optional stock, which the board could authorize to the extent of $1,900,000.

When the bids for the 1858 bond issue were made, Forbes initially took $100,000 worth. He was not anxious to become more involved, explaining, "I wish to keep very snug & not go even into good things beyond my ready money." [45] The sale did not go as smoothly as he had first hoped, but by early August Forbes was more optimistic. "The right sort of people are looking into it & it will go at some rate or other," he reported.[46]

The question of what the proper rate should be was an important one. Large lenders wanted the bonds at a sizable discount, but if they insisted on too great a one the chances of a rapid rise in the bonds' market value would be diminished. "If Barings & the right set take them," Forbes declared, "I would not like to buy them below 70 — but this is a matter for consultation among the bidders & I don't care *much* what rate they put it at so we get the money to open the Road promptly! as we must & shall!!" [47]

The resources of the Forbes group were put to the test in this instance, but the outcome was satisfactory. Forbes finally took for himself and Paul S. Forbes $150,000 of the 1858 bond issue, a New Bedford man (probably Edward L. Baker) was put down for $160,-000, the Barings had accepted $200,000, John C. Green would reportedly take $70,000 to $80,000,[48] and others, including the Forbes-managed American Stock Investment, were similarly interested. Al-

* Forbes's calculations were based on the following figures:

Full paid stock	$1,900,000
State bonds (six per cent)	3,000,000
Land bonds (seven per cent)	5,000,000
Convertible bonds to be issued in settlement with contractors (seven per cent)	310,000
Total	$10,210,000
Estimated value of land	6,000,000
"Cost"	$4,210,000

though he had to borrow to take his share, John M. Forbes had not been forced to go in as deeply as he had feared. If he had had to do so, he wrote Paul Forbes, he would have "made the recusant stockholders *suffer* dreadfully in the rate — in fact transferring a good deal of the *ownership* from the Stockholders to the new Bondholders, but some large outsiders came in & the rate fixed was a fair one . . ." [49]

Forbes had been determined to push the Hannibal through to its terminus on the Missouri River at the first opportunity, and all his financial operations in connection with the road were directed to that end. The goal was achieved on February 13, 1859, early enough to get a favorable start over steamboat traffic.[50]

Although initially there was heavy competition from the steamboats, supported by commission and insurance agents who were interested in them, the railroad gradually proved its superiority. In the meantime, before the steamboat association broke up in August, tariffs had been cut to the bone and the Hannibal was forced to subsidize its own line of boats. Furthermore, much of the construction work done by Duff was poor, and in the haste to complete the road the Hannibal company's own contractors did not do a thorough job. In repairing these deficiencies a heavy load was placed on a management already fully occupied in the struggle to divert trade from the old to a new route. Despite the unfavorable situation, the Hannibal's general agent and superintendent concluded his 1859 report optimistically: "With a little careful attention to secure the proper connections, our road should become the great thoroughfare for Eastern and Western travel, and will soon take rank among the most valuable roads in the country." [51]

West to the Missouri: the Burlington and Missouri River Railroad of Iowa

The kinds of pressures and expectations that had led the Forbes group into railroads connecting Chicago with the Mississippi, and then into the Hannibal and St. Joseph, at the same time also drew them into Iowa. Just as the C. B. & Q. promoters looked to the territory west of the Mississippi to feed their growing system, so the promoters of the Chicago & Rock Island Railroad had found promise there. Henry Farnam, who was doing a yeoman job of construction on the Rock Island, saw a possible feeder in the Mississippi and Missouri Railroad, chartered by a Davenport, Iowa, group in February 1853.[52] The chance that the Rock Island in alliance with the Michigan Southern might tap trans-Mississippi traffic via this local road was not lost on the key figures of the Michigan Central and C. B. & Q.

A potential counter to this competitive threat existed in the Burlington and Missouri River Railroad, a locally promoted Iowa road occupying a strategic location with respect to the emerging C. B. & Q. system. In early 1853 the B. and M. R. was anxious to begin construction but lacked the means.[53] As the promoters of the road scrambled for local support, while pressing their claims in Washington for a land grant, Robert B. Forbes arrived in the state. He was so impressed with Iowa land that he purchased some, and in June 1853 recommended to John M. Forbes, his brother, that the B. and M. R. was worthy of assistance.[54]

The subsequent course of events was similar to the one that carried the Forbes group from Chicago to the Mississippi River. In July 1853, John W. Brooks and James F. Joy came to an agreement with the local B. and M. R. managers; both were elected to the board of directors, and Brooks became president. These arrangements were completed just as the rival Rock Island-Michigan Southern group prepared to bridge the great river.*

The appearance of Brooks and Joy was a preparatory move, and Boston investors only gradually involved themselves in the fortunes of the Burlington and Missouri River road. In June 1854 George Sumner of Boston was employed as subscription agent, and the following month John M. Forbes and others offered to advance $25,000 on the security of Des Moines County bonds and to raise an equal amount by similar means. In 1855 a contract was let to complete the road between Burlington and the Skunk River in Henry County within two years.[55] In May 1856 Congress granted public lands to the state of Iowa to aid four Iowa roads, including the B. and M. R.,** [56]

* The Rock Island Railroad bridge, the only one completed across the river during the decade, was finished in April 1856. (Robert E. Riegel, "Trans-Mississippi Railroads During the Fifties," *Mississippi Valley Historical Review,* X [September 1923], 154 n. 2.)

** The B. and M. R. was allotted 3,840 acres of land for every mile of road built. However, most of the land along its route was already taken up and the directors petitioned Congress for land elsewhere in the state. (B. and M. R., *Annual Report,* 1858, 7). The final grant to the road amounted to 389,989 acres. (Henry G. Pearson, *An American Railroad Builder, John Murray Forbes* [Boston, 1911], 85, n. 1.)

and the stage was finally set for more rapid progress in reaching the Missouri.

Although the B. and M. R. managers sought loans in New York,* they also turned to Boston. Since 1855 the C. B. & Q. had had a terminus on the Mississippi River at Burlington, opposite the point where the B. and M. R.'s route started. James F. Joy, C. B. & Q. president, therefore could be confident of a sympathetic audience when he hurried to Boston early in 1857 to seek more active help from Forbes and Brooks.[57]

Fully convinced of the soundness of an east-west strategy of railroad extension, Forbes was prepared to take action. Writing to Erastus Corning in May 1857, he declared: ". . . the Iowa Road with its rich and populous country, and its 300,000 acres of *Free Soil* seems to me so very important an extension of our lines that I cannot help taking rather more than my share there . . ." [58] To fail to extend aid, he felt, would be like having allowed the Michigan Southern to monopolize the route around the foot of Lake Michigan or having permitted the Aurora and Military Tract roads to become feeders of the Rock Island. Although some of the large C. B. & Q. stockholders seemed reluctant to enter this new field, and John E. Thayer, now approaching the end of his life, was setting them an example in this respect, Forbes felt the B. and M. R. "too good to let go without a try!" [59]

Forbes offered land speculation on favorable terms as an inducement to his followers to participate in the "try." The Missouri Land Company was organized in September of 1857 by the Hannibal's eastern directors to deal in the road's lands. Commenting on the comparable prospects of the B. and M. R. in this respect, Forbes noted, ". . . we intend to have some Land Depot Speculations which will give good results to Stockholders *pro rata*." [60]

Once having decided to commit himself, Forbes acted in typical fashion by insuring control of the road. In May 1857 Edward L. Baker, the trusted New Bedford banker who was connected with most of the Forbes roads, was elected the new president of the B. and M. R. He was authorized to call meetings where and when

* In 1856 the B. and M. R. had mortgaged the first section of its road and its rolling stock to Charles Butler of New York. In January 1857 it added a further mortgage in favor of Francis A. Palmer of that city. (*Trust Mortgage. Burlington and Missouri River Railroad Company to John M. Forbes, Henry P. Kidder, and John N. A. Griswold* [New Bedford, 1858], 3–4.)

he pleased, provided three directors approved. In practice, thereafter, major decisions were made in Boston.[61]

Meanwhile, President Brooks of the Michigan Central and President Joy of the C. B. & Q. jointly issued a circular to their stockholders urging them to subscribe to the B. and M. R.'s stock. They suggested that "If each stockholder in our roads would devote the *probable* earnings on his stock to this subscription, for one year, it would go far toward securing control of the Iowa road, — *a feeder of 280 miles*." In their view the intrinsic merits of the road, quite apart from its land grant, seemed greater than those of their own roads at their inception. "Since then," they pointed out, "experience has proved the superiority of Prairie roads to all others viewed merely as railroads, while the example of the Illinois Central shows what effect a grant of land has upon the value of railroad stock." [62]

At this time only about thirty-six miles of the B. and M. R. had been completed, and to earn the land grant seventy-five miles had to be finished by December 1859. The backers of the road were outwardly confident that the necessary funds could be easily raised through stock subscriptions from counties along the route and from the sale of railroad bonds on favorable terms. As in the case of the Hannibal, they held forth the promise of proceeds from land, after the road was done, as a bonus of $4,000,000 to $5,000,000 and as a cushion to absorb unexpected construction costs.[63]

Forbes succeeded in disposing of $1,500,000 of B. and M. R. stock, on which over $300,000 was paid by June 1858.[64] The source of these funds is suggested by the slate of eastern directors chosen at the annual meeting in that month: the Forbes brothers, Corning,* Nathaniel Thayer, Brooks, Joy, and Baker.[65] In a mortgage, executed October 1, 1858, to secure bonds for the completion of the road to Ottumwa and thus to assure earning the granted lands, the trustees were John M. Forbes, Henry P. Kidder,** and John N. A. Griswold.[66] This group apparently "had personally to absorb many bonds." [67]

Despite his commitment, Forbes for some time was not sure that the road could be pulled through to a "profit-paying point." At the beginning of 1858 he was depressed by the size of the B. and M. R.'s old debts, the costs of building, and the slowness with which money

* Corning & Co. supplied spikes for road construction.

** Kidder (1823–1886) also served as trustee for the Hannibal and the C. B. & Q.

was coming in.[68] During the year, short crops and heavy rains affected traffic and construction adversely. Since the road was not well known in the market, Forbes realized that the 8 per cent mortgage bonds of 1858 would sell only at a large discount. To reduce his own liabilities, he proposed to turn back half of his B. and M. R. stock holdings, which had so far been assessed 40 per cent of par value.* [69]

Although the B. and M. R. finally reached Ottumwa in September 1859 and traffic increased greatly during 1860, the company was still struggling to pay its interest in early 1861. Forbes described the road as like "one of the *promising* young men that holds out hope but does not yet *quite* pay its debts." [70] As a matter of fact, it was not until January 1870 that the road reached its goal at Council Bluffs on the Missouri River.[71]

As in the China trade, Forbes wanted a trusted representative in the management of the roads in which he had a large interest. In the case of the Burlington and Missouri River, Forbes forged a strong link in the persons of Charles Russell Lowell and later Charles Elliott Perkins. Lowell (nephew of James Russell Lowell, the poet and diplomat, and grandson of Patrick Tracy Jackson) had achieved a brilliant record at Harvard and for a brief period thereafter had served in Forbes's Boston office. Later, Forbes offered him the post of assistant treasurer of the B. and M. R. at Burlington. Lowell accepted and assumed the new position in the summer of 1858. When the land department was established in the following year he was placed in charge.[72] However, he left in 1860 for a position at the Mount Savage Iron Company, whence he departed for the war, from which he never returned.

A significant step for the future of the whole C. B. & Q. system was taken by Forbes and Lowell in June 1859 when they invited Charles E. Perkins, an eighteen-year-old cousin of Forbes,** to serve as Lowell's assistant. In a letter of June 28, 1859, Lowell described to the Cincinnati youth both the road and the duties of the assistant: "In winter and spring it [B. and M. R.] means seventy-five miles of mud and water between Burlington and Ottumwa — in summer

* Forbes held 500 shares worth $50,000 at par; he had paid in 40 per cent (i.e., $20,000) and was liable for the additional $30,000. He proposed to apply the $20,000 he had paid to 250 shares ($25,000 par), return the other 250 shares, and thereby reduce his further liability to $5,000. (J. M. Forbes to P. S. Forbes, September 21, 1858. Forbes MSS., typescript. Baker Library.)

** Perkins' grandfather, Samuel G. Perkins, was John M. Forbes's uncle.

and autumn it is seventy-five miles of as pretty rail and ties as you would wish to see." Outlining Perkins' duties as cashier, Lowell concluded: "It would leave you time to study the details of the Freight and Passenger business — and on our short road this would naturally be more open to you than a long road, where there is more subdivision of labour and more red tape." [73]

Forbes also encouraged his young kinsman to accept the post. "The B & M Railroad is under the direction of myself and my friends a good deal," the Bostonian wrote, "and if you can make yourself useful there, you would certainly stand a good chance of having your services recognized by pay and promotion when the proper opening comes." [74] With such encouragement Perkins did not hesitate to make the change from Cincinnati to Burlington. Thereafter he took an increasingly important part in the affairs of roads in which Forbes was interested, and in 1881 he succeeded Forbes as president of the C. B. & Q. and retained the post for twenty years.[75]

Forbes saw the similarity between western railroad management and the China trade, where, for lack of rapid communication, heavy reliance had to be placed in the man on the scene, and personal links with subordinates were valuable. On one occasion he wrote a friend: "I think the mistake we have made on our R. Rd. lines was in not bringing up youngsters we know something about as foremast hands, for the change of picking our good mates and captains just as the old-fashioned shipowners used to do in taking green hands at six dollars a month." [76] In sponsoring Lowell and Perkins, Forbes had followed just such a course, and they were not the only beneficiaries of his search for managerial talent.

The Panic of 1857 and Forbes Roads East of the Mississippi

Both the Michigan Central and the Chicago, Burlington & Quincy were hard hit by the Panic of 1857, and Forbes was forced to take an active role in extricating them from near-collapse. At the same time, of course, he was struggling to keep the Missouri and Iowa roads afloat.

Under John W. Brooks, who had succeeded Forbes as president in 1855, the Michigan Central was put heavily in debt to make various physical improvements and also to gain control of the strategically located Joliet and Northern Indiana.* No sinking fund had been created, and dividends had been continued at the rate of 5 per cent semiannually. As soon as Forbes saw the report of this situation, he suggested that stocks or bonds be issued to fund the floating debt and that dividends be reduced.[77] No action was taken, however, and Forbes failed to press for it.

In August 1857 a money panic struck New York, and within a month the Michigan Central, under pressure from a large floating debt, was in serious danger of joining the hundreds of firms falling under the impact. "We are in such a crisis as only those who went through 1837 can conceive of," Forbes reported on September 28. "New York Central Railroad has run down from 87 to 55, and Michigan Central from 95 to 45, while the weaker concerns are clear out of sight — Erie 10, Southern Michigan 10–15." [78]

It was a time for decisive action, yet the circumstances were far from propitious. John E. Thayer, who would normally have been the pillar of any refinancing effort, was mortally ill. One of the New York directors was on the verge of resigning — an act which would have further shaken public confidence in the Michigan Central. Treasurer Isaac Livermore was, in Forbes's words, "nervous and timid," while Brooks was "overworked, and inexperienced in finances." [79] It seemed that Forbes alone would have to devise and execute a strategy to save the road from disaster, and, although he might have avoided the responsibility without great personal loss,** he felt a moral obligation to "hold on at least through the squall, and when we go leave the ship in a safe place." [80]

Forbes's remedy, as proposed to J. N. A. Griswold, was to save the road by any steps necessary short of liquidation. "I can myself see no way," wrote Forbes, "but to advertise for proposals for a new loan, make it safe with sinking-fund, tempting in its terms, and accept a low price, shut off construction, and in fact take any steps

* The Joliet and Northern Indiana ran westward from the Lake Station of the Michigan Central and provided connections with the Illinois Central, the Chicago, Alton and St. Louis, and the Rock Island. It was jointly leased by the I. C. and M. C. in September 1854. Since the contract required the leasing roads to pay 8 per cent interest on $312,500 of J. and N. I. stock, the M. C. found it preferable to purchase a majority of the stock. (Michigan Central, *Annual Report,* 1855, pp. 9–10; 1856, p. 6.)

** As of September 1, Forbes had $421,000 in "good" bills receivable, $154,000 in ships, merchandise, and bank stock, not to mention valuable residential, mining, and manufacturing property. His current liabilities were only $272,000. He was, he said, in a "pretty well fortified" position. (John M. Forbes to Paul S. Forbes, October 16, 1857. Forbes MSS., typescript.)

(not suicidal) that money-lenders may dictate." [81] To make such a plan work, he realized that he and the Thayers must be prepared to "take a large slice" of the loan. His most daring proposal, however, was to ask Baring Brothers to take hold, a possibility that few who knew the Barings' jaundiced views on American railroads were optimistic enough to visualize.[82]

On October 10 the *American Railroad Journal* contained a frank exposition by President Brooks of the Central's financial position and of the steps needed to improve it. He pointed out that the road up to this time had found no difficulty in selling bonds at par to refund those maturing, and that the floating debt, largely incurred for construction, had been carried without difficulty at an average cost of less than 9 per cent. Now, in a tight money market, the road had to meet $855,050 in bonds maturing before July 1858, as well as a floating debt of $1,789,846. To cover these obligations in the next ten months, the company proposed to raise about $2,000,000 by sale of bonds* and the remainder from cash on hand and earnings of the road. Brooks urged shareholders to subscribe to the bonds at the rate of $1,000 for each 30 shares they held.[83]

Meanwhile, before leaving for England to raise funds, Forbes worked feverishly and effectively. On September 29, 1857, he, Nathaniel Thayer, and H. Hollis Hunnewell became trustees under a trust mortgage deed, covering $3,160,000 convertible 8 per cent bonds from which the required $2,000,000 was to be obtained.[84] Forbes himself subscribed for $250,000 and, believing it to be a favorable time to obtain good investments cheaply, he put Paul S. Forbes down for $50,000 without any specific authority to do so. He took ship early in October, knowing that already $1,100,000 was subscribed, and learned by telegraph at Halifax that William Appleton was working actively to further success of the issue.[85]

The Barings had aided Forbes in the past. They had accepted bonds of his roads as collateral for debts incurred in purchasing rails, had taken part in one Michigan Central bond issue, and had brought for resale in the United States some Michigan Central and Joliet and Northern Indiana securities. In 1856 they had taken $250,000 worth of Hannibal and St. Joseph bonds. But on the basis

* The *American Railroad Journal* endorsed the issue, pointing out that the bonds had a first lien on a road costing $14,000,000 and earning 25 per cent annually on this amount. (*American Railroad Journal,* XXX [October 10, 1857], 649.)

of experience and the advice of William Swift and S. G. Ward, they lately had steered clear of American railroad financing.[86]

In the fall of 1857 the Barings were especially worried about the firm of John E. Thayer & Brother, which J. M. Forbes counted a mainstay in his effort to raise funds for the Michigan Central. John E. Thayer died late in September; his firm was indebted to McCalmont & Company for over £525,000 during the most critical period, and the Barings, in turn, held £150,000 in bills on the McCalmonts. To meet emergencies and protect their investment, they extended a special credit of £100,000 to Thayer & Brother.[87] It was amid such adverse circumstances that Forbes arrived in England.

What success the Bostonian had with the Barings is not clear. When first approached, they declined to take the new Michigan Central bonds because there was no provision for a sinking fund or for payment of interest until after outstanding bonds due in 1860 were covered.[88] However, a China merchant, Edward Cunningham,* then in Europe, helped Forbes make some sort of arrangement with Baring Brothers;[89] on his return voyage, Forbes reported that he had "*succeeded* at my end of the rope." [90] Presumably, then, he disposed of his assignment successfully with or without benefit of the Barings' direct purchase of the Michigan Central bonds.

Meanwhile, bids opened in the United States on November 10, 1857, proved satisfactory. The first bonds went at 70, even though, with the suspension of specie payments, the Michigan Central had been forced to announce on October 10 that it could not pay interest on its floating debt.[91]

Forbes expressed complete optimism and events soon proved him justified. From London on November 8, he wrote: ". . . good railroad securities would be depressed by the discredit of the bad ones & there will be *great bargains*." And again, "The moment the M. Central [bond issue] is *done* it will command a profit & so it will be with the C. B. & Q." Within a month his prophecy had been fulfilled. Forbes had given Paul S. Forbes assurance concerning the bonds taken for him: "I shall make a handsome thing of it — not less than 10% on cost after charging you the heavy interest on such part as I have had to advance. I have sold about half at 80 & upwards." [92] This favorable turn of events was strengthened by a traffic agreement

* Cunningham (1823–1889) was a neighbor of Forbes in Milton, Massachusetts, and a partner in Russell & Co., whose service he had entered as a clerk in 1845.

between the Michigan Central and the Michigan Southern. It divided through passenger traffic equally between them and stipulated that when the Southern did over 42 per cent, the road with the excess should pay 30 per cent of it to the other.[93]

The Michigan Central had been saved by "boldness" which J. M. Forbes described as "*true* prudence";* [94] now Forbes could turn his attention to the C. B. & Q. "The C. B. & Q. are [*sic*] safe I believe for the present," he observed in November 1857, "& I hope can get along until I get the Mich. Central *right* & then I shall have means to help them in common with other large stockholders." [95]

The C. B. & Q. at the end of 1857 was preparing to fund its floating debt, refund outstanding bonds, and to obtain funds for further construction under a single sinking-fund mortgage. For immediate purposes $400,000 was to be raised.[96] In Forbes's view, despite their probable lack of immediate salability for investment or even speculation, the C. B. & Q. 8 per cent bonds at 70 would be better than the Michigan Central's at 80.[97] The *American Railroad Journal* fully agreed. "We think there can be no question as to the value of the security offered," it observed editorially. "The road, in proportion to its cost, has had the largest earnings, we believe, of any in the United States, and we see nothing likely to interfere with it in the future . . . The stockholders should not hesitate in taking the loan and paying off the floating debt." [98]

While in London in the late fall of 1857, Forbes had feared that his group — Paul S. Forbes, King, Griswold, Thayer, and Green — might have to carry the C. B. & Q.'s floating debt, "taking pay at panic rates." [99] However, as it turned out, Forbes' fears were not realized: readiness for bold action was all that was required.

During the 1850's the Forbes group of investors had begun to build a railroad system. They had created an integrated rail network extending from Chicago to Burlington and Quincy on the Mississippi River and organized a company to hold and manage it. Contemporaneously, as individuals, they had begun to take an interest in weak, young roads across the river which formed logical extensions to the evolving C. B. & Q. system. Thus, on the eve of the Civil War, Boston capital was represented in the first railroad to reach the banks

* Forbes later felt he had too much prudence. In February 1858 he declared: "If I had had more courage I might have made quite a pretty thing out of the panic." (John M. Forbes to Paul S. Forbes, February 23, 1858. Forbes MSS., typescript.)

of the Missouri River — the penetrating edge of east-west railroad construction that, together with other forces of transportation, helped establish the basic contours of western economic growth in the first postwar decade.

Central to this process were the financial arrangements directed from Boston, underpinned by growing reliance on public aid and foreign capital. The continuing importance of Forbes' personal influence, as well as his maturing strategic and long-run concepts, were revealed by his response to the financial problems created by the Panic of 1857. By reacting boldly, maintaining his optimism, and demonstrating his confidence by example, he was able to aid the roads in which he was interested and even to turn a personal profit in the process. Perhaps at no other time in the history of these roads was the importance of the individual capitalist-entrepreneur shown to better advantage. Underlying it, in addition to large personal resources and important contacts, was a developmental view toward westward railroad expansion that did not give way in the face of adversity.

Chapter 9

Prewar Railroad Investors: A Brief Appraisal

IN RAILROAD history, as in so many other aspects of national development, the Civil War was a boundary between two different, albeit related, sorts of experience. Therefore, having discussed the step-by-step involvement of various Boston-based capitalists in prewar western investment, it is appropriate to pause here to review their policies and practices in a more analytical way, emphasizing the entrepreneurial processes and the investment patterns which are the primary concern of this study.

THE PROCESS OF INVOLVEMENT

Bostonians' prewar involvement in western railroads was gradual. Major capitalists did not make a sudden, massive switch of investments from their existing commitments to railroads, let alone to railroads west of the Alleghenies. Steam transportation was tested in Massachusetts, chiefly for the transportation savings or advantages that it might bring to those living and doing business there. For this reason capitalists who had earlier turned from foreign trade to textile manufacturing took an interest in local roads, though, with a few exceptions, not on a scale sufficient to alter their major interest. Others, like John Bryant, William Sturgis, and David Neal, who did not move out of foreign trade until the 1830's, also found in local railroads an outlet for their capital and talents in varying degrees. By a process of gradual involvement they developed ties with eastern railroads outside Massachusetts.

Meanwhile, a younger generation of Boston merchants still found ample challenge and rewards in the China trade. A decade or more passed between the time when railroads became a significant factor in the Massachusetts economy and the time when Boston capitalists trading to the Far East found in them an appealing field for investment. In the interim, however, a fund of experience with railroad transportation had accumulated in Boston, and a demand and opportunity for the experience to be applied was emerging in the West.

Developments in the 1840's favored commitment of Boston-based private capital to the West. The collapse of state-backed western internal improvement projects in the aftermath of the Panic of 1837, Boston's prominence as a center of capital and railroad knowledge and the eagerness of her capitalists, large and small, for "a speculation," all stimulated a major response by Bostonians to demands and opportunities for improved western transportation.

In examining the process of their involvement it is clear that whether investors were large or small, they initially moved into western railroads on an opportunistic basis. Boston capital was lured westward by short-run opportunities to participate in projected or existing roads on terms that minimized risk relative to potential returns. Investment of Boston capital in western internal improvements, for example, followed public endeavors in this area and benefited from them.

Naturally, in a new region, the prospect of long-run economic growth was also an ingredient of investment decisions, but the importance attached to this consideration in a specific case was more a function of the investor's personality and the particular situation than the result of familiarity with the West. Moreover, unlike later pioneering railroad investment in relatively unsettled areas west of the Mississippi and Missouri Rivers in the postwar era, the existence of established and growing settlement and mounting production in the Old Northwest reduced doubts about the long-run demand for railroad services there. In this situation, opportunistic investment on a short-run basis was encouraged.

At the very outset Bostonians' involvement in western railroading seems to have been more the product of their having excess funds and a desire to employ them than any prescient view of the developmental consequences of providing the West with more transportation facilities. Accordingly, it was the western promoter who provided an important link between East and West. Bostonians did not have to seek out western railroad investment opportunities; their possession of capital drew one promoter after another to offices within sight or sound of the maritime activity to which most Boston capitalists traced their wealth. For example, John W. Brooks and James F. Joy brought John M. Forbes into the Michigan Central and continued to seek new projects for his appraisal. Promoters of the Little Miami and the Mad River & Lake Erie likewise sought funds in Boston, appealing to a lesser group of capitalists than those of Forbes's circle. Once involved, however, the Boston investor might himself become a promoter of sorts, seeking to ease his burden or share his good fortune by extolling the promise of western investment — first with friends and business associates, and then with the general public. In this way an involvement easily and gradually begun might become a preoccupation.

The Opportunistic Investor

The strategy of western railroad investment by Bostonians following their first major commitment depended on many interwoven elements. In any given instance it was in various degrees determined by the character of the initial investment decision, the size of the investor's resources, and his personal feelings about their use; as well as by conditions over which he could exercise little or no control. The opportunistic investor of small means was automatically limited in the possibilities of surviving adversity. Reverses for a railroad on which such an investor pinned his faith might quickly eliminate him. Others with more extensive interests and experience, like David A. Neal, might weather such a storm or, through a better developed sense of investment timing, anticipate and avoid it.

Neal's career might stand as the archetype of a consistently opportunistic Boston investor in the pre-Civil War West. Sailing and trading from Salem, he made a small fortune in India and the East Indies trade in his early manhood. By 1846 an inheritance from his father and his various investments in railroads in New England, Pennsylvania, Michigan, and Ohio had raised his resources to some $125,000.[1] With his entry into the Illinois Central, his holdings of railroad securities increased from less than $108,000 at the end of 1851 to almost $290,000 one year later.* By the end of 1853 his west-

* These are Neal's own (presumably conservative) valuations. Like the rest of the financial data which follow, they are taken from the few journals and the ledger in the Neal MSS. By December 1852 his bonds (aggregate valuation: $53,000) were principally those of the Mad River, the Illinois Central, and the Michigan Central; and his principal stocks ($236,000) were in order of importance: Mad River, Philadelphia and Reading, Buffalo and Rochester, Rochester & Syracuse, Illinois Central, Philadelphia, Wilmington and Baltimore, and the Eastern. [Neal MSS., vols. 8, 9, and 10. Baker Library.]

ern investments had grown remarkably. Total gross assets of $564,-000 included Illinois Central bonds valued at $123,000 and stock at $55,000, plus $75,000 in Mad River & Lake Erie stock and $11,200 in the same road's bonds.

Two of Neal's transactions in the early 1850's are of particular interest. One was his acquisition, in 1852, of over $20,000 of stock in the Buffalo and Rochester Railroad; the next year this road became part of that profitable consolidation, the New York Central. Neal obviously knew a good speculation when he saw — or was told about — one. A second notable feature was his heavy sales of Illinois Central bonds in 1854 and 1855. Neal's valuation of these holdings declined from $123,000 to less than $7,000, apparently reflecting his switch to private land speculation and his congenital unwillingness to stick with a project that demanded more than a short-run commitment of capital to realize his estimate of its potential. In any event, by January 1, 1855, with a falling off in his portfolio of railroad securities, Neal's investments in western lands stood at more than 50 per cent (almost $98,000) of his holdings in western railroads.

Clearly, by temperament, Neal was an opportunistic investor, accepting the environment as it was, seeking to extract from it relatively short-run profits, and moving from one geographical area to another as new opportunities appeared. In the process he contributed to western development in numerous ways, for opportunism was not necessarily an obstacle to economic growth — in fact, it might stimulate such growth. Thus, Neal's policies in the organization, financing, and early land sales of the Illinois Central, a new transportation facility in a region that needed it, presumably made a greater social contribution than his next move into land speculation for himself. Guided by opportunism, he decided to profit from the "inside" knowledge and information gained in the first connection. But, in terms of economic growth, the extent of the difference between the impact of his activities as a corporation official and as a land speculator would be difficult to measure.

The Developmental Investor

The developmental investor, who looked to long-run economic growth for his major rewards and consciously strove to transform the environment in the light of this vision, was more often made than born. Force of circumstance might work the transformation from an opportunistic to a developmental investment approach — a transformation that involved increasingly closer entrepreneurial and managerial ties with an enterprise that was once only the object of a short-run pecuniary interest. Furthermore, the transformation might only apply to this one area of investment; elsewhere the investor might act in a highly opportunistic manner, seeking to reduce risk in his main endeavor by smartly timed complementary or consequential investments of comparatively low risk, or by rank speculation in the hope of high returns. Therefore the distinction that has been drawn between developmental and opportunistic investors applies primarily to the main elements in their respective portfolios — in this instance western railroads — and the importance attached to them as shown by investment behavior over time.

Although some became developmental investors because at a critical point this was the only alternative to losing their previous investment, for others the transition, in some degree at least, was influenced by birth and training. The accident of birth was the key to wealth for most Boston China merchants of the second generation. Birth was also a factor in the assimilation of the moral and financial values of a socially elite merchant class in Boston which, at least by the mid-nineteenth century, could afford to see a relationship between the two. In practical terms, access to the wealth of this group during the intermittent, short, but severe, downward fluctuations of the economy in that era was also sometimes essential to a developmental investor's survival. Finally, training in trade over the world's sea lanes refined entrepreneurial and managerial skills that could be adapted to developing a speculative western railroad promotion into a continuing and profitable transportation enterprise.

If David A. Neal can be regarded as the archetype of the Boston opportunistic investor, then John M. Forbes fills a similar role for the evolution of the developmental investor. Much of the story of the Michigan Central, the Chicago, Burlington & Quincy, the Hannibal and St. Joseph, and the Burlington and Missouri River has thus far been told in terms of Forbes. To review the early history of these roads is to see that Forbes's strategic decisions provided the mold within which a series of corollary, supporting tactics were shaped. While his associates had much to do with identifying promising investment opportunities and subsequent physical, legal, and organizational developments, Forbes made the critical entrepreneurial decisions, which were basically financial in character.

In the terms of our conceptual framework, Forbes became increasingly a developmental investor during the 1850's, partly through force of circumstance and partly by a conscious determination to make western railroad investment a continuing and major sphere of his activity. While his involvement in the Michigan Central was initially opportunistic, the circumstances of his involvement soon caused him to take a longer view.

Forbes's early commitment west of the Alleghenies in a road with an east-west orientation was extremely important in terms of his subsequent strategy. The Michigan Central was oriented to the great channels of trans-Allegheny trade and migration, which even before the coming of the railroad were beginning to compete strongly with the north-south river route for the great prize of interregional commerce. As a consequence, the Michigan road and its owners could hardly have failed to experience the pull of western trade, the growing competition for its control, or the temptation to take advantage of its cumulative expansion. Thus they followed a logical policy of sequential railroad construction.

Competition was also an important factor affecting Forbes's choice of railroad investments. Once he had determined to reach Chicago, a move virtually preordained by his initial investment decision, actions of the Michigan Southern and the Rock Island forced him into a complicated series of moves, all carrying him farther westward. Although he had railroad interests across the Mississippi before his line was completed east of it, the Michigan Southern had already preceded him. Direct competition between the two routes, therefore, was an important factor in pushing Forbes westward.

To become a major road, the Michigan Central had to reach Chicago. Having reached this goal, the road then needed feeders to tap the flourishing agricultural area at least as far west as the Mississippi. This sequence might have been anticipated, but the manner of meeting the associated requirements was not predetermined, and strategy west of the Mississippi certainly was not.

Forbes was on numerous occasions quite specific in stating his belief that the direction of economic development lay along an east-west axis. To some extent the validity that he attached to this view can be tested not only by his significant interest in strategic east-west roads but also by his avoidance of roads which attracted other Bostonians. The Illinois Central, for example, like the Little Miami and the Mad River railroads in Ohio, ran, broadly speaking, along a north-south axis. In the prewar economy there was less scope or pressure for sequential and cumulative expansion of these roads than of those running east-west. The north-south roads might fit in with existing trade arteries; they might offer great possibilities of stimulating economic expansion in the areas along their rights of way; but from the standpoint of the most dynamic trade routes of the time and of sustained developmental entrepreneurship outward from a base, they did not, in John Murray Forbes's words, "run in the right direction." Therefore he did not become heavily involved in any of them. In his metamorphosis from an opportunistic into a developmental investor, then, one of the most important factors was the geographical alignment of his initial venture and his growing conviction that its extension westward was the path to the future.

Training, experience, and personal values derived from Boston's social and business aristocracy also helped shape Forbes's inclination to view his major commitments in the context of the long run. Therefore he believed in building a road substantially, though where the element of time became critical for tactical reasons — as in the Hannibal — he would, to some extent, compromise with this principle. However, his standards of sound investment made him unwilling to be identified with a speculator's road. He believed that an investor should have enough confidence in a road's management to buy its stock; otherwise purchase of its bonds was unwarranted speculation. As he put it, "If a Road cost *10 millions* & had a 1st mortgage for 1,000,000 I would not buy the bonds as Investments unless I had confidence eno[ugh] to own some of the Stock & use influence as to management." [2] Such sentiments echoed the attitude which had led Bostonians to rely so heavily on equity financing in the early years of Massachusetts railroads.

In roads where he held a substantial interest Forbes insisted that managerial control should be in dependable hands. Thus John W. Brooks, James F. Joy, and Edward L. Baker are consistently found in the top ranks of Forbes's railroads. Young relatives like Charles E. Perkins or promising Boston youths like Charles R. Lowell were placed in the lower positions with an opportunity to prove themselves. Forbes's own service as president of the Michigan Central until 1855 was not typical of his general practice.

While Forbes had an eye for the long run in his major investments, he was also alert to short-run peripheral profits where he could find them. As his roads moved farther west, he put increasing emphasis on the possibility of gains to be made from land sales and speculation. In March 1857, for example, he wrote Paul S. Forbes that he was considering selling his "more saleable & settled R. Rd. stocks" and moving into the "*wilder* & more promising ones having some *Land* basis attached." [3] As already observed, Forbes also made complementary or consequential investments in iron, timber, and copper that sometimes carried him further afield than he had anticipated. Nevertheless, his opportunism never extended to the point of endangering his basic strategy that emphasized long-run gains derived from providing sound transportation service to a developing economy.

Forbes remained cautious in entering any new railroad situation, generally requiring some prior assurance of financial support from New York and favorable reports from men on the scene in whom he had confidence, such as Brooks and Joy. In addition, he wanted a demonstration of substantial local support for the roads in question. When dealing with trans-Mississippi roads in areas where settlement was still thin and where priority of entry rather than the immediate prospect of traffic was the major consideration, he also wanted guarantees of state aid plus substantial land grants. In these ways he sought to minimize risk as much as possible before committing his own resources. Once committed in a major way to a given road, however, Forbes accepted any risk necessary to insure its survival. His actions, therefore, backed his increasingly explicit concept that related personal profits to westward expansion, railroad development, and economic growth.

As Forbes put it time and again, "true prudence" lay in acting "boldly," and here was the test of his nerve as an investor and his allegiance to the developmental concept. This frequently involved a willingness to expand his personal commitments of time and resources in the face of adversity or uncertainty—as with the Michigan Central's building into Illinois without a charter; Forbes's agreement on behalf of his road to accept $2,000,000 in Ilinois Central bonds without prior approval of his own board; and his willingness to shoulder personally the responsibility of pulling the Michigan Central through the crisis of 1857.

Forbes was able to step into critical situations because he had sizable personal resources, not all of which were allocated to railroads. His relative liquidity in 1857, for example, permitted the steps that saved the Michigan Central. In addition, of course, he was in direct control of the extensive funds of Paul S. Forbes and the American Stock Investment, both of which came into his possession from the China trade. But, in the last analysis, it was Forbes as a person who commanded respect and confidence, and this fact gave him command of others' funds. He always sought "substantial" allies in western railroads. Rather than pushing ahead with unreliable support in the Hannibal, for example, he was willing to wait until the "right sort" of people took hold of it. And because of the standards that he set for his own investment, he was usually able to carry a group of substantial Boston, New York, and European investors with him.

The private activities of Boston investors in prewar western railroads thus present a reasonably distinctive pattern. This pattern was not to be repeated in the postwar environment, although there were broad and important similarities. On the whole, the differences were the result not so much of any spontaneous change in policies and practices as of a transformation of the context within which investment policies were formulated.

Following Appomattox, the nation underwent a transportation revolution which multiplied its western railroad mileage at an accelerating rate and knit the area west of the Missouri River to the rapidly industrializing East. In 1865 there were only 3,272 miles of track west of the Mississippi; by 1890 there were more than 72,000. The incentives for this great expansion were many, as were the ways in which they were translated into railroad networks. As a matter of national interest, the federal government liberally encouraged the construction of railroads to link the East and West. As a matter of local pride and ambition, innumerable communities sponsored or aided railroad construction. As a matter of short-run profit-seeking, shrewd manipulators of securities entered the race. As a matter of long-range investment, other capitalists carefully developed railroad systems with an eye to their future as well as their current values. Finally, as was the case before the war, Bostonians were eager to take advantage of these opportunities.

The picture that emerged from the mélange of motives and the strategy and tactics that they encouraged was complex and confusing. The unrestrained railroad onslaught on the huge, undeveloped domain of the western United States contributed substantially to the growth of the nation and its economy in the postwar era. Yet it was an erratic kind of growth, reflecting the different interests at work and their interaction. In some instances railroads were overbuilt, public resources were turned to private gain, stockholders and bondholders were duped, settlers were defrauded, and communities were exploited. The national economy suffered periodic setbacks that were at times attributed to excessive railroad expansion, though cyclical fluctuations had also characterized the performance of the economy prior to the advent of steam locomotion. Nevertheless, tracks were laid in virgin territory, settlement followed, production spurted, and the nation applauded. The undesirable side effects were largely considered to be the price of reliance on personal interest as the mainspring of a public policy aimed at stimulating rapid economic development. Whether the cost was too high is still debated; in the context of mid-nineteenth century America the cost was subordinated to the immediate national goals of rapid economic development.

The West itself acted like a magnet; with every mile of road constructed westwards, the attraction to areas farther west increased. The idea that the Atlantic and Pacific oceans should be joined by rails was virtually as old as railroads in this country, and with each advance of sequential building the desire to make the next step longer was increased. By the 1860's continuation of the old pattern of building relatively short lines and extending them slowly across the country seemed to challenge destiny. The nation was ready to link East and West without regard to the frontier of settlement, and there were railroad builders ready to accept the challenge if offered the right incentive. Once the race into virgin territory was started, only bankruptcy or exhaustion slowed its hectic pace.

After 1865 the changed environment challenged the concept of prewar developmental railroad investment with its emphasis on high-quality, sequential construction against a background of steady, sustained growth. The pattern of railroad construction in the West after the Civil War was different in many ways from that of prewar years, and this fact obviously affected the investment activities of Boston capitalists. Prior to 1860 the western railroad network had been built largely in the wake of immigration flows (although it is still considered possible that immigration was attracted by the economic opportunities, including the trend of railroad investment, inherent in the United States). In the first postwar railroad boom that lasted from 1867 to 1873, however, much western railroad construction more obviously anticipated settlement. Federal aid stimulated rapid construction and increased competition, which raised new and difficult problems for investors accustomed to a slower pace of development.

These postwar problems were presented first and in their most exaggerated form by the construction of the Union Pacific Railroad, a major link in the route between the Missouri River and the Pacific Coast. The Ames group of Boston investors found in it both challenge and profit-making opportunities. By the very fact of the Union Pacific's existence, the Forbes group, which had helped to lead the march of sequential railroad building in the prewar years, was confronted with major strategic decisions. Should they become involved in this or any other transcontinental? Should a connection with it become the dominant consideration in the strategy of their existing roads? Alternatively, was the soundest strategy to concentrate on the development of territory already penetrated and a continuation of the prewar pattern of sequential construction? Or, finally, were non-transportation investment opportunities opened up by extensive railroad construction to be preferred to railroading itself? These questions and the pace of postwar western railroad construction forced a rapid reappraisal of investment attitudes that had grown out of prewar experience.

Elsewhere, in the Atchison, Topeka & Santa Fe, another group of Boston investors took hold of an attractive opportunity in Kansas railroads only to find that the new environment obliged them to rethink both outlook and policy. This rethinking, in turn, led not only to the creation of a transcontinental system but to the creation of even greater problems of investment and management. These processes and the resulting problems increasingly and significantly overlapped with those of the Forbes group and of the Union Pacific.

PART V The Era of Systems

Chapter 10

Bostonians and the Union Pacific Railroad, 1862–1873: Construction and Conflict

THE RAPIDITY with which rails were laid between the Missouri River and the Pacific Coast in the post-Civil War decade is one of the epic episodes of American economic and business history. Government aid, as a matter of national policy, helped to speed the completion of the first transcontinental railroad. But the construction of the Union Pacific Railroad, a key link in this long chain, afforded an invitation to private opportunistic investment on a grand scale. The resulting attempt to weld national transportation objectives with private investment incentives produced one of the great financial scandals of the nineteenth century. This chapter reviews the general historical background of the building of the first transcontinental railroad and analyzes the process by which a group of opportunistic Boston investors became involved and helped to finance the road to completion. These developments not only affected the later history of the U. P. but also the role of other Boston investors in the railroad expansion of the postwar era in the trans-Mississippi West.

THE PACIFIC RAILROAD ACT OF 1862

By 1862 the American public had been well prepared for a transcontinental railroad. To the mounting impatience of Californians for a rail connection with the rest of the country, innumerable spokesmen for regional and business interests added their appeals. Still, in succeeding Congresses during the 1850's the increasing tension between the North and South made agreement on a route impossible. It was not until war removed the southern delegations from Washington that Congress was able to approve a transcontinental line.

The first formal proposal for a transcontinental railroad had envisaged construction by the government, but by 1853 it was being suggested that private enterprise, aided by the government, should undertake the task. This form of mixed enterprise was adopted in the 1862 legislation, which chartered the Union Pacific Railroad Company to build to the California state line, there to connect with the Central Pacific Railroad being built eastward from Sacramento.

Except for the Hannibal and St. Joseph, which had reached the Missouri River in 1859, the western frontier of sequential railroad construction was still largely at the Mississippi River. New York and Philadelphia had been linked to St. Louis, whose spokesmen sought to promote a connection with the Union Pacific via Kansas City. The eastern systems that centered on Chicago had been connected with the Mississippi River towns of Dubuque, Rock Island, Quincy, and Burlington, and from these points feeders were slowly being pushed westward across Iowa. These and almost every other Iowa and Missouri town on the great river wanted connections with the transcontinental line.

The congressional designation of railroads to connect with the Union Pacific was of considerable importance to investors in the lines already poised on the banks of the Mississippi, and to the trade centers they served. In specifying the proposed location of the transcontinental route, the House of Representatives had favored Kansas City as a starting point. This decision was reversed in the Senate, which placed the initial point at the 100th meridian, well beyond the western terminus of any prewar railroad with connections to the East. The statute then read that the eastern terminus of the U. P. was to be between the "south margin of the valley of the Republican River, and the north margin of the valley of the Platte River, in the Territory of Nebraska." This provision favored roads radiating from Chicago over those fanning out from Kansas City — a fact of major importance in the later strategy of the Forbes group of Boston railroad investors.

Financial Aspects of the 1862 Law

In 1862 the foreseeable income to a transcontinental railroad from traffic alone hardly seemed to justify risking major commitments of private capital. During the debate on government aid, several New England congressmen revealed their skepticism about the economic prospects of the road. Referring to the proposed land grants, Justin

S. Morrill of Vermont predicted that capitalists would seize the lands at each end of the line without completing the through rail route. "As a commercial or economical question, such a road is utterly defenseless," Morrill said.[1] F. A. Pike of Maine echoed these sentiments: "I ask where is the great interest in this country or combination of interests that is to furnish $75,000,000? Can any gentleman tell me? There is no travel from the Pacific coast to justify it. Here are 1800 miles of railroad through *an uninhabited country.*"[2]

In rebuttal to such arguments, Congressman Timothy G. Phelps of California declared: "There are . . . two good reasons why we should pass this bill, either one of which is sufficient to justify its passage, namely, *it is a military necessity*; and *secondly, it is absolutely essential to our internal development.*"[3] In one sentence Phelps had summed up both the immediate and the long-run justifications for government aid to promoters and investors who would complete the final link between the nation's East and West coasts. In the Senate, Henry Wilson of Massachusetts, who had earlier advocated government construction, took up this theme. In his remarks on the transcontinental railroad he said: "If by the liberality of this government, either by money or land, we can induce capitalists to put in the money necessary to complete this road, we shall have achieved something for the country."[4]

In general, the need and justification for government support to a transcontinental line were not seriously questioned in Congress, but the form that the aid should take and the anticipated response of investors to it were subjects of controversy. As it turned out, there were good grounds for anxiety on both scores.

The legislation adopted in 1862 authorized federal aid consisting of land grants plus the loan of government bonds amounting to some $60,000,000. To secure the bonds, the government would have a first-mortgage lien on the whole line and all company property. As work progressed, the railroad company could qualify for specific installments of bonds, different in amount according to the presumed difficulties of construction. Under the law, forty miles of track and telegraph line had to be completed to the satisfaction of government commissioners before the road received the first installment of aid. Amounts due the railroad for services rendered to the government, such as carrying mail and transporting troops and supplies, were to be retained by the government and applied to the retirement of its subsidy bonds and the payment of interest on them. Furthermore, at least 5 per cent of the road's annual net earnings was to be used for this purpose.

The authorized capital stock of the railroad company was set at $100,000,000 divided into 100,000 shares of $1,000 each. Stock was to be sold at par and for cash. The first 10 per cent was to be paid at the time of subscription and the balance in semiannual installments of 5 per cent each. When 2,000 shares had been subscribed and the first installment paid, stockholders were to elect at least thirteen directors, who in turn were to appoint officers of the company. At the same time the President of the United States was to appoint government directors.

Investor Reaction to the Act of 1862

Among the board of commissioners named in the Pacific Railroad Act to obtain subscriptions to U. P. stock was Thomas C. Durant, who subsequently became a major figure in the financing of the road. Born at Lee, Massachusetts, in 1820, Durant had some experience in medicine, which brought him the title of Doctor. He had been associated with his uncle in trade and then became involved in railroading, starting with the Chicago & Rock Island in 1851. In association with Henry Farnam he had helped to construct the Mississippi and Missouri Railroad across Iowa. Looking to the future, the partners during the late 1850's had also sponsored surveys west of the Missouri River. Thus it was logical that both men should be among the Union Pacific commissioners.

It was necessary to obtain subscriptions to $2,000,000 worth of stock to organize the company, but progress was slow. Durant took fifty shares. Few Bostonians seemed interested. Nathaniel Thayer of the Forbes group subscribed for twenty shares; Charles A. Lambard of Boston took twenty, but the names of major Boston investors are conspicuously absent from the list. However, some of John M. Forbes's out-of-state associates, Erastus Corning of Albany and George Griswold of New York, subscribed.[5]

The difficulties of attracting private capital at this stage of the project were vividly recalled by Durant in 1873. The railroad promoter stated then that he had succeeded in interesting potential investors only by loaning them the money to make the initial 10 per cent payment on their stock subscriptions. Efforts to win support in Boston and Philadelphia "did not succeed very well," Durant said. "I finally got my friends to make up subscriptions to the amount of $2,180,000 by furnishing three-fourths of the money to make the subscriptions myself." [6] By such means the first requirement of the 1862 act was met.

The Union Pacific Railroad Company was thus organized and the first board of directors chosen in October 1863. Nathaniel Thayer was elected but declined to serve. Major General John A. Dix, former president of the Mississippi and Missouri, was appointed president; Durant became vice president; the former editor of the *American Railroad Journal,* Henry V. Poor, was named secretary; and a New York banker, John J. Cisco, treasurer.[7]

Since subscriptions to the minimum number of shares had been obtained only with difficulty, it was abundantly clear that the incentives offered by the 1862 act were insufficient to attract sizable amounts of private capital to the Union Pacific. Quite aside from the construction risks, the government's first claim on assets discouraged investors. In addition, amidst the uncertainties of wartime conditions, government currency bonds were selling at a discount, and construction costs were rising. The obvious solution was to get Congress to make private investment in the enterprise more attractive. Representatives of the various interests involved swarmed into Washington, and the product of their efforts was the second Pacific Railroad Act, signed into law on July 2, 1864.

The Pacific Railroad Act of 1864

The 1864 legislation, amending the act of 1862, increased the amount of government aid and eased the conditions of obtaining it. Although the U. P.'s capitalization remained at $100,000,000, the par value of shares was reduced to $100 per share. As specified in the 1862 act, the stock was to be sold for cash and at par; the first 10 per cent was to be paid at the time of subscription and the balance in semiannual installments of 5 per cent each. The books were to be kept open until the entire capitalization had been subscribed, a seemingly innocuous provision that later proved very important.

To facilitate the construction of the road, the conditions of the government aid were liberalized. The government's lien was subordinated to first-mortgage bonds which the company could issue up to an amount equal to that of the government bonds. Both U. P. and government bonds could be released for sale by the U. P. upon acceptance of each twenty-mile section of track by the government commissioners. Finally, the land grant was doubled, and instead of the 1862 requirement that all compensation due the company from the government for services had to be applied against retirement of the government bonds, only one half of the compensation had to be so applied. Against this background of governmental encouragement, promoters of the U. P., led by Thomas C. Durant, formed plans for building the road.

Durant may or may not have had faith in the eventual success and profitability of the transcontinental road, but his plans for financing construction were certainly designed to be profit-bearing in their own right. The first contract for the construction of the Union Pacific set the pattern for all the contracts that followed. In effect, the promoters made the contracts with themselves, ensuring that they would have an opportunity to make a profit on the construction. The resulting Hoxie, Ames, and Davis contracts led to one of the best publicized and most notorious financial scandals of the century. They also led to the rapid completion of the Union Pacific line across the vast hostile area that lay between the Missouri River and the Great Salt Lake.

The Hoxie Contract

The first U. P. construction contract, made in the fall of 1864, was with a Herbert M. Hoxie, a man of no financial means[8] who served as a willing tool for Durant. Hoxie himself apparently did not even sign the contract: it was signed for him by H. C. Crane, an attorney and financial aide of Durant's.[9] Even before its formal acceptance by the U. P., the contract was assigned to Durant and his associates.[10] As the contractor, Durant agreed to build and equip 100 miles of road, to purchase $500,000 of U. P. stock, and to provide the funds for construction, taking as security first mortgage U. P. bonds, the government subsidy bonds at 80, and land-grant bonds at 70. In return, he would be paid $50,000 per mile, and the company would have the option of paying him in the bonds given as security, at the prices named, or of paying him in cash. The contract was signed on September 23, 1864; on October 4 following, it was extended to cover the entire 247 miles from Omaha to the 100th meridian.[11]

The Hoxie contract price was very considerably above the costs predicted by civil engineer Peter Dey, who resigned his post as chief engineer of the U. P. rather than be a party to the operation. Later, Dey's estimate of $30,000 per mile construction cost was proven substantially correct.[12]

Durant's immediate problem was to raise the funds that the Hoxie contract specified would be provided by the contractor. Durant and his associates (Cornelius S. Bushnell, Charles A. Lambard, Henry S. McComb and H. W. Gray) agreed to put up $1,600,000 for the construction work, and they paid the first installment of 25 per cent in cash.[13] Construction, financed in this manner, proceeded until a shortage of funds was imminent. Durant then called for the next installment, but his friends stated that they did not wish to go in any farther, as they were afraid of not getting their money back. They did indicate, however, that if their personal liability were limited to the amount of their investment, rather than to the full extent of their property, they would be willing to go on.* According to Durant, it was to accomplish this limitation of personal liability that the Credit Mobilier of America was employed.[14]

The Credit Mobilier of America

In March 1864 Durant had purchased the charter of the Pennsylvania Fiscal Agency, which had been chartered originally to build railroads in the South and West,[15] and renamed it the Credit Mobilier of America. A year later the Hoxie contract was transferred from the general partnership to Credit Mobilier, and the construction work continued under its auspices. When the Union Pacific paid the Credit Mobilier for this work, it paid the cash portion by check; Credit Mobilier then used the check to purchase U. P.

* Under the terms of the U. P. charter, any stockholder was liable for the company's debts to the full extent of his resources. (Durant testimony, in House Select Committee (No. 2) on the Credit Mobilier, 42 Cong., 3 Sess., *Report* (1873), 64. Hereinafter cited as Wilson Report.)

stock,[16] which purchase had also been part of the Hoxie agreement.* This transfer was carried on the books as a cash transaction, and successfully circumvented the U. P.'s charter requirement that stock be sold only for cash and at par. The participants in Credit Mobilier in this way succeeded in limiting their liability and put themselves in a position as U. P. stockholders to reap both short- and long-run profits, if there were any.

The success of this plan hinged on several factors. Profits to Credit Mobilier depended on the approval of contracts allowing a wide spread between contract prices and actual construction costs. Therefore there had to be an identity of stockholder interest between the Union Pacific and Credit Mobilier. This was accomplished by inviting all those who had subscribed to U. P. stock to subscribe also to that of the construction company. If they declined, an effort was made to buy them out.[17] According to Benjamin Ham, Credit Mobilier's assistant secretary and treasurer, Credit Mobilier began to buy U. P. stock in December of 1864, and continued to buy it until the desired identity of interest was achieved.[18]

Credit Mobilier immediately needed funds to finance construction. However, government aid required completion of twenty-mile sections, as did the release of U. P. bonds for public sale. And, to sell these bonds successfully in the open market required that the investing public develop a feeling of confidence in the U. P. project — a feeling which in turn depended in large measure on the success of construction. The crucial maneuver, therefore, was that of financing construction work until the time was ripe to issue the bonds; if the bonds were issued prematurely, and sold at large discounts, the whole construction project would have been endangered.

* During the latter half of 1866, Credit Mobilier distributed to its stockholders over $5,000,000 in U. P. stock. Credit Mobilier had purchased stock from the original stockholders (to create an identity of interest), and had also subscribed to U. P. stock. (For amounts and dates, see Wilson Report, 745–748.) The company sold or transferred this stock to its stockholders for $1.00 a share. Since the stock was still subject to a call for $70.00, Credit Mobilier, using checks received from the U. P. for construction work, purchased U. P. stock scrip, which could be used to make outstanding shares full paid. The scrip was sold to Credit Mobilier stockholders for cash at a 95 per cent discount (*i.e.*, scrip worth $100 when applied to stock could be purchased for $5.00). Thus, for $3.50, a stockholder could purchase enough scrip to pay up the $70.00 due on a share of U. P. stock. Credit Mobilier stockholders, in effect, acquired each U. P. share (par value $100) for $4.50. (See Durant's testimony in Wilson Report, 66, 133, and in House Select Committee to Investigate the Alleged Credit Mobilier Bribery, 42 Cong., 3 Sess., *Report* [1873], 168. [Hereinafter cited as Poland Report.] Also see Ham's testimony in Wilson Report, 378–382, 384.)

In meeting this challenge in the spring of 1865, Durant adopted several approaches. An attempt to market U. P. stock was a complete failure,[19] but John Pondir, a securities broker, succeeded in negotiating a $1,000,000 loan for the U. P. through the New York Bank of Commerce.[20] The most substantial portion of the financing, however, came from a group of Bostonians whom Durant persuaded to subscribe to Credit Mobilier stock. Through Oakes Ames, whom the U. P. promoter had first met in Washington in the fall of 1863,[21] Durant was successful in drawing a large amount of Boston capital into the road for the first time.

The Ames Group

Oakes and Oliver Ames were partners in the family firm, Oliver Ames & Sons, manufacturers of shovels and tools in North Easton, Massachusetts. The Ames brothers had been interested in the construction of railroads in Iowa since 1856, and had provided financial backing for railroad construction that promised short-run profits. The Ameses had been drawn into opportunistic investment in western railroading by John I. Blair, of Blairstown, New Jersey, who had close relations with men promoting the Galena & Chicago Union Railroad Company. Blair's policy was to buy into weak, locally-promoted railroads in promising areas. He saw that profit could be made not only from land grants, but also from organizing an associated company to perform the actual construction of the roads. The completed lines could then be leased or sold to the system into which they best fitted.

Following this scheme, Blair had pushed the Galena road, via leased lines, across Iowa ahead of any other Chicago-based system. In the process, Blair, the Ameses, and their associates invested in the Chicago, Iowa and Nebraska Rail Road, incorporated in 1856 to connect Clinton, Iowa, on the Mississippi, with Cedar Rapids; and the Cedar Rapids and Missouri River Rail Road, organized in 1859, to complete the route to the Missouri River. In these and their other roads, the promoters acted as contractors also; in the construction work they were associated with John Duff, the Boston contractor with whom the Forbes group had trouble in the Hannibal and St. Joseph. The Ameses, then, had some experience with the kind of operations devised by Durant for the U. P.

Oakes Ames was a respected Massachusetts businessman and had entered politics in 1860 as a member of the Massachusetts Executive Council. Two years later he was elected to Congress, where, appropriately, he served on the Committees on Manufactures and on Pacific Railroads. Presumably it was in the latter connection that Durant first made his acquaintance. Their resulting business association inaugurated a new, and in many respects an ill-fated, relationship between Boston capitalists and the West.

Durant drew Ames into Credit Mobilier because he believed that the Massachusetts congressman had large means of his own, as well as important influence with the monied men of Boston.[22] Both assumptions were correct. The men with whom Ames apparently had the most influence were not, however, the Boston men discussed in earlier chapters.

The Boston group that subscribed to Credit Mobilier stock in March of 1865 were substantial, opportunistic investors. Like Forbes, Oakes Ames turned to his relatives, friends, and business associates for capital. His brother Oliver subscribed for 2,000 shares of Credit Mobilier. John Duff took 1,000 shares, as did Charles A. Lambard, a merchant and broker. J. M. S. Williams and William T. Glidden, partners in a famous Boston firm operating clipper ships, also subscribed for 1,000 shares. Benjamin E. Bates, president of the National Bank of Commerce (Boston), Samuel Hooper and Company, and the partnership of Joseph and Frederick Nickerson, shipowners and merchants, each took 500 shares.[23]

During the summer of 1865 additional Bostonians were drawn into the promotional group. The most important of these were John B. Alley, Elisha Atkins, and Ezra H. Baker.

Alley, a Massachusetts congressman, had been associated with Oakes Ames in Iowa roads and at this very time was involved in a construction contract that Ames had with the Hastings & Dakota Railroad.[24] Alley had not been favorably disposed toward the Union Pacific because of the legal requirement that the subscription books be kept open until the $100,000,000 capital was subscribed and paid.[25] If followed literally, this provision would have meant that the promoters had to put up cash and take all the risks while others might reap the rewards. Credit Mobilier, however, had provided a means of circumventing this provision. According to Alley, Ames approached him in the summer of 1865, emphasized the patriotic character of the undertaking, and stated that with the aid of the construction company the building of the road could be made a safe thing promising a reasonable amount of profit. Ames offered his personal guarantee of an investment in Credit Mobilier, and Alley subscribed for $50,000.[26]

Another Bostonian drawn into the U. P. group at this time was Elisha Atkins. Born at Truro on Cape Cod in 1813, Atkins was a successful merchant. He had entered a dry goods business in 1829 and when the proprietors moved into shipping and other mercantile activities, he went along. In the early 1830's he took over the business, but he failed in the Panic of 1837. A new firm of Atkins & Freeman was organized in 1838 and developed a successful trade with Cuba and the West Indies, especially in sugar. In 1849 Freeman withdrew and in subsequent years the firm became Elisha Atkins & Company.[27] Atkins initially subscribed for 100 shares of Credit Mobilier.[28]

Still another member of the Boston group was Ezra H. Baker, a merchant, shipowner, and a director of the Tremont National Bank. By May 1866 he had acquired 313 shares of Credit Mobilier.[29]

Oakes Ames's motives in becoming connected with this giant construction enterprise, a connection which eventually cost him his reputation, a good share of his fortune, and, in a sense, his life, have often been questioned. No single explanation can be satisfactory, and toward the end of his life Ames underlined this fact in his own testimony. Reportedly, President Lincoln in January of 1865 had asked Ames to "take hold" of the Union Pacific.[30] In January 1873, the Wilson Committee of Congress asked Ames whether he had undertaken the enterprise "from a motive of patriotism." His reply was: "I never thought of that, and I do not think I ever said it." [31] This statement seems to indicate that Ames saw the Union Pacific strictly as a business proposition. But in a written statement submitted to the Poland Committee of Congress in December 1872, he clearly implied that he believed business and patriotism were in this instance closely linked. "Those of us who were willing to aid this great enterprise were under the impression our acts were praiseworthy and patriotic," the former congressman wrote. "We certainly hoped we would make a profit, but we knew the risk was enormous." [32]

Ames's conflicting statements and actions suggest that his plunge into Union Pacific affairs reflected a combination of opportunistic and developmental impulses and objectives. Considering Ames's involvement in Iowa roads, his move into the transcontinental was a logical extension of his previous interests. In any event, there can be little question that in the beginning opportunistic motives dominated. This was a familiar pattern, even for a John Murray Forbes. However, construction of the Union Pacific was not the type of investment in which a seasoned railroad investor like Forbes would risk his capital.

Even with the support of the Ames group, the U. P. faced serious financial difficulties. By September of 1865 only eleven miles of road had been completed, and no part of the government loan had yet been earned. By the end of the year, with forty miles of track completed, there still was no market for the railroad's securities,[33] and the government subsidy bonds of $16,000 plus twenty sections of land per mile were far from adequate to pay the full costs of construction.

To obtain money for continued track-laying, the builders had to hypothecate the U. P.'s first-mortgage bonds and to pay 18 or 19 per cent interest for short-term loans in New York. Oliver Ames, who became president of the road in November 1866, later testified to the financial difficulties during the early stages of construction. "We were deeply in debt," he said, "and very much embarrassed, and we were using our credit to the utmost extent in driving the work along. For a period previous to the Ames contract [August 1867], and for six months afterward, I think there was none of us who was not willing to have gone out at the loss of half of what we had paid in." [34] Despite financial problems, construction was pushed vigorously and by October 1866 the road had been completed for the 247 miles to the 100th meridian, the stretch covered by the Hoxie contract.[35]

Conflict Among the Promoters

During this period, serious friction developed between Durant and the Ames group, whose financial participation had increased rapidly. By May 1866 the Ameses had invested $402,500 of their own in Credit Mobilier and had brought in about $400,000 through friends and associates.[36] In the succeeding twelve months the financial investment of the Ames group increasingly overshadowed that of Durant and his allies. With the election of Oliver Ames and Sidney Dillon to the board of the Union Pacific and the former's elevation to the presidency in October 1866, the Durant group began to lose control of the situation.

At the time of Ames's election to the U. P. presidency, the road had reached the 100th meridian, and a new contract was needed for continued construction. The U. P. directors authorized Durant, the vice president, to make temporary contracts subject to their review. The board presumed that arrangements similar to those of the Hoxie contract — a greatly inflated price for each mile constructed — would be made. Durant, however, saw an opportunity to wreak havoc with the Ames group's plans by making contracts at a much lower price. And this he proceeded to do.

Durant's opposition to the Ames group may have been the result of jealousy.[37] He had been the original promoter of the U. P. construction plan and had exerted considerable efforts in its behalf. He had set up Credit Mobilier, negotiated the first contract, invested all of his own resources, and persuaded others to follow suit. Now his position was being threatened by late-comers. His actions can therefore be interpreted as a natural reaction to the increase in the power and control of the Ames group.

On the other hand, Durant's opposition to Ames can be also interpreted as an extension of their different attitudes toward the Union Pacific. Durant, some have claimed, was not interested in the operation of the road *per se;* he did not believe that the road would be a commercial success, and felt that any profits to be made had to come from construction. Ames, however, seemingly believed in the eventual profitability of a transcontinental line, and he certainly insisted on higher standards of construction than Durant favored. Such differences on strategy undoubtedly contributed to their bitter struggle.[38]

Whatever his motives, Durant battled domination by the Ames group, apparently in hopes of eventually forcing them to allow him to resume complete leadership. He had enough power to block the plans of his adversaries, and he used it skillfully.

Durant's first move to thwart the Ames "crowd" was to negotiate a contract with L. B. Boomer of Chicago. It covered the first 150 miles west of the 100th meridian at a price of $19,500 per mile to the north branch of the Platte River, and $20,000 per mile west of that point (but not including any station building or other appurtenances, estimated at an additional $7,500 per mile).[39] These prices were barely adequate to cover construction costs, and allowed little if any profit.

The U. P. board did not accept the Boomer contract, although 58 miles were built under it during the fall of 1866. Instead they voted, in Durant's absence, to extend the Hoxie contract to cover these 58 miles, obligating the U. P. to pay $50,000 per mile for a road it had cost about $27,500 per mile to build. When Durant learned of the board's action, he obtained a court injunction and successfully prevented this extension of the Hoxie contract from going into effect.[40]

Meanwhile, the directors of Credit Mobilier had assumed that any construction contracts made by the U. P. would be assigned to them, and, accordingly, had increased Credit Mobilier's capital stock by 50 per cent (from $2,500,000 to $3,750,000) late in 1866 to provide additional funds needed to carry on the construction. To induce stockholders to enlarge their holdings, the Credit Mobilier directors offered a $1,000 first-mortgage U. P. bond free with every $1,000 of new Credit Mobilier stock subscribed.[41]

The newly authorized capital stock was prorated among Credit Mobilier's existing stockholders, each of whom was thus offered an opportunity to increase his holdings by 50 per cent. Lack of confidence in the future of the enterprise is suggested by the refusal of the offer by fifteen Credit Mobilier stockholders.[42] The stock they refused, between $130,000 and $140,000 worth, was eventually placed with persons previously unconnected with Credit Mobilier, and the entire $1,250,000 was, in this way, subscribed.[43]

The money raised by Credit Mobilier in this manner was transferred to the Union Pacific as part of a complicated loan agreement made in February of 1867 and never fully carried out. The Union Pacific was, at this time, heavily in debt,* and badly needed additional funds. Credit Mobilier, composed of U. P. stockholders, offered to take approximately $6,000,000 in U. P. securities ($3,000,-000 in land-grant bonds at 80, $2,060,000 in the U. P.'s first-mortgage bonds at 80, and $750,000 in certificates convertible into first-mortgage bonds at 80), and to lend the U. P. $1,250,000 for four months

* Durant estimated that the U. P. was in debt "four or five million dollars." (Poland Report, 171). Bushnell put the figure at $3,500,000 or $4,000,000. (Wilson Report, 40).

at 7 per cent per annum and 2.5 per cent commission, the loan to be secured by first-mortgage bonds at 66⅔.[44] The conditions of the agreement were that the U. P. pay its balance due under the Hoxie contract for construction east of the 100th meridian, and extend the Hoxie contract to cover construction west of that point for a distance of one hundred miles at $42,000 per mile. Durant again blocked the signing of a formal construction contract, and the transactions called for in the agreement, with the exception of the loan, did not take place.

During the first half of 1867 the Bostonians tried without success to get a formal construction contract past Durant. On March 1 J. M. S. Williams of Boston, one of the Credit Mobilier "insiders," offered to sign a construction contract covering 267.4 miles, including those miles already built under the Boomer contract. He agreed to assign the contract to Credit Mobilier, if he got it, and the price was set at $42,000 for the first 100 miles, and $45,000 for the remainder. The contract was accepted by the U. P. board, but blocked by another injunction obtained by Durant.[45] In May Durant was ousted from Credit Mobilier's board, and in June Williams again offered to make a contract, this time at a price of $50,000 per mile. But again Durant was successful in blocking it.[46]

Durant justified the use of injunctions to prevent adoption of these contracts by claiming that he was seeking to protect the minor U. P. stockholders, whose interests were not represented on the board of directors. He therefore demanded the written consent of every U. P. stockholder for a new construction contract,[47] and promised to kill every contract not meeting this condition. Despite Durant's protestations of concern for the small stockholder, it seems likely that he was primarily interested in discrediting the Ames group on any grounds he could.

The stalemate between Durant and the Ames group continued through the spring and summer of 1867, but the financial condition of the U. P. improved considerably as a result of the successful marketing of its first-mortgage bonds in mid-June and July. During the spring the U. P. had exhausted the $1,250,000 that it had borrowed from Credit Mobilier, and current construction was being financed by borrowing against first-mortgage bonds at high rates of interest. As an alternative, Cornelius Bushnell persuaded the U. P. directors to let him undertake a campaign to sell the first-mortgage bonds.[48] Although his associate John Duff was pessimistic about the prospects, Bushnell refused to be discouraged. "I went to work," he later said, "employed an advertising agent, and started advertisements in every leading paper in the Northwest and New England, and I sent traveling agents to every leading city. My most sanguine expectations were realized, and in less than six months I sold ten millions of bonds, and put the price up from 90, at which we had started, to 95. That furnished us with money, so that we were out of the woods so far as financial difficulties were concerned." [49]

With this successful campaign, the Union Pacific project took on a new look. For the first time the general investing public had demonstrated confidence in the venture and this virtually assured funds for completing the construction. The market price of the bonds held, and the Union Pacific-Credit Mobilier promoters were finally in position to begin to reap the large profits for which they had hoped.

The Oakes Ames Contract

With a fresh source of funds available, the Ames and Durant groups were under pressure to compromise and adopt a construction contract acceptable to them both. The stalemate was resolved with the adoption of the so-called "Ames contract." This contract was made by the U. P. with Oakes Ames, who was not on the board of either the Union Pacific or Credit Mobilier at the time.[50]

At this point Durant had little choice but to capitulate. He had had sufficient strength to block the actions of the Ames group through his use of injunctions. He could not, however, regain control by purchase: his financial resources had previously reached their limit. For purposes of obstruction, he had put as the condition of peace the written consent of every U. P. stockholder for every construction contract made.[51] When the Ames group agreed to this condition, Durant had to forego further obstructive tactics. The Boston group, on the other hand, had not been able to make contracts freely, and it needed a formal contract badly by this time; they, also, had to accept a compromise.

Ames agreed to assign his contract to seven trustees, who would administer the contract and divide any profits among members of Credit Mobilier. Of the seven trustees, three were from the Ames group (Oliver Ames, John B. Alley, and Sidney Dillon), three from the Durant group (Durant, Cornelius S. Bushnell, and Henry S. McComb), and one was presumably independent (Benjamin E. Bates).[52] Bates may not, however, have been entirely neutral; as president of a Boston bank it seems more than likely that he leaned toward the Ameses. If this was the case, the Ames group did, in fact, control the trustees, since its business could be conducted with the concurrent assent of four members.

Construction prices under the Ames contract ranged from $42,000 to $96,000 per mile, payable in government bonds at par, first-mortgage U. P. bonds at 90, and U. P. stock. The total distance covered by these terms was 667 miles, including 138 miles already built.[53]

Emboldened by the favorable turn of events, the Ames group made one final effort to rid themselves of Durant. In May they had ousted Durant and his associates from the board of Credit Mobilier;[54] a similar coup was attempted at the election of U. P. directors on October 2, 1867, the day after the Ames contract was adopted. Durant obtained yet another injunction and thereby secured his position in the U. P. for at least one more year. By October 15 the written approval of all U. P. stockholders had been obtained, and the Ames contract was assigned to the trustees.[55]

The conditions of the contract were such as to give the trustees absolute control over the construction of the road and any profit derived from it. Proceeds from the contract would be paid only to stockholders of Credit Mobilier, and only to those who surrendered irrevocably to the trustees their voting rights for six tenths of any U. P. stock they then held or might later acquire through Credit Mobilier.

That the Union Pacific stockholders were, in effect, making a contract *inter se* was clearly understood at the time. Bushnell stated in 1873 that "the owners of the Credit Mobilier, being the owners of the Union Pacific Railroad stock, felt perfectly satisfied that there would be no arrangement made to the prejudice of the common interest . . . It was understood that . . . the interest of all would be protected." [56] He pointed out that at one time the Union Pacific attempted to make a contract directly with Credit Mobilier, and Durant had interfered on the grounds that they should not make a contract among themselves. Bushnell went on to explain that the trusteeship arrangement was devised to meet Durant's demand. But that the trustee arrangement was a subterfuge was known and understood by all parties to it at the time.[57]

The Ames contract was the major source of profit for the Union Pacific *cum* Credit Mobilier stockholders. Although Credit Mobilier itself paid only one cash dividend formally designated as such,[58] the trustees of the Ames contract distributed to Credit Mobilier stockholders large amounts of U. P. securities received as payment for the construction work. The amounts involved are not entirely clear. However, it appears that in December 1867 the trustees distributed U. P. first-mortgage bonds, equal in amount to 60 per cent of Credit Mobilier's capitalization and U. P. stock worth, at par, another 60 per cent. The next month, U. P. bonds worth 20 per cent were divided pro rata. In June of 1868 there was a further distribution of U. P. stock equal at par to 40 per cent, and cash equal to 60 per cent of Credit Mobilier's capitalization. In July a cash distribution of 30 per cent (to be paid from the sale of U. P. stock at not less than 40) and a 75 per cent dividend in first-mortgage bonds (changed to income bonds in September 1869) were declared. Finally, a distribution of U. P. stock worth double the Credit Mobilier capitalization was made in December 1868.[59] Thus, a Credit Mobilier stockholder received dividends worth, on paper, $545 for every $100 he had invested.*

Credit Mobilier was able to distribute such impressive dividends largely because the actual costs of construction were considerably less than originally anticipated. When the transcontinental road was first envisioned, the crossing of the Rockies was thought to be a major barrier; building a road across the continental divide would, the promoters believed, be difficult and extremely costly. In reality, the U. P. was pushed across the Rockies with comparative ease, saving considerable time and large sums of construction money.

Evans Pass made these savings possible. Whether this particularly easy route was known to the promoters at the time of the Ames contract was once the subject of considerable debate. The Ames brothers disclaimed prior knowledge of this route. Oliver Ames stated that they "had an idea that the country was pretty rough over the mountains, and that it would cost a great deal to go over

* From other sources, the promoters are known to have distributed, irrespective of U. P. stock, at least $9,475,000 in cash plus first-mortgage bonds. See Robert W. Fogel, *The Union Pacific Railroad, A Case in Premature Enterprise* (Baltimore, 1960), 71.

them." [60] Recalling the situation, Oakes Ames said that they had expected to make a profit of about 20 per cent, but in fact had made close to 300 per cent because of the unexpected ease of building over the mountains.[61] Since the U. P. directors formally adopted the Evans Pass route on January 5, 1867, there is actually little question that the route was known months before the Ames contract was made. And government surveys dated November 23, 1866 gave the physical details of the route.[62]

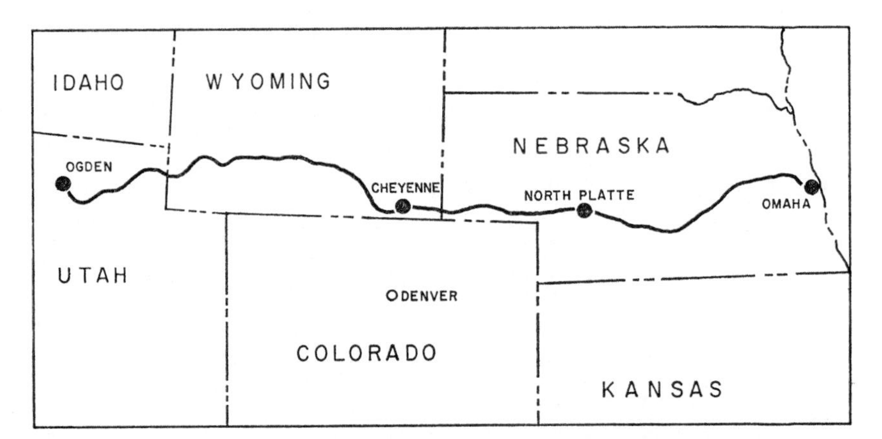

ROUTE OF THE UNION PACIFIC RAILROAD AS COMPLETED MAY 10, 1869.

The Union Pacific met the Central Pacific at Promontory, Utah, on May 10, 1869. The final 120 miles were built under the Davis contract, signed on November 1, 1868, and assigned to the trustees the following week.[63] The terms of this contract were such as to make it, in effect, an extension of the Ames contract.

THE FISK RAID

Following the Ames contract, the price of stock in Credit Mobilier had risen considerably. In the fall of 1867 it went to 160 or 165, and by December stockholders valued it at approximately double par value; in the next two months, its value rose even more.[64] The appreciation of the stock was not widely known, nor did the promoters wish it so. They desired to keep the operation among themselves, but in this they were not entirely successful.

The notorious Jim Fisk, of Erie fame, had learned of the large profits being made in construction of the U. P. and tried to obtain a part of them for himself. He demanded $75,000 as the price of silence. Otherwise, he threatened, he would bring a suit against the U. P. in Judge Barnard's court, and the judge was known to be well disposed toward Fisk and his claims. Despite the risk of the suit, the U. P. did not pay Fisk, who in July 1868 made good his threat.

Taking advantage of the charter requirement that the U. P.'s books be kept open until the entire $100,000,000 capital stock was subscribed, Fisk claimed that he had attempted to subscribe to 20,000 shares in September of 1867, and had been refused. He also claimed that he owned six shares of U. P. stock purchased on the open market, and therefore was injured by the Ames contract.[65]

Oliver Ames later testified that Fisk was paid $50,000 to withdraw his suit, and that Fisk went back on the U. P. by not doing so.[66] In any case, the suit continued; in March 1869 Judge Barnard issued injunctions preventing the scheduled election of a board of directors, the issuance of any more bonds, or the transaction of any more business. Furthermore, he obligingly appointed William M. Tweed, Jr., "Boss" Tweed's son, receiver for Credit Mobilier.[67]

The company disregarded the injunctions and continued business as usual. The judge directed the sheriff to enforce the injunctions, but the U. P. officers received a warning in time to leave their New York office for New Jersey just ahead of the sheriff. In their haste, they misplaced or lost over $400,000 of government bonds and first-mortgage bonds, thus further complicating the financial records and transactions of the company. Shortly thereafter the Union Pacific petitioned Congress for the right to establish offices in any city in the country; this petition was granted and in 1869 Boston became the official headquarters of the U. P.[68]

The Fisk raid severely shook the market for U. P. securities. C. S. Bushnell reportedly spent approximately $76,000 supporting first-mortgage bond prices,[69] but the public's new reluctance to take the bonds resulted in another U. P. financial crisis.

The Fisk raid made it necessary, according to Oliver Ames, to distribute securities on hand to the stockholders on a pro rata basis.[70] Actually, during the summer of 1869, the trustees attempted to raise needed funds by offering appealing stock-and-bond combinations to the stockholders of Credit Mobilier. For this purpose the trustees purchased $275,000 in U. P. land-grant bonds at 85 and an equal amount of first-mortgage bonds at 55 (total cost to the trustees: $385,000). In a circular dated August 11, 1869 the stockholders were offered one $1000 land-grant bond, one $1000 first-mortgage bond, and stock worth $5000 at par, for $2000.[71] The stock was, in effect, thrown in free.

A month later a similar offer was made, this time on a much larger scale. The U. P., still desperately in need of funds, authorized $10,-000,000 in income bonds. The trustees bought $5,840,000 worth of this issue at 60, paying $3,504,000, and sold the bonds pro rata at 80 with a "bonus" in U. P. stock of double the amount of the bonds. Again, the stock was virtually given away. In a circular dated September 22, 1869 the U. P. offered two $1000 U.P. income bonds and 40 shares of stock for $1600, payment to be made periodically between then and the middle of the following February.[72] The promoters obtained $4,672,000 on this transaction.[73] Of the total of $5,222,000 received in these two operations, $3,889,000 went to the U. P. in payment for the bonds. Later accusations in the New York newspapers indicating that the deals had involved $10,000,000 in land-grant and $10,000,000 in first-mortgage bonds appear to be greatly exaggerated.

Repercussions of Opportunistic Investment: Trouble with the Government

The Union Pacific ran into major trouble with the government when Attorney General Boutwell ruled late in 1870 that the United States should retain the entire compensation due the U. P. for movement of government goods and personnel. This compensation would then be used on a current basis to pay interest on the government bonds loaned to the railroad and the remainder, if any, would be held as a sinking fund to retire the bonds. Prodded by vigorous lobbying, Congress in March 1871 reversed this ruling. But it was only the beginning of controversy over the terms of government aid and its repayment, which became a continuing source of friction between U. P. management and government officials.

In 1872 the unpredictable consequences of opportunistic investment became even more alarming to Bostonians in the U. P. A quarrel between members of Credit Mobilier over division of the spoils of success and Oakes Ames's placement of the construction company's stock with members of Congress brought the construction contracts into full public view and provoked a storm of protest. Ames, once hailed as a benefactor of his country, found himself the target of congressional action and public condemnation.

From the start Ames had pursued the policy of interesting members of Congress in Credit Mobilier. Samuel Hooper, William Appleton's son-in-law, was a representative from Massachusetts, and Ames had induced Samuel Hooper & Company to take 500 shares of construction company stock in March 1865. This amount had risen to 750 shares in May 1866, and was still at that level a year later. Senator James W. Grimes of Iowa was on Credit Mobilier's books for 250 shares in May 1866, having been guaranteed 10 per cent on his money. John B. Alley, Massachusetts congressman, had 500 shares at that time.[74]

Subsequently other members of Congress had accepted or solicited Ames's investment advice, and he had recommended Credit Mobilier. For example, a gift of money raised by friends of Senator Henry Wilson of Massachusetts to honor his wife was invested in the stock. When Wilson, worried by the possible repercussions, later objected, the money was returned. In December 1867 Congressman Henry L. Dawes of Massachusetts had sought to purchase a Cedar Rapids bond from Ames, who had recommended Credit Mobilier as a better investment. This transaction was also subsequently canceled.[75] Other members of the government involved in some degree with Credit Mobilier were: Vice President Schuyler Colfax; Senators James W. Patterson (New Hampshire), and John A. Logan (Illinois); Congressmen James G. Blaine (Maine), W. D. Kelley (Pennsylvania), James A. Garfield (Ohio), James Brooks (New York), G. W. Schofield (Pennsylvania), and John A. Bingham (Ohio).

The stock that gave rise to the scandal came from Credit Mobilier's treasury and amounted to 650 shares. Ames and Durant had each wanted it to fulfill obligations that they had incurred, and it was purportedly divided between them at a meeting in New York early in 1868. Meanwhile, H. S. McComb, one of Durant's early associates, claimed that he was entitled to 250 shares. Angered at the summary dismissal of his claim, he instituted legal proceedings. An affidavit filed in 1872 claimed that the stock had been set aside for Ames specifically to distribute to members of Congress, and that the stock had been sold to congressmen at considerably less than its market value — the difference representing a gift. The 100 per cent increase in the value of Credit Mobilier stock between early 1867 and early 1868, resulting from the Ames contract and the distributions declared by Credit Mobilier and the trustees, threw a suspicious light on the "gift." Ames claimed that his commitments had been made before the picture was so bright; McComb claimed that they were made later for the purpose of influencing congressional action.

McComb's charges, first filed in 1868, remained quiescent for several years. They found a wide popular audience in the election year of 1872, following publication by the New York *Sun* in September of an exchange of letters between Ames and McComb. The House of Representatives therefore resolved to investigate the transactions. A committee of five members, headed by Luke P. Poland of Vermont, was appointed for the purpose. In January of 1873 another Congressional committee, headed by J. M. Wilson of Indiana, was appointed to probe the relations between Credit Mobilier and the the Union Pacific.

Ames was confronted by damaging circumstantial evidence. For example, McComb had written Ames in January of 1868 complaining that New Englanders were receiving all the stock. Ames had replied that he was in a better position to judge where it should be "placed." The worst interpretation was given to this phrase when the letter was introduced before the congressional investigators. Other letters also contained remarks that could easily be interpreted to reflect adversely on Ames. His protests and explanations did not find a sympathetic audience.[76] Whatever his motives and objectives, involvement with politicians in this compromising relationship proved to have been a serious mistake.

The Poland Committee found that Ames had tried to use Credit Mobilier stock to exert improper influence on his congressional associates. Accordingly it recommended that both he and James Brooks, a congressman from New York and former U. P. government director who was implicated in the same manner, should be expelled from the House. The House Judiciary Committee, however, found that this action went beyond the powers of that body. Therefore, both men were subjected to votes of censure. The

Wilson Committee concluded that Credit Mobilier had defrauded the government and recommended legal action. Crushed by these indictments, both Ames and Brooks died shortly thereafter.

The Boston group who undertook construction of the Union Pacific clearly acted on an opportunistic basis, which brought them trouble as well as profit. The contributions to economic growth of these men lay in the construction of a strategic railroad where there had been none before. Though they charged a high price for their services, the nation at first encouraged and applauded their accomplishment. When the work was done and a political issue broadcast the facts of its questionable financing, praise turned to vitriol. It is appropriate, therefore, to examine what risks, if any, these men had accepted.

The Question of Risk

There is contemporary testimony that investment in the Union Pacific was, at least up to the Ames contract, regarded more as a rash gamble than even as an opportunistic speculation. "I would not have put a dollar in the enterprise," Horace F. Clark, Cornelius Vanderbilt's son-in-law, testified in 1873, "because it occurred to me that it was a wild waste of money to think of doing such a thing." [77] Oakes Ames himself testified: "People thought I was crazy to make such contracts and to go into such an enterprise." [78] William F. Weld of Boston, who was certainly not averse to taking risks, in 1865 thought the undertaking "too vast" for private capitalists to carry out.[79] John M. Forbes refused to touch it.[80]

The Wilson Committee of Congress, which investigated the Credit Mobilier in 1873, in retrospect saw the investors as completely protected. "We think they differed from other capitalists, not in taking a risk, but in having discovered that the road could be built at vast profit without risk, the resources furnished by the government being more than ample for the purpose," the committee's report said.[81] The committee's position was that the government had authorized the project and provided aid to it. This left the promoters and their followers in the role of agents of the government. If the law or subsidy was inadequate, the committee argued, the investors should have sought changes from Congress rather than adapting their operations to the existing statute.

The Credit Mobilier stockholders viewed the situation differently. In their eyes, the government had invited private capital to build the Union Pacific. The conditions of the offer had little appeal for most investors, and those who became interested properly took every precaution that they could to reduce their risk as far as possible. These measures were extremely effective as it turned out, but the risk was there. The satisfactory outcome could not have been foreseen. Therefore the promoters felt justified in reaping commensurately large rewards.

Reviewing the history of construction work, this argument is particularly relevant to the situation prior to 1867. U. P. securities were generally unmarketable and the enterprise was still so uncertain in early 1867 that some Credit Mobilier stockholders refused to increase their participation.

On the other hand, the risks were relatively well insured under the Ames contract. The chief uncertainty in mid-1867 had been whether the market would support U. P. first-mortgage bonds. This it did both before and throughout the life of the Ames contract, as well as during the ensuing Davis contract, under which the road was completed. Apparently, then, the investing public changed its view in the spring of 1867 about the risks of building the Union Pacific. And it was the willingness of the public to buy Union Pacific bonds that underpinned much of the financial success of the Ames contract.[82]

But success for the contractors also hinged on the spread between the actual costs of construction and the prices specified in the contract. The uncertainties which the spread in prices covered were, in John Duff's words, "the character of the country, the poor quality of most of the land, the difficulty and expense of getting lumber and materials there, the Indians, the alkali plains, and the Rocky Mountains." [83] To be safe, the Ames contract included 138 miles of road already built; therefore the Union Pacific paid almost double the actual cost of the road for those miles.[84] The difference between the amount specified in the Ames contract and the actual construction costs was a generous "bonus," offsetting any risks the contractors could not foresee.

Of the physical obstacles to construction, the mountains were the most crucial. As already indicated, however, the Evans Pass route was known and had been adopted by the directors in January 1867.

If the Ames group in the fall of 1867 was not betting on a sure thing, at least the odds were not heavily loaded against them, and they had taken ample precautions to compensate for any miscalculation.

Durant maintained that the uncertainties of further construction made the inclusion of these profits a condition of Ames's taking the contract. He distinguished between the "light work" of crossing Nebraska and the "heavy work" of Wyoming and the mountains. According to his testimony, the Ames contract was arranged to average the two and produce about a 20 per cent profit.[85] This interpretation was corroborated by Oakes Ames's own testimony.[86] Although he admitted that actual profits might have been as much as 300 per cent, he noted that they were dependent both on the market for securities and the unexpected ease with which the "heavy" work was actually done.

The precise amount of profit accruing to investors in Credit Mobilier is, however, far from clear. Estimates depend in part on ascertaining market values of Union Pacific securities, and the stock was not publicly listed until 1871. Also, poor bookkeeping and contradictory statements by principals leave major questions about what was paid to whom and in what amounts. It is quite clear that a congressional committee's 1873 estimate of $23,366,319.81 in cash profits to the promoters was incorrect. The lowest estimate of profits has placed them at $8,141,903.70.[87]

Robert Fogel has meticulously attempted to calculate what would have constituted a "reasonable" profit in view of the nature and extent of the promoters' risks. He has placed the figure conservatively at $11,100,000 and estimates that actual profits were between $13,000,000 and $16,500,000.[88] In any event, since the maximum capital investment in Credit Mobilier did not exceed $4,000,000, the return, however figured, was very substantial.

Although the activities of some of the members of Credit Mobilier showed flagrant disregard for even the loose business standards of the day, these activities were a logical response to prevailing political and economic attitudes which encouraged rapid growth through private enterprise with government aid and a minimum of safeguards. It is only necessary to turn to the historical record to find that the promoter and opportunistic investor were invited to undertake a task that neither the federal government nor more conservative capitalists would tackle. However crass the motives of its builders or objectionable their financial methods, the Union Pacific Railroad was a major creative achievement and developmental agency. For its Boston owners the costs of its opportunistic beginnings were not soon nor easily forgotten. For other railroad investors in the West, and particularly the Forbes group, completion of the Union Pacific created new and difficult problems of strategy.

Chapter 11

The C. B. & Q., 1865–1873: Conflicting Strategies of Expansion

THERE WAS room for both the opportunistic and developmental railroad investor in post-Civil War America, but the accelerated rate of postwar railroad construction made it increasingly difficult to maintain long-run developmental attitudes amidst the struggle for short-run competitive advantage. The completion of the Union Pacific, the imperatives of new competitive situations, and the enticements of land speculation raised major problems about the strategy and tactics appropriate for the Chicago, Burlington, & Quincy. To a significant degree these decisions revolved about the relative merits of continuing sequential construction westward or buying and building roads along a north-south axis, which seemed to some to offer better short-run profit opportunities. They also reflected an intensifying competitiveness in railroad construction which disturbed the orderliness of expansion and created an environment in which entrepreneurs were reluctantly obliged to overbuild. Here, in a very real sense, was a test of the relative weight accorded developmental and opportunistic goals by members of the Forbes group, and it led to a clash that split the group.

The Burlington and Missouri River Railroad (Iowa)

The Forbes group of Boston investors, starting in Michigan in the 1840's, had reacted to a combination of competitive goads, visions of economic growth, prospects of profit, and favorable public policies by extending their main line westward and enlarging their holdings to form the C. B. & Q. system of roads. By the outbreak of the Civil War individual investors in this group were also interested in the Hannibal and St. Joseph, which had reached the Missouri River, and in the Burlington and Missouri River Railroad, which was being pushed slowly across Iowa.

The essence of John M. Forbes's postwar strategy centering on the

B. and M. R. was adumbrated by Bernhardt Henn in 1858. Henn, a congressman from Iowa who had been influential in obtaining the 1856 land grant for the road, extolled the advantages of its route across Iowa.[1] It would, he said, provide one great thoroughfare, the route of which would "be determined by *population — quickness of transit — certainty of arrivals* and cost of construction — all of which again depend, in a great measure on Climate & Soil . . ." And he enthusiastically noted that the east-west route of the road lay along the 41st parallel of latitude, toward which western immigration tended to gravitate. The prospects of the B. and M. R., he felt, were heightened by the fact that this route had the advantage of *"a settled country"* and was *"already a thoroughfare."* In addition, an east-west railroad also had the advantage of draining arteries of trade provided by nature.

Even in the absence of a transcontinental line, Henn stressed the necessity for pushing the road to the Missouri River. If the B. and M. R. became a thoroughfare across Iowa, he predicted, "Three embryo cities of importance on that River — Nebraska City — Omaha & Council Bluffs — will throw their trade into this Channel, and will open up a career of prosperity — second only to such thoroughfares as the N. Y. Central — the Penna. Central & the Balt. & Ohio roads." To stop short of the river, however, would be to invite other roads to seek this traffic and to condemn the B. and M. R. to the status of a *"mere branch"* of the C. B. & Q.

When John M. Forbes and his associates decided to take firm hold of the road in 1857, the B. and M. R.'s location, as well as its land grant, had been primary considerations. A circular of that era addressed to prospective stockholders and signed by Forbes emphasized the potential value of the land but also declared that "this road is located where it ought to be, and can be made as profitable as any of the Illinois Roads." [2] It seems, then, that the Bostonian, while not overlooking the land aspect, shared the Iowan's view about the strategic importance of a route across Iowa.

At the time of the Pacific Railroad Acts the most westerly point of the B. and M. R.'s route was Ottumwa, Iowa, which had been reached in 1859. To encourage extension of the road in conjunction with the U. P., Congress in 1864 increased the land grant in Iowa and added a grant of land in Nebraska Territory. This encouragement came at a critical time in the B. and M. R.'s fortunes. Although

Iowa's population had more than tripled in the fifties, the southern market for her corn had been cut off by the outbreak of war and the road had felt sharply the loss of freight.[3] Retrenchment and refinancing had been necessary.

Writing to bondholders in 1863, Edward L. Baker, president of the company, again made the point that extension would be the salvation of the road. "The advance of the Burlington & Missouri River Road not only saves it from threatened danger," he wrote, "but will also increase the value of its lands granted by Congress [in 1856], which all lie beyond the present terminus westerly, and are held, and will be, for a sinking fund for the redemption of the bonds." [4]

The additional land grant of 1864 spurred action. In the spring and early summer of 1865 a new effort was made to get on with construction. The new B. and M. R. president, John W. Brooks, a long-time Forbes associate, in his annual report threatened recalcitrant bondholders with repudiation of the second mortgage if they did not consent to refunding to expedite the next moves. Under this pressure, the bondholders capitulated. On June 15, 1865, the board of directors, meeting in Boston, approved the C. B. & Q.'s offer to accept in the form of securities half the payments due on account of joint traffic. In addition, the directors agreed to issue $600,000 of income bonds and whatever amount of common or preferred stock was necessary to extend the road to qualify for the additional Iowa land offered in the 1864 act.

The decision to move ahead came none too soon to suit Iowans, who had a significant financial as well as strategic interest in the B. and M. R.* The road's prolonged failure to extend its line had begun to cause local dissatisfaction. Charles E. Perkins reported to Forbes at the end of March 1865 that there was talk of constructing "a perfect network of [competing] railroads in southern Iowa." [5]

Competitive pressures indeed underscored the need for more aggressive action. The B. and M. R. was threatened with invasion of its territory by the Keokuk & Des Moines and the Mississippi and Missouri railroads. President Brooks had good reason to declare in his 1865 report: "To live and support itself, our road must be extended, and be also connected with the Chicago, Burlington & Quincy road

* Iowa counties and the city of Burlington, for example, had subscribed $502,865.85 to B. and M. R. common stock, compared with a nonresident subscription of $680,546.50.

by a bridge at Burlington, affording to all southern Iowa a direct and uninterrupted route to and from the great business centre and mart of the West, Chicago." [6]

It was to realize this potential that the resources of the C. B. & Q. were placed behind the Iowa road in the early summer of 1865. The first destination of the B. and M. R. was Chariton, fifty-six miles west of Ottumwa; fifty miles beyond that lay the Iowa lands granted in aid of construction. By moving ahead, Brooks wrote, "We make our lands worth enough in a few years to pay off our mortgage, at the same time that we have a road which will, like the Chicago, Burlington and Quincy road increase in value yearly with the development of the country which it serves." [7] In his 1865 report he noted that there was also a land grant of 3,000,000 acres waiting for the road in Nebraska. However, in keeping with the philosophy of sequential construction, the land could wait. "We have too much on our hands in Iowa, just now, to do more than the preliminary work in Nebraska for the present," Brooks declared.[8]

In the year of Appomattox, then, the directors of the C. B. & Q. endorsed the same pattern of sequential construction that they had followed before the war. Oakes Ames and his followers might seek glory and profit from such a vast undertaking as the Union Pacific, but John Murray Forbes and his closest associates preferred to extend their system a piece at a time. They relied primarily on the development of traffic, not whirlwind construction profits, to vindicate their judgment and investment. But on one point Forbes was adamant: The path of extension should continue to be westward along the east-west axis to which he had committed himself years before. In 1866, however, this guiding precept was severely challenged by some leading members of his group.

Boston Investors and Kansas City Railroads

In the summer of 1866 the Forbes group of investors faced an important strategic decision. Although construction gangs were pushing the B. and M. R. westward across Iowa, their progress was halting. Meanwhile various Kansas towns were vying with one another for railroad connections with the East. The possibility that the Union Pacific's main line might be turned southward to Kansas City, as originally contemplated in the House bill of 1862, had not been completely forgotten. For the Forbes group these developments posed the question of whether to concentrate on pushing the B. and M. R. through to a connection with the transcontinental at Council Bluffs or to listen to the entreaties of Kansans and concentrate on making that connection via the Hannibal and St. Joseph, which was already at the Missouri River. The alternatives were debated with increasing fervor within the group that had moved together from Michigan to the Missouri River with comparatively little friction.

In 1866 Leavenworth was engaged in a bitter rivalry with Kansas City for railroad favor and, therefore, commercial predominance. Charles E. Perkins reported in the summer of that year that both towns were anxious for a connection with the Hannibal and St. Joseph road. "The people of the two towns hate one another bitterly," he wrote, "and it is amusing to hear them talk." [9] Since the Hannibal was reportedly on the verge of signing an agreement with Leavenworth, Kansas City boosters saw they had to act quickly. Accordingly, Kersey Coates, an easterner who had settled in Kansas City, and two other local promoters were dispatched to Boston to seek postponement of the Hannibal's contract to build to Leavenworth in favor of a renewal of a prewar contract that would favor Kansas City.* In Boston the Hannibal directors referred Coates and the Kansas City group to James F. Joy, president of the C. B. & Q. and of the B. and M. R., as well as chairman of the Hannibal and St Joseph, and up to this time the chief western strategist of the Forbes group.[10]

Joy was already interested in Kansas City from a personal investment standpoint. Early in 1866 he had begun to buy shares in the West Kansas City Land Company, which proposed to develop rich land west of the hills on which the city was located. The value of these lands would be enhanced by railroad development that members of the company sought to influence. Joy was also familiar with the Kansas City-Leavenworth railroad controversy, as was John W. Brooks, who was at this time incapacitated by illness.[11]

The C. B. & Q. president set the terms on which the Hannibal

* Coates had gone West in 1855 to guide the investments of Philadelphia capitalists and encourage the influx of free-state settlers into Kansas. He had remained and purchased property on the outskirts of Kansas City, Missouri, which as agent he had originally acquired for a syndicate. Because of his family ties in the East, "he was able to become a kind of ambassador of the Kansas City business community to Eastern financial and political circles." (Charles N. Glaab, "Business Patterns in the Growth of a Midwestern City . . . ," *Business History Review*, XXXIII [Summer 1959], 169.)

would favor Kansas City over Leavenworth. The Forbes group was anxious for congressional authorization of a railroad bridge across the Mississippi River at Quincy, Illinois. In exchange for support in this endeavor, Joy had offered his aid in obtaining a land grant to the promoters of the Kansas and Neosho Valley Railroad (later renamed the Missouri River, Fort Scott and Gulf), projected to run from Kansas City to the southwest. Before committing himself and the Forbes group definitely to a connection of the Hannibal and St. Joseph with Kansas City, however, Joy also wanted federal approval of a railroad bridge across the Missouri River at Kansas City. He therefore recommended to his Boston associates that a final decision be deferred until Congress acted on the bridge question.[12]

In August of 1866 Joy and Perkins toured the new route by which the Union Pacific, Eastern Division (Kansas Pacific) was being built west from Kansas City.[13] During their trip together, Perkins noted that Joy was much interested in a road northward from Kansas City along the Missouri, that he seemed disposed to favor Kansas City over Leavenworth, and that he would probably also recommend extension of the B. and M. R. for fifty miles beyond Chariton.[14]

Joy had, as previously noted, already recommended the extension of the Hannibal and St. Joseph to Kansas City instead of Leavenworth, subject to congressional approval of the railroad bridges across the Mississippi and Missouri Rivers. When this approval was obtained in late July 1866, the die was cast to connect the C. B. & Q. system with Kansas City.[15]

The Kansas City & Cameron, a locally promoted road running between those two cities, provided the connecting link. In late 1866 the Boston directors of the Hannibal and St. Joseph approved a contract to supply the Cameron road with rails and funds for bridge construction. The following February the K. C. & C. was mortgaged to the C. B. & Q. and the Hannibal, each agreeing to devote 40 per cent of gross receipts from their business with the branch to the purchase of its bonds The directors of the K. C. & C. authorized a $1,200,000 issue of bonds and invited stockholders of the two major roads to subscribe for the securities at 90 on a pro rata basis. The purchaser of each $1,000 bond could also subscribe to five shares of stock in the Quincy Railroad Bridge Company, which had been organized to bridge the Mississippi River at Quincy and there to connect the C. B. & Q. with the Hannibal and St. Joseph.[16] This structure was opened to traffic in November 1868,[17] and the span across the Missouri at Kansas City was completed in July 1869.

The B. and M. R. Versus the Hannibal and St. Joseph

Although the C. B. & Q. was to be linked to Kansas City as a result of Joy's recommendation, the Forbes group was not unanimous on the strategy. In a letter to Joy, dated November 21, 1866, John M. Forbes expressed his concern: "As you put it you seal the fate of the B. & M. [Burlington and Missouri River, Iowa] bond which is your own child and into which you have more than anybody else led the more venturesome of C. B. & Q. stockholders. Your move will delay it and delay is very dangerous." [18] He then went on to emphasize that his own interests were now entirely in the Michigan Central, the C. B. & Q., and the B. and M. R. Since the Hannibal led to competing roads, Joy's strategy directly challenged Forbes's financial interest in the Iowa road as well as his basic philosophy concerning extension. Forbes also feared that Nathaniel Thayer would be drawn increasingly into support of the Kansas project and that this defection would affect adversely the B. and M. R. extension. However, the ex-China trader was not prepared to make any concessions. He concluded his letter to Joy with a reaffirmation that he would not budge in his own dedication to an east-west route and with a plea that the Detroit lawyer not desert him

Thayer's account books indicate that Forbes's analysis of the former's relative interests in the Hannibal and the B. and M. R. was correct.[19] Thayer had gone into the Hannibal and St. Joseph in 1858, with the purchase of 450 shares of common stock and $5,000 (par value) of convertible bonds. At the end of 1860 he had added $30,000 in land bonds at 60. He had gradually increased his holdings during the war, and in 1865 purchased several thousand shares of common and preferred stock. At the time of Forbes's letter, Thayer apparently had a total stake in the Hannibal which exceeded even his investment in the C. B. & Q., and he held only about one fourth as much in B. and M. R. securities. Seemingly, Thayer was following more in Joy's than Forbes's footsteps.

Joy, the C. B. & Q. president, seemed to think that greater opportunities lay to the south instead of west of that system. As revealed in Perkins' recollections of a later date, Joy in 1866 had completely discounted the future of the B. and M. R. and its Nebraska land grant. Writing in 1886, Perkins declared that Joy had shown no interest in the Nebraska lands during their western trip twenty years before. Perkins' interpretation was that Joy did not think that it would pay even to examine these lands, which Perkins noted had since sold for $12,000,000! [20] This story was expanded in a letter by Perkins to the editor of the Des Moines *Capital* in May 1904. In it he recalled that Joy had questioned the wisdom of building the B. and M. R. beyond Chariton and had doubted that "a road through the counties of Clarke, Union, Adams, Montgomery, and Mills [Iowa], could be made to pay in thirty years . . ." [21]

These recollections, though many years after the fact, are in keeping with what we know of Joy's strategy. His first step, after deciding on a Kansas City connection, was to promote a connection of the Hannibal with the Union Pacific. For this purpose the St. Joseph & Council Bluffs Railroad Company was organized in July 1867, to build to the northern border of Missouri, where it would meet the Council Bluffs & St. Joseph, a local road organized in 1858 and a potentially useful link in reaching the eastern terminus of the Union Pacific.

The St. Joseph & Council Bluffs road was initially organized with subscriptions to 800 shares, each with par value $100. Joy took 500 shares in his own name and 50 shares for Thayer.[22] By March 1868, Thayer had 1,325 shares and $265,000 (par value) in bonds of the new road, and during the year he sharply reduced his holdings of B. and M. R. bonds. Forbes's fears about the changed direction of Thayer's primary investment interests were being realized.

As Joy became involved in Kansas roads with interesting possibilities for land speculation as well as for tapping the Texas cattle trade,* he sought to leave the presidency of the B. and M. R. He had to retain that post, however, for another year because Brooks was ill and unavailable.[23] But a realignment of the Forbes group on the basis of developmental versus opportunistic investment attitudes was clearly in progress.

Chairman John N. Denison of the C. B. & Q. noted the drift of Thayer and Joy away from the B. and M. R. in favor of the Hannibal and the Council Bluffs roads. The possibility that this develop-

* Joy was active in promoting Kansas City as a meat-packing center, a development that benefited his investment in the West Kansas City Land Company. (Charles N. Glaab, *Kansas City and the Railroads* [Madison, Wisconsin, 1962], 168.)

ment would undermine the traffic of the Iowa road and the position of the C. B. & Q. in its relations with the Union Pacific alarmed him. Writing to Forbes, August 9, 1867, he said: "Unless we rally our forces, and put the B. & M. through at once, we shall irretrievably lose the grand opportunity which we now have to make its success complete, and establish it and the C. B. & Q. as the great line." [24]

For Forbes, long-run protection of the C. B. & Q. through extension of the B. and M. R. was now a governing consideration, but for investors more concerned with current traffic and earnings, the Hannibal had significant attractions over the Iowa road. The traffic figures for the year ended April 30, 1867, compared with those of the preceding year, showed that the Hannibal had both increased its business with and contributed more to the revenue of the C. B. & Q. than had the B. and M. R. The number of tons shipped from Chicago to the B. and M. R. via the C. B. & Q. increased 25.71 per cent, while to the Hannibal the increase was 48.17 per cent. Traffic for the C. B. & Q. originating with the B. and M. R. had risen only 15.06 per cent compared with 119.27 per cent for the Hannibal. C. B. & Q. earnings derived from business with the B. and M. R. totaled $358,064.84 versus $607,749.46 for the Hannibal.[25] Thayer apparently pointed to these differences in rebutting Denison's position on the primary importance of the B. and M. R.[26]

For those investors whose interests were primarily in the C. B. & Q. and the B. and M. R., the need for reaching the river at Council Bluffs was being increasingly emphasized. The progress of the Chicago and North Western's Iowa lines underscored the urgency of the situation. With support of the Ames group of Boston investors, the Cedar Rapids and Missouri River Rail Road had been pushed forward vigorously, and in 1867 it reached Council Bluffs over a route that was complete with a bridge across the Mississippi and one in progress across the Missouri. Furthermore, as its reward for early completion, it won a contract to haul building supplies for the Union Pacific.[27] Meantime, the Chicago & Rock Island had acquired the Mississippi and Missouri Railroad and, reorganized as the Chicago, Rock Island & Pacific, was pushing west from Des Moines.

Thus, when Denison was writing to Forbes in 1867, Chicago already had one direct connection with the U. P. and another was in prospect. The C. B. & Q. had to move — and quickly — if it was to become the "great line."

With Denison's urging and Forbes's support, important action to this end came in the late summer of 1867. In a circular offering B. and M. R. bonds to stockholders, C. B. & Q. officials outlined the Iowa road's prospects. The C. B. & Q. had originally taken an interest in it for the business to be derived from Iowa. With the passage of the Pacific Railroad Acts and rapid construction on the transcontinental line, however, the Iowa road had assumed a new importance. The C. B. & Q. circular said: "The latter becomes a link connecting our road directly with the main Pacific road, making our route from Chicago to that road as short as any other, and in some respects superior to all others." Participation in through traffic, moreover, would relieve the Burlington's dependence on local crops for traffic and on the fluctuations in revenue that a poor crop year would produce.[28] The same argument had been made twenty years before for westward extension of the Forbes group's first railroad, the Michigan Central.

This circular, which offered $744,000 in 7 per cent B. and M. R. bonds at 85, was signed by Thayer, Bartlett, Forbes, and Joy as officers of the C. B. & Q. All these men, except Forbes, had become interested in a complex of roads centering on Kansas City and therefore were actual or potential competitors of the road whose cause they formally espoused. As Forbes had predicted, Thayer was becoming more interested in this area of investment than in Iowa. At least his accounts do not show that he purchased any of the new B. and M. R. bonds; in fact, he was shortly thereafter reducing his existing holdings.

Other steps were taken in the fall of 1867 to finance and expedite completion of the B. and M. R. The road's capitalization was doubled, and the directors, including Joy, voted for rapid extension. In his 1868 C. B. & Q. report Joy predicted: "With the road [B. & M. R.] opened through, and with a through as well as local traffic the time cannot be far distant when its contributions to the business of our [C. B. & Q.] road must be doubled and trebled beyond what they are now." [29] Meantime the C. B. & Q. had increased its support of the B. and M. R. to the extent that it shortly became the majority stockholder. As the Iowa road neared completion in 1869, the market price of its stock rose to par. Pointing to this rise in values, Joy wrote that it promised the C. B. & Q. would receive full value for its investment in the B. and M. R., in addition to the increased volume of business *"which was the real object of the aid given."* [30]

By the end of the year, the Burlington and Missouri River road had been completed to East Plattsmouth on the Missouri River, connecting with the Union Pacific at Pacific Junction near Council Bluffs via the Council Bluffs & St. Joseph road. The Iowa road was, in effect, now part of the C. B. and Q.'s main line, and that system had thus forged one more link between the newly completed transcontinental and Chicago. The Hannibal and St. Joseph, which Joy had apparently favored over the B. and M. R. for this role, was specifically deemed a "prosperous feeder" by C. B. & Q. chairman J. N. Denison.[31] For the time being, however, the Hannibal continued to be the source of more revenue for the C. B. & Q. than its Iowa rival: for fiscal 1869, $702,975.16 compared to $472,123.24.[32]

Even before the Iowa road reached the Missouri, the need for a decision on extending it into Nebraska became pressing. In 1867 that Territory became a state, and the Union Pacific had already been built more than three hundred miles west from Omaha. The B. and M. R. had been granted land in Nebraska in 1864 to encourage a connection with the transcontinental at a point not beyond the 100th meridian. So long as the Iowa road was short of the Missouri River, however, extension in Nebraska had been largely an academic question. With the decision in 1867 to push the B. and M. R. completely across Iowa, there was renewed interest in its Nebraska grant.

Joy had been skeptical about Nebraska, and Brooks, his successor as president of the B. and M. R., proved almost more so in the spring of 1868. Specifically, he was doubtful about the country, questioned the economics of transporting "cereals" from there to points east of the Mississippi, and feared the reactions of the Union Pacific to the extension of a parallel and competing road in Nebraska. Still, he was willing to postpone a final judgment.[33]

To establish the facts, Charles E. Perkins and Henry Strong, a C. B. & Q. attorney, visited Nebraska in December 1868. They reported: ". . . the South Platte country as far west as 75 or 100 miles from the Missouri River is . . . almost as rich in climate and soil as any part of Iowa, unless it be the Missouri River counties of Mills and Fremont." Therefore, Perkins said, "We believe that the country south of the Platte River in Nebraska will in a short time be able to support several railroads, and that the business of southern Nebraska is worth an effort on the part of the B. & M. to get it." [34]

Forbes accepted this verdict and suggested that a new company be formed to build and operate the Nebraska road, thus keeping its fortunes and risks separate from his other roads. This suggestion was accepted by the directors in February of 1869. In the spring Congress approved, and President Grant signed, a bill to transfer the Iowa road's Nebraska lands to a new concern, the Burlington & Missouri River Railroad Company in Nebraska. Organized in May 1869, its first board of directors was composed of Sidney Bartlett, John M. Forbes, John W. Brooks, John A. Burnham, Charles E. Perkins, and Cyrus Woodman, the former land agent for the Forbes group in Michigan. On July 4, 1869, ground was broken at Plattsmouth to begin construction on the new road.

At this time the wisdom of backing the B. and M. R. rather than the Hannibal was still in doubt if one judged by freight or revenue statistics. In 1869, for example, while the Iowa road carried more tonnage eastward than the Hannibal, the reverse was true for the opposite direction. Total C. B. & Q. revenue generated by the Hannibal road still very considerably exceeded that produced by the B. and M. R. The same east-west traffic and revenue relationships existed until 1872 when the B. and M. R. pulled ahead in all categories as the Hannibal's business declined.

Meanwhile, the Hannibal's management had become the target of stockholder criticism. One shareholder charged that Bostonians Joy, Bartlett, and Thayer were using the Hannibal as a feeder for their other roads with no thought to its welfare and no major investment in it. He charged that the Cameron branch could not compete with the Missouri Pacific or North Missouri roads which made better connections between Kansas City, St. Louis, and the East. And, in his view, the bridge across the Missouri River had been a costly mistake. "Do you not, also, gain new reasons why the annual Reports — which would give the amounts of freight traffic over our road, and its carriage price, in detail, and enable you thus to see how much your milch cow is milked by others — are so persistently repressed, and all information steadily refused?" he asked.[35]

Whether or not these charges were true, the Hannibal did not long retain its attractiveness for "insider" opportunistic investors.

In a report on the situation early in 1870, Treasurer R. S. Watson admitted that business had been disappointing, though he pointed hopefully to the developing western roads with which the Hannibal connected: the Fort Scott and Gulf; Leavenworth, Lawrence & Galveston; Kansas Pacific; Atchison, Topeka & Santa Fe; Central Branch of the Union Pacific; St. Joseph and Denver; and St. Joseph & Council Bluffs.[36] But while the Hannibal occupied a strategic position, it was a closed-end system vulnerable to pressures from major roads which had a choice of routes for through traffic between the Mississippi and Missouri rivers.

Faced with stockholder revolt and declining revenues, the Boston group stepped out of the Hannibal in 1871. Although Joy expressed the opinion at the annual stockholders' meeting, "that if the road is run on its merits, and for the benefit of its stockholders, and not in the interest of any other corporation, the management would be a success, and the road would pay," [37] this was his farewell speech. His name and those of Bostonians Thayer, Bartlett, Burnham, Hunnewell, and Blake disappeared from the directorate.

Completion of the "Joy System"

Joy and Thayer, having challenged Forbes's sequential, east-west construction strategy, showed growing interest in Kansas City* and a railroad net extending southward from it to a vast area of available public and Indian lands. One object of their attention was the Kansas and Neosho Valley Railroad, organized by local interests in 1865 and aided a year later by congressional and state land grants. Congress authorized the road to extend through Indian Territory to Texas, giving ten sections of land per mile as soon as this Indian country became public land of the United States. In addition, the road was given the authority on its own behalf to negotiate additional land purchases from the Indians. The claim to a right of way through Indian Territory and the land subsidy there, however, were on condition that the road reach the southern boundary of Kansas in the Neosho Valley before any other road.[38]

In August 1866, as Joy was pondering his recommendations on the relative merits of extending the B. and M. R. or aiding the Han-

* Thayer's ledger shows that he purchased $20,000 of Kansas City bonds at 80 on April 15, 1867.

nibal, the United States received in trust from the Cherokee Indians 8,000,000 acres in Kansas, the so-called Neutral Tract. Almost immediately the land was sold to the American Emigrant Company, but the terms brought so much public protest that the sale was soon canceled. Since the land involved lay along the proposed route of the Kansas and Neosho Valley Railroad, it offered a temptation to an active railroad promoter like Joy and an opportunistic investor like Thayer.

The challenge of acquiring the Kansas lands called for the political skills that had made Joy so valuable to the Forbes group. By the beginning of 1867 he was hard at work attempting to acquire the Cherokee Neutral Tract. In this effort Joy was aided by the presidents of three Kansas roads: James Craig of the Hannibal and St. Joseph and its connecting roads to Council Bluffs; Kersey Coates of the Kansas and Neosho Valley; and William Sturges of the Leavenworth, Lawrence, and Galveston, which proposed to parallel roughly Coates's road, starting at the rival city of Lawrence instead of Kansas City.[39]

The first goal of these railroad presidents was to prevent the sale of the Neutral Tract to the Atlantic & Pacific Railroad, which had been chartered in 1866 to build from Springfield, Missouri, to the West Coast. The ironical arguments that the A. & P. did not even touch Kansas and that it was a speculative land-grabbing enterprise apparently had some weight. At least, that sale was rejected by the Senate on April 17, 1867.[40]

The following October, Secretary of the Interior Browning agreed to sell to the Joy group for $1.00 an acre cash all lands in the Neutral Tract not occupied by settlers.[41] These were more onerous terms than those earlier given the American Emigrant Company, which had not yet relinquished its claim to the lands. By a complicated series of maneuvers, however, the Emigrant Company's claim was disposed of, payment for the land was spread over a period of seven years, and congressional criticism was avoided.[42] In these maneuvers Iowa congressman Josiah B. Grinnell, C. B. & Q. lawyer Nehemiah Bushnell, and his law partner, Secretary Browning, were most helpful. The sale was completed in June 1868.

In October of 1868 the Kansas and Neosho Valley Railroad Company became the Missouri River, Fort Scott, and Gulf Railroad Company. Capital stock to the extent of $4,000,000 was authorized, and

Joy applied familiar fund-raising techniques. He was successful in obtaining $750,000 in loans represented by city and county bonds. As of January 1, 1869, the railroad company issued first-mortgage, 10 per cent, 30-year bonds to the amount of $5,000,000; another $2,000,-000 of 10 per cent, 20-year bonds followed in April 1870.[43] Thayer's accounts show that he advanced $215,000 cash on the road's bonds in the fall of 1868.

Joy, Thayer, and their associates were now fairly well defined as the more opportunistic members of the Forbes group. The Boston directors of the Fort Scott and Gulf in 1870, for example, were Thayer, William F. Weld, John A. Burnham, and H. H. Hunnewell. A year earlier this same group was among the stockholders of the St. Joseph & Council Bluffs listed as approving the consolidation of that road and the Council Bluffs & St. Joseph, with Thayer in his own right and as trustee representing the controlling shares of the latter.[44] In June 1869 Thayer, Hunnewell, and Weld also became directors of the Leavenworth, Lawrence and Galveston, along with Sidney Bartlett and John N. Denison. Joy, Bartlett, Thayer, and Denison, were also still directors of the C. B. & Q.

By 1870 a network of roads, designed by Joy, was centered at Kansas City. The Hannibal and St. Joseph, of which he was chairman of the board, linked the growing city with the C. B. & Q. at Quincy, Illinois. In 1870 the Council Bluffs road, connecting with the transcontinental line, was merged with the Missouri Valley road running north from Kansas City. South from there ran the Missouri River, Fort Scott and Gulf, and from Lawrence, the Leavenworth, Lawrence and Galveston, whose cars were also routed into Kansas City over the Fort Scott and connecting lines. With completion of these roads to the southern boundary of Kansas, the Joy system reached its fullest extent.

The Weaknesses of the Joy System

The weaknesses of the Joy design were several. The Hannibal, for example, was loaded with debt, had a high operating ratio, and was dependent on other roads at its termini. While it occupied a strategic position, it could not control its own destiny. Much the same thing could be said of the Kansas City, St. Joseph & Council Bluffs, which was oriented on a north-south axis between competing railroad centers and through routes. Joy was soon forced to concede that the greater efficiency of the Omaha-Chicago roads and the greater activity of the Chicago grain market drew trade in that direction and away from St. Louis, which the Council Bluffs road was best situated to serve. He declared in the 1871 annual report: "In the last three months, for instance, there has been shipped out of Nebraska City 468 car loads of grain. Of these 461 have gone to Chicago by the Burlington and Missouri, and 7 have gone to St. Louis, although the rates from Nebraska City to both cities are the same, and the distance to St. Louis more than a hundred miles less." [45]

He also said of the Chicago-based lines, "These roads are managed with system and vigor, and the transportation of freight is as regular and as much on time, as a rule, as their passenger trains." [46] By contrast the St. Louis roads, terminating at Kansas City or Leavenworth, were managed in relation to connections with the Kansas Pacific. The resulting delays and missed connections with roads coming from the North, in addition to the greater cost of handling grains in St. Louis, affected the Council Bluffs road adversely.

Whereas this road depended heavily on east-west connections, others running on that axis could easily send off feeders to compete with it. In 1873 the B. and M. R. was siphoning off business from Nebraska City, the Rock Island's Chicago & Southwestern was tapping Leavenworth and Atchison, while the Hannibal and St. Joseph had also extended its line to Atchison, Ruefully, Joy commented: "None of these roads were [*sic*] in contemplation when the road of this company was undertaken, and though possibly one of them might have been foreseen, could the financial condition of the country been foreknown, yet no possible wise foresight could have predicted or apprehended that all of them would be built." [47]

This statement is open to question. Forbes, for example, had recognized the long-run logic and advantages of adhering to an east-west construction pattern; Joy had seen more short-run advantages in departing from it. His self-confessed lack of foresight might better have been termed lack of long-run time-perspective, which was a characteristic of opportunistic investors.

By 1873, however, Joy saw long-run economic development as the salvation of the Council Bluffs road. He remarked. "While . . . these causes have been at work taking away a part of the business properly belonging to the road, and diminishing the rates at which the remainder must be done, the natural increase of the country has been such that in no year has its business fallen off, and during the last year, as has been stated, it has largely increased." [48] Nevertheless, for the preceding two years the road had been unable to pay expenses and interest on its whole debt. August 1, 1873, on the

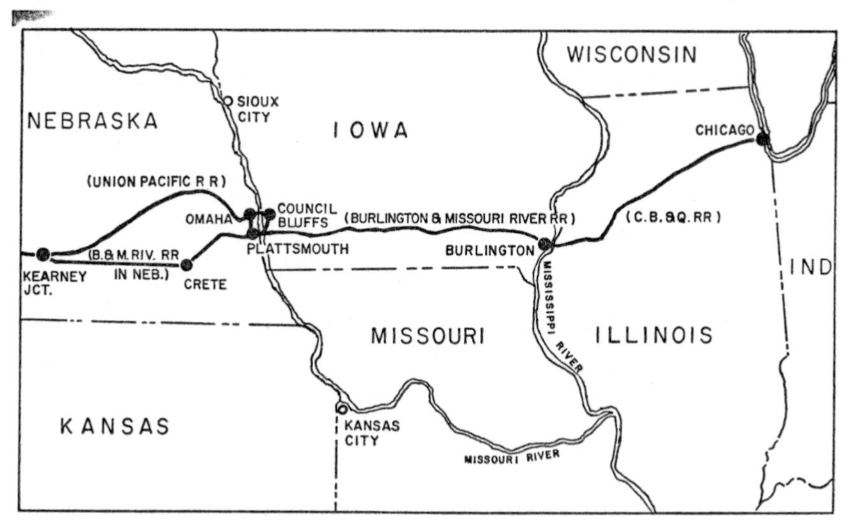

Through routes to the Union Pacific from Chicago over the C. B. & Q. and the Burlington and Missouri River roads in Iowa and Nebraska, 1873.

eve of a general financial crisis, the company defaulted on interest due, except on the mortgage of the former Council Bluffs & St. Joseph. The directors funded coupons on first-mortgage bonds for the next two years into ten-year notes and exchanged coupons on second- and consolidated-mortgage bonds for preferred stock. Thayer replaced Joy as president, though Joy remained on the board for two more years. The capitalist thus succeeded the promoter.

The Council Bluffs road survived in this way, and the growth of the country eventually fulfilled Joy's premature expectations. The increase in grain shipments was most notable. In 1873 the road had carried only 22,585 tons of wheat; in 1878 the figure was 108,430 tons. The amount of general merchandise nearly tripled during the same period.[49]

The passage of time and accompanying railroad developments

gave the Council Bluffs road a new importance for the C. B. & Q. The Burlington missed an opportunity to obtain a lease in 1878, but in the following year, with Jay Gould's purchase of the Missouri Pacific threatening the entire C. B. & Q. system, the Forbes group had to protect its flank. An arrangement was then made to exchange C. B. & Q. stock for the stock and income bonds of the Council Bluffs road by August 1, 1880. In Julius Grodinsky's words: "The Burlington's hand was forced. It was now defensively following in the footsteps of Gould — buying roads with poor earnings at high prices." [50] As we shall see, this was but one area of conflict between Gould and Boston developmental investors, who, under the pressure of the times and the place, were being forced in self-defense to act increasingly opportunistically.

The rapid expansion of the railroad network in the decade after 1865 provided a severe test of long-run investment strategy. John M. Forbes was deeply committed to the C. B. & Q. system, which ran along an east-west axis of westward immigration. This commitment governed his attitude toward postwar expansion, but the commitment itself reflected strategic decisions consciously made long before the outbreak of the Civil War. Therefore the sequential extension across Iowa and Nebraska at a relatively unhurried pace in the immediate postwar years marked no significant departure from long-established developmental policies.

James F. Joy was the architect of much of the C. B. & Q.'s basic strategy, but he had performed more in promotional and managerial capacities than in entrepreneurial-ownership ones. Therefore, when the opportunity offered to combine all these roles with increased emphasis on the latter, he seized it. While strategic considerations which could have aided the C. B. & Q. were involved, the lure of cheap lands, the opportunity to create a new system of roads in which he would be the major figure, and other considerations increasingly led Joy away from Forbes and toward a north-south axis of railroad investment. The effects were undeniably developmental to the extent that rails were laid into virgin territory with all the corollary effects, direct and indirect, that encouraged economic development. But the resulting financial difficulties of these companies represented an investors', and perhaps a social, cost of overly rapid expansion in an attempt to realize opportunistic expectations.

An expanding element of the Forbes group followed Joy and

Thayer into these new ventures without completely severing their ties with the C. B. & Q., and eventually the impact of changing times brought their respective strategies closer together. Amidst intensifying competitive pressures, the C. B. & Q. was forced to act opportunistically in self-defense, while the Joy group found that it had to adopt increasingly long-run, developmental policies to salvage their early investment. However, the wisdom of Forbes's commitment to the east-west strategy and reliance for profit on traffic development is suggested by the relative strengths of the C. B. & Q. and Joy systems at the end of a decade of expansion. Matters of timing, resources, and the general behavior of the economy were involved, but it does not seem too much to suggest that the differences also reflected private investment decisions as they related to anticipated rates and directions of postwar railroad expansion.

Chapter 12

The Union Pacific Railroad, 1873–1890: Consolidation and Conflict

BOSTONIANS HAD played a leading role in the construction of the Union Pacific and thereby established a relationship with the first transcontinental railroad that remained significant for several decades. In 1884, for example, over one third of the railroad's stock was held in New England. Among these shareholders were the former members of the Credit Mobilier group, or their descendants, as well as distinguished members of the Boston aristocracy, such as Charles Francis Adams, Jr.

Although the Union Pacific had found its way into the portfolios of conservative investors, it had far from outlived its legacy from the era of frenzied construction and complex finances. Opportunities for financial manipulation in the U. P. continued. After 1873 a key role in its activities was played by Jay Gould, an outstanding speculator and railroad strategist. His keen strategic sense, as well as financial acumen, led to the 1880 merger of the Kansas Pacific and the U. P., offering new opportunities for securities speculation. In these maneuvers he was actively aided, or unsuccessfully opposed, by various Bostonians whose interest in the road's management dated from Credit Mobilier days. During the same period, Gould also attempted with less success to outwit and outmaneuver the Forbes group of Boston investors in the C. B. & Q.

Both the U. P. and the C. B. & Q. fought their battles in a rapidly changing environment. Mounting railroad competition and cyclical movements of the economy forced the abandonment of developmental investment strategies in some instances and in others required opportunistic investors to accept long-term involvements. In the case of the U. P., for example, extensive railroad construction opening virgin territory gave way to intensive building of feeders to protect that territory. Thus Gould, when he turned to other things, left the U. P. with a burgeoning network of branch lines, as well as ownership of the previously competitive route of the newly merged Kansas Pacific.

Although Charles Francis Adams, the Bostonian who succeeded to command of the U. P. in 1884, continued the policy of intensive building, he was eventually unable to cope with its consequences amidst increasing competition, declining revenues, and mounting troubles with the federal government. When Adams left the management in 1890, Gould, who had helped to engineer the situation, moved in to salvage what he could. During the preceding two decades, however, the U. P., whatever its problems, had contributed significantly to the development of the expanding territory that it served. This chapter deals with these varied facets of the U. P.'s transformation into a developmental agency backed by continuing injections of Boston capital.

From Credit Mobilier to Jay Gould

The strategic location of the Union Pacific and its initial monopoly of transcontinental rail traffic west of the Missouri insured interest in it by the directors of eastern trunk lines. Moreover, the transcontinental's financial difficulties afforded these individuals an opportunity to express their interest. In 1871 a group representing the Pennsylvania Railroad came to the aid of the financially embarrassed Boston promoters of the U. P. As a result, for a short time the Pennsylvania was able to use the western road as part of a through route from New York to Denver. This development, however, threatened the Vanderbilt interests, and they displaced the Pennsylvania group in 1872. Horace F. Clark, Commodore Cornelius Vanderbilt's son-in-law, then became president of the U. P.

The company's position at that time was precarious. There was a large floating debt, directors held substantial notes against the company, and a sizable amount of income bonds was coming due in 1874. This bleak financial picture was made worse by the government's action in withholding all compensation for services rendered by the railroad and in declaring the issue of land-grant and income bonds illegal. Whether for these reasons or not, before he died in 1873, Clark had begun to put his U. P. shares on the market. Jay Gould began to acquire them on a falling market that reflected the road's continuing financial difficulties as well as the general oversupply of railroad securities.[1]

Gould had had a phenomenal career as a stock market manipulator and speculator in the East. He came to public notice in 1869 by his attempt, with James Fisk, to corner the gold market. Associated with Fisk in a struggle for control of the Erie Railroad, Gould was also actively interested in New York street railways, telegraph companies, and the Pacific Mail Steamship Company.

Once involved in the U. P., Gould's first action was to deal with its most pressing financial problems. Aided by Boston directors Oliver Ames, Elisha Atkins, and Franklin Dexter, he succeeded in transferring the floating debt into 8 per cent sinking-fund bonds and in reducing the high rate of interest being charged by directors for endorsing the company's notes. Meanwhile, he added to his own holding of U. P. stock, was elected to the board of directors, and became a member of the executive committee, whose membership still included former members of Credit Mobilier. The unity of this Boston group was soon revealed by their refusal to support Gould's demand that beneficiaries of the Ames and Davis construction contracts be sued by the U. P. for recovery of their profits.[2]

Gould's Strategy

For the remainder of the decade Gould sought to increase the earning power of the Union Pacific and to use the expanding system as a fulcrum to obtain securities profits from other opportunistic ventures. Much of his strategy centered around the Kansas Pacific Railroad, another product of the Pacific Railroad legislation and opportunistic promotion.

It will be recalled that the Pacific Railroad Act of 1862 established the eastern terminus of the Union Pacific at the 100th meridian, well beyond the existing railroad network but generally favoring roads radiating from Chicago over those centering on Kansas City. One of the latter was the Leavenworth, Pawnee & Western, which the 1862 legislation authorized to extend from Kansas City to meet the U. P. at its starting point. In 1866 Congress agreed that this road, now known as the Union Pacific Eastern Division, could build fifty miles west of Denver before connecting with the transcontinental.

To aid this work the federal land grant was increased to apply to the whole route, though the original bond subsidy remained unchanged. Three years later the road was renamed the Kansas Pacific and authorized to connect Denver, Colorado, with Cheyenne, Wyoming. In short, congressional action instead of creating a feeder for the U. P. had created a competitor, a fact brought home to both roads when they tapped Denver in 1870 and offered alternative routes to the Missouri River and the East.

To deal with this challenge, the Union Pacific, ignoring provisions of the 1864 act intended to prevent such tactics, took advantage of its monopoly west of Cheyenne to discriminate against K. P. shipments moving past that point. In 1875 Gould offered to relieve this pressure on the hard-pressed K. P. by consolidation, but the negotiations collapsed. A rate war ensued, followed by a traffic agreement between the two roads.

Another thorn in Gould's side was the Burlington and Missouri River Railroad in Nebraska, which threatened to invade U. P. territory. This road was subjected to the same treatment as the K. P. Gould also threatened reprisals against the C. B. & Q., which was allied with the B. and M. R. through common ownership. The management of these Boston-backed roads, however, refused to be intimidated.

Charles E. Perkins, B. and M. R. general manager, took such a strong stand that Gould decided to change his tactics. In 1877 he bought sizable blocks of shares in the Chicago, Rock Island & Pacific and the Chicago and North Western, the other members of the "Iowa Pool" formed by Chicago-based roads in 1870 to divide U. P. traffic moving eastward. Gould, Sidney Dillon, and Oliver Ames were soon seated on the boards of these two roads, whose representatives joined the U. P. board. Gould proposed a quintuple contract among all the roads concerned * and emphasized his power by having Dillon route U. P. traffic away from Omaha and over the Hannibal and the Wabash. Perkins naturally resisted this effort to break the Iowa Pool and, despite the presence of the Gould representatives, he found enough support to save it.[3]

Gould then launched a campaign to outflank the Burlington. He

* Union Pacific; Burlington and Missouri River; Chicago, Burlington & Quincy; Rock Island; and Chicago and North Western.

first attempted to purchase the Hannibal, which had been sold by its Boston owners in 1871. When this maneuver failed, he moved into the K. P., which was in the hands of Carlos Greeley and Henry Villard as receivers. Gould reversed his late strategy and now emphasized the Omaha traffic to put pressure on the Kansas City–oriented line. Villard fought back by proposing a reorganization of the K. P., accepting the rate war, and unsuccessfully appealing to Boston capitalists William Endicott, John M. Forbes, and Thomas H. Nickerson for aid. While the rate war continued, Gould organized a successful pool to acquire K. P. stock and bonds in the spring of 1878.[4]

To free himself for a new attack on the western railroad problem, Gould began to sell his U. P. stock. These holdings were sizable, since he owned 200,000 out of a total of 370,000 shares.[5] In February 1879 a syndicate led by Russell Sage and James Keene relieved him of a significant number, but Gould retained approximately 90,000 shares and remained a U. P. director.[6]

In effect, Gould exchanged a major part of his interest in the U. P. for a dominant position in the K. P., which he planned to merge with the former on terms that would more than compensate him for his trouble. After finally reaching an agreement with Villard, Gould obtained control of the K. P. in the summer of 1879. He also acquired the Denver Pacific, which linked the K. P.'s Denver terminus with Cheyenne, and became an important influence in the South Park, a road which challenged the Atchison, Topeka & Santa Fe's access to Colorado mine traffic. With these properties in hand, he approached the other directors of the U. P. in September 1879, proposing that they purchase the K. P.

When this proposal was rejected, Gould demonstrated his brilliance as a railroad strategist and tactician. From Oliver Ames II he purchased control of the Central Branch. This move put an end to Commodore C. K. Garrison's hopes that the Missouri Pacific could be extended west of Kansas City, and Garrison's St. Louis–based road fell to Gould. Controlling the K. P. and the Wabash, and having already eliminated possibilities of the U. P.'s reaching St. Louis via a branch between St. Joseph and Denver City, Gould was in a strong position to deal with his fellow-directors of the U. P. They now had little alternative but to accept his terms for consolidating the K. P. and U. P. The agreement, which was most favorable to the Kansas Pacific and therefore to Gould, who had invested heavily in it, was signed in January of 1880.

Part of Gould's maneuvering had been designed to induce co-operation from the U. P.'s Boston directors. Therefore it is necessary to examine their response to his alternate use of goads and lures.

Gould and His Boston Associates

Some of the Bostonians who had participated in the construction of the Union Pacific as an opportunistic venture remained active throughout this period. When Gould became interested in the company, he discovered that "Oliver Ames and Sidney Dillon were the two (directors) that could be relied upon." The former's interest in the U. P. was managed by his son, Frederick Lothrop Ames.[7] Oliver Ames II, son of Oakes Ames, acted as trustee for what was left of his father's investment in the transcontinental. Although the Panic of 1873 wiped out the father's holdings of U. P. stock, the son had retained about 3,500 Credit Mobilier shares and some of the Central Branch. Since the Credit Mobilier still had significant claims against the U. P., Gould tried hard to get these shares. It was his refusal to sell, young Ames thought, that caused Gould to drop him from the U. P. board in 1876.[8] But in the sale of the Central Branch several years later the Bostonian obtained ample revenge.

Frederick L. Ames testified in 1887 about his relations with Gould, whom he had met when the latter went on the U. P. board. Three years later, in 1877, Ames took his father's place as a director, and the following year he also became a director of the Kansas Pacific. In April 1879 he contributed $100,000 to a pool arranged by Gould to purchase Kansas Pacific Denver extension bonds.* In return for this and other financial aid, Ames received K. P. securities,[9] which were also distributed among the other Boston U. P. directors as part of Gould's carrot-and-stick technique.

According to Ames, by October of 1879 the Boston directors favored the consolidation with the Kansas Pacific, but not on the terms proposed by Gould. They felt that he overvalued K. P. securities because his own position in them was greater than in those of

* Other members of the pool included Russell Sage, Dillon, and St. Louis parties. Later, Gould bought out the stockholdings of the original K. P. backers in St. Louis.

the U. P., whereas their position was the reverse of his. During December 1879 and early January 1880 the Boston directors had frequent interviews with Gould in New York and succeeded somewhat in modifying his views on the relative values to be assigned the securities of the two roads in consolidation. Nevertheless, according to this account, the Bostonians remained lukewarm about the proposition. Gould forced them to accept it, Ames claimed, by threatening both to revive the litigation concerning the prorating of traffic between the Kansas Pacific and Union Pacific, and to build branches to draw traffic away from the U. P.[10] Gould also held over the heads of the Boston directors the possibility of extending the Kansas Pacific to Ogden; this move would have provided a direct connection with the Central Pacific and given him, with the Missouri Pacific, a through route from St. Louis to the Pacific Coast.[11]

But Ames testified that fear of the C. B. & Q. also influenced the directors' attitude toward consolidation. He referred to the Burlington and Missouri River in Nebraska, which was threatening to build branches down into the territory lying between the Union Pacific on the north and the Kansas Pacific on the south. "And," said Ames, "we urged it on Mr. Gould to join the [U. P. and K. P.] properties together, thinking that together we could, with his help, make a stronger front towards protecting the country against the Burlington and Missouri invasion." [12]

Frederick Ames felt that the consolidation had proved worthwhile and he defended his part in it as being in the U. P.'s best interests. However, the investigators who elicited this testimony clearly believed that Gould and his associates had planned the consolidation primarily for profits in securities. Therefore, they tried to get Ames to admit that he had profited similarly.

Although he stated that prior to the consolidation he had an interest of $4,830,000 in the U. P. and $828,000 in the K. P., Ames denied that he had acquired the latter interest for speculative purposes or that his position on consolidation had been influenced by it. Instead, he said, he had retained all of his U. P. stock, including that for which the K. P. stock had been exchanged. The picture that emerged from Ames's testimony was one of cooperation with Gould, but more to protect Ames's interest in the U. P. than to gain securities profits directly from the consolidation.[13]

Franklin G. Dexter, another Boston director of the U. P., supported Ames's testimony. Admitting participation in the pool of 1879, he also reinforced Ames's claim that the activity of the Forbes group had actually precipitated the consolidation of 1880. Dexter recalled that he had heard rumors that the C. B. & Q. was about to expand, and he asserted that it was this rumored expansion of a rival system, in which incidentally he was also a stockholder, that finally induced the Boston directors of the U. P. to settle with Gould.[14]

Gould had clearly hoped to win over the Bostonians by appealing to their pocketbooks, but their holdings in the U. P. were so substantial that speculation in K. P. securities was no lure if it hurt their primary interest. When it became clear that they were not going to capitulate, Gould had showed his hand. As Dexter remembered it, "Mr. Gould said he was going to Kansas, and I thought he had his war paint on and his trunk in hand . . . I was a great deal disturbed about it, because I recognized Mr. Gould's energy and ability; and with him as an enemy with the Kansas Pacific to fight us with, it was a serious matter." [15] It was indeed serious, for Gould proceeded to carry out the series of moves that increasingly threatened the U. P. and culminated in his purchase of the Missouri Pacific.

Oliver Ames II later told the Pacific Railway commissioners, "If you had seen those Union Pacific directors, as I did, just about the time the consolidation took place, you would have pitied them." [16] Following the Missouri Pacific purchase, Ames felt that Gould had the Boston U. P. directors in his power and that they knew it. "I know I saw Sidney Dillon and Dexter and Fred Ames as gloomy and unhappy a set of men as I ever saw," he declared.[17]

This member of the Ames family had reason to be pleased with his own role in the preliminaries to the consolidation. He had made the Central Branch Railroad important to Gould. This road, part of the original U. P. construction plan, ended one hundred miles from Atchison, Kansas, until Ames in 1877 had formed a construction company and obtained $2,500,000 in subscriptions to extend the line. To counter this threat, Gould had commenced to extend the Kansas Central on a parallel route not twenty miles distant. According to Ames, the Boston U. P. directors had urged him to see Gould and attempt to end this competitive construction.[18]

Ames's report of his interview with Gould, Dillon, and Russell Sage early in November 1879 gives a glimpse of Gould in action. As the Bostonian recalled it, "Mr. Gould said he did not think much of agricultural roads. I told him I saw he did not, but I noticed he was building all the time. Said he, 'I build them as feeders and not as main lines.' Mr. Sage had the impudence to say to me if I would sell him the road he would give me back the land assets in payment." [19]

Angered by such remarks, Ames retorted that he was ready, able, and willing to extend his road to Denver if need be. His firmness paid off; Gould needed the Central Branch in connection with his larger strategy. The next day he and Ames came to an agreement. The Bostonian and his group were paid $250 a share for 6,250 shares of the Central Branch,* plus a 50 per cent division of the profits for extensions that Ames already had under contract and payment for the equipment that his group had leased to the road.[20] Although Ames had a small amount of U. P. stock, he was not thereafter vitally involved in the consolidation question. As he put it, "I was an outsider, and could see it all and enjoy it all." [21]

Gould's strategy also paid off. A new corporation, the Union Pacific Railway Company, was formed, with a capital stock equal to the sum of the stocks of the constituent companies — the Union Pacific, Kansas Pacific, and Denver Pacific. This stock was exchanged on a dollar-for-dollar basis with the old stocks, a feature of the agreement to which subsequent investigators gave considerable attention, for it put the earning power and credit of the dividend-paying U. P. behind the securities of the virtually bankrupt K. P.[22]

Opportunistic Profits from Consolidation

Gould managed to make the consolidation pay handsomely for the costs of bringing it about. His interest in the Central Branch and the Kansas Central (acquired to threaten the Missouri Pacific and the Central Branch) was advantageously exchanged for new U. P. stock in the case of the former, and bonds of the U. P. and the K. P. in the case of the latter. In addition to these roads, Gould for good measure also included the St. Joseph and Western and the St. Joseph Bridge Company in the consolidation.[23] Although he denied that he had made money out of the operation itself,[24] Gould received

* Ames testified that in addition to the shares he had inherited from his father, he bought a considerable amount of Central Branch stock for about $50.00 a share in 1878 and sold it to Gould for $150–$250 a share a year or so later. (Pacific Railway Commission, II, 804, 810–812.)

stock in the consolidated companies equaling the par value but worth more in the market than the Kansas Pacific stock which he had acquired at twelve cents or less on the dollar. And this was only one of the securities from which he stood to benefit. Any attempt to realize these profits at one time would have been disastrous, so Gould gradually disposed of his U. P. stock over the next three years on a rising market and in 1883 stepped out of active participation in the road for the remainder of the decade.[25]

The Boston directors were in a position to share in the windfall that Gould had engineered, but it is difficult to determine how much they actually profited from it. Frederick Ames and Franklin Dexter both testified in 1887 that they had retained substantially all their U. P. holdings.[26] Ezra H. Baker, president of the American Loan and Trust Company in Boston, a former member of Credit Mobilier, and a U. P. director since 1876, had done likewise.

Bostonian Elisha Atkins, also an investor in Credit Mobilier, a U. P. director since 1869, and a vice president since 1874, not only kept his stock but added to it. Somewhat more active than Dexter, he confined his attention primarily to financial matters and apparently negotiated most of the Union Pacific's short-term loans.* Between 1880 and 1887 he nearly tripled his personal holdings on U. P. stock. "I stood by the ship," he declared.[27] Atkins declined to condemn Gould's activities, about which he professed to know little. In connection with the securities operations accompanying the consolidation, he said that he had done nothing different from his associates.[28]

Gould had called the tune to which the Boston U. P. directors had danced, some a little more reluctantly than others. But in retrospect, and at least for the public record, all the Bostonians agreed in 1887 that while Gould had left them no alternative to consolidation of the U. P. and K. P., they had desired it anyway. Their complaint was with his initial proposal. The final terms, they claimed, were satisfactory.

* Among the institutions from which Atkins borrowed for the U. P. was Baker's American Loan and Trust, of which Atkins was himself a director. He testified that he also used other banks in Boston. "We would take money wherever we could get it at a fair, moderate price," he said. The highest rate paid was 6 per cent, according to his testimony. In major negotiations the finance committee turned to Kidder, Peabody and to Blake Brothers. On some occasions the individuals pledged their personal securities as collateral and charged the Union Pacific a commission for this service to the company. (Pacific Railway Commission, II, 767–768, 775.)

As president of the Union Pacific, Charles Francis Adams, patrician descendant of American presidents, testified in 1887 that he also believed the consolidation had proved beneficial. Among other things, he cited the favorable basis on which bonds had been turned in at the time of the consolidation, reducing the company's debt burden appreciably. Furthermore, he reported that the Kansas Pacific had pulled its weight in the consolidation and that its price had not been unreasonable in terms of its earning capacity.[29] Adams' views could be accorded some consideration since he was a railroad expert and, though not involved in the consolidation, he had had to deal with its consequences. As ex-president, however, Adams changed his tune and told Clarence Barron in 1892 that Gould had "saddled" the U. P. with the Kansas Pacific when he should have let it go into bankruptcy.[30]

Charles Francis Adams, Jr., and the Union Pacific

Adams, an investor with varied western interests, was drawn deeply into the Union Pacific by its apparent success in the years immediately following the consolidation. Since the acquisition of the Kansas Pacific had eliminated the only immediate threat to the U. P.'s through traffic in the prosperous early eighties, it was possible to increase rates and pay dividends on the capitalization of the consolidated company. Net earnings rose steadily in 1880, 1881, and 1882. So did the price of U. P. securities, reflecting not only heightened expectations as to earnings but also the speculative stock market activity which accompanied the fast-paced revival from the aftermath of 1873.

In the autumn of 1882, however, U. P. stock began to decline, and Adams, who apparently had first become seriously interested in the road as a government director in 1878, decided to examine its prospects for himself. He spent a fortnight traveling over the system in October 1882 and returned to Boston reassured that its condition was improved and that the country it served and the business of the road itself were developing satisfactorily. Consulting with Frederick Ames, a friend and neighbor, he concluded that rumors of falsified earnings, over-issues of stock, and an enormous floating debt were baseless. He therefore attributed the weakening of the market price to the manipulations of Wall Street operators "bearing" the market.

Adams was so confident of his findings that he incorporated them in a letter to the Boston *Advertiser* in December 1882. In words he was later to regret, Adams praised the U. P.'s development and urged that New Englanders seek control of the system. "It is but necessary to quietly take the stock at the price at which the Wall Street bears offer it," he said. "It has already been drifting to Boston in considerable quantities. The object of my present writing is, in so far as I can, to cause it to drift here faster." [31] Apparently such an unqualified recommendation from such a distinguished figure led many New Englanders to follow his advice.[32] In 1883 he became a private director of the company.

By the spring of 1884 Adams was forced to admit that he had been overly optimistic. Gould had sold out, the U. P.'s affairs were in a tangle, and recession had settled on the country. To ascertain how bad the situation was, Adams journeyed to Omaha with Fred Ames. There he found things in "a shocking bad way." In his words: "The concern was threatened with summary proceedings on behalf of the United States Government, its service was demoralized, it had just backed down before its employees in face of a threatened strike, and it was on the verge of bankruptcy, with a heavy floating debt." [33]

Adams' enthusiasm for the U. P. a few years earlier had not only discounted fluctuations in the economy but had seemingly ignored the new look in transcontinental transportation. In 1881 the Southern Pacific was completed to a connection with the Atchison, Topeka & Santa Fe at Deming, New Mexico, offering a through route from Kansas City to the Pacific coast. In the spring of the following year the C. B. & Q. was completed to Denver, where it connected with the Denver & Rio Grande, offering access to Ogden. In the next two years more competing routes were opened. The Atlantic & Pacific was completed from the Pacific Coast to a connection with the Atchison at Albuquerque, and the Southern Pacific was extended from Deming to New Orleans. Meanwhile, the Northern Pacific was finally completed to the Pacific coast.

These roads, built at less cost per mile than the U. P., could afford to cut rates to attract traffic, and the U. P. had no alternative but to follow suit. While competition cut into through business, feeders of these and other lines were luring away local traffic which might otherwise have gone to the U. P. Quite aside from the general recession in business, the impact of these developments, plus a heavy capitalization and a floating debt that approached $7,000,000, left the U. P. a weak-kneed giant in the spring of 1884.

Relations with the Government

Relations with the federal government became a major concern of U. P. management during this era. Government aid had helped to make the construction of the U. P. a profitable private undertaking, but succeeding generations of management had to meet the accompanying obligations incurred by the promoters. The complications mounted rapidly after 1873 and had become acute when Adams became president of the U. P. in 1884.

The central issue of these years was how the government's loan for construction work should be repaid. Under the act of 1862, payment of interest by the company on government subsidy bonds was presumably deferred until maturity of the bonds. The Secretary of the Treasury had challenged this interpretation in 1870, but Congress took the company's side. In 1873, however, the legislators in the heat of the Credit Mobilier revelations reversed their position. The Secretary was authorized to withhold all government compensation due the company until interest on the government loan was paid. Pending satisfaction of this obligation, no dividends were to be paid, and the company's financial affairs were circumscribed in other ways. The company challenged this restraint, and in 1875 the Supreme Court decided in favor of the company.

While this matter and repayment of the principal of the loan were awaiting another review in the courts, Congress acted once more. Under the Thurman Act of 1878, a sinking fund was established into which was to be paid an amount sufficient to make annual payments equal to 25 per cent of net earnings. Half of the compensation due from the government for services was to be paid directly on the bonds; the other half was to be invested in the sinking fund. This fund remained the property of the company, but it was to be administered by the Secretary of the Treasury, who was required to invest it in United States bonds.[34]

The Thurman Act defined "net earnings" as the amount derived by deducting from gross earnings the sum of operating and maintenance expenses and interest on first-mortgage bonds. This provision was particularly hard on the U. P., which was spending large amounts to build branch lines and was now prohibited by law from subtracting these outlays from gross earnings in accounting with the government.* In 1879 the Supreme Court, deciding the case brought under the 1873 law, removed a large part of this inequity. However, the Court also upheld most of the government's contentions and ruled that for the period 1869–1874 the U. P. owed more than a million dollars in repayment of subsidy aid.[35]

Although the Supreme Court sustained the constitutionality of the sinking fund provisions of the Thurman Act,[36] the U. P. refused to make payments into the fund, claiming that certain expenditures challenged by the government should be allowed as deductions in arriving at the amount to be paid. As a result, the U. P.'s delinquency on this score had reached nearly $1,700,000 by 1883, and the government brought suit to recover this amount. By the spring of 1884 congressional action to force payment, and perhaps to increase the amount, was threatened. Union Pacific stock by the end of June had fallen to 28 from 131¾ in early July 1881.[37]

With government relations overshadowing all other aspects of the U. P.'s operations, Sidney Dillon resigned the presidency and Adams, who was presumed to have considerable influence in Washington, succeeded him. Major concessions had to be made quickly to stave off a disastrous government attack. Accordingly Adams offered to pay the government's maximum claim for the year 1883, pending a decision by the Court of Claims; to allow the government to retain all payments due for transportation; and to discontinue the payment of dividends for the remainder of 1884. The Senate Judiciary Committee accepted these terms as a *quid pro quo* for withholding action and gave Adams time in which to reorganize the company.

Adams, with the support and advice of Boston directors whose ties with the company went back to Credit Mobilier days, made remarkable progress in meeting the U. P.'s immediate financial problems. During his first six months in office he reduced the floating debt by more than half. By the end of 1886 there was a balance of more than $1,250,000 above current liabilities. Nevertheless, net earnings slowly declined in the general recession of the period.[38]

For the long run, however, Adams still faced two major, inter-

* The U. P. charter prevented the road from consolidating with others not named in the charter. Therefore it had to control the stock of branches and use that control to vote leases to the U. P.

related problems. First, he had to reach an understanding with the government that would allow the management of the U. P. to adjust to mounting competition. Basically this meant freeing enough resources from government claims to allow continued development of the branch line system now carrying the lifeblood of the Union Pacific. Second, to accomplish the first objective Adams had to convince the public and Congress that the U. P. was not the plaything of Wall Street speculators.

Adams had a "model" of investment and investors with which he attempted to explain the evolution the Union Pacific to skeptical congressmen. In his words, "The venturesome constructor [Ames] made way for the speculative capitalist [Gould]; he in due time sold out at his own price to the *bona fide* investor." [39] Thus, the initial step of constructing the U. P. was pictured as a "business gamble." Adams wrote: "In any other country than the United States it [the U. P.] would therefore either have remained unbuilt, or it would have been built by the Government, and purely as a military way. Here, in accordance with the spirit of our institutions and our people, a different course was adopted. A corporation of citizens was organized; and with that corporation the Government proceeded to make the best terms it could." [40] The U. P. president declared, "Enterprises in unknown fields are not gone into by prudent men, or on a six per cent profit basis." Accordingly those "who went into it did so looking for large profits, or a total loss." The fact that the gamble paid off, in Adams' view, caused the general public to feel mistakenly that success had been preordained and the government defrauded.[41]

According to Adams, Gould had acquired the shares pledged as collateral by Oakes Ames, who forfeited them as a result of his personal difficulties amidst general financial crisis. Then, as a consequence of the encouraging results of the U. P.'s operations, stock prices advanced to the point where it paid Gould to sell out and where it attracted small investors to buy. This was the group that Adams declared he represented.

Supporting this claim in a letter to the chairman of the board of government directors of the U. P., apparently written in late December 1884, Adams reported the regional distribution of stock holdings in the U. P. Two separate stock ledgers were maintained; one contained the names of stockholders living in Boston and eastern New England; all others were shown on the New York books. In 1875, the Boston books listed the names of 95 New Englanders, representing 67,121 shares of stock, or an average of 706.5 shares per person. Five years later, at the time of the consolidation, this list had grown to 507 names, representing 93,972 shares. As of late 1884, the Boston ledger contained 5,145 names, representing over 231,000 shares. Of the 95 Boston names of 1875, however, only 33 were still on the books. Of 30 Massachusetts towns outside Boston proper the largest holdings were in Cambridge and Salem. In all, the stockholders shown in both the Boston and New York books totaled 7,713, representing 608,685 shares. According to Adams, only 128,863 of them were held on speculative "Wall Street account." [42]

Adams realized that the claim that U. P. stock was now widely held by small investors, including women, would be disbelieved and held up to ridicule as a "widow and orphan racket." Therefore, in addressing himself to government officials, he did so in the name of business. "No railroad is operated for fun, or for patriotism, or for philanthropy," he said. "Railroads are always operated in order to make money." The alternative to managing a railroad legitimately was to let it pass into the hands of those he termed "Wall Street wreckers." Accordingly he told a congressional committee, "The widow and the orphan, the 'trustee,' the small *bona fide* investor and the stockholder for income, — sneer at them, flout at them, as the wrecker does and may — these none the less constitute the one real protection which the Government has. Their only chance is in legitimate management. If they save anything, the Government must save all." [43]

Adams attacked the provisions of the Thurman Act as contrary to the best interests of the territory served by the U. P., of the U. P. itself, and of the Government. This was so, he argued, because the Thurman Act required the company to place 25 per cent of its net earnings in a sinking fund invested in United States securities yielding less than 3 per cent. This money, in his view, might better be invested in branch lines, the construction of which had consumed a significant share of U. P. earnings since 1880 and had become a mainstay of the U. P.'s business.* In a letter to Senator Hoar of the

* The profit on main-line business contributed by branches was nearly 11 per cent of the investment in branch lines in 1886. (Testimony of Oliver Mink, Pacific Railway Commission, II, 617.)

Senate Judiciary Committee in February 1885, Adams wrote: "Every dollar of money, therefore, which is taken out of our business annually, is so much which could be applied to the development of the country, not only to the great advantage of the Union Pacific, but to the increase of the security of the government so far as the ultimate recovery of its debt is concerned." [44]

A year later Adams repeated these arguments before the Committee on Pacific Railroads. At that time he proposed that the U. P. pay the government $1,500,000 per year. As he put it, "Our proposition, therefore, is that a portion of the principal shall be paid off before any of it would be regularly due, and that the balance unpaid in 1897 shall be renewed, and gradually extinguished through a period of a little over two generations." This was a business proposition, Adams maintained, and a sensible solution to a mutually distressing problem.[45]

This proposal was not accepted, but legislation was introduced in the House and Senate to fund the U. P.'s debt and transform payments to the government into fixed amounts payable in semiannual installments over a period of seventy years. The fact that the U. P. was known to favor this legislation apparently contributed to arousing opposition.[46] In any event, no action was taken at that session, and Congress, to gain more information, in the following session authorized an investigation of the Pacific railroads that had received government aid.

The investigating committee, known as the Pacific Railway Commission, was appointed by President Grover Cleveland and headed by Governor Robert E. Pattison of Pennsylvania. It spent much of 1887 on its assigned task. Extensive testimony was taken from those associated with the government-aided Pacific railroads, and government accountants combed their books. Of the final nine volumes of testimony and exhibits, four were devoted entirely to the Union Pacific.

The Commission presented a majority and a minority report. The majority, consisting of E. Ellery Anderson, a New York lawyer, and David T. Littler, an Illinois lawyer and politician, arrived at a neatly balanced verdict. They found that the 1880 K. P.–U. P. consolidation had probably been beneficial but that the manner of its execution and the resulting financial burden that it placed on the U. P. were open to criticism. Similarly, while conceding that the policy of acquiring branches initiated by Gould was a desirable one, they felt that the implementation reflected manipulation. Though the majority concluded that the road was generally well equipped and operated, they also found that its management had engaged in practices which just skirted the edges of legality. In this connection they maintained that the payment of dividends while the floating debt was mounting and the government's claims were ignored was unjustifiable. The lobbying activities of the U. P. and its pooling and rebate arrangements were also targets of criticism, though there was nothing strictly illegal in any of them.

Adams' administration received praise. The majority report stated: "The administration has devoted itself honestly and intelligently to the herculean task of rescuing the Union Pacific Railway Company from the insolvency which seriously threatened it at the inception of its work; that it has devoted itself, by rigid economy, by intelligent management, and by an application of every dollar of the earning capacity of the system to its improvement and betterment to place the company on a sound and enduring financial foundation." Finally, as Adams had hoped, the majority recommended that the debts owed by the Pacific railways to the government be funded.[47]

Governor Pattison, who had taken an active role in support of Pennsylvania oil producers in their fight against Standard Oil and railroad discriminations in favor of the Trust, found a completely different meaning in the evidence. He condemned the branch-line policy, pooling, and rebating, and refused to give Adams a clean bill of health. Finally, he opposed funding the debt to the government, favoring instead revocation of existing charters, recovery of the government's money, and leaving the future of these properties strictly to private enterprise.[48]

President Cleveland submitted the Commission's conflicting conclusions to Congress with the admonition that the public interest demanded prompt action. However, despite a new legislative effort, no action was forthcoming.

Adams had tried repeatedly to reach some agreement with the government that would remove the continuing uncertainty between them. However, though virtually every government body or official that had investigated the Union Pacific problem prior to 1888 had recommended corrective action, none had resulted.[49] Therefore, the company's obligation to the government had continued to increase; the sinking fund established under the Thurman Act had failed to keep up even with the interest charges.

Despairing of government action, the U. P. directors in 1888 at last decided to take a step which had been indicated for some time — the establishment of their own sinking fund. But this decision came too late. A decline in net surplus revenue from 2.55 per cent on capital stock in 1888 to 1.88 per cent in 1889, plus the expenses of development along the main line and at Omaha, caused the directors to reconsider their action. The initial $165,000 earmarked for the supplemental sinking fund was not paid in, and further action under this plan was deferred.[50]

Branch Lines and Financial Difficulties

Branch lines were the salvation of the Union Pacific and also the cause of Adams' downfall. Adams pointed out to the Committee on Pacific Railroads in 1886 that the 1,600 miles of main line were supported by 3,000 miles of branch lines: ". . . it is these branches and not the subsidized lines which are now to carry the Union Pacific through," he said.[51]

One of the most important of these branches was the Oregon Short Line, built and controlled by the Union Pacific. Its purpose was to give the U. P. access to the Pacific coast by a route other than that of the Central Pacific, which in 1884 came under the control of the Southern Pacific. The Oregon Short Line was completed in 1882 from the Union Pacific main line at Granger, Wyoming, to Huntington, Oregon, where it joined the Oregon Railway and Navigation Company. The latter road completed the route to Portland, Oregon in December 1884. Three years later the Railway and Navigation Company was leased to the Short Line, which guaranteed R. & N. bonds and a 6 per cent annual dividend. The following year other branch roads were consolidated with the Short Line to form the Oregon Short Line & Utah Northern Railway Company.

Since the Northern Pacific appeared interested in gaining control of the Railway and Navigation Company, the U. P. directors decided to prevent any such development. This decision seemed to be justified on financial grounds alone; the purchase of the R. & N. Company could be made with money borrowed at 5 per cent, while indirectly under its existing agreement with the Short Line, the Union Pacific was guaranteeing a 6 per cent dividend to owners of the Oregon road. The Short Line was therefore authorized in 1889 to acquire the R. & N.'s stock in the interest of the U. P. for approximately $12,000,000. To cover this expenditure the U. P. proposed to issue 5 per cent collateral trust bonds.[52]

This move, plus subsequent ones toward the Gulf of Mexico and alliances with midwestern roads, threatened to upset the whole railroad picture in the West. This development alarmed Jay Gould, who became increasingly anxious to displace Adams at the helm of the U. P.

Adams shortly ran into difficulties that culminated in his resignation from the Union Pacific presidency. The bonds for the acquisitions in the Northwest sold so poorly that the company withdrew them from the market and proceeded to borrow on them, pending an upturn in financial conditions. Instead of improving, conditions grew worse. In October 1890 the stock market collapsed; Adams was desperate. He asked Drexel, Morgan & Company and the Vanderbilt interests for aid in carrying the floating debt, offering them control in return. When both groups declined this proposition, Adams reluctantly turned to Gould who, with Dillon and Frederick Ames, had taken advantage of the slump to buy U. P. stock. Gould stepped in, made arrangements with leading creditors of the company, and assumed responsibility for management.[53] Charles Francis Adams, a disillusioned man, ended his efforts to realize the U. P.'s promise, which had so filled him with hope eight years before. At the time of his resignation, about one third of the U. P.'s capital stock was held in New England, one third in New York, and the remainder abroad.[54]

In 1892 Adams explained to Clarence Barron, the Boston financial writer, the troubles that had led to his resignation. Adams attributed much of his difficulty to W. H. Holcomb, the western manager of the U. P. He charged that Holcomb failed to operate the road at full efficiency and was lax in the control of employees. However, he also admitted that the floating debt problem was serious. He had relied on Kidder, Peabody & Company and on Baring Brothers for financial aid. The collapse of the Barings had blocked this avenue of relief, and the refusal of the Drexel, Morgan firm and of Vanderbilt to come to the U. P.'s aid had sealed another. Under these conditions, Adams claimed, attacks by Gould on the road and its management left him no recourse but to resign.[55]

Taking a more unsympathetic viewpoint, Boston financier F. H. Prince thought that Adams' cardinal error was in not properly timing the sale of bonds.[56] Adams indirectly and partially admitted the justice of the criticism. Of his inability to meet the floating debt of some $10,000 000 he was reported to have said: "Had we sold our bonds we would have been all right, or had our earnings been large we could have carried our debt easily, or perhaps sold some of our bonds by reason of our large earnings, but the combination of bad earnings and of bad bond market was a double blow." [57]

Adams left the incoming Gould administration with a slightly larger floating debt than the one he had inherited in 1884. Although he had worked diligently in the interim, the Bostonian had not overcome the burdensome legacy, financial and governmental, that the preceding administration had left. By his own admission, however, eastern control of western operations had not been as strong as it should have been, and he admitted errors in selecting managerial personnel and in financing acquisitions. On the other hand, the growth of competition and the continuing uncertainty that characterized the U. P.'s relations with the government had provided an inauspicious background against which to reach sound decisions or to do long-range planning.

The Gould group also inherited a situation difficult to handle. Some progress was made up to 1893, but the general financial collapse of that year brought down the U. P. amidst the wreckage. Gould had died the preceding year, and Frederick Ames in September 1893. However, their sons remained associated with the road, as did the son of Elisha Atkins.

The Union Pacific and Economic Development

The Union Pacific, conceived as a project for national development but activated for military, political, and speculative purposes, had a major impact on the area that it opened to settlement and development. One rough measure is the expansion of mileage. Although the Union Pacific Railroad Company (the main line) only increased its operated mileage from 1,039 in 1869 to 1,821 in 1890, the Union Pacific Railway System (the company plus branches and feeders) increased operated mileage from 2,766 in 1880 to 7,563 in 1890.

Another measure of the U. P.'s impact is the trend in tonnage carried and the rates at which it moved. In the 1870's total ton-miles of freight carried by the company quintupled while rates decreased. During the next decade, as branch lines expanded, the number of ton-miles of freight carried by the system nearly tripled and rates continued to decline. As a result, much more traffic was carried for relatively less at the end of the period than at its beginning. Both the Union Pacific and the Kansas Pacific also disposed of a vast amount of land, which contributed to the area's development, but from the companies' standpoint the direct proceeds from land sales were minor, compared to freight receipts.[58]

By an ingenious system of calculation, Robert W. Fogel has estimated the social benefits accruing from the construction of the Union Pacific. Employing the theory of rent, he was able to figure the increase in national income, aside from the U. P.'s receipts, "due to the opening up of lands in states through which the railroad passed." Using the strip of land extending forty miles on each side of the Union Pacific from Omaha to Ogden for this purpose, Fogel found that its value in 1880, given the labor and capital of that year, would have been $5,800,000 in the absence of the railroad. With the railroad, its value was $158,500,000 (in 1869 dollars). The increase in national income for 1880 due to the presence of the railroad came to $15,630,000. Adding the net earnings of the U. P., Fogel estimates that between 1870 and 1880 the annual social rate of return on the capital expended for construction ranged from 15.3 to 42.3 per cent, with a decadal average of 29.9 per cent. And these estimates, for lack of data, do not include savings to shippers, to the government, and to other elements in the economy affected directly or indirectly by the existence of the railroad.[59]

While these estimates suggest only roughly the order of magnitude of economic gain attributable to the U. P., they indicate that the government was indeed justified in aiding the road's construction. That this aid might have been extended in different ways and in different forms, resulting in a more efficient use of capital, public or private, is also beyond question. But it is also beside the point. Given the political system of the United States, the allegiance to private economic decision making, the wartime situation, and the lack of prescience that existed in the early 1860's, the plan that was actually adopted in financing the construction of the U. P. was as logical as any of the proposed alternatives involving private enterprise. Indeed, it was more logical than one that would have assigned primary responsibility to the government.

The particular plan of government aid that was actually adopted provided the framework for the private investment decisions that created the Union Pacific. The Boston investors who became involved with the railroad's construction phase may have initially been interested only in short-run profits from that work. Nevertheless, a number of them and their descendants remained active in the management and ownership of the company as extensive economic growth gave way to intensive economic development. While their abilities, personalities, investment philosophies, and commitments naturally varied, these investors as a group became more concerned with realizing the long-run developmental possibilities of the U. P. than Thomas Durant and Jay Gould; on the other hand, these two men respectively devised much of the basic strategy of construction and of expansion.

The fact that the Union Pacific aided the development of the area it served by opening it to settlement and by providing transportation at a constantly decreasing cost was not, as Charles Francis Adams pointed out, the product of altruism; the rise of competition left the management with little alternative but to meet it. The inherited costs with which they were saddled and those that they chose to assume to meet new threats, however, made the Union Pacific a highly unstable investment. This characteristic in turn fostered speculation which increased the instability.

Throughout this period, the government's role was a further unstabilizing influence. Instead of treating the Union Pacific as an agency of economic development, government officials seemed to regard it as a faithless partner in a business "deal." In part this attitude was a reaction to the behavior of those who constructed the road as a business "gamble." The gamble was neither completely lost nor won. The Union Pacific ruined Oakes Ames and disillusioned Charles Francis Adams, but they and other Boston investors in the system contributed materially to altering the landscape of the American West and increasing the productivity of that region and of the nation.

Chapter 13

The C. B. & Q., 1874–1890: Completion of the System

THE EVOLUTION of the Chicago, Burlington & Quincy system in the era from 1874 to 1890 was in many respects typical of other major western roads. Extension westward continued at different rates, but the specific directions and dimensions of this expansion reflected not only appraisals of economic growth possibilities but offensive and defensive moves to counter competing roads. As a result, the problems of living with competition — by attempts at conciliation and cooperation or by vigorous infighting — assumed an importance that overshadowed many of the earlier problems of western railroads.

As systems enlarged, so did the range of factors affecting individual investment decisions. This meant that personal investment policy had to be flexible. Though a major investor's basic policy might still be developmental in orientation, he might have to act opportunistically in dealing with situations over which otherwise he would have no control. For example, it was necessary for railroad strategists to anticipate and react to competitors' moves, even though the results provided only tactical, short-run advantages. Also, the size of major railroad companies made widespread public ownership and the use of financial intermediaries increasingly important, and the institutionalizing of financial functions in turn diminished to some degree the influence that any one element of ownership, even a John M. Forbes, could exercise. In short, the growing complexity of the railroad industry resulted in a sharper cleavage between the functional role of railroad ownership and that of participation in strategic entrepreneurial and managerial decisions; yet the exercise of any one of them had important repercussions on the others.

The C. B. & Q. had to face these demands of the new era along with a host of other roads, but the particular way in which it reacted was the product of important decisions by Boston investors and their representatives in management. Therefore this chapter analyzes changes in that group, the pattern that they gave to continued expansion of the C. B. & Q., the financial structure and policies they developed, and the significance of these changes for the economy of the region served by the C. B. & Q. system.

Realignment of the Forbes Group

The different investment approaches represented in the Forbes group had been revealed in the first flush of the postwar railroad boom. Joy and Thayer had led part of the group into north-south roads from which Forbes could see little benefit to the C. B. & Q. system. His concern was with protection and development of the main line, and he could not see the advantage of sacrificing this policy to the uncertainties of short-run opportunistic investment in the roads running south through Kansas, no matter how glowing their immediate prospects appeared. The Joy group therefore proceeded into the new area of investment without the encouragement or financial support of John M. Forbes. It was a path that eventually led to an open break in the relations of the Michigan promoter with the Boston capitalist.

One of Joy's major contributions to the C. B. & Q. was a plan for assisting the construction of roads which might become rivals and in the process converting them into allies. In its simplest terms this plan put the C. B. & Q.'s credit behind these new roads by agreements to buy their bonds with a certain percentage (usually 40 per cent) of the revenues from traffic that they sent over the C. B. & Q. As Joy put it in a letter to John Newell of the Illinois Central, "In other words, we make a perpetual treaty of alliance to work together, and thus we have a friend and ally, instead of a rival." [1] This procedure became standard for the C. B. & Q.,[2] but its specific application in the early 1870's brought to the final breaking point the split that had developed in the ranks of the Forbes group.

The roads in question were the Chicago, Clinton & Dubuque and the Chicago, Dubuque & Minnesota, projected to run end-to-end up the west bank of the Mississippi River from Clinton, Iowa, to Minneapolis and St. Paul. These so-called "River Roads" promised to be useful feeders for the Chicago traffic of the C. B. & Q., but there was also the possibility that their business would be lost to competing systems.

The key person in this particular situation was J. K. Graves, a Dubuque businessman of many interests who was president of the two railroad companies and also of the Iowa-chartered construction company that was to build them. As was the case in many other roads, the construction company was to build the road and take its stocks and bonds in payment. The opportunistic character of the enterprise was noted by Joy in a letter to Nathaniel Thayer in 1875: "The hope doubtless, and the expectation of making a profit induced men to take stock in a Construction Company, who would not subscribe to stock in the Railroad Company where they would pay par for stock, and the chance for profit was less . . . "[3] In microcosm it was the old story of Credit Mobilier and the Union Pacific.

A group of large C. B. & Q. stockholders, led by Joy, took a majority of the stock in the construction company. The purpose, so Joy later said, was to preserve the C. B. & Q. policy of controlling roads with which it had traffic contracts. In addition to Joy, the Burlington's directors who also became directors of the construction company were John W. Brooks, John N. Denison, Sidney Bartlett, and John A. Burnham — the last three being associates of Joy and Thayer in the Kansas roads.

As in the case of Credit Mobilier, the construction company became a channel for the distribution of stocks and bonds issued by the railroads. For the Chicago, Clinton & Dubuque, the construction company provided $140,000 in return for railroad securities and a land grant of 38,000 acres.[4] Investors in the C. B. & Q., accepting their directors' endorsement of the River Roads, took some of the railroads' bonds. Forbes later claimed that he and J. N. A. Griswold had approved the sale to C. B. & Q. stockholders without knowing that their associates were intimately connected with the construction company.[5]

From 1871 to 1873 the C. B. & Q. stood solidly behind the construction work on the River Roads, lending short-term capital to Graves to get on with the job.[6] Denison was the most conservative of the C. B. & Q. "insiders" in the construction company, and by early 1872 he was becoming alarmed at the abandon with which Graves was spending money. "We ought never to put our money into another man's hands without constant supervision and control," he wrote Joy.[7] James M. Walker,* a New Hampshire-born Chicago lawyer, who had succeeded Joy in the C. B. & Q. presidency, appeared not to be so concerned. He wrote to Brooks in October 1872: "So far as I can judge our programme is being strictly carried out as arranged in Boston." [8]

By mid-1873, however, Forbes was becoming skeptical about Walker, whose selection as C. B. & Q. president had been backed by Thayer and Joy. In June 1873 Forbes wrote to John C. Green, "I was never in favor of replacing Joy, a 1st class lawyer, by Walker a 2nd class one." [9] In July he wrote: "We know next to nothing and we trust the administration of this mammoth enterprise 1000 miles off to a man [Walker] who has no experience in the details of R.R. business, and who represents at least two other companies whose interests *may be* conflicting . . . " [10] When Forbes discovered that the C. B. & Q. had advanced the money to pay interest on the River Roads' bonds, his mounting suspicion that something was wrong was confirmed. The panic of September 1873 brought these roads to the brink of disaster, and tardily Forbes hurried to the West for a first-hand investigation of the situation.

Forbes's worst fears were soon confirmed. According to the opinion he formed, Graves had been "loose in his notions of administration, loose beyond the imagination of the ordinary mind to conceive of." [11] It appeared that Graves as railroad president had been paying himself in his capacity as president of the construction company without accounting to anyone. Graves admitted this fact and also that the construction company's assets, except for a part of the land grant, had been expended while the roads were yet unfinished. Subsequently it was discovered that the contract for building the roads relieved the construction company from responsibility for completing them after it had used up its money.[12] Furthermore, whatever earnings there were went to the construction company instead of to bondholders.[13]

Reflecting his sense of personal financial responsibility for the enterprise, Forbes felt that the directors of the C. B. & Q., including himself, should make some reparation to investors for the damage that had resulted from this contract. He was outraged by what he regarded as a betrayal of his trust and the interests of C. B. & Q.

* Walker was also president of the Kansas City Stockyards Company, indicating the close ties that the concern had with railroads and Boston capital.

stockholders. Reviewing the event, he wrote Joy in 1875: "I then found to my *utter* surprise that you and all the other active directors upon whose judgment I had relied were interested in contracts for building the roads . . . that you were practically sellers of the bonds to us outside the ring, and that they and all the assets of the company had belonged to you as contractors — on such terms that with ordinary care you ought (in *my* judgment) to have made among you over a million of dollars by the bargain." [14] Although Forbes attempted to reach a satisfactory arrangement with his "friends" involved in the construction company fiasco, he was unsuccessful. Therefore in early 1875 he decided to purge them from the C. B. & Q. board.[15]

In this major contest, John N. A. Griswold was Forbes's trusted ally. On February 14, 1875, a few days before a meeting of disgruntled Dubuque bondholders was to convene in Boston, Forbes outlined alternative courses of action to Griswold. President Walker of the C. B. & Q. had not been directly involved in the Dubuque contracts; he would be offered an opportunity to join the Forbes group. But if he stayed, responsibility for railroad operations would be put in the hands of a vice president. In Forbes's view, Burnham, Joy, and Thayer had to go. The remaining question was whether Brooks or Bartlett, both of whom had been in the construction company, should be dropped from the board.* Although Forbes was greatly irritated with Brooks, he preferred to have him, rather than Bartlett, remain as a director.[16]

In a discussion of the report of an investigating committee, Forbes and Joy got into a heated controversy. Forbes declared that the contract in question was the most atrocious one he had ever seen or heard of in the railroad business and he denied that he had had knowledge of it when he had endorsed the River Roads' bonds. Joy protested his good faith and that of Burnham, Bartlett, Thayer, Hunnewell, Brooks, and Denison in their association with the construction company. He asked, "What better evidence of our sincerity can there be possibly given to any body of bondholders than that we have not only taken our share of the bonds [as C. B. & Q. stockholders], but that we have taken outside and lost $240,000,

* The C. B. & Q. directors as of 1872 were Erastus Corning, John C. Green, Sidney Bartlett, John W. Brooks, John A. Burnham, John N. Denison, Nathaniel Thayer, Robert S. Watson, James F. Joy, Chauncey C. Colton, James M. Walker, and John M. Forbes.

which we have put in for the purpose of helping the enterprise along?" Joy referred to the stock as a "barren" investment, but Forbes interjected that the land involved (which was sold at $3.00 to $6.00 an acre) did not fit this characterization. It was a dramatic scene between two men who had worked closely together for thirty years and now found that their attitudes toward investment and the responsibilities of management clashed beyond hope of compromise.[17]

Since the meeting of bondholders produced no satisfaction for Forbes, he determined on a proxy fight against Joy at the C. B. & Q. meeting on February 24, 1875. With the aid of his son, William H. Forbes, and John N. A. Griswold, Forbes was victorious in this contest, though his group did not succeed in placing all its candidates on the board until the following year. Burnham and Joy were ousted and replaced by Charles J. Paine of Boston, W. J. Rotch of New Bedford, and Griswold. Brooks and Bartlett survived the purge.[18] In 1876, however, Denison's name disappeared, as did Thayer's and Colton's. They were succeeded by Thomas Jefferson Coolidge of Boston, and Peter Geddes and Robert Harris of Chicago. President Walker was downgraded to general solicitor. Harris, who had been general superintendent of the C. B. & Q. since 1865, moved up to the presidency, and Charles E. Perkins became operating vice president.[19]

Thus 1875 was a turning point in the management of the C. B. & Q. It had taken Forbes three years to repair the damage that resulted from his failure to keep close check on the system. However, his sense of ethics was vindicated and his goal that the C. B. & Q. should be in the hands of competent and reliable managers, who placed the long-run welfare of the system above short-run opportunities for personal profit at its expense, was brought closer.* More importantly, the old Forbes-Joy-Brooks combination which in thirty years had pushed rails from the western border of New York state to Nebraska — and produced through routes from New York City to the West via Chicago, Council Bluffs, and Kansas City — was

* Forbes wrote Brooks November 12, 1875, "We all agree we needed more R. Roadmen in the concern. On the Board here in the East we have absolutely none if we count you out as for your sake we ought to do when it comes to work. We have plenty of law, finance etc. but no R. Road skill whatever." (Quoted in Thomas C. Cochran, *Railroad Leaders, 1845–1890: The Business Mind in Action* [Cambridge, Massachusetts, 1958], 335.)

broken. A new generation of managers, personified by Charles E. Perkins, began to take over responsibility for integrating and operating the system that the old team had created.

Gould Forces the Issue of Expansion

The C. B. & Q. had pushed westward along the line projected by Forbes and his associates in the 1860's. As of January 1, 1873 the B. and M. R. (Iowa) and the C. B. & Q. subsidiary lines in Illinois were formally merged into the Chicago, Burlington & Quincy Railroad Company. The Burlington and Missouri River Railroad in Nebraska was not formally joined to the system until 1880. It had reached a connection with the Union Pacific at Kearney Junction, Nebraska in 1872 and during the remainder of the decade the Nebraska road acquired five feeders which connected the original line with points on the Platte River and on the Kansas border, including a branch to Atchison.

The B. and M. R. in Nebraska and its Boston backers, however, found themselves confronted with a powerful antagonist in Jay Gould. As we have seen, when Gould in 1874 assumed a leading role in the Union Pacific, he proceeded to utilize his power to the disadvantage of the competing Kansas Pacific and the B. and M. R. The Union Pacific discriminated against the K. P. on shipments coming from or going to points west of Cheyenne, and the B. and M. R. in Nebraska suffered from the same type of discrimination at Kearney.

The future of the Nebraska road thus became a matter of concern to leading C. B. & Q. officials who, as individuals, owned its controlling shares. In 1875 they protested without success against the practice of the U. P. and then, along with the K. P., turned to Congress for relief. No satisfaction was obtained, and in 1877 a majority of the board voted to lease the B. and M. R. in Nebraska to the U. P. However, the opposition of the powerful team of Forbes and Griswold was sufficient to table this proposal, which would have played directly into Gould's hands.[20]

While there was trouble at the western end of the C. B. & Q. system, there was some comfort in the situation that existed between the Missouri River and Chicago. At Council Bluffs, three major systems — the Rock Island, the North Western, and the Burlington

— shared the U. P. traffic. To live with this situation they had formed the "Iowa Pool" in 1870 and agreed to divide Omaha-Chicago business equally. The pool functioned with surprising success, but it was an arrangement which could easily be disturbed by an aggressive promoter and strategist like Gould.

Disappointed in his effort to lease the B. and M. R. in Nebraska and angered by efforts of the C. B. & Q. to force the U. P. to prorate its tariffs on traffic interchanged with the Nebraska road, Gould threatened reprisals. While Forbes tended to be conciliatory, Perkins refused to be intimidated. He saw the need to move beyond alliances with other roads to a program of aggressive construction and purchases.[21] From 1877 to 1882 a test of strength pitted Perkins against Gould. As already noted, Gould failed to break the C. B. & Q. by attacking its position in the Iowa Pool, but by 1880 he had succeeded in merging the Union Pacific and Kansas Pacific, posing a major threat to the Burlington.*

While Gould was thus setting the broad contours of western railroad competition, the C. B. & Q. was reorganizing and strengthening its management structure. Following the ouster of Joy in 1875, the separation between finance and operation was clarified. The executive and finance committee (J. N. A. Griswold, John M. Forbes, Sidney Bartlett, and Charles J. Paine) was relieved of direct operational responsibilities by the creation of a western executive committee (J. M. Walker, Robert Harris, C. E. Perkins).[22]

Meantime, the acquisition of branch lines proceeded apace in Iowa and Illinois as well as farther west. Explaining the conflicting considerations affecting policy in this area, the directors in 1876 declared: "The true policy of the Company undoubtedly should be against extensions or additional branches, and this will be adhered to so long as may be without serious detriment to the property." On the other hand, they pointed out: "In a new country, such as is traversed by our Road, especially in Iowa, and with Roads in embarrassed circumstances coming upon the market at prices so largely below the cost of construction, an absolutely passive policy would seem to be unwise."[23]

Among the more important acquisitions of this period was the St. Louis, Rock Island & Chicago Railroad Company, which ex-

* In March 1880 the *Commercial & Financial Chronicle* (XXX [March 27, 1880], 308) estimated that Gould controlled about one tenth of the railroad mileage in the United States.

tended from the Chicago and North Western line near Sterling, Illinois to St. Louis, crossing the main line of the C. B. & Q. in five places. The lease of this road in 1876 helped to stabilize rates and gave the C. B. & Q. an entrance to St. Louis. In addition to linking the Upper Mississippi Valley with that city, it provided the C. B. & Q. with access to the South for traffic coming from Council Bluffs and more western points on the B. and M. R. in Nebraska.[24]

Although the leading investors in the Chicago, Burlington & Quincy by 1880 controlled a well-integrated system that extended from mid-Nebraska to Chicago and St. Louis, Forbes had proceeded conservatively. In early 1879, for example, he had noted the upturn in western business and its significance for further expansion, but he declared, " . . . we must limit ourselves strictly to *the unquestionable wants* of our Road, and to its means of payment." And he restated a familiar policy of expansion, "Our policy has been, and is, to avoid any possible outlay of money so long as we are justified in doing so, while taking broad views of the future as well as of the immediate interests of the company." [25] Forbes again expressed a familiar philosophy when he wrote in the 1878 C. B. & Q. report, "The point to aim at is one in which our interests are identical with those of the people around us . . ."

But these generalized developmental views clashed with the hard reality of Gould's maneuvering. The New York promoter was forcing the pace, and the C. B. & Q. had little recourse other than to meet his challenge, though Forbes moved reluctantly. On December 27, 1879, for example, Charles E. Perkins, general manager of the B. and M. R. in Nebraska and a vice president and director of the C. B. and Q., wrote: "Gould is determined to keep us out of Denver if he can, and questions are certain to come up in the discussion with him, which the B. & M. and C. B. & Q., if they remain single, may, indeed I fear must, disagree about." [26] The following year the Nebraska road was merged into the larger system to eliminate this danger.

Young Perkins had been urging on Forbes the need for aggressive action, but the old China trader was still not anxious to get into the Kansas City nexus of roads which his early associates had put together thirteen years before. "I want to see our main line through and local lines strengthened — rather than exhaust ourselves too much to the S. West," he wrote in July of 1879.[27] But times and competition had changed. Perkins pointed out in November 1879: "If we don't get it [the Council Bluffs road] Gould will or the Rock Island will or the Alton will — and we have got to consider the effect of any such purchase on us." [28] Two days later he again emphasized the urgency of action, writing to Forbes: "The process of grouping into systems is going on faster than I supposed it would . . . We cannot take these Roads without taking some risks of course, but it may be a question of whether we do not take more risk if we let them go into the hands of powerful rivals." [29] It was an interesting correspondence. Forbes was dragging his feet while his young relative used the same type of arguments that Forbes himself had once advanced with equal vigor about roads in Illinois and Iowa twenty-five years before.

Although Forbes preferred alliances to consolidations,[30] the first major step to meet Gould's challenge was to consolidate the B. and M. R. in Nebraska into the C. B. & Q. This proposal was ratified on February 28, 1880, and added 836 miles of operating railroad and 109 miles of new construction to the C. B. & Q. system.[31]

With the consolidation of the Nebraska company, the posts of C. B. & Q. general manager and vice president, both of which Charles E. Perkins had held since 1876, were separated. Under him as vice president were placed two general managers, one for lines east of the Missouri River, the other for lines west of it. This change reflected the growth of the system. Between 1874 and 1880 mileage operated by the C. B. & Q. had increased from 1,268.25 to 2,511.74.[32]

The die had been cast for the C. B. & Q. to compete and expand vigorously. In 1880 the directors also took steps to secure control of the Kansas City, St. Joseph & Council Bluffs road, which would in some measure offset Gould's recent acquisition of the Missouri Pacific. But they were now reacting to pressures that did not permit adherence to a long-run developmental plan.

Before the end of 1880 further management changes signalized the new strategy. John M. Forbes, dissatisfied with Harris, had taken over the C. B. & Q. presidency himself in 1878. Now, however, he stepped down from that post and was succeeded by Perkins.[33] It was with genuine regret that he faced the inescapable fact that the C. B. & Q. had to meet Gould on the latter's terms. He wrote Frederick L. Ames in September 1880, "I want peace but I see breakers ahead." [34]

Perkins was ready for a fight. He wrote Forbes: "If I were as rich as Vanderbilt, and owned half of the C. B. & Q. I think I should fight Mr. Gould now & *whip him* but I don't know that the mass of C. B. & Q. stockholders would favor it." He added: "It is quite obvious also that our Atchison friends are very anxious not to have us extend into Colorado and Kansas because they fear it would wean us wholly away from them, and no doubt the Atchison element among our stockholders and Directors would strongly favor a compromise." [35]

During the remainder of 1880 and early 1881 there were various efforts to reach some kind of settlement between the C. B. & Q. and Gould's roads. The decision to extend the C. B. & Q.'s line to Denver hinged on whether or not Gould's Wabash and the Union Pacific would cease efforts to invade Burlington territory east of the Missouri. A territorial agreement was made between these roads in October 1880, and an uneasy peace prevailed for a time. In June 1881, however, the news that Gould was preparing to extend the Missouri Pacific (which was not a party to the territorial agreement) as far as Omaha ended the truce. Though the U. P.'s Boston directors had protested Gould's move, pointing out it was certain to bring retaliation from the C. B. & Q. and invasion of U. P. business at Denver, their arguments were in vain. Perkins was equally adamant that the C. B. & Q. must go through to Denver. There was no turning back from the decision that had elevated Forbes to chairman of the board and placed Perkins in the presidency to pursue a policy of aggressive action.[36]

On September 28, 1881, C. B. & Q. stockholders in a special meeting ratified several important strategic decisions that had grown out of these developments. The first was to extend the main line to Denver. The second was to acquire by lease or purchase the Burlington & Southwestern (organized in 1880 as the Chicago, Burlington & Kansas City), which ran from Laclede, Missouri, on the Hannibal and St. Joseph to a connection in Iowa with the C. B. & Q.'s Keokuk line. The purpose of this move was to frustrate the dual threats that the Hannibal, in which Gould had acquired significant influence, might build from Quincy to Chicago, and that the C. B. & K. C. might be extended into Kansas City.[37] Clearly the Hannibal, whose early development owed so much to the Bostonians who later abandoned it, was now assuming major importance in the strategic power plays of the new era.

The extension to Denver was completed and opened for service on May 29, 1882. Over its own rails, the C. B. & Q. then offered through service between Denver and Chicago and shared transcontinental traffic between Denver and the Midwest.

The important results of extension west of the Missouri were reflected in freight earnings from a wider area of staple crops, which were still the mainstay of C. B. & Q. traffic. Despite a poor crop-year in Illinois, Iowa, and northern Missouri, earnings for 1882 were up. Perkins observed in the annual report for that year: "Our loss of business east of the river has been more than made up by the large gain west of the river, not wholly due to additional mileage, but in part to the growth of the country generally, which has had good crops and is steadily increasing in population and wealth." [38] The C. B. & Q., while reacting to pressures from opportunistic promoters like Gould, was still serving and profiting from western economic development.

Ironically, the final tactical move of the early 1880's was to acquire the Hannibal and St. Joseph which the C. B. & Q. had relinquished a decade earlier. It was no longer possible, as Forbes had earlier done, to ignore the Southwest to which the Hannibal gave access. The growth of that region and of Kansas City, which Joy had foreseen but over-anticipated, demanded recognition. In September of 1880, therefore, a traffic agreement was concluded between the C. B. & Q. and the Hannibal, which the president of the latter believed would add $400,000 a year to his road's revenues.[39] In June 1883 the Hannibal became once and for all part of the C. B. & Q. system. In the words of Charles E. Perkins, "The acquisition of the Hannibal & St. Joseph Railroad was believed to be the best solution to the Southwestern question, and it places us in a strong position at Kansas City, the great and growing commercial centre of that region." [40]

During the remainder of the decade the C. B. & Q. extended in several directions. In 1886 the Chicago, Burlington & Northern was opened to tap the spring wheat and lumber traffic at Minneapolis–St. Paul and to bring those products to Chicago over rails controlled by C. B. & Q. By the end of the decade a new line had been completed across Nebraska to Cheyenne, Wyoming and another had been thrust into South Dakota. Ultimately, in 1894, this branch was extended to a connection with the Northern Pacific at Billings, Montana, giving direct access from points in the Northwest to the major centers served by the C. B. & Q. in the central part of the country.

The Financial Aspects of C. B. & Q. Expansion, 1874–1890

Between 1874 and 1890 the C. B. & Q. system had grown from one operating 1,268 miles of railroad to one with 5,216 miles. Expansion was virtually a condition of survival in this highly competitive era, and it was expensive. This fact is reflected in the financial history of the C. B. & Q. In 1874 capital stock stood at about $26,-600,000 and funded debt was nearly $21,000,000; by 1890 capital stock had tripled and funded debt had quintupled.[41] In 1890 there were over 11,000 individual shareholders, more than half owning 25 shares or less and only 244 owning 500 shares or more each.[42] As of September 1890 Bostonians held 485,903 shares (a decline of 8,588 since June 1889), New Yorkers owned 269,168 shares, and Chicagoans, 8,855.[43]

Most of the financing of this period centered on capital needed for construction. From 1860 to 1872 more funds were raised from stock issues than from bonds; from 1872 to 1874 bonds were predominant, reflecting a consolidated mortgage issued in 1873; from 1874 to 1886 stock and bonds about kept pace with each other, but after 1887 bonds exceeded stock.

Between 1863 and 1879 some 95,000 shares of new stock were issued by the C. B. & Q. In each instance (1863, 1864, 1869, 1871, 1878), the stock was offered to stockholders at par, and apparently none of it had to be sold initially on the open market. Between 1881 and 1884 an additional 14,207 shares were issued and sold to stockholders at par. Stock dividends were paid in the 1860's and in 1880. As various lines were merged into the C. B. & Q., their stock was exchanged for that of the parent road and retired.[44]

A major financial step of this era took place in the depression year of 1873. One third of the bonds secured by the $30,000,000 consolidated mortgage of that year was intended to finance construction in Illinois; the remaining two thirds was to meet other obligations, including maturing debt of branch lines. No provision was made in this reserve for construction in Iowa, where surplus earnings provided necessary funds. However, in the next five years only $2,490,000 obtained from the sale of the consolidated mortgage bonds was actually expended.[45]

Meanwhile, the directors had cause to re-examine their debt policy. Market evaluations of some C. B. & Q. bonds did not compare favorably with those of other high-grade securities. Part of this reaction, in Forbes's view, reflected the absence of a sinking fund for nearly 75 per cent of net funded debt. Also, the high rates of interest on C. B. & Q. bonds caused them to sell at a premium and kept them out of the portfolios of "Trustees and other conservative investors." [46] In view of this situation, the C. B. & Q. board decided in 1878 to raise money for the coming year by issuing new stock rather than by marketing more of the 7 per cent consolidated mortgage bonds of 1873.* [47] The following year, to meet construction costs in Iowa, a new mortgage issue was authorized bearing only 5 per cent interest.[48] This issue of $3,000,000 was bought by Drexel, Morgan and by Winslow, Lanier & Company of New York.[49]

Forbes was pleased with the financial picture as it stood in 1879. In his annual report, he declared: "Our accounts for the past few years show that with average crops, in a rapidly growing country, there is every promise of our being able to pay fair dividends upon the whole cost of our road. The rates at which we are doing our business are moderate, and the facilities which we are giving to both freight and passengers seem to be satisfactory to the public, while our rate of dividends is less than the average rate of interest at the West on good security, and very much less than the returns which enterprising men claim upon all investments involving risk."[50]

Forbes seemingly had no reason to revise his long-held view that the C. B. & Q. could be a profitable investment if it were managed soundly as a transportation agency. That policy, which had guided Forbes's personal railroad investments, had been explicitly recognized in the C. B. & Q.'s 1871 corporate report. It predicted that competition would inevitably increase and therefore location and economy of operations, coupled with improved facilities, would be the

* Apparently there were some doubts among board members as to the proper relationship between stock and bonds. In 1878 Forbes noted that John L. Gardner might make a good successor to President Walker but was "perhaps a little stiff in his notions as to proportions of debt and stock." (John M. Forbes to John N. A. Griswold, November 18, 1878, quoted in Cochran, *Railroad Leaders,* 336.)

key to future profits.[51] The fulfillment of this prediction, which C. B. & Q. managers consciously tried to validate, was reflected in the 1879 report. There Forbes pointed out that the gross earnings per ton per mile of that period would have fallen considerably short of paying operating expenses thirteen years earlier.[52]

The year 1880 marked not only the culmination of pressures forcing the C. B. & Q. to act aggressively to defend its territory but also the increased participation by investment bankers in raising capital to carry out these plans. John E. Thayer & Brother before 1865 and Kidder, Peabody & Company after that date had generally acted as transfer agents for C. B. & Q. stock. Kidder, Peabody had sold C. B. & Q. bonds in 1872 and 1873, but the consolidated mortgage bonds of 1873 and an 1875 issue to cover bonds acquired with the lease of the Albia, Knoxville & Des Moines were sold by public bid. Bonds issued for the St. Louis, Rock Island & Chicago in 1877 were sold through Morton, Bliss & Company of New York and London. Lee, Higginson also participated in this issue, for which the New England Trust Company was trustee. In 1880, William Endicott, Jr., an earlier associate of Forbes in the anti-slavery movement, later president of that bank, and associated with the Higginsons, appeared on the C. B. & Q. directorate. One of his functions was to supervise the financial operations of the C. B. & Q.[53]

Conditions of financing had changed greatly over two decades; more especially, reliance on financial intermediaries had increased. In 1863, for example, funds for extending track from Aurora to Chicago were raised by selling stock directly to existing stockholders. It was possible at that time to claim that purchase of stock was "the easiest, and to them [the existing stockholders] most agreeable mode of raising the money." No intermediaries were needed or employed. Stockholders who did not wish to subscribe for new stock were advised to dispose of their rights themselves.[54] As late as 1871 the urgent need for funds with which to double-track this route was met in the same manner.[55]

As the system increased in size, financing had moved from a personal to an institutional basis involving investment bankers, but John M. Forbes understandably wanted to preserve as much freedom of action as possible. In the early years he had personally mobilized capital for his railroad ventures, calling on friends, relatives, and business associates who relied on the ex-China trader's judgment and often on his personal guarantee. Even then, of course, the Thayer and Baring Brothers' banking houses had played an important, though not controlling, role. When financing of his railroads became too large an operation for an individual to handle, Forbes did not propose to surrender the job to a single investment banking house. He wrote Endicott in 1881, "We want two strings to our bow Europe & America and must not here be *tied* to one House." [56] This policy was apparently followed during the remainder of the decade. Bonds issued to finance the extension through Nebraska, for example, were handled by August Belmont; Lee, Higginson; Kidder, Peabody; Brown Brothers; and Berliner Handels Gesellschaft. As in preceding issues, the New England Trust Company was trustee.

Forbes continued to look on equity investment as an evidence of developmental interest in a road, but he also recognized that it increasingly offered an avenue to opportunistic manipulation by outsiders. In 1880, for example, William Vanderbilt bought 10,000 shares of C. B. & Q.[57] Apparently it was an investment of the type Forbes eschewed. Writing to John N. A. Griswold in May 1880, the Bostonian declared: "Vanderbilt or Gould have a great advantage over us in these stock operations — they can buy and sell millions of company stock as if it were their own. We have never done it. . . ." Reflecting what appeared to him to be the standards by which he would be judged in his own community for such actions, Forbes added, perhaps regretfully, "And while I agree that it might be legitimately done in this case under cover of the Council Bluffs trade I fear the effect of it, especially as I know how such operations have always been looked upon in Boston." [58]

Forbes regarded a common interest stock ownership between roads as a guarantee against such speculative raiding. In November of 1880, for example, he wrote President Roberts of the Pennsylvania Railroad to this effect, pointing out, "The solid R. R. companies want all the conservative influence against their raiding and speculating neighbors which such joint ownership tends to build up." [59]

But the old China trader still had a sense of humor and some of the opportunistic spirit that saved him from stodginess. In March 1881 he was writing in this less familiar vein: "I rather have a notion that there will not be a chance for more than one more stock dividend before bars and barriers are put up, and do not quite like the idea of doing it half way, the one thing is to water and pray, which we saints are doing." * [60]

The greatest increases of C. B. & Q. stock coincided with the consolidations and extensions of the early 1880's. Accompanying the B. and M. R. consolidation, there was a 20 per cent stock dividend. The purchase of stock and income bonds of the Council Bluffs road occasioned a further increase in stock. Two years later the issue of $7,895,000 of stock in connection with the extension to Denver, plus conversion of old bonds and a further 10 per cent increase in equity, brought total capital stock to slightly over $70,000,000.[61] Still, the road paid 8 per cent dividends regularly and had such a good reputation that its bond issues carrying a 4 per cent interest rate found a ready market.

Preference in new issues was given to existing stockholders. For example, the owner of 70 shares of C. B. & Q. stock received the right to subscribe to a $1,000 Denver Extension bond plus 10 shares of stock scrip for $1,000.[62] As a result of its rapid expansion, the C. B. & Q. in 1882 had the largest capital of any road except the major eastern trunk lines — the Pennsylvania, the New York Central, and the Erie.[63]

From 1878 through 1887 the C. B. & Q. paid its usual 8 per cent annual dividend, but in 1888 this figure slipped to 5 per cent, and in the following year to 4 per cent. Charles E. Perkins in the 1888 *Annual Report* stated: "After many prosperous years the Chicago, Burlington and Quincy Company has experienced a year of serious reverses." [64] After paying fixed charges and the 5 per cent dividend, the company had to meet, from accumulated surplus, a deficit of over $4,300,000. In part this situation resulted from a strike of engineers and firemen, but the impact of competition and federal and state regulation, which Perkins had vigorously opposed, also contributed to the setback.

The widespread ownership of C. B. & Q. stock as well as the small stockholders' personal image of the large corporation were revealed in a flood of letters directed to John M. Forbes. A widow wrote

* Perkins thought stock-watering legitimate. "It is not any dilution of real strength," he wrote Forbes in November 1880, "but rather increases borrowing power because people are apt to consider the relative amount of stock & debt." (Perkins to John M. Forbes, November 4, 1880. C. E. Perkins letters, 1880–1901, in possession of Richard C. Overton. By permission.)

about her distress caused by the cut in dividends. "I have always voted for you," she wrote, "and know of no other name to apply to for information." Another woman wrote that if she lost her investment in C. B. & Q. she would be left almost penniless. Forbes published these letters and his reply, which placed much responsibility on ill-advised legislation, in the Boston *Daily Advertiser* of January 25, 1889. In addition, he included Perkins' answer to a "large stockholder" who complained about reports by Interstate Commerce Commissioners that western roads were doing business at rates below cost.

Perkins' reply was a dissertation on the problems of railroad competition. In his view a road had to take whatever steps were necessary to secure business that would help to cover fixed costs. With an overabundance of roads, many of them having little economic justification, scrambling for traffic, railroad management had to meet the threat by cutting rates. "It was plain," he wrote, "that, if other roads paid commissions and otherwise bought business, the C. B. & Q. would be compelled to do the same thing, or fail to secure any share of the competitive traffic." Pooling provided a partial answer, but government intervention closed this avenue to peaceful coexistence of weak and strong roads. Perkins concluded, "You will see from what I have written that I regard the situation, rather than the managers of the railroads, as to blame for the existing state of things . . ." [65]

The impact of competition is shown by a comparison of the rates of the C. B. & Q. east and west of the Missouri. The average freight rate per ton per mile east of the river declined from $1.90 in 1874 to a low point of 79 cents in 1890. West of the river, however, the figure for 1880, the first year the B. and M. R. in Nebraska was part of the system, was $3.15 and for 1890 it was $1.49.[66]

With declining rates, the volume of traffic rose until the troubled late 1880's. From 2,420,628 tons of freight carried by the system in 1874, there was a continued increase until a peak of 9,752,325 tons was reached in 1887. A sharp drop in 1888, reflected in the reduced dividend rate, was followed by a recovery in 1889 and a new peak of 11,201,874 tons in 1890.[67]

The various branches constructed by, or sought by, or forced on the C. B. & Q. had aided the system in maintaining its competitive position and over-all earnings, but they produced only a small direct

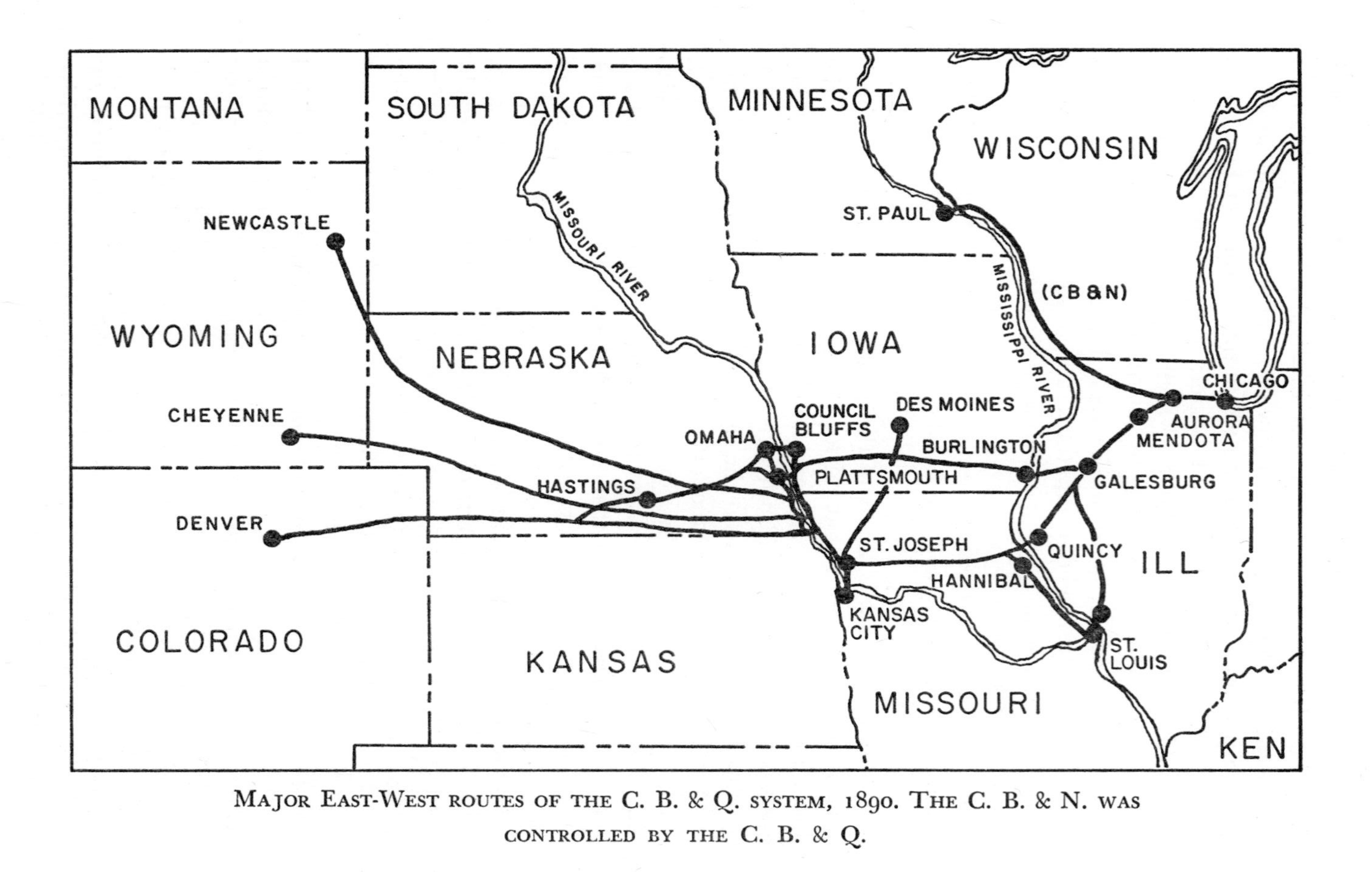

Major East-West routes of the C. B. & Q. system, 1890. The C. B. & N. was controlled by the C. B. & Q.

return on investment. The *Commercial & Financial Chronicle* praised the ability of the Burlington to maintain 8 per cent dividends, cover fixed charges, and add to surplus, but noted in 1887 that branch lines showed small direct returns. In fact, the only direct return on this $26,000,000 branch-line investment, which was part of the $100,000,000 increase in stock and debt in the course of a decade, was a 5 per cent dividend on Council Bluffs stock amounting to $263,075.[68] Nevertheless, the C. B. & Q. as a system had proved a profitable investment for those who had held their stock for the long term. From 1873 through 1890 it had paid a total of 84 regular cash dividends, most of them averaging at least 8 per cent annually, amounting to 271.75 per cent of the original capitalization of $85,357,123.[69]

In reviewing the operations of 1890, President Perkins condemned government intervention which forbade pooling and expressed the philosophy of the capitalists who had given shape to the systems he headed. He pointed out that "Railroad transportation is a commodity created by private capital for sale, and reasonable prices for it are such as tend to encourage trade in it, that is, the creation and sale of it by private capital, and the purchase of it by the public . . ."[70] But he also claimed that western railroad investment paid less than other western investments, a fact reflected — he thought — by the lack of western capital in western railroads.

Implicitly, Perkins seemed to be arguing that eastern capital invested in western railroads at rates below those obtainable in other western investments, had developed the West. This was a tenuous argument. To some extent, certainly, its validity hinged on the yardsticks used as a basis for comparisons. A lucky strike in western mining, for example, might bring an investor fabulous rewards, but as Boston investors in early copper mines had found, the odds were against even recovering their capital. The absence of large amounts of western money in western railroads is susceptible of many explanations, including a shortage of capital. The continued presence of large amounts of eastern money suggests that alternative uses of capital did not consistently offer a higher return. In the case of the C. B. & Q., at least, the steady 8 per cent dividend probably compensated investors as well as, if not better than, other western investments of comparable risk. And this, after all, was the objective of developmental investing.

The C. B. & Q. in Perspective

The C. B. & Q. system was rooted in the corn and spring wheat states of Illinois and Iowa. These staples formed the bulk of its eastern traffic, and for the first twenty years of its existence, which included the advent of transcontinentals, the C. B. & Q. concentrated primarily on developing traffic in these two states. The Burlington, for example, ranked second among railroads bringing corn to Chicago in 1872, transporting 20.82 per cent of the total received there.[71]

The managers of the C. B. & Q. deliberately put heavy emphasis on local traffic, which provided higher earnings than through movements per ton–mile. It is not surprising therefore, that most of the increase in the system's mileage until 1880 was in the form of branches. In the decade from 1863 to 1873 mileage operated by the C. B. & Q. more than doubled; in the next four years it more than doubled again, yet the road still had not been extended west of the Missouri. By 1882, after the consolidation of the B. and M. R. in Nebraska and the extension to Denver, mileage doubled once more.

During the rest of that decade the rate of expansion slowed, but mileage rose from 3,229 in 1882 to 5,217 in 1890. Much of this expansion, as we have already discussed, was in response to competitive pressures which forced the C. B. & Q.'s strategists to recognize the fact that comparatively slow sequential building, accompanied by development of local traffic, was no longer adequate to protect existing investment. Still, Forbes never dreamed of, nor sought, an empire of transcontinental proportions. As late as 1888 he wrote Perkins, "Thank Heaven the cup passed our lips however tempting. I hope the Adams apple [Union Pacific] and other Paradise fruits may not tempt us into the dream of universal empire." [72]

Such attitudes characterized not only the C. B. & Q.'s long-term strategy but the financial policy of its leaders. The point was well made by Charles E. Perkins in a letter of 1883 to William Endicott, Jr., explaining why the Burlington declined to buy into the Northern Pacific. "I consider that it would be better for the C. B. & Q. to pay a higher price later, when the real value of the property can be better known, than to go in now, at the present seemingly low price," he wrote on this occasion. "This has been the policy of the C. B. & Q.

in the past, and it is, undoubtedly, the conservative and probably sound policy." [73] Expansion for expansion's sake, or for securities manipulation, was not part of the C. B. & Q. philosophy.

Although C. B. & Q. management as early as 1855 had explicitly recognized the importance of through traffic, changing personnel did not change the fundamental principle that the system was a regional one and would stand or fall on that basis. In the words of Charles E. Perkins, "A railroad must, for its own sake, do all it can to build up the business of the region which it serves, to develop its markets and resources, in competition with the markets and the resources of other regions." [74] He was only stating in different words what J. W. Brooks had declared in June 1848 when, as superintendent and engineer of the Michigan Central, he wrote that it was the duty and the interest of the road "to promote the welfare and prosperity of that people, upon whose very prosperity rests the whole value of our enterprise." [75] It was this emphasis on the role of the railroad as a transportation agency, working to develop new territory and thereby to serve its own long-run best interests, that made it possible to finance expansion on favorable terms. Consequently, the interests of investors and of the areas served by their railroad interacted in ways that promoted growth, return on investment, and further expansion.

The C. B. & Q. helped to develop the states it served not only by providing transportation but by disposing of its land grants on a basis that encouraged settlement and the production of traffic. Forbes and associates, following the pattern set by the Illinois Central, also made private speculation in railroad lands a profitable supplement to their primary investment but without losing sight of the priority of relationships. This story has been well told by Richard C. Overton in his *Burlington West.**

If population increase is any index to economic development, the availability and reliability of railroad transportation provided by the C. B. & Q. in Iowa and Nebraska were important, particularly where the railroad was itself encouraging immigration by numerous means. In Iowa, for example, total population increased 36.1 per cent in the decade 1870–1880, but population per 1,000 acres along

* For land operations along the Hannibal and St. Joseph, see Howard F. Bennett, "The Hannibal and St. Joseph Railroad and the Development of Northern Missouri, 1847–1870: a Study of Land and Colonization Policies," (Unpublished Ph.D. dissertation, Harvard University, 1950).

the western half of the B. and M. R. in that state increased almost 100 per cent in the same period. In Nebraska, where total population in 1890 had still not reached that of Iowa twenty years before, the percentage increase per decade was very high — 267.8 per cent, for example, between 1870 and 1880.[76] The population per 1,000 acres on the B. and M. R.'s Nebraska lands south of the Platte River rose seven fold in the same decade. What these settlers did in terms of developing the territory served by the C. B. and Q. can be judged in the upward trend of freight moved.

It might be argued, of course, that any railroad system serving the area covered by the C. B. & Q. would have done as much, or even more, for economic development there. There is no way that this proposition can be adequately tested. Therefore, the best indication of the results of developmental investment must be what a particular railroad system actually did in the territory where it was placed by the decisions of men adopting a long-range viewpoint. This has been the concern of the present chapter and preceding ones on the C. B. & Q.

As a grain, livestock, and lumber carrier, as a route which connected and helped to develop such important regional centers as St. Louis, Kansas City, Denver, and Chicago, the C. B. & Q. by 1890 took its place as a leading American railroad. The C. B. & Q. as an investment, as a transportation facility, and as a factor in economic development reflected the Boston leadership that had guided key decisions over many decades. In 1890 Boston stock holdings still dominated the system which Boston capital, accumulated in world trade, had helped bring into existence. The C. B. & Q. indelibly bore the stamp of John M. Forbes's emphasis on integrity, sound management, and service as a source of profit. These were the qualities and values that had enabled the Forbes group to exert a constructive and profitable influence in the West for over half a century.

Chapter 14

The Atchison, Topeka & Santa Fe, 1870–1883: A New Response to the Transcontinental Challenge

ALTHOUGH BOSTON investors were extremely influential in the postwar development of both the Union Pacific and the Chicago, Burlington & Quincy, the Atchison, Topeka & Santa Fe was even more closely associated with Boston interests. In 1883, for example, some 547,000 of its 569,100 shares were held in that city, while for many years its securities were listed only on the Boston Stock Exchange.[1] The Atchison, moreover, was for some time the largest privately owned railroad in the world. By the end of 1887 it owned or controlled over seven thousand miles of track extending from Chicago and the Gulf coast to the Pacific shores of Mexico and California. And, in the nature of extensive systems, it passed through a wide variety of topographical and economic regions, each with its own peculiarities and its own transportation problems. This fact, together with the vicissitudes of its own development, meant that the company and its leading figures underwent business experiences which in many ways reflected the factors shaping many American railroad enterprises in the years after the Civil War.

In general terms, as happened with other railroad ventures, the final form and function of the enterprise differed markedly from the original expectations of the promoters and capitalists. And, again, it was the adaptation of expectations to the reality of new situations that produced the managerial changes underlying the transformation. More specifically, the Atchison's top management was pulled in two complementary directions. First, as with the prewar Illinois Central, under the pressure of circumstances, it had to extend both its commitment and its ambition. Second, as with the postwar C. B. & Q., it found that the increasingly complex web of competitive railroads in the West made it difficult to adhere to plans for orderly, sequential growth: offensive and defensive construction was increasely part of the postwar railroad picture.

The sheer size of the Atchison — in terms of both miles of track and geographical area served — was the outcome of an interplay between entrepreneurs and situation. Unlike the Union Pacific, the concept of a transcontinental system in this instance emerged only with time and changing circumstances; it was not a significant element in either the original planning or the original investment. The evolving situation encouraged and even necessitated a transition from opportunistic to developmental entrepreneurship.

In the process of the transition, the Atchison's management and principal owners seemed to combine the contrasting prewar policies of the Michigan Central and the Illinois Central. Like the former, they responded to the demands of strategy by transforming the road into an open-ended system, undertaking a cumulative extension along the line of its original construction. Like the latter, with an abundant land grant in a very fertile state, they could hardly fail to respond to the needs of intrinsic development by encouraging settlement and agricultural production in Kansas and by considerably extending trackage in the state.* Once again conflicting opportunistic and developmental objectives influenced the behavior of interested investors.

The Origins of the Atchison and the Emergence of Boston Control, 1859–1871

Boston capitalists made their preliminary entry into the Atchison at the end of the 1860's. Before that, even though a charter had been in existence since 1859, the road had been little more than an idea. As such, it was the brain child of Cyrus K. Halliday, an eastern-born Kansas pioneer and politician, and an active promoter of railroads and development, whose political resourcefulness and local support were not matched by his access to capital. Moved by a vision of a trans-state railroad over the old Santa Fe trail from Atchison to

* The implicit contrast with the Illinois Central which, prior to the Civil War, did not create an extensive system, presumably rests more on the different periods, rather than the different managements involved. In the postwar world, under postwar pressures, the Illinois Central did in fact expand into a north-south system of over 3,500 miles.

Topeka and thence to the western border of Kansas in the general direction of Santa Fe, New Mexico, Halliday had obtained, in 1863, a Congressional land grant equivalent to 6,400 acres per mile of line. The grant required the road to be completed from Atchison to the Colorado line within ten years; yet by June 1869 there existed only seventeen miles of track.[2]

The Atchison had its real beginning in the railroad boom which commenced in the late 1860's when the retarding influence of the Civil War was no longer felt and when Kansas itself was reasonably well populated.* As with most trans-Mississippi railroads at this time, it was apparently the prospect of obtaining cheap land that gave the road new life. In July 1868 Congress granted the company permission to purchase land of the Pottawatomie Indians at $1.00 per acre on six years' credit at 6 per cent, and some 340,000 acres were so acquired.

The fertile Pottawatomie lands were at that time eminently more attractive than the earlier land grant, for they were close to Topeka, and, because of the denser settlement in northeast Kansas, readily and quickly marketable. The land was therefore most useful as a source of ultimate income (it was sold at an average price of $5.00 an acre, on long credit) and more immediately as security for bond issues.

The group that undertook to push the Atchison forward in the late 1860's, although largely drawn from outside Kansas, contained a sprinkling of New Englanders. A construction company, the Atchison Associates, was organized, with its leadership in the hands of H. C. Lord of Cincinnati, A. E. Burnside of Rhode Island, and Henry Keyes of Vermont and Boston. Lord, who was a member of Dodge, Lord & Co., the contractors for the initial mileage, became president of the Atchison, Topeka & Santa Fe in September 1868, when the Associates had their first meeting. Henry Keyes, together with Emmons Raymond, also from Boston, obtained short-term financing for the road by borrowing on personal notes from Boston banks.

* In 1860 the state had only 107,000 inhabitants and in 1865 only some 140,000. But by 1870, when the Atchison's construction was properly under way, there were some 360,000 people in Kansas. (U.S. Bureau of Statistics, *Report on the Internal Commerce of the United States for the Fiscal Year 1889,* by William F. Switzler [Washington, D.C., 1889], 270.)

The decisive entry of Boston capitalists, however, appears to have come early in 1870 when the Associates withdrew because of financial difficulties. Early in that year construction was taken over from them by the Atchison, Topeka & Santa Fe.* Lord was replaced as president by Henry Keyes, who was president of the Connecticut & Passumpsic River Railroad (a Boston-controlled line in Vermont).** Boston's importance to the Atchison grew markedly: the head office was in Boston, and of the twelve directors besides President Keyes, who was listed as a Vermonter, three were from Boston — Emmons Raymond, Alden Speare, and Carlos Pierce. Another Bostonian, Charles W. Pierce was secretary and treasurer. A New Yorker, Henry Blood, was vice president.

Very shortly after he assumed the presidency, Henry Keyes died, and in September 1870 his place was taken by Ginery Twichell of Boston. Twichell (1811–1883) was a railroad man of some experience. He had been president of the Boston and Worcester from 1857 to 1867, and was to be president of the Atchison until 1873 and a director until 1877. He also served in Congress from 1867 to 1873. According to one contemporary source, Twichell had "the confidence of capitalists and R. R. men to as great an extent as any man in the country." [3]

At the same time (September 1870) the Boston house of Kidder, Peabody & Company became financial agents of the road.[4] This firm had been founded in 1865 as a direct outgrowth from and successor to John E. Thayer & Brother. The new organization was established by a partner of the older firm, Henry P. Kidder, and two employees, Francis H. Peabody and Oliver W. Peabody. They carried on a

* The balances from the Associates' books were not transferred to those of the railroad until May 1871, at which time it appeared that they had issued over $1,000,000 of stock and just over $900,000 of bonds. Some $750,000 had been expended on construction and almost $1,100,000 distributed in bonuses in connection with the sale of securities. They recorded a loss of over $80,000. See Interstate Commerce Commission, *Reports,* Vol. 127, Valuation Docket No. 625, "Atchison, Topeka & Santa Fe Railway Company" (Washington, 1927), 360–361.

** This railroad played a significant part in the early history of the Atchison. Besides Keyes (who was originally from Vermont), the following directors of the Connecticut & Passumpsic were also associated with the Atchison: Emmons Raymond (on the executive and finance committees of the Atchison and president of the Connecticut & Passumpsic by 1872), B. P. Cheney of Boston (Atchison director until 1876), and Thomas Upham of Boston (Atchison director in 1875). The first president of the Vermont road was Erastus Fairbanks, who was an important projector of the Sault Ste. Marie venture.

diverse business, and, like the China merchants before them, had established close and friendly relationships with Baring Brothers of London. They were to sustain an intimate connection with Atchison affairs for a generation. By 1871 the Boston interest in the Atchison — with Ginery Twichell, Francis Peabody, and Joseph Nickerson added to the directorate — was even stronger than it had been under Keyes.

Financing Expansion, 1870–1873

During these early years Atchison securities came onto the market in a limited number of ways. Following the earlier issues to the Associates, and contemporaneously with the entrance of major Boston investors into the road in 1870, Kidder, Peabody contracted to take $200,000 of stock and $1,150,000 of 7 per cent bonds in return for $880,000 cash. The investment bankers were to keep $50,000 of the bonds as commission, while selling the rest at a discount and using the equity as a bonus for bond purchasers.[5] In addition, a substantial amount of Atchison stock went to Kansas counties in exchange for county bonds, which were then given with railroad bonds as a bonus on private stock subscriptions. In fact, the largest issues up to 1873 were all sales of stock at par with large bonuses of bonds and notes. By such means, from 1870 to 1872, $6,855,000 cash was received in return for the issue of 68,550 shares — with which were given as bonuses: $5,787,000 of first-mortgage 7 per cent bonds, $2,960,000 of land-grant 7 per cent bonds, $531,000 of long-term 7 per cent notes, and $502,000 county and town bonds.[6]

The cash was spent to complete the road to the Colorado line, thereby qualifying for the federal land grant. After a slow start (a mere 137 miles had been constructed in 1870 and 1871) the goal was achieved by a crash program, involving a cost of some $600,000 more than had been anticipated. On December 28, 1872 the Atchison ran cars over the entire line from the Missouri River to Colorado.

Meantime, the road also belatedly joined the town of Atchison (on the Missouri) and Topeka. The company thereby secured direct access to the big lines east of the river, — the Hannibal and St. Joseph, the Rock Island, the Chicago, Burlington & Quincy, and the Missouri Pacific. The Atchison, Topeka & Santa Fe itself now had a main stem of 469 miles, and a branch line 28 miles long.

The rapidity of this physical expansion had outpaced even the extensive campaign to float additional securities. As capital was poured into construction in 1872, the floating debt grew to a dangerous size. By 1873 money could not be found to pay the interest on this debt, and twice in the course of that year bonds were issued at a 50 per cent discount and either exchanged against outstanding interest coupons or sold to fund the floating debt. At some cost, which was in part due to the unpropitious coincidence of the 1873 crisis, the Atchison finally obtained the means of payment for the trackage it had constructed in the previous year.

Boston Influence in the Atchison, 1873–1883

The spurt of construction in 1872 not only exhausted long-term funds, but led, through the need to relieve the ensuing financial strains, to the intensification of Boston's managerial dominance. In May 1873 Twichell and Blood were replaced as president and vice president, respectively, by Henry Strong, who had spent some years with the C. B & Q., and Thomas Nickerson of Boston. Twichell remained on the board, and Francis Peabody, the Boston banker, moved up to become chairman of the finance committee. The next year Nickerson was elected to the presidency and Peabody to the vice presidency. By 1873 ten of the fourteen directors were Bostonians.* It was Thomas Nickerson who solved the immediate problem by inducing the bondholders to buy new issues in order to pay off the dangerously large floating debt.[7]

In the 1870's the Atchison was closely associated in the public mind with the Nickerson family of Boston. Thomas Nickerson, born in 1810, entered western railroading late in his career. He retired from his mercantile business in 1875, and was president of the Atchison from 1874 to 1880. Even after his retirement from the parent company's presidency at age seventy he was president of three important subsidiaries: the Mexican Central (1880–1884), the Atlantic & Pacific (1880–1881), and the California Southern (1881–1884).Thomas Nickerson's brother Joseph was an Atchison

* Besides Thomas Nickerson, Peabody, Twichell, and Strong, there were: Joseph Nickerson, Isaac T. Burr, Alden Speare, B. P. Cheney, George W. Wilbur, and Charles W. Pierce (secretary and treasurer).

director until 1877, and another brother, Frederick, was a director of the Union Pacific. In 1883, three years after Joseph's death, the Nickerson family still had large holdings of Atchison stock.[8] In the mid-1880's a member of the second generation, Albert W. Nickerson, was the dominant figure on the board.

Thomas and Joseph Nickerson, in association with Kidder, Peabody & Company and other Bostonians, were responsible for the early, rapid surge of construction.[9] Apparently neither they nor the original promoters had conceived of the Atchison as a transcontinental road. While they planned to extend the line a considerable distance into Colorado and the Southwest, they apparently envisaged the road primarily as a large trans-state line. Even in this limited context, however, it had two outstanding locational advantages: its connection with the complex of lines and trade routes centering on the Missouri River at Atchison and at Kansas City; and its route through the most fertile areas of Kansas along the valleys of the Cottonwood and Arkansas Rivers, which generated abundant local traffic as settlement increased.

Counting on the Missouri River connection, the management expected great things of the cattle trade, particularly from Texas. The *Annual Report* for 1873 predicted that "The shipment of domestic cattle . . . must eventually form a very large portion of our business . . ."[10] But, in fact, the cattle trade never came to play its expected role. As Texas cattle found alternative ways to market in the 1870's, the Atchison, Topeka & Santa Fe emerged as a railroad quite different in character from one which could have relied on cattle shipments for a major part of its receipts.

The Atchison as a Developmental Agency in Kansas, 1870–1880

The length and location of the Atchison's line identified it with the leading agricultural products of Kansas — cattle and grainstuffs. The state's cattle production just about doubled between 1870 and 1880; the output of corn increased almost sevenfold, and wheat almost tenfold. By the end of the decade, with a population which had increased from 364,000 to almost 1,000,000, Kansas produced 109,917,000 bushels of corn and 23,400,000 bushels of wheat — which reflected a rate of increase exceeding that of Illinois in the

1850's.* Even at the beginning of the decade there were spectacular changes: between 1870 and 1874 the acreage under oats, corn, and wheat alone boomed from 871,000 to 2,760,000.[11]

The Atchison was bound to serve and develop an agricultural purpose in such a state. The road's *Annual Report* for 1875 stated that wheat was the surest and most valuable traffic.[12] In the next two years, however, corn overtook wheat. Eastern shipments of corn averaged 75,759,000 pounds in 1876 and 1877, while wheat averaged 71,817, 000 pounds.[13]

As with the Illinois Central at an earlier date, these changes in agricultural output were accompanied by conscious efforts on the part of the railroad's management to facilitate them. That is, the Atchison, Topeka & Santa Fe, on the basis of its land grant, operated as a development agency in Kansas during the 1870's and early 1880's.

Under the terms of the 1863 congressional land grant of 6,400 acres per mile of road between Atchison and Colorado, the railroad got just under 3,000,000 acres of land. Much of the land was concentrated in the fertile valleys of the Cottonwood and the Arkansas Rivers. Up to March 1872 about 74,250 acres had been sold, but the real boom started in 1873. The following table illustrates the gross sales, and declining prices, of the 1870's and 1880's.

The Atchison's management, while anxious to profit from land holdings in their corporate capacity, bent most of their efforts to sound and substantial settlement rather than short-run profit-taking. "We have a reasonable right to expect," wrote the president in the *Report* for 1873, "that with the development of the country, and the settlement of our lands, the business of the road will steadily increase." And, in comparison with the Kansas Pacific, for example, the Atchison was a far better land holder in local estimation. It took title to and paid tax on its lands earlier; it sold its lands more

* Kansas agricultural statistics are in Julian D. Morgan, *Some Controlling Factors in Kansas Population* (Lawrence, Kansas, 1953), 23, 34, 76. For Illinois: U.S. Census Office, 7th Census, 1850, *Abstract,* 89, and 8th Census, 1860, *Agriculture,* 35. The comparisons are as follows (corn and wheat output in bushels):

Factors	*Illinois: 1850*	*and 1860*	*Kansas: 1870*	*and 1880*
Population:	851,000	1,712,000	364,000	996,000
Corn production:	57,647,000	115,175,000	15,960,000	109,917,000
Wheat production:	9,415,000	23,837,000	2,418,000	23,400,000
Bushels of corn and wheat per capita:	78.8	81.2	50.5	133.8

TABLE 2. Land sales of Atchison, Topeka & Santa Fe Railroad, March 1, 1871—December 31, 1886.

Year	Acreage rounded to nearest acre	Average price (dol.)	Year	Acreage rounded to nearest acre	Average price (dol.)
1871	71,801	5.91	1879	104,744	4.72
1872	45,238	5.90	1880	78,241	4.98
1873	133,507	5.61	1881	50,033	5.22
1874	200,459	4.54	1882	189,830	4.71
1875	75,415	5.59	1883	431,755	3.56
1876	122,201	5.44	1884	353,090	3.36
1877	85,047	4.98	1885	770,494	2.66
1878	267,122	4.52	1886	347,321	2.44

Source: Paul W. Gates, *Fifty Million Acres: Conflict over Kansas Land Policy, 1854–1890* (Ithaca, New York, 1954), 271.

quickly and at lower prices; it had a more vigorous settlement policy; and it was more understanding of the position of settlers.[14]

Land Sales: Organization and Procedure

By this time the organization and procedures for selling railroad lands had become fairly standardized. The precedents established by the Illinois Central were followed by the Boston backers of roads affiliated with the C. B. & Q. and that experience was transferred directly to the Atchison through A. E. Touzalin, formerly land agent of the Burlington and Missouri River Railroad in Nebraska, who became commissioner of the Atchison's land department.

The Atchison's land sale campaign was familiar and effective. Commission agents were appointed in both West and East — by 1875 there were 23 local and 60 out-of-state agencies. A vast amount of literature singing the praises of Kansas was distributed in the United States. Within 14 months of the establishment of a London office in 1880, over 300,000 pamphlets were also distributed throughout Europe. Colonization meetings were organized and visits of journalists from Europe and from more settled parts of the United States were subsidized. Contacts were established with ocean shipping lines, and favorable rates of transportation were offered to people seeking land. Credit was liberally extended and a variety of purchase arrangements were offered to buyers, ranging from a 20 per cent discount for cash to the deferment of principal payments for four years and then a repayment of the 7 per cent loan over eight years.

Block sales were also employed to establish Mennonite colonies on Atchison land. Touzalin not only corresponded extensively with the leaders of Mennonite groups in Russia but in 1873 hired a specialist, C. B. Schmidt, to aid in this work. By these means 100,000 acres were sold to the Mennonites in 1874, and the railroad chartered a steamer to bring their household equipment across the Atlantic, shipped the cargo from Philadelphia at its own expense, provided free transportation of building materials for one year, and guaranteed aid in the event of any disaster. By 1883 some 15,000 Mennonites lived along the Atchison line.[15]

In the fall of 1874, when the first large groups began to arrive in Kansas from Russia, Kansas (along with other western areas) suffered from a drought followed by a devastating plague of grasshoppers which destroyed crops, drove livestock frantic, and frightened many settlers into moving back East. New settlers in the western corn regions, relying on their first crop for subsistence, were particularly hard hit. In the resulting relief measures, the Atchison, Topeka & Santa Fe played an important part by carrying all supplies, except grain and coal, free of charge, and carrying the latter at drastically reduced rates.[16]

In spite of the disaster, long-run growth trends were not affected. In the summer the land department organized an extensive tour by three hundred out-of-state newspapermen, and the public relations endeavor seems to have had a good effect in reasserting Kansas' attractions.[17]

That the company's land policy went beyond boosterism, extravagant advertisement, and grand gestures, was shown by other aspects of the colonization campaign. For example, six tracts, each of twenty acres, were set aside in 1873 to serve as experimental stations and to be shown to the large groups of potential settlers which were organized and conducted on tours of the road's lands.

As with the Illinois Central in the late 1850's, the average size of each sale was kept small to facilitate actual settlement and early production. The annual average sale between 1871 and 1879 varied in size between 114.97 and 164.79 acres, for a decadal average of 142.79.[18] The company was not so eager for sales that potential settlers were misled. It advised immigrants not to come without the financial means to tide them over the pioneering period. One pamphlet mentioned minimum capitals of at least $800 to $1000 for married men and $500 to $600 for single men. Even then, it warned, "it will require plenty of grit, hard work and rigid economy to get through the first year or two . . . If you are happy in the East, stay there . . . Living costs are moderately high [in Kansas]." [19]

Using these methods, the company forged ahead in the task of disposing of its land on a reasonably sound basis. By the end of 1885, a most successful year in which some 770,000 acres changed hands, the original land grant was nearly all sold.

Developmental Results of Land Sales

The Atchison became a powerful force for the development of Kansas during the 1870's. The counties through which the main stem ran had just under 6,000 farms in them at the start of the decade; the number had risen to just over 21,500 at its end. The increase of farms in the region west of Emporia — largely empty in 1870 — was, of course, more impressive: from 473 to 11,873. The significance of the Atchison is partially indicated by Table 3.

Table 3. Percentage growth rates in Kansas, 1870–1880.

Location	Population	Number of farms	Corn output	Wheat output
State	173	263	589	867
Counties along A. T. & S. F.	204	263	349	735
Counties along A. T. & S. F. west of Emporia	2,124	2,410	1,507	2,638

Source: University of Kansas, Bureau of Business Research, *Kansas Statistical Base Book* (Lawrence, 1954), 11, 87.

Of course, the Atchison was not the only railroad in Kansas. In the 1870's the state's total mileage expanded from 1,500 to 3,400 and by 1888, with about 9,000 miles of track running through all but five counties, Kansas had more miles per capita (5.5 per thousand population) than any other state in the Union or any country in the world.[20] "The railroad system," an official observer wrote in

1889, "has made it possible for the Kansas farmer to be a true agriculturalist, instead of a mere shepherd or herder. He and his brother Western farmers have driven the Eastern farmer out of wheat-growing and corn-raising, the fattening of pork, and the killing of beef, as a business." [21] Kansas, with its grain yield the highest in the country in the early 1880's, with almost 40 per cent of its acreage under corn in 1880, and its packing industry booming, was an outstanding example of the economic effects of the railroad.

From Kansas Line to Transcontinental System

Although the force of circumstances in the early and mid-1870's had turned the attention of the Atchison management inwards to the agricultural development of the regions through which their newly constructed line ran, it did not anticipate that the railroad would or could be entirely self-contained. The managers still entertained the idea of an "open-ended" system linking up with and extending into Colorado and even New Mexico. Between 1872 and 1879, however, only two significant additions were made to Atchison mileage. Slowly, operating through the Pueblo & Arkansas Valley Railroad, the Atchison interests pushed 150 miles into Colorado, reaching Pueblo and thereby tapping the tourist trade as well as the traffic in minerals, timber, wool, cattle, and hides. At the same time they also obtained access to Kansas City by leasing the 67-mile Kansas City, Topeka & Western Railroad — thus competing with the Kansas Pacific for eastbound traffic to that city.

In spite of the relative slowness with which these extensions were made, the bases for a new strategy were emerging. The Atchison, originated as a Kansas railroad line, was in the course of becoming a regional railroad system. Controlling over 700 miles of track, mostly on the rich soil of Kansas, the embryo system had a good strategic position for ultimate growth.

Until about 1877 there is no evidence that the chief figures in the Atchison, Topeka & Santa Fe envisaged more than a sectional role for their railroad: to connect the Missouri River and the Rocky Mountains would appear to have been the limit of their expectations. Nevertheless, in the course of the next ten years the railroad expanded both extensively and intensively to a remarkable degree. By 1882 it owned or controlled more than 2,600 miles of road. By the end of 1887 its trackage covered more than 7,000 miles and led, in the largest transcontinental system in America, from Chicago to the Missouri River and from the Missouri to the coasts of Texas, Mexico, and California.

The executive most directly associated with the transformation was William B. Strong, general manager and vice president from 1877 to 1881, and president of the company from 1881 until 1889. Like Touzalin of the land department, Strong had close ties with Bostonians of the Forbes group. After beginning his railroad career with the Chicago, Milwaukee & St. Paul and serving a stint with the Chicago and North Western, he had moved to the Chicago, Burlington & Quincy in 1870. In 1874 he became general superintendent of the Michigan Central and the next year moved back to the Burlington, where he stayed until he joined the Atchison in 1877. Thus Strong was a connecting link in the chain of personal relationships that Charles Francis Adams saw when he subsequently attributed to Kidder, Peabody, the Nickersons, and other Boston businessmen the general achievement of making the Atchison "one of the most brilliantly successful [railroads] in the business history of the country." [22]

Alternative Routes to the Pacific, 1880–1882

According to one story, Strong had said that when a railroad ceased to grow it began to decay.[23] He certainly seems to have acted on that assumption. As general manager he began to frame aggressive plans to extend the railroad further into Colorado and across the mountains into New Mexico, aiming ultimately at a Pacific connection. For these purposes the Atchison undertook a violent and successful rivalry with Jay Gould's Denver & Rio Grande (which was building south from Denver) for control of mountain passes. In February 1878 a charter was obtained from the New Mexico Southern Pacific Railroad Company, and this offshoot of the Atchison pushed on through New Mexico. By February 1880 a branch line had at last reached the original goal of old Santa Fe; two months later the main line reached Albuquerque; by October 1880, 350 miles had been built in New Mexico, and early the next year an Atchison subsidiary reached Deming in southwest New Mexico. At Deming, according to previous agreement, the Atchison linked up with Collis P. Huntington's Southern Pacific, running across Arizona to Los Angeles and San Francisco. The Boston-backed road thereby established itself as an important element in a new transcontinental route. The way had been cleared by an 1880 agreement with the Denver & Rio Grande and the Union Pacific for each to respect the others "territory" and avoid construction in it.[24]

The Atchison's strategists were not content, however, to rely on the Southern Pacific alone for concessions and transcontinental traffic. And, in fact, Huntington refused to cooperate: the Southern Pacific proved reluctant to make favorable rates for the Atchison.[25] The latter therefore sought further outlets to the sea. The Atchison managers had already organized another company, the Sonora Railway, to build northwards through Mexico from Guaymas on the Gulf of California, aided by a subsidy from the Mexican government. Construction commenced in 1880, and it was the knowledge that the Atchison group would be able to make a direct connection with the Sonora that induced Huntington to sign a joint trackage agreement giving the Atchison rights for the 174 miles of Southern Pacific line between Deming, New Mexico, and Benson, Arizona. The Atchison group then chartered another company, the New Mexico and Arizona Railroad, to build some 90 miles southwards from Benson to Nogales on the Mexico-Arizona border. In March 1882 the Atchison officially acquired the Sonora by an exchange of stock, guaranteeing just over $4,000,000 of 7 per cent bonds. The completion of this road in October of 1882 gave the Atchison direct access to the Pacific from the Missouri River over a fully controlled line.

Meanwhile, the Atchison's interests in Mexico were being further extended. In February 1880 the Mexican Central Railway Company was formed under Massachusetts law to construct a line northwards from Mexico City. The company, controlled by the Atchison interest, secured tax and customs exemptions and a subsidy of just over $15,000 per mile from the Mexican government. Thomas Nickerson became president of the road in May of 1880. The concession was extended, allowing the line to reach El Paso, on the New Mexico border, and branches to be extended to the Gulf of Mexico and the Pacific. Over $31,000,000 was raised between February 1880 and January 1883, and by April 1884 the main line was

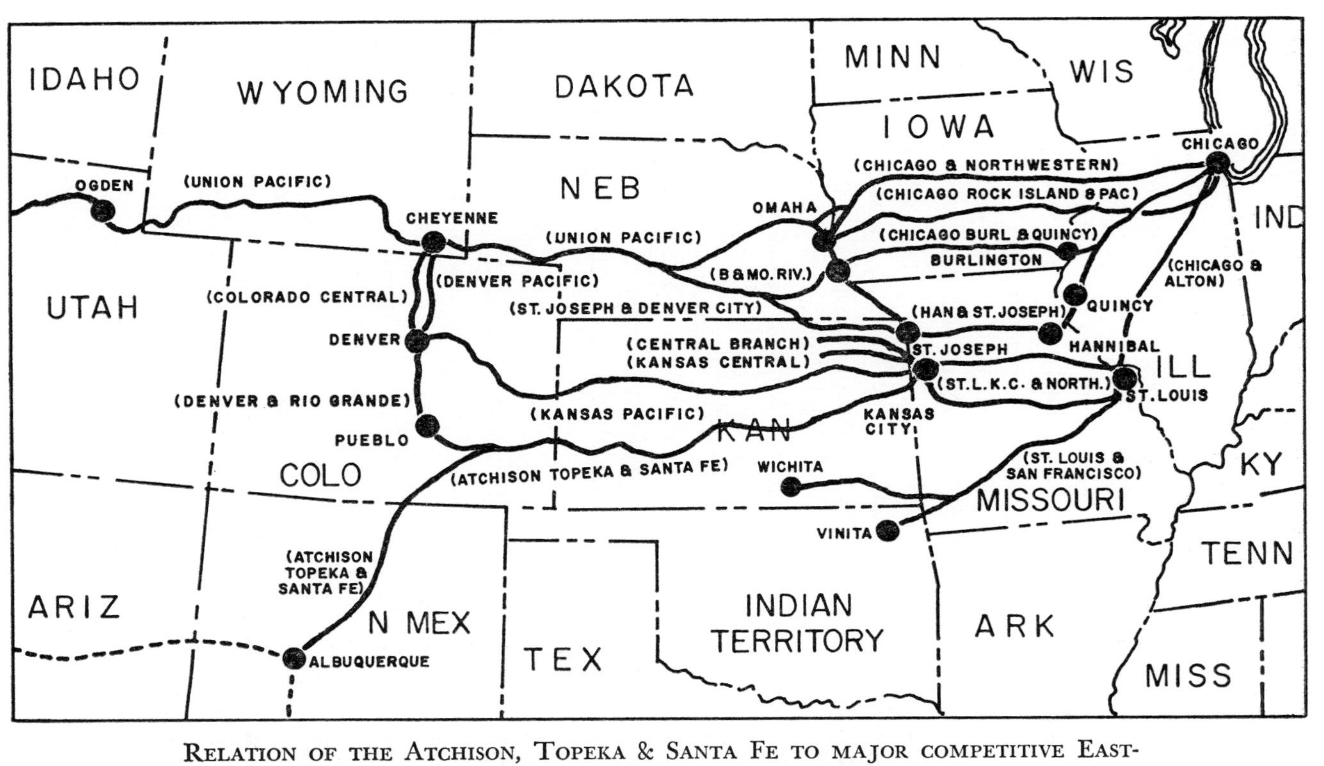

Relation of the Atchison, Topeka & Santa Fe to major competitive East-West routes in the central United States, 1880. Dotted lines indicate routes under construction.

completed and in operation. The Mexican Central continued as an intimate ally of (although not legally related to) the Atchison.

Neither the connection with the Southern Pacific, running across Arizona and California, nor the control of the Sonora, which provided an independent connection with the Pacific, was sufficient comfort to the Atchison in its search for a transcontinental line. The S. P. link was dependent on a potentially (and sometimes overtly) hostile group, and the Sonora reached the coast too far south to be of any great value in tapping the principal routes of the California trade. Hence, even before these two connections were fully under way, the Atchison group was looking for still another transcontinental route.

In 1866 Congress had chartered the Atlantic & Pacific Railroad to build a line from Springfield, Missouri, via Albuquerque to the Colorado River at the California state line, and thence by the best available route to the Pacific. In spite of its very abundant land grant, admittedly in less-than-fertile areas, the road showed relatively little progress of its first decade. It emerged from its bankruptcy of 1875 under the control of the St. Louis & San Francisco Railway Company. The Frisco, as it was known, even though in poor financial circumstances, announced that it intended to push its line through westwards.

In part as a reaction to this threat, coupled as it was with the danger that the Southern Pacific forces would cooperate and thereby pre-empt the Atlantic & Pacific route, the Atchison managers opened negotiations with the Frisco and reached an agreement in January 1880.[26] The Atchison and the Frisco took command of the A. & P. on equal terms, Thomas Nickerson became its president, and plans were made to expedite the construction of the 600-mile Western Division, leading west from the Atchison's line in central New Mexico. This union of capital was basically one between Boston and New York, since the Frisco was controlled by capitalists from the latter city led by the banking house of J. & W. Seligman & Company.

By the end of 1881 the Atlantic & Pacific line was nearing the Colorado River, and, if its new owners' plans materialized, the A. & P. would constitute a threat to Huntington's Southern Pacific and to Jay Gould's Texas Pacific. Huntington and Gould therefore moved in January 1882 to buy control of the Frisco, thereby securing themselves places on the directorate of their rival, the A. & P. Once placed in this position of strength, Huntington was able to attain his immediate objective of keeping the projected extension of the Atchison out of his own territory. Late in the winter of 1882 it was agreed that Atchison construction should stop at the California line and that the Southern Pacific should build a branch from its own main stem to give the A. & P. a direct connection with the Pacific. Following these plans, the two lines were joined in August 1883, and another route to Southern California had been completed. Meantime, of course, the Atchison had completed its own link with the Pacific Coast via the Sonora.

THE ROLE OF COMPETITION IN THE DRIVE FOR TRANSCONTINENTAL STATUS

The emergent transcontinental ambitions that lay behind the series of moves by the Atchison's managers in the early 1880's clearly did not operate in isolation from the activities and attitudes of other railroad leaders. One demonstration of this was the attempt by Huntington and Gould to block the advance of the Atlantic & Pacific at the California state line. While some investment interests in Boston were reported to be ashamed of the resulting compromise, which they regarded as a blow to the Hub's financial prestige,[27] the reporter of this reaction also took pains to indicate that not only did the Atlantic & Pacific retain its right and its ability to build to the coast, but that the Atchison had more than one alternative route to the Pacific.

Of the no less than four possible routes, three (the arrangement with the Southern Pacific, the sharing of the Atlantic & Pacific's franchise, and the allied Sonora Railway) have already been mentioned. The fourth was the California Southern Rail Road Company, which had been formed by an Atchison syndicate in October 1880,* and had constructed 210 miles from National City to Barstow by November 1882. It was ultimately fully incorporated into the Atchison system, forming the last link in that system's first wholly-owned line to the California coast.

It was, however, more than pressure in California that explains the Atchison's drive to transcontinental status. Prior to the Civil

* The syndicate, signing an agreement in July 1880, consisted of: Thomas Nickerson, Kidder, Peabody & Co., B. P. Cheney, George B. Wilbur, and Lucius G. Pratt, all of Boston.

War most western roads, whether running through relatively settled areas or opening up new tracts of land and creating fresh traffic, did not have to consider the direct impact of competition. Increasingly in the postwar environment, the strategy of rivals had to be taken into account: actual or threatened competition became a powerful influence on the growth of railroad lines and systems. In particular, companies found that they were obliged to extend their systems in order to protect the profitability of the base from which they were expanding. As President Strong of the Atchison wrote in 1882, "It has been found in the United States that the power of a Railroad to protect and increase its business depends much upon its length, and the extent of the territory it can touch." [28]

As the Union Pacific, and more particularly the Kansas Pacific, became increasingly aggressive in the trans-Missouri area, as competition for through traffic grew, as Jay Gould stepped up the pace of his volatile activity, as the Southern Pacific began to push eastward and the Texas Pacific westward, the Atchison management had appreciated that it could not stand still. Having the potentiality to become a transcontinental line, it was bound to translate this into a reality; it had to place itself in a position where it would have more to offer roads running into Kansas City, lest it be forced into a position where it could only offer less.

Expansion in Kansas, 1868–1882

While the Atchison drove to the Pacific by a variety of routes after 1877, it was also rounding out and intensifying its network in Kansas. Indeed, just as the situation along the Atchison's eastern portions helped stimulate new developments in the West, so these new developments themselves helped enforce a more aggressive expansionist policy in the East. To understand the interrelationship it is necessary to deal with some antecedent developments in Kansas, where the Atchison group of Boston investors cooperated with the most opportunistic members of the Forbes group led by Joy and Thayer. In the early postwar period these latter Bostonians had seen more promise in Kansas than in Nebraska. But their subsequent experience there reflected the problems of investing opportunistically in truncated and state or regional roads in the era of transcontinental and interregional systems

The Boston investors who followed Joy and Thayer into the Leavenworth, Lawrence & Galveston and the Kansas City, Fort Scott & Gulf roads, primarily on the basis of possibilities of their Texas cattle trade and land speculation, had found these Kansas ventures disappointing. The way in which the Joy group had acquired control of the Cherokee lands provoked legal opposition and physical violence on the part of settlers who felt that their efforts had given value to the land and who were not ready to pay Joy premium prices for it. Troops were required to maintain order in the Cherokee Neutral Tract in 1869 and were kept there until 1872. Joy and his associates fought the opposition with a subsidized press, railroad passes, other assistance to key political figures, and a powerful lobbying group.[29] Although the United States Supreme Court in November of 1872 upheld the legality of the land sale to Joy, the Fort Scott road failed to qualify for a land grant that would have carried it to the Gulf. Its cattle traffic was lost to roads like the Atchison and its financial problems multiplied. In 1877 what remained of its federal land grant was returned to the government, and in March 1878 suit was brought to foreclose two mortgages on the road. The company and its property were sold in February 1879 to the Boston bondholders: Nathaniel Thayer, John A. Burnham, H. H. Hunnewell, F. Gordon Dexter, and Charles Merriam. In 1881 extension of the road to Memphis was undertaken, and this link was completed in 1883.

Both the Leavenworth, Lawrence & Galveston backers and the early promoters of the Atchison had found common cause in an attempt to acquire Osage reserves. In 1868 William Sturges of the L. L. & G., cooperating with the Joy group, had arranged a treaty that would have given them 8,000,000 acres of Osage lands at twenty cents an acre in a deal that would have required little cash. The Osage treaty, however, came into question at the same time that the Cherokee Neutral Tract matter was in progress. Hostile congressmen used the give-away Osage treaty as a basis to demand land reform and to attack the policy of selling Indian reserves to railroads. Under this attack, the Osage treaty was dropped for the rest of 1868. It was revived again the following year under the sponsorship of six railroads, those with the largest claims being the L. L. & G. and the Atchison. In February 1870 the treaty was again withdrawn and was not revived. The Osage land was sold by the government to settlers at $1.25 an acre. The practice of acquiring Indian lands by treaty for the benefit of railroads had, as a result of these experiences, been thoroughly discredited and within a few years was formally abandoned.[30]

The failures of the Joy group helped set the scene for the Atchison's expansion. Other railroad systems were actually or potentially interested in acquiring "territory" in Kansas, both because it was an intrinsically fertile area which could generate much freight and because not only length but feeder territory was important to the power of competing roads. The Atchison therefore found itself fully committed to a strategic struggle of important dimension in the early 1880's.

In 1879 the Leavenworth, Lawrence & Galveston had been reorganized as the Kansas City, Lawrence & Southern Kansas Railroad, extending 305 miles from Lawrence to the southeast corner of Kansas. In 1880, in one of its largest single acquisitions of the period, the Atchison purchased the stock of this Kansas road with a $3,743,000 issue of 5 per cent bonds. In the words of the *Annual Report* for 1880, "In unfriendly hands, it might have interfered and seriously with our business, while it could, under proper management, become a valuable property." [31]

The Atchison was clearly attracted by the potentialities of the Kansas City road, and, as with the C. B. & Q. in its purchase of the Council Bluffs roads, there was little alternative. Jay Gould had defeated the Burlington in a struggle for control of the Missouri, Kansas & Texas in the winter of 1879–1880.[32] Once that strategically placed road was in potentially hostile hands, the Atchison was virtually obliged to secure a line which could compete for the business of Southern Kansas and Indian Territory. The acquisition of the Kansas City, Lawrence & Southern Kansas was a logical response to Gould's move.[33]

At the same time as this purchase, the Kansas City, Burlington & Santa Fe was also acquired. This road, although still relatively short, had posed another potentially strong threat to the Atchison since it was projected from Kansas City to Santa Fe and was actively soliciting funds. Looking back on the acquisition of the two Kansas railroads, the *Commercial & Financial Chronicle* said: "These were both rivals of the Atchison in Southern Kansas — only in a limited way as yet, but they threatened to expand and become troublesome.

As the easiest way to avoid the threatened encroachment on its business, the Atchison bought them both up." [34]

These Kansas acquisitions of 1880 served to emphasize an important fact: the Atchison, Topeka & Santa Fe, in spite of its transcontinental connections, was still to a great extent a locally-based enterprise. In 1883–1884, for example, it was estimated that less than 10 per cent of its gross earnings came from transcontinental traffic. In the mid-1880's the most abundant source of traffic for the road remained the fertile and developing lands of Kansas itself. And this was substantiated by mileage statistics: at the close of 1882 more than half the Atchison's trackage of 2,600 miles was in Kansas.* The parallel with the C. B. & Q.'s deep-seated regional attachment is obvious.

From one viewpoint the Atchison's extensions and acquisition in Kansas in the early 1880's can be seen as a response to competitive pressures; from another standpoint, however, they were part of a general spurt in railroad construction which characterized the economic upswing from 1879 to 1882 — an upswing in which the word "boom" was used for the first time to describe an economic phenomenon.[35] Prosperity radiated through the farming west: while the national acreage under wheat had been about 26,000,000 in the mid-1870's, it was some 37,500,000 in the period 1880–1882; between the same two periods the value of the wheat crop surged from just under $270,000,000 to almost $460,000,000.[36] Linked with such a forward thrust, systems like the Atchison could not help but expand.

The C. B. & Q. and the Atchison, 1880–1881

The management of the Atchison did not, of course, divide its problems into those of the East and those of the West. The Atchison had to be appraised as one system, and the *Annual Report* for 1882 did this in reassuring, if general, terms. After emphasizing that "The territory tributary to this road" could be better protected against "invasion" than most, it went on to emphasize the importance of Boston support: "Thirteen years ago [i.e., in 1870], the Atchison, Topeka & Santa Fe Railroad, a line then twenty-eight miles in length, under the same general direction which now governs its af-

* Of the 2,621 miles of track in the Atchison system, 1,365 were in Kansas, 580 in New Mexico, 282 in Colorado, 262 in Maxico, and the rest in Arizona, Missouri, and Texas. These statistics exclude the closely associated but independent Mexican Central road, and the jointly-owned Atlantic & Pacific.

fairs, asked the confidence and support of the Massachusetts public in the execution of the project it contemplated. Through good and evil times, that support has always been readily given and that confidence has never been broken; and, as a result, those who have followed the fortunes of the Company have shared in its prosperity." [37]

Symbolic of this relationship was the election, in May 1880, of Thomas Jefferson Coolidge, son-in-law of the late William Appleton, to the presidency of the Atchison. Coolidge had left active commerce in 1857 at the age of twenty-six. Within eleven years his interests in textile manufacturing, in railroad investment, in banking, and in wartime commodity speculation, had augmented his fortune to some $360,000. After becoming a director of the C. B. & Q. in 1876, he traveled extensively in the West, familiarizing himself with that section. By February 1870, a year before he became president of the Atchison, Coolidge, according to his own valuation, was a millionaire. His investments in 1880 reflected his new allegiances: those in textiles and western real estate and stockyards were reasonably stable at just over $500,000 and $200,000 respectively; non-western real estate and non-western railroads both declined in amount, but his capital in western roads expanded from $261,500 in February to $1,377,000 in November.[38]

This extraordinary increase stemmed in the main from the acquisition of stock in the C. B. & Q. and the Atchison. While he had no more than $28,500 in bonds in the two systems, his equity holdings were:

Road	February 1879	February 1880	August 1880	November 1880
C. B. & Q.	$63,000	$80,000	$120,000	$465,000
A. T. & S. F.	$239,500	$59,500	$69,000	$718,500

Two facts follow from these data: first that Coolidge's principal acquisitions of Atchison stock came after he became president of the company and, second, that his holdings show a volatility which can best be explained by an opportunistic approach to railroad investment. This assumption is strengthened by the fact of his small investments in eastern lines and by his tendency to buy stocks rather than bonds.

The election of a Boston man to head the Atchison immediately occasioned discussion of the relationship between that company and the other Boston-controlled railroad system, the C. B. & Q. Under ordinary circumstances, the *Commercial & Financial Chronicle* held, the normal friendly relationships between them would not grow too close, since each had to maintain friendly relationships with other lines, either east or west. On the other hand, the *Chronicle* argued that if the Union Pacific should ever become too closely identified with the Wabash or any other system east of the Missouri River, "and seek to control the course of traffic going either east or west, the Burlington & Quincy and the Atchison, prompted by self-interest, would probably find it advantageous to combine forces, in order the more effectively to resist and oppose the common foe . . . But the ability to do a thing is often tantamount to doing it, and the Burlington & Quincy and the Atchison may never be called upon to counteract undue aggression in the direction indicated.[39]

In fact, at this time Charles E. Perkins of the C. B. & Q. was thinking seriously of a merger or close working relationship with the Atchison as an answer to Gould's threat. On May 15, 1880, for example, he wrote Peter Geddes, a director of the C. B. & Q., "The C. B. & Q. had better hitch horses with the Atchison after cementing its Rock Island relations." [40] In November he urged on John M. Forbes the importance of consolidating with other systems, most notably the Rock Island, the Atchison, and the New York Central. Of the Atchison, Perkins wrote, "We know the road, its stock & debt & its present earning power & the market price of its securities. Are not our stockholders and the public ripe for a trade & considering Gould's operations & Rock Island probabilities, had we better not trade now while all hands are in the humor & take the risks necessarily involved in buying it than to wait and take the other risk of having to pay much more or not getting it at all?" [41] But once again the conservative influences which up to that time had restrained the C. B. & Q.'s expansion were still operative and no formal action was taken to implement Perkins' suggestion.

Coolidge's election to the Atchison presidency exemplified the growing western interests of an opportunistic Boston investor; his brief tenure in this post reflected his distaste for managerial duties. With disarming honesty, Coolidge outlined the reasons for his resignation from the Atchison's presidency in 1881: "I found the work not only fatiguing but unprofitable, because as director and president I felt that my duty to . . . the shareholders, prevented me from taking advantage of any facts not known to all, and cut me off from speculations which might have been advantageous. I resigned as soon as I could . . . "[42] After his resignation Coolidge remained one more year as chairman of the board, and then severed his official connection with the Atchison, Topeka & Santa Fe. After Coolidge, William B. Strong, former C. B. & Q. official who had been the real managerial power in the Atchison for some years, assumed the formal position of power and remained president through the turbulent 1880's.

Regrouping and Further Advance, 1883–1887

The development of the Atchison had proceeded in sharp bursts of costly construction and acquisition, followed by periods of relative quiescence. One such burst had carried the line across Kansas in 1872; another had carried it to California and across Mexico ten years later. After that there was a brief pause before yet another hectic bout of expansion.

The very rapidity of the growth between 1878 and 1882, as was the case in 1872–1873, had naturally imposed some strain on financial resources. The strain was met satisfactorily, at least at the time, even though this meant a great increase in outstanding securities, particularly in stock. Shares were both sold to raise cash and exchanged against the stock of acquired railroads. Although there had been no augmentation of capital between 1872 and 1879, from 1879 through 1883 over $48,000,000 par value of stock was issued: $15,447,600 for cash, $11,381,900 against the stock of acquired roads, $18,077,150 as a stock dividend, and $3,391,500 in exchange for Atchison bonds.[43] Bond liabilities had also been increased. Table 4 indicates the changes which had taken place in ten years.[44]

Table 4. Growth of Atchison, Topeka & Santa Fe Railroad, 1873–1883.

Date	Mileage	Capital (dol.)	Shareholders	Bonds (dol.)
January 1, 1873	470	8,615,000	336	14,108,000
January 13, 1883	2,620	56,907,100	6,032	45,780,500

Source: Clarence H. Venner & Company, *Facts for Investors Concerning the Atchison, Topeka & Santa Fe R. R. Company* (Boston, 1883).

The exertions by which the Atchison reached its high plateau of development at the end of 1882 were justified by the operating results. The years 1881 and 1882 were most favorable and profitable; tonnage and earnings both boomed. In 1875 the Atchison moved some 250,000 tons of freight; by 1882 that had risen to 1,360,000 tons and net earnings had risen from $822,000 to $6,136,000 ($1,155 to $3,380 per mile).[45] In 1883, with a stationary mileage, net earnings of the parent system rose by more than $1,200,000.[46]

During the depressed mid-eighties (1883–1885) the Atchison management expanded mileage only slightly but took steps to secure "a more compact and therefore more economical organization for the operation of the road," which was "rendered possible from the fact that the construction of extensions had been practically completed."[47] This pause in the course of the system's expansion was no doubt partly occasioned by the need to digest the results of the previous growth. In addition it was presumably influenced by the cyclical downturn of 1883–1885. In this regard, however, it is significant that the Atchison enjoyed a remarkably good financial record among transcontinental systems in these troubled years.[48]

Yet, as happened ten years earlier, this hiatus was merely the prelude to another sudden spurt of activity of the same kind that Charles Francis Adams had found irresistible in the U. P. From 1886 to 1888, the mileage owned or controlled by the Atchison more than doubled, increasing from around 3,000 to almost 7,000 miles, both figures including half the Atlantic & Pacific mileage. Broadly considered, this remarkable expansion was undertaken in four areas: in the far West, where connections with the Pacific were consolidated and increased; in Kansas, where the penetration of the network was even more itensified; and to the northwest and southeast of Kansas, where the Atchison took giant strides to reach Chicago and the Gulf of Mexico.

Conquest in the West, 1883–1885

It will be remembered that in August of 1883 the Atlantic & Pacific was joined to a newly built extension of Huntington's Southern Pacific (the Mojave branch) at the California line. Yet this link merely emphasized an uncomfortable dependence, and the Atchison management decided that it had to have direct control of a California road. Its threat to parallel the Mojave branch quickly secured a lease arrangement, which was tantamount to purchase by the Atchison, and by August 1885 the Atchison had even obtained trackage rights over the Southern Pacific into San Francisco.[49] Once again the importance of a competitive momentum was illustrated: the Atchison had found itself obliged to move forward in order not to retrogress.

Meanwhile, the Atchison took yet another approach to the transcontinental problem. As already described, the California Southern was chartered in 1880 by men intimately identified with the Atchison. In July 1884, however, that road was in difficulties and defaulted on its first-mortgage bonds. Since the Atchison had obtained control of the Mojave branch, it was now clear that something positive might be done to realize the initial promise of the California Southern. Therefore, in the fall of 1884 its stockholders and bondholders offered direct control of the road to the Atchison on the basis of an exchange of securities, a new mortgage, and an extension to meet the Atchison's line at Barstow, on the former Mojave branch. This offer was accepted and, in the words of the committee which had recommended the step to the California Southern security owners, besides being generally attractive to both sides, it gave the Atchison "a key to the Pacific business." [50]

This move marked the beginning of the final stage of the Atchison's striving for independent transcontinental status. By November 1885 the California Southern had been completed, providing an Atchison outlet at San Diego. Moreover, in September 1885 the Southern Pacific had leased equal use of part of its tracks to the Atchison, and this arrangement, in conjunction with its own subsidiary, gave the Atchison direct access to Los Angeles. The Atchison, Topeka & Santa Fe then not only had a fully effective line between the Missouri and the American Pacific shore; it had established a firm foothold in the rich trade of Southern California. It was only a matter of time before entry by its own tracks into the other California metropolis, San Francisco, was attained.

Expansion in Kansas and Access to the Gulf, 1884–1886

During 1884 and 1885 a modicum of local construction took place in Kansas. Then, early in 1886, the Atchison announced the imminent construction of 450 miles of new line in the state, and raised $5,600,000 for the purpose. "The various lines," said the *Report* for 1885, repeating a familiar theme, "while self-sustaining . . . will no doubt add considerably to the earnings of the Atchison Company, and will also protect its present property." [51]

The new corporate device selected for controlling these additions was the Chicago, Kansas & Western Railroad. By the end of 1886 this company had 401 miles of road; one year later it controlled 903 miles. It is clear that this move reflected the new and rapidly changing situation of the 1880's: other entrepreneurs and other roads were increasingly foraging into the rich territories of Kansas. From the east came the Burlington, the St. Louis & San Francisco, the Rock Island, and the Missouri Pacific. To "protect its present property" the Atchison was forced to expand intensively. More than this, however, it was forced to continue expansion along extensive lines. In 1886 and 1887 this led to moves in two directions: to the Gulf and to Chicago.

In 1884 the Atchison's Southern Kansas system, acquired four years earlier, began a drive south by obtaining congressional approval to build from Kansas into Indian Territory. Two years later the Atchison acquired the Gulf, Colorado & Santa Fe, then building northward from Galveston. In 1886 and 1887 the newly acquired road was extended northward to connect with the Atchison's line in Indian Territory, and northeastwards to link with the Atchison's ally, the St. Louis & San Francisco. As reasons for this move, Atchison executives pointed to the growth of Dallas and Fort Worth, the potential of Texas agricultural lands, and the importance of Galveston as the country's third largest cotton port. In their view it would prove beneficial "from the direct business gained as well as in the strengthening of the Atchison's connections . . . " And they went on in a now-familiar vein: "It will secure to the Atchison Company independence against any attempt of rival lines to close the doors of trade against us or to cripple or embarrass our business." [52]

The Thrust to Chicago, 1886–1887

The second push was even more dramatic. For some time the Atchison's strategists had envisaged their road as running west from the Missouri — at first to the Rockies and then to the Pacific. However, the railroad situation in the 1880's changed. Gould was a catalyst, but others illustrated the same trend. Strategists of major systems, either taking the initiative or reacting against aggression, were no longer satisfied with uni-regional systems.

The Atchison's leaders eventually became convinced that their system could not terminate at the Missouri: roads from the East were not observing that river as a boundary to their westward expansion. The Atchison's *Annual Report* for 1886, however, argued that the need for an independent line to Chicago only became apparent towards the end of 1886: "The lines east of the Missouri River having assumed an aggressive position, three having already invaded our territory in Kansas, or preparing to do so, thereby not only dividing the business, but also placing us with our vast interests beyond in an inferior position as regards the power of making rates, it became necessary to your Directors to determine what course should be pursued." [53]

Rejecting the alternative of a traffic agreement which "at best is always uncertain and unsatisfactory, and generally becomes neglected or odious," * the board settled on an independent line to Chicago. Dismissing the possibility that the proposed extension would provoke retaliatory incursions into Atchison territory, the management argued that past experience had shown "that in no case has the policy of inaction proved a defence." It mentioned the Missouri Pacific, the Rock Island, and the Burlington as encroachers and claimed that "it would seem to be a fact that we had tempted these invasions by our own inertness rather than challenged them by an aggressive disposition." Above all, it was held that the extension would bring independence as well as protection: "We shall be able to do what no other line can; namely, make our own rates over our own lines between the Pacific Coast and Chicago . . . and between the Gulf of Mexico and Chicago."

Charles E. Perkins of the C. B. & Q. had attempted to dissuade President Strong of the Atchison from this move, and he had used his influence with Henry L. Higginson, the Boston banker, against financing it. To Higginson he pointed out: "There are plenty of roads between Chicago and Kansas City for the Atchison to use, and it can get the use of any one or all of them at about its own terms."

* It was pointed out that such contracts were breached as soon as it was in the interests of one party to do so, and that legal enforcement was doubtful "since the law looks with disfavor upon such contracts as contrary to the public interest."

Therefore he urged the banker, in justice to the C. B. & Q., to refrain from participation in the Atchison's extension.[54] To Strong, Perkins stressed the folly of competitive construction. Reporting this conversation to Forbes, Perkins said that he had told Strong that "It might be well for the interest of the property under his [Strong's] control not to be antagonistic to the C. B & Q., occupying, as it does, on the whole, the strongest position of any line west of Chicago and owned as it is by the same people who own the Santa Fe!" [55]

But the Atchison top management, despite the presumed identity of ownership of the two systems, was not to be turned from its goal by such arguments. The state of railroad competition would not permit it. In the summer of 1886 an official of the Atchison had outlined the problem in a bellicose nutshell: by building to Chicago, he argued, "we shall be on an equal footing [with other systems], and can say to them if they demoralize our Kansas business we will hurt them equally as bad in Missouri, Iowa and Illinois." [56] In fact, as early as 1883 the Atchison had tentatively located two lines from Kansas City to Chicago.[57] Nothing further had been done until the capital market recovered from the depression of 1884–1885 and until the pace of competitive change quickened and the reasons for growth became even more compelling. Once decided upon, action was swift: final locations were made by November 1886, and within a year, in the name of the Chicago, Santa Fe & California Railway Company, the whole 450 miles had been constructed, while expensive terminal facilities had been acquired in Chicago by another subsidiary. The Atchison, Topeka & Santa Fe, its management pulled by ambition and pushed by change, had emerged as the world's greatest railroad system, spanning, within eighteen years of its effective beginning, the vast western and southwestern part of the continent.*

Reprise

The connection with Chicago completed a considerable and even spectacular achievement. That it involved hardly less spectacular

* The Atchison mileage as of December 31, 1887, including 919 miles of the Atlantic & Pacific (jointly owned with a company which the Atchison was soon to acquire), was 7,374. Of this, just over 2,000 miles was in the Atchison system proper, just over 1,000 in the Gulf, Colorado & Sante Fe, and over 900 each in the Southern Kansas and the Chicago, Kansas & Western.

costs will be seen in the following chapter. But the financial difficulties which the Atchison management encountered were the result, even on the worst interpretation, of carelessness and overoptimism rather than corruption or manipulation. In nearly every respect the company had dealt fairly with investors and the region through which its system ran. And, in retrospect, even the carelessness can be partially justified by the pressure of events and the nature of real or threatened competition described in the foregoing pages.

At the end of the 1860's and in the early 1870's, when Boston capitalists took hold of the Atchison and drove forward the initial stage of its construction, their vision of a through-state road principally oriented around Kansas' needs and potentialities was both realistic and conservative. Yet, in a sense, it was cast in a mold more appropriate to the prewar than the postwar railroad situation. And when the environment of entrepreneurial decision making changed in the course of the 1870's and 1880's, the original expectations of the entrepreneurs involved were bound to be frustrated.

It says much for their ability that this clash between expectations and reality was resolved by a confident and drastic shift in policy and practices. The pressure of strategic competition in this process should not be exaggerated: there were positive as well as negative reasons for the extension of the Atchison system. But the framework within which the search for profits and positions of strategic strength was pursued was the shifting one of postwar railroad competition — competition in transcontinentals, in the intensive construction of intrastate and regional feeders, and in through routes to the Great Lakes. In all these areas the threats and promises of rivalry were interrelated and therefore cumulative: strength in one had to be protected by building up further strength in another; Kansas traffic had to be bolstered by a transcontinental system; the latter, in its turn, demanded further extension in Kansas; and both ultimately had to be served by a route to Chicago.

To a large extent John Murray Forbes's dictum that true prudence consisted of boldness was borne out by the Atchison's strategy in another region. Investment in western railroads was no longer principally a reflection of the potentialities of a relatively limited area of land. It had become a response to the actions of other railroads and part of a systematic and massive campaign for interregional and transcontinental traffic. This transition had been perfectly exemplified by the Atchison, Topeka & Santa Fe and its Boston management. It was, therefore, only logical that the outstanding nature of their achievements in this respect should also involve them in financial difficulties and make them representative of the changes in institutional and financial arrangements which marked the end of an era.

Chapter 15

The Atchison, Topeka & Santa Fe, 1880–1890: Financial Aspects of Expansion

IN THE words of a Boston journalist, the Atchison had emerged by 1880 as "the splendid child of Boston energy and enterprise." [1] The *Commercial & Financial Chronicle* maintained in December 1880 that the Atchison was the "only formidable competitor of the Gould system west of the Mississippi and Missouri Rivers" and that "in the Boston party Gould has no mean antagonist . . . They are enterprising, alert, energetic, aggressive, and are backed by abundant capital." [2] In barely a decade the Atchison's Boston owners and managers had established their system as a major force in western railroading. In the following decade, as just described, they both consolidated and extended this position.

Like the C. B. & Q., the Atchison acted as a developmental agency in the territory where it had its roots, but, unlike the Burlington, it had been tempted by what John M. Forbes called "the illusory paradise fruits" of transcontinental status. The financial demands involved in pursuing this goal, plus those occasioned by intensive building to protect Atchison territory against competitors, created burdens that the system found increasingly difficult to bear. That decade of frenetic railroad building in the 1880's exacted its toll from the Union Pacific and the Chicago, Burlington & Quincy, as we have seen. For the Atchison it brought major reorganization, change in management, and the assertion of investment-banker control, signaling the beginning of a new era in western railroads and an end to their attractiveness for Boston investors.

FINANCIAL CONTROL AND FINANCIAL CRISIS

While the Atchison, Topeka & Santa Fe underwent rapid growth in the 1880's, it lost little of its Boston emphasis. In 1887, for example, of fifteen directors, ten (the same number as in 1873) were from Boston and the rest were from Kansas.* And in a comprehensive listing of Atchison stockholders for October 1883 there is further evidence of Boston orientation: of 569,100 shares, 546,707 were registered in Boston, 14,397 in New York, and 7,996 in Chicago.[3]

It is clear from the stock list that the Nickersons were still important influences in the Atchison: Albert held 8,469 shares, George 6,499, and Thomas 2,100. As late as 1888 a Kidder, Peabody partner complained that "Jesse [Seligman] is the Frisco board and Albert [Nickerson] is the Atchison board; and they carry on their little deals together, regardless of everybody else." [4]

Benjamin P. Cheney was the largest individual holder of stock, with 12,755 shares. Cheney had started driving a stage in New Hampshire at sixteen, and developed an express business that was merged into the American Express Company in 1880. Active in the Northern Pacific and Kansas roads, he was a major Atchison stockholder and director through the 1870's and 1880's. However, as the Atchison expanded, it challenged the resources of such individuals. Like many other large corporations of the late nineteenth century, the Atchison was growing beyond the point where major managerial and financial decisions could be the responsibility of a single individual.

The stock list shows that Baring Brothers, with 22,300 shares, and Kidder, Peabody, with 8,470, controlled significant amounts of equity.** Lee, Higginson & Co. held 2,397. As financial intermediaries with practiced access to English as well as American capital, these houses had come to assume vital functions for an enterprise like the Atchison, with its large size and appetite for capital, and with its many small shareholders, whose confidence had to be created and justified. In these and other tasks the Boston and the London firms worked in close cooperation with each other, starting in the late 1870's and extending over many years.

From the surviving confidential letter books of Kidder, Peabody & Company, there emerges a picture of investment bankers who,

* The Boston residents were: William B. Strong (president), Isaac T. Burr, Alden Speare, B. P. Cheney, Albert W. Nickerson, Warren Sawyer, George O. Shattuck, C. R. Codman, W. R. Wharton, and George Sealy. Of these men, Strong, Burr, Speare, and Cheney had been on the board in 1873.

** Possibly the most extensive business in which these firms were in partnership related to foreign exchange and the sale of letters of credit for the use of travelers and international merchants.

while they did not completely dominate the Atchison in the 1880's, played an active and important part in the shaping of its policy. The partners never had any hesitation in bringing pressure to bear with regard to such important matters as building to the Pacific or to the Gulf — the former being urged and the latter opposed in 1885.[5] In 1886 Oliver W. Peabody was enthusiastic about the planned Chicago branch and the possibility of his firm, the Barings, and Lee, Higginson syndicating the relevant loan. "The property is increasing rapidly and largely in value and in influence," he wrote, "and has, on the whole, I think, the most honest and able management that I know of, of any railroad property here. We ought to keep it to ourselves." [6]

If this confidence in the Atchison management included a feeling that nothing serious could go wrong with the system's finances, then the bankers were due for some rude shocks. Hints of financial difficulties were recognized in late 1887 and early 1888. They were followed by an agreement between the Barings and Kidder, Peabody and the railroad to market more Atchison securities, although it was stipulated that no more bonds should be issued during 1888 by the Atchison Company without the bankers' consent, and no plans for extensive or large outlays were to be entered into until the credit of the company was better established.[7] In October 1888, Kidder, Peabody & Company informed president William B. Strong that it was worried about the Atchison's earnings and floating debt, and advised him to pay a dividend of no more than fifty cents a share. Yet within a week of sending this letter it was found that the situation was far worse than had been imagined: the floating debt was some $6,000,000 and the Atchison faced a real financial crisis.

The very speed with which the system and its subsidiaries had expanded had imposed severe financial strains. Between 1885 and 1888 the Atchison group's bonded indebtedness (excluding that of the Atlantic & Pacific) tripled, rising from just under $52,000,000 to about $154,000,000. And as expansion had often taken place by the issue, on the part of subsidiaries, of fixed-interest securities for which the Atchison was responsible, the annual obligations mounted rapidly. In addition, a good deal of new, as indeed some of the old, mileage was initially unproductive of net revenue, while competition and rate wars aggravated the situation. In 1888, within the Atchison, Topeka & Santa Fe system, the Atlantic & Pacific lost over

$1,500,000, the Gulf, Colorado & Santa Fe more than $1,300,000, the Chicago, Santa Fe & California some $440,000, and the Sonora over $350,000. Even so, the directorate paid a total of 5¼ per cent in dividends — subsequently a cause of considerable criticism.

But whatever the disadvantages of the speed with which expansion had taken place, the difficulties encountered by the Atchison, along with other systems, are most directly attributable to a general collapse of freight rates amid intensive competition. Table 5 illustrates the pressures and troubles of the period as reflected in falling freight rates. Between 1881–1885 and 1886–1890, rates on the Atchison and the U. P. declined by more than one third. From 1881 to 1888 they had fallen by no less than 46 percent.

TABLE 5. Ton-mile freight rates, 1871–1890 (gold values in cents).

Years	Pennsylvania Railroad	Illinois Central	C. B. & Q. (east of Missouri River)	C. B. & Q. (west of Missouri River)	U. P. and A. T. & S. F.
1871–1875	1.18	1.90	1.71	—	2.21
1876–1880	0.89	1.60	1.22	4.02	2.15
1881–1885	0.82	1.41	1.04	2.73	1.83
1886–1890	0.71	1.02	0.86	1.68	1.19

Source: Fred A. Shannon, *The Farmer's Last Frontier: Agriculture, 1860–1897* (New York, 1945), 269–297.

Looking back on the miserable events of 1888, the *Annual Report* blamed the Atchison's misfortunes on a variety of factors, while at the same time it defended the management's policy against the obvious charge of impetuosity.[8] Considering the short-run decline in traffic — a physical decline whose financial repercussions were compounded by a fall in freight rates — the management first of all blamed the subnormal crops for two successive years "and the consequent depression of all kinds of business throughout our entire territory." Secondly, the decline in earnings* was blamed on

* Earnings in 1886–1888 were:

Year	*Gross*	*Net*
1886	$15,984,000	$7,863,000
1887	18,461,000	8,604,000
1888	15,613,000	5,225,000

(A. T. & S. F., *Annual Report,* 1887, 9; 1888, 9.)

the construction of new lines in Kansas by rival companies, which the report said, "have covered our territory with a network of railroads reaching almost every point of consequence on our lines, and dividing with us the business which has heretofore sought our road." The resulting competition, complained the report, resulted in lower rates which, under the provisions of the Interstate Commerce Act, entailed "proportionate reductions to and from almost all other points on our lines, whether they were reached by our competitors or not." And since the Act precluded any division of traffic, the Atchison management reported gloomily, "competition was continued with the usual result of loss to all interests and advantage to none." Finally, the payment of dividends was explained somewhat lamely as an anticipation of improved earnings, which, in fact, never materialized.*

Having dealt, at least to its own satisfaction, with short-run problems, the Atchison management turned to a longer view of the railroad situation and particularly to its own policy of seemingly continuous expansion. Here it touched on familiar and important themes. The 1888 *Annual Report* pointed out that the experience of western railroads demonstrated that success depended on rapid expansion, "often in advance of actual business necessity." It argued: "This was the policy of the Atchison Company from the first. It led the way. It built, not upon assured returns of profit, but upon a faith which time had abundantly vindicated, — that the great Western and South-western regions of the country were rich in possibilities and that the company which first occupied the territory would reap the first and greatest rewards." [9] Reaffirming the wisdom of past decisions, the management maintained that expansion was a condition of both vigor and growth. It did not cease to be a prudent policy when the road linked the Missouri and the Rockies, nor when the system became fully transcontinental. Arguing that there was territory "naturally tributary" to the Atchison's line, the *Report* claimed that the line "should not be left a single thread extending from the Missouri River to the Pacific Ocean, liable to be cut by rival lines." Inaction in such circumstances would not only deny the

* The seasonal increase in net earnings from the first to the second half-year had been almost $1,500,000 in 1885 and over $1,900,000 in 1886. In 1887 this had slumped to a bare $204,100. (A. T. & S. F., *Annual Report,* 1888, 15.)

Atchison the existing business from adjacent regions but make it "lose the opportunity of securing it in the future." The threatened inroads of other lines made further territorial occupations "an obvious duty." [10]

According to the directors, the expectation that prompt action "would deter other companies from building" had not been realized. Asserting that the decisions to expand had been based on the best available information, they maintained that no one could have known that droughts, crop failures, excessive competition, falling rates, "unwise legislation," strikes, "and other calamities" would not only occur, but occur more or less simultaneously. Nevertheless, they argued, these difficulties, and the concomitant financial losses, were temporary in nature. Accordingly, they urged stockholders to take the long view, to remember the potentialities of "the growth of States and communities." It was worth remembering that: "Every mile of our new roads has been built by the Company itself; and no construction company has been interposed to increase their cost, thus securing to our stockholders the actual value of every dollar which has been expended upon their property. Since their construction, repeated failure of crops has prevented these extensions from showing their real earning capacity. With fair conditions and the natural growth of the country, we do not doubt that they will prove valuable additions to our system, though this result will be retarded by the competition of other lines which have built into the territory which they occupy." [11] Well reasoned and sensible as was this apologia, it represented an optimism that seemed poorly based in view of the existing situation. For whatever the rationale of past policies or the hopes for future income, the Atchison had a very serious immediate problem.

In the nature of the crisis, the solution did not lie in management's hands; it lay, if anywhere, in the hands of its bankers. On October 9, 1888, Kidder, Peabody wrote to Baring Brothers tentatively considering a second mortgage, and concluding that "The consequence of the failure of this great concern would be so disastrous in many directions that the situation calls for careful handling. The directors show good courage and are putting in their own money freely." [12]

This description of the directors' reaction to crisis is doubly significant. First, it reflected an attitude and a mode of behavior already familiar from the earlier example of the Illinois Central management and John Murray Forbes and his colleagues. Faced with a crisis or a frustration of initial hopes, capitalists of this type did not hesitate to commit even more of their resources to an enterprise which they viewed as, in the long run, developmental. Secondly, the very fact that the Atchison' plight was the subject of remedial planning by two investment banking institutions reflected the fact that the individual attitudes and private resources which at an earlier date might suffice to salvage a railroad or fulfill original hopes were no longer enough. Railroad systems had become too large and too competitive. Rescue operations could only be satisfactorily undertaken by banking houses enjoying a significantly new relationship with American and overseas capital markets.

Within a week of Kidder, Peabody's communication to the Barings, first steps had been taken. Kidder, Peabody offered help on three specific conditions: George C. Magoun,* one of their New York partners, was to be placed on the finance committee; Joseph W. Reinhart was to be employed to make the Atchison bookkeeping system similar to that of the Pennsylvania Railroad, and any expenditure exceeding $25,000 beyond normal operating and maintenance expenses had to be authorized by the finance committee in Boston. In addition, the banking house delivered a brief but firm lecture on the necessity of covering fixed charges with "actual available cash" in the succeeding five months, and of the need for the strictest economy "throughout the entire system." [13] These conditions were accepted, and as a stopgap measure $7,000,000 of 6 per cent three-year notes were floated.[14]

More far-reaching and permanent changes were still to come. When figures became available for the Atchison's 1888 performance, they showed that although the system had increased by 1,700 miles between 1887 and 1888, net earnings had dropped by more than 40 per cent, falling by about the same percentage below annual fixed charges (which then stood at $10,918,558). For the first eleven months of 1888 the Atchison, together with its auxiliary lines and

* Magoun (1841–1893) was born in Cambridge, Massachusetts, and was working as a clerk for Kidder, Peabody in 1867. In 1868 he was with the New York branch and later became a member of the partnership which replaced the branch. Subsequently, in 1891, he helped found a successor firm, Baring, Magoun & Company.

its proportion of jointly owned roads, sustained a net loss of almost $2,500,000.*

By April 1889 it was obvious that Kidder, Peabody and Baring Brothers were determined not to leave management matters as they were. On hearing that they had called for proxies, the *Commercial & Financial Chronicle* praised their motives. It drew a distinction between financial methods by which bankers, having marketed securities, "reap their own handsome profit, and then get out, leaving the bondholders in the day of trouble to look out for themselves," and those by which bankers "stand by a company, raise money for it to tide over hard places," and, if reorganization becomes necessary, step in to protect first-mortgage claims.[15] Institutionally they were prepared to do what developmental investors were no longer capable of doing as individuals.

Having realized that outside finance and advice no longer sufficed, the two investment houses with major interests in the Atchison moved strongly and directly into the sphere of management. At the annual meeting of May 9 their representative, Thomas Baring, voting 442,520 shares out of the 621,811 represented, elected "the Kidder Peabody ticket" without opposition. Six new directors (two of them members of Kidder, Peabody) came onto the Atchison Board:** Thomas Baring, William Libbey, and John J. McCook from New York, Oliver W. Peabody and George C. Crocker from Boston, and Edwin H. Abbott from Cambridge, Massachusetts. With George Magoun, who now became chairman of the board, the bankers controlled four seats on the seven-man executive and financial committee. At the same time the president's office was moved from Boston to Chicago and, reaffirming the general implication that Strong was now in a subordinate executive position, the board chairman was given charge of financial matters and the president was alloted the task of "running the property." [16] Within four months Strong, who had led the drive for aggressive expansion, re-

* The net loss included a surplus of $1,066,000 for the Atchison system proper. Auxiliary and jointly owned roads made good $1,915,505 of their losses by virtue of the fact that construction costs fell below original estimates. Net floating debt on November 30, 1888, stood at $5,185,892 — against which could be reckoned $6,300,000 of uncalled (reserve fund) notes. (*Commercial & Financial Chronicle,* XLVII [February 23, 1889], 236–237.)

** The directors resigning were: Albert W. Nickerson, George O. Shattuck, Isaac T. Burr, Warren Sawyer, C. R. Codman, and W. R. Wharton.

signed from an intolerable position and was replaced by a thoroughgoing railroad man: Allen Manvel, who had been general manager of the St. Paul, Minneapolis & Manitoba under James J. Hill. When this news was announced, Atchison stock "ruled quite strong," and Kidder, Peabody and the Barings tightened their control of management even further by securing the election of Francis H. Peabody as a director.[17]

Management changes, however, were merely the prelude to further action. During the summer months of 1889 it was "evident that a readjustment of the company's finances was inevitable." [18] In October the plan for financial reorganization was announced. Carried out under the auspices of Kidder, Peabody and directly overseen by their nominee, Joseph W. Reinhart, the plan was eminently a large-scale success. It was designed to reduce fixed charges, consolidate a bewildering complexity of issues, simplify corporation structures, and fund the floating debt. Including stocks, $250,000,000 of securities were involved. With almost forty types of bond issues current, it was proposed that these be exchanged — in different amounts depending upon the type — against 4 per cent general first-mortgage bonds and 5 per cent income bonds. The terms were such that no assessment was to be levied on stocks or bonds. In only three minor cases was there to be any reduction of the principal of security holders.

The main sacrifice involved in the reshuffling of securities was to be made by current bondholders. They were to agree to have part of their interest payments depend on current earnings, if available, rather than on a legal obligation. Indeed, the reorganization was so planned that security holders were to have precisely that amount of new bonds and notes which would yield the same income as their old bonds. And since the new securities, designed to run for one hundred years, were to be issued at a lower rate of interest, this naturally involved an increase in fixed debt. Nevertheless, because the disposition of claims as between property and earnings was altered, the necessary fixed charges were reduced from the existing $11,157,770 to an estimated $7,352,390. The plan provided for possible total issues of $150,000,000 general mortgage bonds and $80,000,000 income bonds. Even if all interest were paid on the latter, this still only increased charges to a slight amount above pre-existing definite obligations. And even this was a specious increase, since not all the new securities were to be exchanged: part were to be sold for cash, yielding the wherewithal to retire floating debt and to provide in addition some $5,000,000 of new liquid capital.[19]

As already intimated, the plan was an immediate success and this on a voluntary basis. It was announced on October 15, 1889; by December 14, holders of $128,860,700 out of a possible $148,000,000 of bonds had given their assent.[20] However, Kidder, Peabody & Company could not be content with these financial arrangements alone. As early as October 23, 1889, Francis H. Peabody was suggesting a three- or five-year voting trust "for protection of the property." [21] In December, Peabody, writing to George Magoun, expressed fears that Gould would make a successful attempt to acquire the Atchison in the next few years: "If he should do so, it would not only be a great disaster to the property, but a terrible mortification for K., P. & Co., who would practically have cooked the goose for him to eat." Peabody therefore suggested a ten-year trust as a means of frightening off speculative interests. He put forward a detailed plan, which included proposals for the support and manipulation of the market, to get a majority of the stocks within the trust.[22]

The first proposals for a voting trust were not well received, but by January a second plan was going well. However, no action was taken by management or stockholders at the annual meeting in May 1890. At that time Levi C. Wade, president of the Mexican Central, replaced F. H. Peabody on the board. Joseph W. Reinhart, after his successful handling of the reorganization, was promoted from fourth to first vice president.[23]

While plans for the financial reorganization were being successfully put into operation, the new management interests in the Atchison were effecting large-scale changes in the administrative organization. It was clear that the new exchange of securities, substituting two for thirty-six, would itself simplify financial administration and thus economize in that area. Operational savings and increased efficiency would also result from the consolidation of some sixty separate organizations: reducing the number of employees, systematizing the work, and tightening control of operating expenses.[24]

The Atchison's *Annual Report* for 1890 reviewed the changes that had taken place. Stressing the stockholders' interest, the management reported: "a policy was adopted in the management of your properties which was believed would be productive of the most satisfactory results in carrying on the business of such an extensive Railway System as that owned by your Company."[25] The president had been relieved of the administration of the financial and accounting branches of the business. These functions were placed under a vice president in Boston, who was subject to the immediate direction of the chairman and board, "thus permitting the attention of the president to the operations and general physical benefit of properties."

A considerable amalgamation of separate properties had also been effected. The operation of the Chicago, Santa Fe & California Railway (formerly managed at Chicago) was assigned to the management office of the main line at Topeka. The Chicago, Kansas & Western and the St. Joseph, St. Louis & Santa Fe were consolidated into the Atchison system proper, as were other, smaller, Kansas roads. The California Southern, the California Central, and the Redondo Beach roads were consolidated into the Southern California Railway Company. In May 1890 the Atlantic & Pacific and the St. Louis & San Francisco were both acquired, and their management was transferred to Atchison officials. Their traffic offices were also merged and their New York offices absorbed by the Atchison's Boston offices. A new accounting system was instituted in July 1890. Altogether the board simplified and economized operations, made administration more efficient, and reduced duplication of terminal facilities.

Despite these significant achievements, the assumption of power by the bankers did not end the Atchison's troubles. The acquisition of the Atlantic & Pacific and the St. Louis & San Francisco (the latter with very heavy fixed charges) in 1890 did not prove particularly astute decisions. Neither did the various reorganizations prevent even worse difficulties soon afterwards. While earnings picked up markedly in the short run, the system entered the slump of 1893 under a crippling weight of bonds (a burden increased by an unwise refunding of income bonds into fixed-interest bonds in 1892) and rapidly declined into bankruptcy, receivership, and bitter controversy among the bondholders. This part of the Atchison's story need not be told here.[26] In the crash of the company may be seen not only the mistakes of individual managers but also a repercussion of the general economic situation which produced the crisis of 1893 and sent some one third of American railroads into bankruptcy during the 1890's.

The financial and managerial reorganizations of 1889–1890 mark a convenient terminating point for this narrative, for they reflect a transition from one style of entrepreneurship to another and therefore coincide with the ending of the sort of Boston influence with which we have been concerned. In a way, the reorganizations were a logical accompaniment of the inevitable growth of the Atchison system and its attempt to survive in a new environment of railroad competition. In more general terms they exemplified the passing of a distinctive era in western railroading.

In the last four chapters we have noted the extent to which the postwar environment transformed the nature of developmental investment and policies. In the case of the Atchison this meant that the original, and relatively circumspect, outlook was changed by actual or potential competition until a transcontinental system had been created. The inflexible logic of competition meant, further, that such a system continued to grow in the 1880's — intensively, by tapping regions adjacent to its lines, and extensively, by driving west to the Pacific, south to the Gulf, and northeastwards to Chicago. As had been the case for some time, therefore, developmental entrepreneurship responded to need by increasing its commitment and protecting the long-run interests of its enterprise. By the 1880's, however, such consistency of outlook and action forced management into situations fraught with financial insecurity. Other railroads and railroad systems were also expanding, and for the same reasons, at a speed and to a point at which overbuilding and shaky financing threatened many with ruin.

Before the Civil War to a large extent, and even after the war to some extent, Boston capitalists such as Forbes and members of the Atchison group seemed to be able to control the circumstances in which they operated. But consistency brought its own nemesis. The march of events got out of hand, and the outlook and policies appropriate to an earlier phase of railroading no longer sufficed. The railroad was no longer a pioneer in the West.

In spite of their troubles at the end of the 1880's, however, it would be misleading to say that the Boston management of the Atchison had "failed." Urged on by the necessities of postwar railroad strategy, and after many well-fought and successful battles, it had constructed a great railroad system. Its financial plight at the end of the campaign was different only in degree from that of other systems, like the C. B. & Q. and U. P., which had been inexorably caught up in the same scramble of overbuilding merely to protect what already existed. Its stupendous growth in a brief period had coincided with so many other changes that the company could not avoid a massive attempt to tailor its managerial and financial structures to its new needs. But this, combined with the situation's threat to so many security holders, depended on a new relationship with capital markets and on a new executive command. Hence the transition to institutional rather than individual control. Kidder, Peabody & Company and their London associates moved in decisively to discard a large part of the old-line Boston management.

Naturally enough, Bostonians did not cease to invest in the Atchison, or other western roads, after 1889. But the ejection of the old Atchison management and the broadening of financial and managerial influences clearly delineate a new phase in the road's history—one in which its control and administration were far less insular and far less personalized. Moreover, even as the two financial houses stepped in, the great epoch of Boston investment in the West was drawing to a close, and for related reasons. The primary-producing West, whose rapid development had been the rationale of so much railroad construction between the 1840's and the 1880's, had fulfilled its principal initial functions in American economic growth. The symbolic concept of the closing of the frontier in 1890 is not entirely devoid of realistic content. About that time, even while obvious signs of railroad overconstruction were appearing, the economy was undergoing a surge of development associated with new industries — chemicals, utilities, petroleum, steel — largely centered in the East, although also springing up in the West. Now that the railroads had more than succeeded in the West, and had even competed themselves into a severe crisis, now that more impersonal financial interests moved to salvage and bolster large parts of the railroad network, an increasing amount of Boston capital was turned to these new types of investment.

PART VI Conclusion

Chapter 16

The Nineteenth-Century Railroad Investment Process: An Overview

After tracing the activities of representatives of one eastern center of capital through half a century and over more than half the continent, we think some general conclusions about nineteenth-century railroad investment processes are justifiable. Although broad generalizations would appear to be warranted, they do not come easily. Investment decisions are human decisions. The personalities and backgrounds of nineteenth-century decision makers, the situations they confronted, and the general march of events over which they had no direct control conditioned their specific policies. In this book we have dealt at length with many investment decisions and have made some attempt in each case to appraise their origin, their cumulative consequences and significance. It is now appropriate to consider them in other terms, and, while focusing on decision making, to find common denominators that give us insight on the way men appraised profit-making opportunities and implemented their decisions in a leading sector of nineteenth-century economic growth.

To make such an analysis carries us away from the empirical data that form such a large part of the study. Even in this move toward abstraction, however, an actual historical process, involving the interaction of men and their environment, and continuity and change in such interaction, holds the center of our attention.

The Environment of Nineteenth-Century Decision-Making

If ever there was a time in American history when private economic decision making could be done under favorable external conditions, it was during the period under review. The political, economic, and social environment encouraged the unrestrained and imaginative exercise of private initiative. A vast undeveloped continent, rich in natural resources, provided an opportunity and a continually unfolding incentive. Innovation in the application of steam to transportation as well as to manufacturing gave men a new source of power. A growing population, accustomed to hard labor, was eager to improve its standard of living. These were only some of the factors in the well-known but nonetheless unprecedently favorable combination of elements conducive to successful private investment and enterprise.

For these reasons it is tempting to minimize the role and the creativity of individual capitalists. However, the existence of a favorable environment does not automatically put capital to work. Although there was no shortage of entrepreneurial talent to take advantage of positive environmental factors, there was, from time to time, or in particular sectors, a shortage of domestic capital; and the state of institutions for mobilizing and channeling it into productive uses was primitive. For this reason it would be easy to magnify the role of individual capitalists.

We have attempted to maintain a balanced position, emphasizing the importance of the investment environment while insisting on the human element in both molding and adapting to it. Men built on what they and their predecessors, as well as nature, had created, and in the process they altered over time their own environment and their own ways of looking at and dealing with it. It is the latter aspects of the investment process that interest us most.

Types of Investors

We have shown that private decision making in the transportation sector of the economy created a surprising similarity of results, if we take one geographical group of investors as our subjects and the development of major railroad systems in the West as our criterion. The post-Civil War experience of the Union Pacific, C. B. & Q., and Atchison fits this generalization. But, in keeping with our argument that the results were not predetermined except in the very broadest sense — an expanding economy in a rich continent was bound to be supplied, ultimately, with transportation services organized into integrated systems — it is necessary to provide a framework for a retrospective analysis of the complex investment process whereby these systems were actually created.* For this purpose we have attempted to differentiate between two general types of investors, the opportunistic and the developmental, on the basis of their investment expectations and in terms of their image of the changing environment in relation to their investment decisions.

That these typological categories are analytical constructs — useful only for points of departure — is illustrated by the refusal of much of our empirical data to be forced neatly into one or two boxes. The investor's time-horizon, for example, might appear to be a basis for a separation of types; but in practice an opportunistic investor might look to the future quite as much as his developmental counterpart. As in the case of Joy and Thayer, the question was where the future lay. Size of resources might be another important criterion: the larger the investor's resources, the more he might be expected to adopt a longer time-horizon in appraising his capital commitments. While we have shown that there is a limited validity for such distinctions, it also appears that men with large resources were sometimes — especially in boom times — just as opportunistic and had just as short time-horizons as those with modest resources. This was certainly the case with John M. Forbes in the 1840's.

The element of personal involvement in making an investment productive is yet another yardstick that can be applied. And here a more useful distinction, though again a qualified one, can perhaps be drawn. The opportunistic investor did not typically anticipate any long or intimate involvement with entrepreneurial decisions in order to make his investment profitable. Rather, as the basis for his returns he looked primarily to the immediate environment or to foreseeable changes in it wrought by others. A good example is David Neal's departure from the Illinois Central to engage in private land speculation. The stock speculator, using borrowed money in a search for short-run returns, might come closest in reality to the "pure" type of opportunistic investor.**

The developmental investor, on the other hand, was more likely to commit himself only when he had the opportunity to participate

* It is worth repeating that both authors, when they started the study, were unaware of the extent to which Boston capitalists were involved in the creation of the major railroad systems covered in this book. They started with the individuals and not with the systems.

** Dun and Bradstreet records for the 1850's make a similar distinction between investing in an "operation" and in a "speculation."

in entrepreneurial decisions that would influence the productiveness of his investment. Nevertheless, since an opportunistic investor might also commit himself on the same basis, further differentiation is necessary. It hinges on the investor's expectation of a need to *change* the environment to realize a profit and to manage his investment actively to this end. Therefore, a capitalist committing a large part of his personal resources, taking part in the entrepreneurial decisions affecting their use, and doing so with the expectation of consolidating and improving his position in the same enterprise by helping to change its environment over the long run, comes closest to the "pure" type of developmental investor. John M. Forbes, of course, is our best example of this type, though he often departed from it in practice.

It might be said that there is an implicit value judgment in the selection of terms such as "opportunistic" and "developmental"; yet one conclusion of this study is that such judgments are not justified in aggregate growth terms. The opportunistic investor, actuated by the most selfish short-run motives and having little or no concern about the effect of his actions on others, contributed significantly to American economic development. He moved into areas and activities that developmental investors would not touch. Even bearing in mind the social costs and economic waste of some of this activity, one cannot ignore the fact that short-run investment that exploited particular situations created by a benevolent or corrupt government, gullible white men, or hapless Indians, "plugged" new resources into the economy and introduced rails and economic activity into areas where none had existed before.

All opportunistic investment did not have these baneful side effects, but even where this was the case, it was a logical — and in many cases, productive — adaptation by individuals to the opportunities created by the nation's reliance on decentralized, private decision making for rapid development of the economy. Whether the costs were too high is, in one sense, irrelevant. The fact is that a good part of the job of developing the nation's resources took place through opportunistic investment.

The Development of the Investor

The actual decision that turned a Boston capitalist into an active investor in western railroads was frequently the product of a number of factors — some noneconomic in character — but it was certainly the product of a process over time. The men whose activities we have traced most closely derived their capital from mercantile trade, and especially the trade to the Far East. Their experience with conducting a large business at a distance, and the close ties that it produced, not only among the group but with foreign sources of capital, were well suited to the demands of domestic railroad investment. However, the process of their involvement with deepened commitment to, and personal participation in, western roads was both gradual and varied. There was, in short, no sudden, massive switch of Boston capital from trade to railroads.

It is significant that, certainly in the prewar era, Boston capitalists who became involved in western railroad investment initially tended to be passive with respect to the uncovering of opportunities for such investment. A vital role in the investment process was therefore played by men like Joy and Brooks who lived or traveled in the West and spotted opportunities that they brought to the doors of State Street counting houses. Without active promotional activity of this kind, Boston capital that went into western railroads in the 1840's might have been funneled in different directions. Supporting and supplementing such promotional activity were investment houses like that of John E. Thayer & Brother, whose livelihood involved the flotation and sale of securities.

THE IMPORTANCE OF GROUPS

Although we have dealt at length with specific individuals, we have also shown that they tended to cluster in identifiable groups which were central to the involvement process. In this sense, investment decisions had social as well as economic dimensions. Kinship as well as business connections had a role in the formation and behavior of these groups, and group support and sanctions were not insignificant considerations in individual investment decisions, particularly initiatory ones.

The case of John M. Forbes is again relevant. While seeking a railroad post for his seafaring brother and a good return on his capital, he wanted the approval of a group based on his China trade affiliations and he wanted that group to share with him the risks of entering the Michigan Central. Decades later he hesitated to water stock for fear of what "Boston might think." The Boston that he had in mind, of course, was the band of merchant princes and the upper crust of Boston society to which he belonged. His outrage at the way in which Joy and other directors of the Burlington handled the River Roads in the 1870's was the fruit of his personal sense of ethics, reinforced by the code of his group, which in railroad matters he, though not all of his associates, extended to embrace investors of all kinds in the C. B. & Q.

It is important, then, to bear in mind that we are dealing with investors and businessmen deriving their outlook and personal potentialities, as well as their wealth and command over others' wealth, from a close-knit and quite distinctive community. Boston capitalists, operating through a series of closely interlocking groups, owed their economic strength, and in some measure their behavioral characteristics, to the social background and cohesiveness of Boston's mercantile inheritance.

These characteristics were important in all phases of the investment process, and they were particularly relevant to the mobilization of capital. In an age when institutional arrangements to facilitate the flow of capital into new ventures were embryonic, the role of the individual mobilizer of capital and his place within a social grouping were crucial. Hence the tendency of Boston investment to "bunch" in particular sectors and enterprises. The C. B. & Q. and the Atchison were Boston ventures because investment tended to be a cumulative social process in an environment lacking an impersonal, national money market.

In this environment, investment leadership was by example. Because Forbes had an excellent reputation with members of his group, he was able to mobilize their resources when he needed them. But his ability to do this was contingent on his own willingness to go in as deep or deeper than any on whom he called. Although he played a major role in investment decisions by others, important reciprocal obligations existed between him and his group. The same seems to have been true of Thomas Nickerson when he obtained a further injection of capital for the Atchison in 1873, after a rapid and expensive bout of construction.

The critical importance of the individual in an investment process that involved group relationships also had peculiar relevance to the strategy by which capital was placed. With personal reputation and responsibility as a fiduciary agent resting on such decisions, the mobilizer of capital was under numerous constraints to proceed with caution. This should have discouraged the more flagrant kinds of opportunistic investment and been conducive to developmental attitudes. Such a policy was revealed in the careful, solid, sequential construction at a moderate pace that characterized the evolution of the Burlington system and to a considerable extent the Atchison's, though the latter's environment was significantly different and its leading Boston backers somewhat more opportunistic than the latter-day Forbes.

Failure to recognize the personal obligations imposed by the investment process severely handicapped the promoters of the Illinois Central. Their initial reluctance to commit their own capital dampened enthusiasm of others to do so. In the Union Pacific, the narrowness of the group concept — and its polarization around the Durant and Ames factions — contributed materially to the road's difficulties.

THE TRANSFORMATION OF THE INVESTOR

Although the capitalist's initial decision to make a significant capital commitment might be founded on short-run expectations of profit, or other considerations, the ensuing reality could move his investment decision making in several directions. If the short-run expectations were fulfilled, this was a persuasive argument for increasing his commitment and his expectations of the future. With this kind of commitment, there was reason to take a more active role in decision making within the firm to protect past investment, as well as to make decisions with respect to a longer time span. And, as the span lengthened, changes in the environment became more relevant to the decisions. Thus a passive capitalist could be transformed into an opportunistic investor and then into a developmental one. Clearly this was the case with Forbes, the Griswolds, and, in a significant sense, the Ames brothers. Alternatively, the success of one opportunistic venture could lead to the liquidation of that investment and the search for new opportunities to repeat the coup with augmented resources. H. H. Hunnewell and David Neal in the Reading and Jay Gould in the Kansas Pacific come to mind in this connection.

The short-run reality could also fall far short of expectations. This could mean catastrophe for the small capitalist, as in the case of Dr. Estes Howe and the Mad River road in Ohio. On the other hand, for one of larger means such reverses might mean the end of only that particular investment, or the prelude to increased commitments of capital and participation in entrepreneurial decision making. Both reactions characterized investors in the Joy system when it collapsed and in the Illinois Central when it encountered severe financial difficulties.

CONSEQUENTIAL INVESTMENT AND INVESTMENT STRATEGY

No individual whom we have studied was completely opportunistic or developmental in his portfolio of western investments. For example, the enforced conservatism of a developmental role in a railroad could induce opportunistic investment elsewhere. Such opportunities naturally followed from the opening of new territory by a railroad — town lot, agricultural land, minerals, stockyard, and other investments presented themselves as a consequence of railroad investment decisions. This study shows that a practical differentiation can be drawn between opportunistic and developmental railroad investors, up to the 1880's at least, on the basis of whether such consequential investment, as a personal rather than corporate venture, replaced primary concern with development of an open-ended railroad system.

Because extension of a railroad almost inevitably opened new opportunities for consequential investment, a basic strategy of opportunistic investors was to skim the cream off those chances offered in any one period. Some, like David Neal, became too engrossed with consequential investment to continue in railroads. Others, like Forbes, did not allow themselves to be diverted from a primary interest in the development of a transportation system, yet took advantage of consequential investment when they could. Still others, like Nathaniel Thayer, tried to straddle the fence. Each in his own way contributed to the process of the economic growth.

The System Concept and Investment Strategy

The evolution of the railroad–system concept after 1850 did much to transform opportunistic into developmental investors, for there was a geographical dimension to nineteenth-century investment in western railroads. Commitment on an opportunistic basis to a single road that was open-ended to either East or West typically led in a series of steps to the idea of building or combining roads between major nodal points.

Viewing western railroad investment in these terms, the initial investment decision assumes added significance. Commitment to a closed-end road running athwart rather than along the main paths of western development from East to West made the emergence of a system concept less likely. The investor who became heavily involved in such roads had fewer opportunities to reorient his investment strategy than one who committed himself to an open-ended road stretching westward. For example, once roads intended to connect the Great Lakes with a major waterway such as the Ohio River were completed, there were both physical and economic impediments to further expansion. This was generally true of roads oriented along a north-south axis until extensive railroad construction westward began to generate interest in protection of these systems along their flanks. Then, of course, the existing east-west systems dominated the resulting strategy. The major exception that we have discussed is the Illinois Central, but the circumstances of its birth largely explain the outcome. Even so, for individual investors the experience of the I.C.'s early years fitted the pattern we have ascribed to north-south roads generally.

The open-ended system, on the other hand, tended to generate the incentives, the opportunities, and the requirements for deepening capital commitments and to provide recurring opportunities to apply accumulated investment knowledge and entrepreneurial skills under new conditions. The extent of Boston interest and influence in the development of such major systems as the Atchison, the Burlington, and the Union Pacific is evidence of the self-reinforcing characteristics of investment in open-ended systems.

From these conclusions it follows that the initial placement of a Bostonian's capital in western railroads was important in determining whether he would follow it with more. An early investment in an east-west road was more likely to lead to a long-run developmental commitment than when capital was placed in a north-south one. This fact goes far toward explaining why Bostonians came to play such a prominent and continuing role in the major western systems that we have traced over a comparatively long span of time. It also bears repetition in this context that the timing of initial commitments by major Boston capitalists to western railroads was fortuitous in the over-all timing of western development and was a product of Boston's place as a capital center, based largely on its prominence in earlier overseas trade.

RISK, UNCERTAINTY, AND THE INVESTOR

While commitment to an open-ended railroad system tended to generate its own imperatives over time, investors' portfolios had an extensive geographical dimension that told something about the investor himself. This was so because risk-taking in railroad investment varied as one considered roads in terms of their relation to a moving population frontier. For example, the point of departure for Bostonians considering new investment in the 1840's was a 6 per cent return, which could be obtained in the immediate area with little or no risk.

As an individual's geographical investment horizons widened, a higher rate of return was used in evaluating opportunities for investment. For example, an anticipated 10 per cent return helped to lure Forbes into the Michigan Central which, though distant from Boston, was available at a price in keeping with its capital assets and in an area already settled. Here, in short, was a calculable risk. Two decades later, Forbes declined to invest in the Union Pacific, where genuine uncertainty about its completion through a vast undeveloped area attracted investors whose *minimum* expectation was a 20 per cent return on short-run investment. While other factors contributed to Forbes's specific decision against the U. P., it does seem clear that one rough measure of an investor's degree of opportunism — at least up to the 1880's — was *how far* West his major railroad investments extended.

Within the context of over-all investment strategy, and regardless of the geographical area, both opportunistic and developmental investors sought to minimize the risks accompanying any significant commitment of either their time or their resources. In general, as investment opportunity moved along the continuum from the "sure" thing to the outright "gamble," the greater became the effort to shift risk-bearing to others and the greater became the substitution of promotional and entrepreneurial skills for personal capital. The promotion of the Illinois Central is a case in point.

Of course, the type of individual and the extent of his resources were frequently as relevant as geography to such substitutions. Still, the *degree* to which an investor sought to shift risk-bearing to others is another indicator of *how* opportunistic his own goals were.

Equally relevant to the practical differentiation between opportunistic and developmental investors, and again a matter of degree, was how investors sought to minimize risk-bearing in given situations. Both types sought to use government influence, for example, but a distinction can be drawn between those to whom this was the pivotal point of a whole strategy and those to whom such influence supplemented strategy devised on other grounds. As indicated earlier, participation in active management was also a way of minimizing risk-bearing for both types of investors.

It was characteristic of developmental railroad investors that as long as the environment permitted it, they systematically aimed at minimizing and controlling risks. In spite of their expectation and encouragement of long-run regional growth, these investors made decisions on the purchase, construction, or extension of roads with an eye to relatively short-run projections from the availability of existing traffic. In the postwar environment the intensification of a new type of railroad competition did lead to increasingly risky ventures and to overcommitment. However, aside from situations such as those of the Union Pacific or the later extensions of the Atchison, there were few examples of pure "building ahead of demand."

Transformation of the Railroad Sector

In the nineteenth century, as in any period of economic development, the interaction between an investor's expectations, his strategy, and its consequences operated at many levels. So far in this chapter we have dealt with one set of changing relationships between expectations and reality. It is now appropriate to re-emphasize another level, one exemplified by the impact of competitive and environmental differences in the prewar and postwar railroad scenes.

Economic development is a dynamic process. In terms of railroad investment between the 1840's and the 1880's, this fact had a twofold implication. First, the outcome of similar investment decisions changed over time, so that familiar beneficial consequences no longer flowed from traditional patterns of behavior. Second, as the competitive pressures on and environmental incentives to investment changed, so the nature and structure of that investment were also obliged to change.

In the post-Civil War period both extensive and intensive railroad construction reached a peak. This was partly due to the quickened pace of economic development and appetite, which stimulated construction beyond the Mississippi and to the Pacific. But it was also due to the attraction of massive supplies of capital, to the rival pressures of different entrepreneurial groups competing until they had constructed intertwined yet hostile railroad systems.

Before the war the problems of railroad extension could on the whole be met in terms of the orderly, sequential expansion of lines. Increasingly in the postwar period, however, to protect what they had built and to insure against the future, western railroad managements were obliged to overbuild, to assume new risks and new obligations because of the strategic risks of failing to do so. As the West became the arena for a newly intensive competition, therefore, some railroads were forced both to build ahead of any substantial demand for their services and to extend branches beyond the point which optimistic projections of existing demand even in settled regions would have justified. The postwar growth of giant systems, illustrated by the Union Pacific, the C. B. & Q., and the Atchison, was one symptom of the new situation. The intrusive and disturbing operations of Jay Gould was another. And, significantly, the extent to which Boston investors, otherwise closely allied, fought each other with extensions and rate-cutting — as happened between the Atchison and the C. B. & Q. — was a third.

In retrospect, it is clear that the unco-ordinated expansion of enterprises with such large burdens of fixed capital to carry, heralded a new period of crisis for the railroad sector of the economy. And developmental investment, even of the most sober and responsible kind, now produced untoward and uncomfortable consequences.

These problems came to a head as a result of the great railroad construction boom of the 1880's. The response to the ensuing problems at a general policy level led to a period of financial reorganization and operating consolidation — although this was not to happen before crisis in the form of bankruptcy and collapse had overtaken a good part of the national railroad mileage. In terms of structures and operations the response was a sharper separation of ownership and management, the replacement of general entrepreneurs by investment banking houses, and a growing professionalization of capital mobilization and control. The gathering, the allocation, and the management of capital became increasingly institutionalized. This, indeed, was perhaps the most important sense in which railroads showed the way to big business in general.

As exemplified in the Atchison, Topeka & Santa Fe, the immediate occasion for this transformation was often a financial crisis of very serious proportions. Yet it would be wrong to attribute such extensive changes in policies, practices, and organization merely to a short-term collapse. Rather, it is important to appreciate the background to the various crises of particular railroad systems. For, at bottom, the extent of their troubles was due in large measure to the inability of their inherited organization and financial procedures to deal with the problems raised by railroad operations in a new age.

Competition between giant systems characterized by problems of large-scale organization and complex management, of increasingly powerful labor groups, and of government regulation at federal and state levels, enforced a departure from traditional, personal management and finance. Indeed, in these respects, it is significant that the Atchison, Topeka & Santa Fe was dependent on the services of an investment banking house from the beginning of its effective development, even though Kidder, Peabody & Co. did not come to play a decisive role until the implications of expansion raised entirely new problems in the 1880's. In that decade it became increasingly apparent that the new scope of railroad enterprise demanded both a new type of management and more appropriate means of obtaining the requisite amounts of capital and of safeguarding it for its owners once it had been acquired.

These kinds of factors, rather than any specific entreprenurial "failure," led to the termination of the era of railroad enterprise which has provided the subject matter of this study. In a way, investors such as those in the Boston-backed systems traced in this book had been *too* successful: the persistence and consistency of their efforts had helped to change dramatically the environment within which new investment decisions had to be made. And, as the investment process changed to adapt to the new environment, so the rationale of the efforts of fifty years disappeared.

In summary, then, the strategy of open-ended systems which emerged in the 1850's and intensified soon after the Civil War was giving way to a new strategy by the late 1870's and 1880's. The new approach was based on the need to protect what had already been created, even when this meant further aggressive (and expensive) expansion. Meanwhile, and as a concomitant of these developments, the demands of large-scale enterprises tended increasingly to diminish the role that any individual investor could expect to play in their affairs. More than this, institutional arrangements had been perfected over the years both to supply capital and to provide entrepreneurial and managerial skills. In an age of investment banking, professional management, and new organizational structures, there were strong forces at work to force the erstwhile active western railroad investor back into the role of the relatively passive capitalist.

In an important sense, with the maturity of the western railroad systems they had helped to create, Boston capitalists had come full circle by 1890. They had contributed significantly to the development of a national transportation network, as well as to the erosion of their own individual position on the investment scene. Their policies had helped transform the West. Some, like Forbes, were active throughout the whole period. Others were descendants of the pioneering investors. Yet others were relative newcomers. But even with these late arrivals a web of mutual relationships within the Boston community of capitalists had directed capital toward goals identified, and along channels developed, by their predecessors.

But now that the job was done, and done so thoroughly that its achievement blocked out any vision of future railroad growth with comparable prospects, capitalists in Boston and elsewhere were faced with two broad (but not necessarily mutually exclusive) alternatives. They could continue to invest, albeit more passively and impersonally, in sectors such as the railroads which were being consolidated; or they could shift their resources into some of the newer sectors of the economy which were undergoing dynamic expansion in the more mature stage of economic evolution. Their reactions to the new problems of choice were varied and comprise material for an entirely different sort of study. But, it may well be claimed, never again would individual investors be faced with choices of the magnitude and scope involved in the development of the western railroad network.

BIBLIOGRAPHY

NOTES

INDEX

Bibliography

Books

Ackerman, William K. *Historical Sketch of the Illinois Central Railroad, together with a Brief Biographical Record* . . . Chicago, 1890.
Adams, Charles Francis. *Charles Francis Adams, 1835–1915: An Autobiography* . . . Boston, 1916.
[Barron, Clarence W.] *The Boston Stock Exchange* . . . Boston, 1893.
Berry, Thomas S. *Western Prices before 1861.* Cambridge, Mass., 1943.
Bidwell, Percy W. and John I. Falconer. *History of Agriculture in the Northern United States, 1620–1860.* Washington, 1925.
Black, Robert L. *The Little Miami Railroad.* Cincinnati, n.d.
Bliss, George. *Historical Memoir of the Western Railroad.* Springfield, Mass., 1863.
Bogen, Jules T. *The Anthracite Railroads: A Study in American Railroad Enterprise.* New York, 1927.
Bradlee, Francis B. C. *The Eastern Railroad: A Historical Account of Early Railroading in Eastern New England.* Salem, Mass., 1922, 2d ed.
Bradley, Glenn D. *The Story of the Santa Fe.* Boston, 1920.
Brownson, Howard G. *History of the Illinois Central Railroad to 1870.* Urbana, Illinois, 1915.
Case, Theodore S. *History of Kansas City, Missouri.* Syracuse, New York, 1888.
Claflin, Helen A. *A New England Family.* Belmont, Mass., privately printed, n.d.
Cochran, Thomas C. *Railroad Leaders, 1845–1890; The Business Mind in Action.* Cambridge, Mass., 1953.
Coolidge, T. Jefferson. *The Autobiography of T. Jefferson Coolidge, 1831–1920.* Boston, 1923.
Corliss, Carlton J. *Main-Line of Mid-America.* New York, 1950.
Crawford, J. B. *The Credit Mobilier of America.* Boston, 1880.
Crawford, Mary C. *Famous Families of Massachusetts.* 2 vols. Boston, 1930.
Cunningham, Edith P., ed. *Charles Elliott Perkins and Edith Forbes Perkins: Family Letters, 1861–1869.* Boston, 1949.
Davis, John P. *The Union Pacific Railway, A Study in Railway Politics, History, and Economics.* Chicago, 1894.
Davis, Lance E., *et al. American Economic History, The Development of a National Economy.* Homewood, Illinois, 1961.
Duesenberry, James S. *Business Cycles and Economic Growth.* New York, 1958.
Eavenson, Howard N. *The First Century and a Quarter of American Coal Industry.* Pittsburgh, 1942.
Emerson, Edward W. *Life and Letters of Charles Russell Lowell.* Boston and New York, 1907.
Fels, Rendig. *American Business Cycles, 1865–1897.* Chapel Hill, North Carolina, 1959.
Fishlow, Albert. *American Railroads and the Transformation of the Ante-Bellum Economy.* Cambridge, Mass., 1965.
Fogel, Robert W. *Railroads and American Economic Growth: Essays in Econometric History.* Baltimore, 1964.

——— *The Union Pacific Railroad, A Case in Premature Enterprise.* Baltimore, 1960.

Forbes, Robert Bennet. *Personal Reminiscences.* Boston, 1882, 2d ed., rev.

——— *Remarks on China and the China Trade.* Boston, 1844.

Fries, Robert F. *Empire in Pine, the Story of Lumbering in Wisconsin, 1830–1900.* Madison, Wisconsin, 1951.

Gara, Larry. *Westernized Yankee, The Story of Cyrus Woodman.* Madison, Wisconsin, 1956.

Gates, Paul W. *Fifty Million Acres: Conflicts over Kansas Land Policy 1854–1890.* Ithaca, New York, 1954.

——— *The Illinois Central Railroad and Its Colonization Work.* Cambridge, Mass., 1934.

Gates, William B., Jr. *Michigan Copper and Boston Dollars.* Cambridge, Mass., 1951.

Gibb, George Sweet. *The Saco-Lowell Shops: Textile Machinery Building in New England, 1813–1949.* Cambridge, Mass., 1950.

Glaab, Charles N. *Kansas City and the Railroads.* Madison, Wisconsin, 1962.

Goodrich, Carter L. *Government Promotion of American Canals and Railroads, 1800–1890.* New York, 1960.

Greenberg, Michael. *British Trade and the Opening of China, 1800–42.* Cambridge, England, 1951.

Grodinsky, Julius. *Jay Gould, His Business Career, 1867–1892.* Philadelphia, 1957.

——— *Transcontinental Railway Strategy, 1869–1893.* Philadelphia, 1962.

Hall, Henry, ed. *America's Successful Men of Affairs.* New York, 1896.

Hargrave, Frank F. *A Pioneer Indiana Railroad: The Origin and Development of the Monon.* Indianapolis, 1932.

Harris, Seymour E., ed. *American Economic History.* New York, 1961.

Hayes, William E. *Iron Road to Empire.* New York, 1953.

Hazard, Rowland. *The Credit Mobilier of America.* Providence, 1881.

Hibbard, Benjamin H. *A History of the Public Land Policies.* New York, 1924.

Hicks, John R. *A Contribution to the Theory of the Trade Cycle.* Oxford, England, 1950.

Hidy, Ralph W. *The House of Baring in American Trade and Finance: English Merchant Bankers at Work, 1763–1861.* Cambridge, Mass., 1949.

Hughes, Sarah Forbes, ed. *Letters and Recollections of John Murray Forbes.* 2 vols. Boston, 1900.

Hunnewell, Hollis H. *Life, Letters and Diary of Horatio Hollis Hunnewell.* 3 vols. Boston, 1906.

Hunter, Louis C. *Steamboats on the Western Rivers; An Economic and Technological History.* Cambridge, Mass., 1949.

Johnson, Emory R., *et al. History of Domestic and Foreign Commerce of the United States.* 2 vols. Washington, 1915.

Kirkland, Edward C. *Men, Cities and Transportation: A Study in New England History, 1820–1900.* 2 vols. Cambridge, Mass., 1948.

Latham, Bryan. *Timber, Its Development and Distribution, a Historical Survey.* London, 1957.

Marriner, Sheila. *Rathbones of Liverpool, 1845–73.* Liverpool, 1961.

Martin, Joseph A. *Seventy-Three Years' History of the Boston Stock Market . . .* Boston, 1871.

McGrane, Reginald C. *Foreign Bondholders and American State Debts.* New York, 1935.

McHenry, George. *Philadelphia and Reading Railroad Company; its Financial History* . . . London, 1878.

Morgan, Julian D. *Some Controlling Factors in Kansas Population Movements.* Lawrence, Kansas, 1953.

Morison, Samuel E. *Maritime History of Massachusetts, 1783–1860.* Boston, 1921.

National Bureau of Economic Research. *Trends in the American Economy in the Nineteenth Century.* Princeton, 1960.

Neu, Irene D. *Erastus Corning: Merchant and Financier, 1794–1872.* Ithaca, New York, 1960.

North, Douglass C. *Economic Growth of the United States, 1790–1860.* Englewood Cliffs, New Jersey, 1961.

Overton, Richard C. *Burlington West, a Colonization History of the Burlington Railroad.* Cambridge, Mass., 1941.

Pearson, Henry G. *An American Railroad Builder, John Murray Forbes.* Boston, 1911.

Poor, Henry V. *History of the Railroads and Canals of the United States.* New York, 1860.

——— *The Pacific Railroad, The Relations Existing between It and the Government of the United States.* New York, 1871.

Porter, Kenneth W. *The Jacksons and the Lees: Two Generations of Massachusetts Merchants, 1765–1844.* 2 vols. Cambridge, Mass., 1937.

Pound, Arthur, and Samuel T. Moore, eds. *More They Told Barron.* New York, 1931.

Professional and Industrial History of Suffolk County, [Massachusetts]. 3 vols. Boston, 1894.

Riegel, Robert E. *The Story of the Western Railroads.* New York, 1926.

Rubin, Julius. *Canal or Railroad? Imitation and Innovation in the Response to the Erie Canal in Philadelphia, Baltimore, and Boston.* (Transactions of the American Philosophical Society.) Philadelphia, 1961.

Sabin, Edwin L. *Building the Pacific Railway.* Philadelphia, 1919.

Shannon, Fred A. *The Farmer's Last Frontier: Agriculture, 1860–1897.* New York, 1945.

Shattuck, Lemuel. *Report to the Committee of the City Council Appointed to Obtain the Census of Boston for the year 1845.* Boston, 1846.

Smith, Walter B. and Arthur H. Cole. *Fluctuations in American Business, 1790 to 1860.* Cambridge, Mass., 1935.

Sumner, William H. *A History of East Boston; with Biographical Sketches of Its Early Proprietors.* Boston, 1858.

Taylor, George R. *The Transportation Revolution, 1815–1860.* New York, 1951.

de Tocqueville, Alexis. *Democracy in America.* 2 vols. New York, 1957.

Youngson, A. J. *The Possibilities of Economic Progress.* Cambridge, England, 1959.

Articles

Albion, Robert G. "New York Port and Its Disappointed Rivals, 1815–1860," *Journal of Economic and Business History,* III (August 1931), 602–629.

Cochran, Thomas C. "The Legend of the Robber Barons," *The Pennsylvania Magazine of History and Biography,* LXXIV (July 1950), 307–321.

Cootner, Paul H. "The Role of the Railroads in United States Economic Growth," *The Journal of Economic History,* XXIII (December 1963), 477–521.

Derby, E. H. "City of Boston," *Hunt's Merchants' Magazine,* XXIII (November 1846), 483–497.

——— "Progress of Railroads in Massachusetts," *Hunt's Merchants' Magazine,* XIV (January 1846), 29–35.

Duesenberry, James S. "Some Aspects of the Theory of Development," *Explorations in Entrepreneurial History,* III (December 1950), 63–102.

Gates, Paul W. "The Role of the Land Speculator in Western Development," *The Pennsylvania Magazine of History and Biography,* LXVI (July 1942), 314–333.

Glaab, Charles N. "Business Patterns in the Growth of a Midwestern City . . . ," *Business History Review,* XXXIII (Summer 1959), 156–174.

Jenks, Leland H. "Railroads as an Economic Force in American Development," *The Journal of Economic History,* IV (May 1944), 1–20.

Joy, James F. "Railroad History of Michigan," Michigan Pioneer and Historical Society, *Collections,* XXII (1894), 292–304.

Kennedy, Charles J. "The Eastern Rail-road Company to 1855," *Business History Review,* XXXI (Spring 1957), 92–123.

Larson, Henrietta M. "A China Trader Turns Investor — A Biographical Chapter in American Business History," *Harvard Business Review,* XI (April 1934), 345–358.

Neu, Irene D. "The Building of the Sault Canal, 1852–1855," *Mississippi Valley Historical Review,* XL (June 1953), 25–46.

Newton, A. W. "The Chicago and Aurora Railroad," Railway and Locomotive Historical Society, *Bulletin,* LXXVI (March 1949), 6–20.

Overton, Richard C. "Charles Elliott Perkins," *Business History Review,* XXXI (Autumn 1957), 292–309.

Raney, William F. "Appleton," *Wisconsin Magazine of History,* XXXIII (December 1949), 135–151.

Riegel, Robert E. "Trans-Mississippi Railroads During the Fifties," *Mississippi Valley Historical Review,* X (September 1923).

Scheiber, Harry N. "New England Capital in Western Banking: The Commercial Bank of Lake Erie, 1831–1843," *Business History Review,* XXXIX (Spring 1966), 47–65.

Schumpeter, Joseph A. "The Creative Response in Economic History," *The Journal of Economic History,* VII (November 1947), 149–159.

Scott, J. W. "Railroads East and West," *Hunt's Merchants' Magazine,* XIII (September 1845), 250–252.

Spriggs, W. M. "Great Western Railway of Canada," Railway and Locomotive Historical Society, *Bulletin,* LI (February 1940), 7–36.

Trottman, Nelson. *History of the Union Pacific, A Financial and Economic Survey.* New York, 1923.

Waters, Lawrence L. *Steel Trails to Santa Fe.* Lawrence, Kansas, 1950.

Waters, Thomas F. *Augustine Heard and His Friends.* Salem, Massachusetts, 1916.

Webster, Daniel. *Writings and Speeches of Daniel Webster.* 18 vols. Boston, 1903.

White, Gerald T. *The History of the Massachusetts Hospital Life Insurance Company.* Cambridge, Mass., 1955.

White, Henry K. *History of the Union Pacific Railway.* Chicago, 1895.

Winsor, Justin, ed. *The Memorial History of Boston.* 4 vols. Boston, 1883.

Unpublished Studies

Bennett, Howard. "The Hannibal and St. Joseph Railroad and the Development of Northern Missouri, 1847–1870; a Study of Land and Colonization Policies." Unpublished Ph.D. dissertation, Harvard University, 1950.

Gregory, Frances W. "Nathan Appleton, Yankee Merchant, 1779–1861." Unpublished Ph.D. dissertation, Radcliffe College, 1949.

Hansen, Walter J. "State Aid to Railroads in Michigan during the Early Statehood Period." Unpublished Ph.D. dissertation, University of Michigan, 1941.

McConkey, M. C. "James F. Joy." Unpublished biography, Michigan Historical Collections, University of Michigan.

Nance, Joseph M. "The Attitude of New England Toward Westward Expansion, 1800–1850." Unpublished Ph.D. dissertation, University of Texas, 1941.

Salsbury, Stephen. "Private Enterprise in Massachusetts, the Beginnings of the Boston & Albany Railroad, 1825–1842." Unpublished Ph.D. dissertation, Harvard University, 1961.

Railroad and Other Company Publications

RAILROAD CHARTERS

Charter of the Boston and Worcester Railroad Corporation . . . Boston, 1859.

The Charter and Laws Relating to the Mad River and Lake Erie Rail-Road Company. Sandusky City, 1847.

Charter of the Michigan Central Rail-Road Company.

RAILROAD MANUALS

Poor's Manual of the Railroads of the United States, 1870–1890.

RAILROAD ANNUAL REPORTS

Atchison, Topeka & Santa Fe, 1873–1890.
Boston and Lowell
  to the legislature, 1834–1836.
  to the stockholders, 1837–1849.
Boston and Worcester
  to the legislature, 1833–1837.
Burlington and Missouri River, 1858–1865.
Chicago, Burlington & Quincy, 1867–1890.
Hannibal and St. Joseph, 1850–1872.
Illinois Central, 1854–1864.
Kansas City, St. Joseph & Council Bluffs, 1871.
Little Miami Railroad, 1843–1845.
Mad River and Lake Erie, 1847.
Michigan Central, 1848–1859.
Missouri River, Fort Scott & Gulf, 1871.
Philadelphia and Reading, 1847–1849.
Philadelphia, Wilmington and Baltimore, 1842–1848.
Union Pacific, 1884–1889.
Western, 1840–1845.

OTHER ANNUAL REPORTS

New York & Boston Illinois Land Company, 1837.
St. Mary's Falls Ship Canal Company, 1858.
South Cove Corporation, 1834.

COMPANY LISTS, CIRCULARS, AND OCCASIONAL PUBLICATIONS

Atchison, Topeka & Santa Fe

Manuscript list of stockholders, October 11, 1883.
Documents Relating to the Atchison, Topeka & Santa Fe Railroad, 1890.
The Atchison, Topeka & Santa Fe Railroad. Boston, 1871 (Brochure).
Clarence H. Venner & Company, *Facts for Investors Concerning the Atchison, Topeka and Santa Fe R. R. Company.* Boston, March, 1883.
Zarah, Its Present and Future, 1871 (Promotional Pamphlet).

Boston and Lowell

Report of a Committee on the Boston and Lowell Railroad, Boston, 1831.

Boston and Providence

Report of the Joint Special Committee to investigate . . . the Boston and Providence, Mass. Senate, No. 50, March, 1840.

Burlington and Missouri River

Circular to the bondholders, October 7, 1863.
Circular to the bondholders, September 20, 1861.

Chicago, Burlington & Quincy

Letter to stockholders, October 12, 1863.
Letter to stockholders, August 15, 1871.
Circular, September 15, 1881.
Circular to the stockholders, February 20, 1868.
Documentary History. 3 vols. Chicago, 1928.
Budd, Ralph, "The Burlington Railroad's Boston Background," an address before the American Newcomen Society, Boston, April 22, 1949.

Chicago, Burlington & Quincy and the Hannibal and St. Joseph

Circular to the stockholders, January 25, 1867.

Eastern

Peabody, George, *Address at the Opening of the Eastern Rail Road Between Boston and Salem.* Salem, 1838.

Great Western

Report Upon the Merits of the Great Western Railroad Canada West: by a Committee of its American Friends. Boston, 1851.

Hannibal and St. Joseph

Circular to the stockholders, January 24, 1870.
A Letter to the Stockholders . . . of the Hannibal and St. Joseph Railroad Company . . . New York, 1870.

Illinois Central

Neal, David A. *The Illinois Central Railroad: Its Position and Prospects.* July 1, 1851.
Documents Relating to the Organization of the Illinois Central Railroad Company. 1853, 2nd ed.
Communication from the President to the Directors of the Illinois Central, August 10, 1853. New York, 1853.
Report to the Board of Directors . . . by a Committee . . . November 10, 1853.
Letter to the stockholders, October 1, 1855.

Rantoul, Robert, Jr. *Letter to Robert Schuyler, Esq., President of the Illinois Central Railroad, on the Value of the Public Lands of Illinois.* Boston, 1851.

Michigan Central

Circular to subscribers to Michigan Central stock, September 12, 1846.

Circular to subscribers to Michigan Central stock, September 14, 1846.

Brooks, John W. *Report Upon the Merits of the Michigan Central Railroad . . .* New York, 1846.

"Statements and Replies in Reference to the Compensation for the Use of the Road of the Illinois Central R. R. Company, from Calumet to Chicago, by the Michigan Central R. R. Company." Boston, 1860.

Philadelphia and Reading

Report of a Committee of Investigation into the Affairs of the Philadelphia and Reading Rail Road Company. Boston, 1846.

Report to the Stockholders of the Philadelphia and Reading Rail Road Company, January, 1850. (Published with *Annual Report,* 1850.)

Neal, David A., *Report Made to the Managers of the Philadelphia and Reading Rail Road Company, September 19, 1849.* September, 1849. (Published with *Report of the President and Managers . . . ,* September, 1849.)

Kidder, Peabody & Co.

Circular, November 1, 1870.

Letter to Stock and Bondholders, California Southern Railroad, October 25, 1884.

St. Mary's Falls Ship Canal Company

Catalogue of 525,000 Acres of Pine Timber Lands . . . 1863.

U.S. Government Publications

U.S. Census Office. 8th Census, 1860: *Agriculture.*

U.S. Bureau of the Census. *Abstract of the Eleventh Census. 1890.*

——. *Historical Statistics of the United States, Colonial Times to 1957.* Washington, D.C., 1960.

U.S. Bureau of Statistics. *Report on . . . Internal Commerce . . . 1889.*

42 Cong. 3 Sess. House Select Committee to Investigate the Alleged Credit Mobilier Bribery. *Report.* Washington, 1873.

42 Cong. 3 Sess. House Select Committee No. 2 on the Credit Mobilier. *Report.* Washington, 1873.

50 Cong. 1 Sess. Senate Ex. Doc. 51. *United States Pacific Railway Commission Testimony.* 10 vols. Washington, 1887.

52 Cong. 2 Sess. Senate. Committee on Finance. *Wholesale Prices, Wages, and Transportation.* Washington, 1893.

U.S. Interstate Commerce Commission. *Valuation Reports.* vol. 127. [Valuation Docket 625, "Atchison, Topeka & Santa Fe Railway Company"]. Washington, 1927.

State Publications

Massachusetts Board of Directors of Internal Improvements. *Report . . . on the Practicability and Expediency of a Railroad from Boston to the Hudson River . . .* Boston, 1829.

Massachusetts Secretary of the Commonwealth. *Statistics of the Condition and Products of Certain Branches of Industry in Massachusetts, for the year ending April 1, 1845.* Boston, 1846.

State of Missouri. Act to Expedite the Pacific Railroad and Hannibal and St. Joseph Railroad.

PAMPHLETS

Adams, Charles Francis, Jr. *The Case of the Union Pacific Railway Company.* Statement before the Committee on the Pacific Railroads, February 24, 1886.

A Few Remarks on the Operations of the Companies . . . Organized for the Digging & Smelting of Copper . . . on Lake Superior . . . by an Explorer. Boston, 1845 (?).

"Our First Men:" a Calendar of Wealth, Fashion and Gentility . . . a List of those Persons Taxed in the City of Boston . . . Worth One Hundred Thousand Dollars, with Biographical Notices of the Principal Persons. Boston, 1846, rev. ed.

PERIODICALS

American Railroad Journal, 1845–1859.
Bankers' Magazine, 1848.
Boston *Daily Advertiser,* 1889.
Boston *Herald,* 1880.
Commercial & Financial Chronicle, 1875–1890.
Hazard's U.S. Register, 1841.
Hunt's Merchants' Magazine, 1846–1854.
New York *Tribune,* 1876.
Niles Weekly Register, 1837.
Railroad Gazette, 1873–1892.

MANUSCRIPT SOURCES

Boston and Worcester Manuscripts, Manuscript Division, Baker Library. Harvard University, Graduate School of Business Administration. (Part of Boston and Albany Railroad Collection.)
Bryant & Sturgis Collection, Manuscript Division, Baker Library.
Cunningham-Overton Collection of Perkins Papers, Lawson Memorial Library, University of Western Ontario.
John P. Cushing Collection, Manuscript Division, Baker Library.
Forbes Collection, Manuscript Division, Baker Library.
Heard Collection, Manuscript Division, Baker Library.
Illinois Land Agency Collection, Manuscript Division, Baker Library.
Kidder, Peabody & Company, Letter Books, Manuscript Division, Baker Library.
Mad River and Lake Erie Folder, Manuscript Division, Baker Library.
Neal-Rantoul Collection, Manuscript Division, Baker Library.
Norcross papers, Massachusetts Historical Society, Boston.
Pepperell Manufacturing Company Collection, Manuscript Division, Baker Library.
Philadelphia and Reading Folders, Manuscript Division, Baker Library.

Notes

Chapter 1
The Problem and Its Setting

1. U.S. Bureau of the Census, *Historical Statistics of the United States, Colonial Times to 1957* (Washington, D.C., 1960), 297, 302, 357, 360, 366, 427. In aggregate terms, between 1839 and 1859 the value of the agricultural output doubled, and those of mining and manufacturing almost quadrupled. (Robert E. Gallman, "Commodity Output, 1839–1899," National Bureau of Economic Research, *Trends in the American Economy in the Nineteenth Century* [Princeton, 1960], 43. Hereafter cited as *Trends in the American Economy*.) As late as 1859 agriculture employed over four times as many workers and produced 75 per cent more net output than did manufacturing. (*Ibid.*, 26, 30.)

2. See the statistics in Gallman, "Commodity Output, 1839–1899," 16, 24.

3. Agriculture employed 72 per cent of the growing labor force in 1820; this fell to 59 per cent in 1860, and to 37 per cent in 1900. (Calculated from *Historical Statistics*, 74.) The output per worker in agriculture does not seem to have changed significantly between 1800 and 1850. In the last half of the century, however, it rose by some 75 per cent. (Gallman, "Commodity Output, 1839–1899," 31; Marvin W. Towne and Wayne D. Rasmussen, "Farm Gross Product and Gross Investment in the Nineteenth Century," *Trends in the American Economy*, 269.)

4. For an analytical exposition of this process, see James S. Duesenberry, "Some Aspects of the Theory of Development," *Explorations in Entrepreneurial History*, III, 2 (December 1950), 96–102.

5. See in particular Robert W. Fogel, *Railroads and American Economic Growth: Essays in Econometric History* (Baltimore, 1964); Albert Fishlow, *American Railroads and the Transformation of the Ante Bellum Economy* (Cambridge, Massachusetts, 1965); and Paul H. Cootner, "The Role of the Railroads in United States Economic Growth," *The Journal of Economic History*, XXIII, 4 (December 1963), 477–521. For an earlier appraisal of the subject, see Leland H. Jenks, "Railroads as an Economic Force in American Development," *The Journal of Economic History*, IV, 1 (May 1944), 1–20.

6. Fishlow, *American Railroads*, 305–306.

7. Joseph A. Schumpeter, "The Creative Response in Economic History," *The Journal of Economic History*, VII, 2 (November 1947), 150–151.

8. See, for example, John R. Hicks, *A Contribution to the Theory of the Trade Cycle* (Oxford, England, 1950), 58–61; James S. Duesenberry, *Business Cycles and Economic Growth* (New York, 1958), 225–235, 268–288.

9. Duesenberry, *Business Cycles and Economic Growth*, 225.

10. Quoted in A. J. Youngson, *The Possibilities of Economic Progress* (Cambridge, England, 1959), 82.

11. *Ibid.*, 82–86.

Chapter 2
Boston as a Center of Capital, 1820–1845

1. Samuel E. Morison, *Maritime History of Massachusetts, 1783–1860* (Boston, 1921), 215.

2. *Ibid.*, 227–228. Robert G. Albion, "New York Port and Its Disappointed Rivals, 1815–1860," *Journal of Economic and Business History*, III (August 1931), 607, summarizes commerce statistics with a note on Boston and Salem.

3. Morison, *Maritime History,* 216.

4. Lemuel Shattuck, *Report to the Committee of the City Council Appointed to Obtain the Census of Boston . . . 1845* (Boston, 1846), 26, 28.

5. See Albion, "New York Port," 609–613.

6. *Ibid.,* 606, 623.

7. Kenneth W. Porter, *The Jacksons and the Lees: Two Generations of Massachusetts Merchants, 1765–1844* (2 vols.; Cambridge, Massachusetts, 1937), I, 747.

8. Joseph A. Martin, *Seventy-Three Years' History of the Boston Stock Market . . .* (Boston, 1871), 66. It should be remembered, however, that the dividends were on an increasing capital stock.

9. George Sweet Gibb, *The Saco-Lowell Shops: Textile Machinery Building in New England, 1813–1949* (Cambridge, Massachusetts, 1950), 73.

10. Frances W. Gregory, "Nathan Appleton, Yankee Merchant, 1779–1861." Unpublished Ph.D. dissertation, Radcliffe, 1949, 428–9. William Appleton's constant concern with Lowell textile affairs is demonstrated by his diary entries. See MSS diary, MSS Division, Baker Library, Harvard Graduate School of Business Administration.

11. See lists in *Professional and Industrial History of Suffolk County, Massachusetts* (3 vols.; Boston, 1894), II, 241–243, 246–247, 249; Gerald T. White, *The History of the Massachusetts Hospital Life Insurance Company* (Cambridge, Massachusetts, 1955), 12–13.

12. Quoted in Michael Greenberg, *British Trade and the Opening of China, 1800–42* (Cambridge, England, 1951), 12–13.

13. Robert Bennet Forbes, *Remarks on China and the China Trade* (Boston, 1844), 29.

14. Sarah F. Hughes, ed., *Letters and Recollections of John Murray Forbes* (2 vols.; Boston, 1900), I, 116.

15. Mary C. Crawford, *Famous Families of Massachusetts* (2 vols.; Boston, 1930), I, 198.

16. This, and other details, are taken from Robert Bennet Forbes, *Personal Reminiscences* (Boston, 1882, 2d ed., rev.), *passim.*

17. Thomas F. Waters, *Augustine Heard and His Friends* (Salem, Massachusetts, 1916), 33–34. When Coolidge first went to China (1832), he carried a letter of introduction from Cushing to Heard. (July 19, 1832, Heard MSS., BM-8. Baker Library, Harvard University Graduate School of Business Administration.)

18. See John M. Forbes's letter to Augustine Heard, August 5, 1843, in Heard MSS, BM-8.

19. See Henrietta M. Larson, "A China Trader Turns Investor — A Biographical Chapter in American Business History," *Harvard Business Review,* XI (April 1934), 345–358.

20. John M. Forbes to Augustine Heard, August 17, 1833. Heard MSS, BM-8.

21. William Sturgis, Accounts Current. Bryant & Sturgis MSS., vol. 14. Baker Library.

22. Thomas T. Forbes to Cushing, July 10, 1829. Bryant & Sturgis MSS., vol. 14. For Augustine Heard & Company, there are isolated estimates. John Heard in his typescript autobiography claimed that his firm's profit in the late 1840's was some $50,000 a year, and a decade later it was between $180,000 and $200,000 a year. In 1860 John Heard, writing confidentially to his brother, attempted to make some estimate of Augustine Heard's assets. In the sixteen years from 1844 (when Augustine left China) to 1860, John estimated that his uncle's profits from the partnership, together with 6 per cent interest on the balances and 20 per cent premium for remittance to America, amounted to almost $250,000, which together with the money which he left in Canton in 1844 brought the total to over $350,000. Typescript "Diary," 1891, 71, 123. Heard MSS; John Heard to "A," November 3, 1860. Heard MSS., BQ-24.

23. John M. Forbes to Augustine Heard, September 18, 1838. Heard MSS., BM-8.

24. Robert B. Forbes to Augustine Heard, May 15, 1850. Heard MSS., BM-8.

25. Accounts of Paul S. Forbes for 1854. Forbes MSS., K-1 (case 2, folder 27). Baker Library.

26. Hughes, *Letters and Recollections,* I, 116.

27. Forbes, *Personal Reminiscences,* 359.

28. *Ibid.,* 361. The change came by the late 1850's. For the financial operations of one English house trading to China, see Sheila Marriner, *Rathbones of Liverpool. 1845–73* (Liverpool, 1961), especially Chapters 12–14.

29. Forbes, *Personal Reminiscences,* 367.

30. Ralph W. Hidy, *The House of Baring in American Trade and Finance: English Merchant Bankers at Work, 1763–1861* (Cambridge, Massachusetts, 1949), 103–104, 191. The Perkins concern paid the Barings $684,839 for the year ending February 28, 1835.

31. *Ibid.,* 107.

32. *Ibid.,* 353.

33. *Ibid.,* 412–413.

34. Porter, *The Jacksons and the Lees,* I, 125.

Chapter 3
Moving into Railroad Investment: Experience in the East

1. Julius Rubin, *Canal or Railroad? Imitation and Innovation in the Response to the Erie Canal in Philadelphia, Baltimore, and Boston* (Transactions of the American Philosophical Society, Philadelphia, 1961), 84, 89–90.

2. *Ibid.,* 89.

3. Massachusetts Board of Directors of Internal Improvements, *Report . . . on the Practicability and Expediency of a Railroad from Boston to the Hudson River . . .* (Boston, 1829), 73. (The controversy over private or state ownership is discussed fully in Stephen Salsbury, "Private Enterprise in Massachusetts, the Beginnings of the Boston & Albany Railroad, 1825–1842." Unpublished Ph.D., dissertation, Harvard University, 1961, 125–168.)

4. Edward C. Kirkland, *Men, Cities and Transportation: A Study in New England History, 1820–1900* (2 vols.; Cambridge, Massachusetts, 1948) I, 118.

5. *Report of a Committee on the Boston and Lowell Railroad* (Boston, 1831), 4.

6. Among the original subscribers were P. T. Jackson, 124 shares; Edwin Munroe, 100; John Lowell, 94; George W. Lyman, 75; George W. Pratt, 75; William Appleton, 50; (Charles Francis Adams, Jr., "The Canal and Railroad Enterprise of Boston," *The Memorial History of Boston,* Justin Winsor, ed. [4 vols.; Boston, 1883], IV, 126 n.1).

7. *Report of a Committee on the Boston and Lowell Railroad,* 6.

8. *Ibid.,* 9.

9. George Sweet Gibb, *The Saco-Lowell Shops: Textile Machinery Building in New England, 1813–1949* (Cambridge, Massachusetts, 1950), 92.

10. Boston and Lowell Railroad, *Annual Report* (to the Legislature) January 9, 1834, in Mass. Senate, No. 26, *Reports of the Boston and Lowell . . . [and other roads],* 1834, 7–8.

11. *Ibid.,* Jan. 1, 1836, in Mass. Senate, No. 49, *Reports of the Boston and Lowell . . . [and other roads],* 1836, 17–18. In 1838, the total authorized capital stock reached $2,100,000. (Henry V. Poor, *History of the Railroads and Canals of the United States* [New York, 1860], 97.)

12. Boston and Lowell Railroad, *Annual Report* (to Stockholders), 1837, 7.

13. Adams, "Canal and Railroad Enterprise," 127 n.

14. Boston and Lowell, *Annual Report* (to Stockholders), 1849, 5–6.

15. Adams, "Canal and Railroad Enterprise," 129, n.2.

16. *Report of the Joint Special Committee to investigate . . . the Boston and Providence* (Mass. Senate No. 50), March, 1840, 18.

17. Adams, "Canal and Railroad Enterprise," 129, n.2.

18. Kirkland, *Men, Cities and Transportation,* I, 125.

19. *Charter of the Boston and Worcester Railroad Corporation . . .* (Boston, 1859), Sections 5, 14.

20. Boston and Worcester Railroad, *Annual Reports . . . to the Legislature,* 1833–1837, *passim.*

21. B. and W. Stock Ledgers A & B, MSS. Division, Baker Library, Harvard University, Graduate School of Business Administration.

22. South Cove Corporation, *Annual Report,* 1834, 5.

23. *Ibid.,* 1836, 9.

24. *Ibid.,* 9–10.

25. *Ibid.,* 1839, 7–8.

26. Salsbury, "Private Enterprise."

27. Adams, "Canal and Railroad Enterprise," 131.

28. *Ibid.,* 132.

29. Western Rail-Road, *Annual Report,* 1840, 22.

30. George Bliss, *Historical Memoir of the Western Railroad* (Springfield, Massachusetts, 1863), 33.

31. See Carter Goodrich, *Government Promotion of American Canals and Railroads, 1800–1890* (New York, 1960), especially Chapters 3–4.

32. *Memorial and Report of the Western Rail-Road Corporation,* January 3, 1838, to the Mass. Senate and House (Senate, No. 8), 5.

33. Adams, "Canal and Railroad Enterprise," 134.

34. Ralph W. Hidy, *The House of Baring in American Trade and Finance: English Merchant Bankers at Work, 1763–1861* (Cambridge, Massachusetts, 1949), 261; Kirkland, *Men, Cities and Transportation,* I, 132–133.

35. Western Rail-Road, *Annual Report,* 1845, 5.

36. J. W. Scott, "Railroads East and West," *Hunt's Merchants' Magazine,* XIII (September 1845), 252.

37. Mass. Sen. Doc. 35, 1841, abstracted in Bliss, *Historical Memoir,* 63, 153.

38. Poor, *History of the Railroads of the United States,* 160–161; Kirkland, *Men, Cities and Transportation,* I, 135.

39. An excellent analysis of the Western's problems and their relation to Boston's prosperity is in Kirkland, *Men, Cities and Transportation,* I, 135–157.

40. Francis B. C. Bradlee, *The Eastern Railroad: A Historical Account of Early Railroading in Eastern New England,* 2d ed., (Salem, Massachusetts, 1922), 9–10.

41. George Peabody, *Address at the Opening of the Eastern Rail Road Between Boston and Salem* (Salem, 1838), 12. See William H. Sumner, *A History of East Boston; with Biographical Sketches of Its Early Proprietors* (Boston, 1858), 612–618.

42. Charles J. Kennedy, "The Eastern Rail-Road Company to 1855," *Business History Review,* XXXI (Spring 1957), 99; Kirkland, *Men, Cities and Transportation,* I, 198.

43. Peabody, *Address,* 10, 17.

44. Kennedy, "Eastern Rail-Road," 117–119.

45. Hidy, *House of Baring,* 413.

46. E. H. Derby, "City of Boston," *Hunt's Merchants' Magazine,* XXIII (November 1850), 486. Population figures based on state census.

47. Lemuel Shattuck, *Report to the Committee of the City Council Appointed to Obtain the Census of Boston for the year 1845 . . .* (Boston, 1846), Appendix EE, 53.

48. *American Railroad Journal,* XXI (December 16, 1848), 802.

49. E. H. Derby, "Progress of Railroads in Massachusetts," *Hunt's Merchants' Magazine,* XIV (January 1846), 31.

50. Compare reports to the Secretary of the Commonwealth for 1837 and 1845 with U.S. Census of 1840. See Massachusetts Secretary of the Commonwealth, *Statistics of the Condition and Products of Certain Branches of Industry in Massachusetts, for the year ending April 1, 1845.*

51. Shattuck, *Report to the Committee of the City Council . . . 1845*, 86.

52. *Hunt's Merchants' Magazine*, XIV (March 1846), 286.

53. Shattuck, *Report to the Committee of the City Council . . . 1845*, 92.

54. William Sturgis to Henry Martin, President of the Attica and Buffalo, February 10, 1849. Bryant & Sturgis MSS., Vol. 11, Baker Library.

55. Ledger dated January 1, 1840, John P. Cushing MSS., Vol. 5, Baker Library.

56. See Irene D. Neu, *Erastus Corning: Merchant and Financier, 1794–1872* (Ithaca, New York, 1960), 61–64.

57. William Sturgis to V. R. Hawkins, June 23, 1843, Bryant & Sturgis MSS., Vol. 11. The company had retained 1,856 shares. (See Sturgis to Oliver Lee, July 22, 1843. *Ibid.*)

58. Sturgis to Lee, June 29, 1843. *Ibid.*

59. Sturgis to Lee, July 12, 1843; Sturgis to Hawkins, July 22, August 7, 1843. *Ibid.*

60. Sturgis to Henry Martin, February 10, 1849. *Ibid.*

61. Sturgis to Committee of the Directors of the Syracuse & Utica Rail Road Corp., December 28, 1842. *Ibid.*

62. See George McHenry, *Philadelphia and Reading Railroad Company; its Financial History . . .* (London, 1878).

63. David A. Neal, *Report Made to the Managers of the Philadelphia and Reading Rail Road Company, September 19, 1849*, published with *Report of the President and Managers . . .* (September 1849), 6.

64. Jules T. Bogen, *The Anthracite Railroads: A Study in American Railroad Enterprise* (New York, 1927), 28.

65. P. T. Jackson to John Tucker, February 17, 1844. Philadelphia and Reading MSS., Baker Library.

66. Neal, *Report*, September 19, 1849, 15.

67. Bogen, *Anthracite Railroads*, 31.

68. Davenport and Bridges, car builders, to John Tucker, September 27, 1845. Philadelphia and Reading MSS.

69. John J. Stackpole to John Tucker, June 1, 1845. *Ibid.*

70. *Report of a Committee of Investigation into the Affairs of the Philadelphia and Reading Rail Road Company* (Boston, 1846), 40–44.

71. Philadelphia and Reading Railroad, *Annual Report*, January 12, 1847, 5–6; Bogen, *Anthracite Roads*, 31.

72. *Hunt's Merchants' Magazine*, XVI (February 1847), 210.

73. John Gihon to John Tucker, March 21, 1847. Philadelphia and Reading MSS.

74. Philadelphia and Reading, *Annual Report*, January 8, 1849, 3–5, 9; Bogen, *Anthracite Railroads*, 32.

75. Bogen, *Anthracite Railroads*, 34–35; Neal, *Report*, September 19, 1849, 36–37.

76. Bogen, *Anthracite Railroads*, 33.

77. *Ibid.*, 35; Neal, *Report*, September 19, 1849, 36, and *Report to the Stockholders of the Philadelphia and Reading Rail Road Company*, January, 1850 (published with Annual Report, 1850), *passim*.

78. Bogen, *Anthracite Railroads*, 35–37.

79. Neal, *Report*, September 19, 1849, 33.

80. Neal Journal (1846–1855), February 19, 25, 1850. Neal MSS., Vol. 8, Baker Library.

81. *Ibid.*, May 31, October 12, December 31, 1850; March 28, 1851.

82. *Ibid.*, December 15, 1853. Neal's Journal for December 31, 1854 showed a loss on his Philadelphia and Reading holdings in the amount of $7,886.99. By August 1, 1855, however, his Journal showed a $7,354.90 profit.

83. Hollis H. Hunnewell, *Life, Letters and Diary of Horatio Hollis Hunnewell* (3 vols.; Boston, 1906), I, 197.

84. Neal Journal (1846–1855), January 16, August 29, December 15, 1853. Neal MSS., vol. 8.

85. *Ibid.*, December 30, 1852; August 29, September 15, December 31, 1853.

86. For a list of important directorships held by Hunnewell, see Hunnewell, *Life, Letters and Diary*, 197–200.

87. Quoted in *Hazard's U. S. Register*, IV (May 1841), 311.

88. Philadelphia, Wilmington and Baltimore Railroad, *Annual Report*, 1842, 4–6.

89. P. W. and B., *Annual Report*, 1848, 4–5; *Hunt's Merchants' Magazine*, XXIII (September, 1850), 351.

90. John M. Forbes to Paul S. Forbes, February 25, 1848, Forbes MSS., typescript, Baker Library.

91. See Neal Ledgers (1846–1855), vol. 10, 17. Neal MSS.

92. Reportedly 86 per cent of the stock was owned in Boston as late as March 1881. *Railroad Gazette*, XIII (March 11, 1881), 150.

93. *Commercial & Financial Chronicle*, XXXII (March 5, 1881), 226. J. J. Stackpole to John Tucker, June 1, 1845. Philadelphia and Reading MSS.

94. *American Railroad Journal*, XVIII (January 9, 1845), 25.

Chapter 4
The West: Experiment and Opportunity, 1830–1850

1. Percy W. Bidwell and John I. Falconer, *History of Agriculture in the Northern United States, 1620–1860* (Washington, 1925), 152.

2. Alexis de Tocqueville, *Democracy in America* (2 vols.; New York, 1957), I, 303.

3. Bidwell and Falconer, *History of Agriculture*, 158–159.

4. See Joseph M. Nance, "The Attitude of New England Toward Westward Expansion, 1800–1850." Unpublished Ph.D. dissertation, University of Texas, 1941, *passim.*

5. *Niles Weekly Register*, LII (April 8, 1837), 89–90.

6. Benjamin H. Hibbard, *A History of the Public Land Policies* (New York, 1924), 295–296; "First Speech on Foot's Resolution," January 20, 1830, *Writings and Speeches of Daniel Webster* (18 vols.; Boston, 1903), V, 253.

7. Paul W. Gates, "The Role of the Land Speculator in Western Development," *The Pennsylvania Magazine of History and Biography*, LXVI (July 1942), 328. See also, Paul W. Gates, *The Illinois Central Railroad and Its Colonization Work* (Cambridge, Massachusetts, 1934), 37, 39.

8. William F. Raney, "Appleton," *Wisconsin Magazine of History*, XXXIII (December 1949), 137, 146.

9. Gates, *Illinois Central*, 37.

10. Larry Gara, *Westernized Yankee, The Story of Cyrus Woodman* (Madison, Wisconsin, 1956), 19–20, 25–34.

11. *Professional and Industrial History of Suffolk County* (3 vols.; Boston, 1894), II, 546, 695.

12. Irene D. Neu, *Erastus Corning: Merchant and Financier, 1794–1872* (Ithaca, New York, 1960), 129–130, 132, 136; Gates, *Illinois Central*, 39.

13. New York & Boston Illinois Land Company, *Annual Report*, 1837, 9.

14. Robert F. Fries, *Empire in Pine, the Story of Lumbering in Wisconsin, 1830–1900* (Madison, Wisconsin, 1951), 11.

15. Coon and Hunter to Charles G. Loring (executor of Rantoul's estate), December 7, 1852. Neal-Rantoul MSS., vol. 18, Baker Library, Harvard Graduate School of Business Administration.

16. Bryan Latham, *Timber, Its Development and Distribution, a Historical Survey* (London, 1957), 114–116.

17. Fries, *Empire in Pine*, 21.

18. *Hunt's Merchants' Magazine*, XIX (July 1848), 31.

19. *A Few Remarks on the Operations of the Companies . . . Organized for the Dig-*

ging & Smelting of Copper . . . on Lake Superior . . . by an Explorer (Boston, 1845 [?]), 2.

20. *American Railroad Journal,* XXIV, January 18, 1851, 47.

21. William B. Gates, Jr., *Michigan Copper and Boston Dollars* (Cambridge, Massachusetts, 1951), 10.

22. Howard N. Eavenson, *The First Century and a Quarter of American Coal Industry* (Pittsburgh, 1942), 290.

23. *Ibid.,* 310, citing the Pittsburgh *Daily Gazette* and the Cincinnati *Atlas.*

24. Emory R. Johnson, *et al., History of Domestic and Foreign Commerce of the United States* (2 vols.; Washington, 1915), I, 222; Louis C. Hunter, *Steamboats on the Western Rivers; An Economic and Technological History* (Cambridge, Massachusetts, 1949), 33–34.

25. Johnson, *History of Domestic and Foreign Commerce,* I, 230; Douglass C. North, *Economic Growth of the United States, 1790–1860* (Englewood Cliffs, New Jersey, 1961), 105.

26. North, *Economic Growth,* 253. One barrel of flour has been reckoned as five bushels.

27. Johnson, *History of Domestic and Foreign Commerce,* I, 238.

28. U.S. Census Office, 8th Census, 1860, *Agriculture,* clvii.

29. See the data in Thomas S. Berry, *Western Prices before 1861* (Cambridge, Massachusetts, 1943), 106–107, 122, 536–537, 564.

30. Quoted in Carter L. Goodrich, *Government Promotion of American Canals and Railroads, 1800–1890* (New York, 1960), 9.

31. *Ibid.,* 135. Most of the following descriptive material on internal improvements is taken from Professor Goodrich's book.

32. *Ibid.,* 137.

33. George R. Taylor, *The Transportation Revolution, 1815–1860* (New York, 1951), 451.

34. John M. Forbes to Paul S. Forbes, October 31, 1847. Forbes MSS., typescript, Baker Library.

35. Seymour E. Harris, ed., *American Economic History* (New York, 1961), 535.

36. Robert E. Gallman, "Commodity Output, 1839–1899," National Bureau of Economic Research, *Trends in the American Economy in the Nineteenth Century* (Princeton, 1960), 24.

CHAPTER 5
WESTERN RAILROAD PROMOTERS AND BOSTON CAPITALISTS, 1845–1848

1. Quoted in *Hunt's Merchants' Magazine,* XIV (January 1846), 102.

2. George Peabody, *Address at the Opening of the Eastern Rail Road Between Boston and Salem, August 27, 1838* (Salem, 1838), 5, 17.

3. J. J. Stackpole to John Tucker, June 1, 1845. Philadelphia and Reading Railroad MSS. Baker Library, Harvard University Graduate School of Business Administration.

4. *American Railroad Journal,* XVIII (January 2, 1845), 13.

5. *"Our First Men:" a Calendar of Wealth, Fashion and Gentility . . . a List of those Persons Taxed in the City of Boston . . . Worth One Hundred Thousand Dollars, with Biographical Notices of the Principal Persons* (rev. ed., Boston, 1846).

6. *Ibid.,* 5.

7. Little Miami Railroad, *Annual Report,* 1843, 8.

8. Robert L. Black, *The Little Miami Railroad* (Cincinnati, no date), 29.

9. *Ibid.,* 62. See *Hunt's Merchants' Magazine* XXI (October 1849), 397, which gives $293,050 as the amount of state aid. Under the provisions of an act of 1842 the state could sell public-aided works, accepting its own bonds in payment.

10. *American Railroad Journal,* XVIII (January 2, 1845), 3.

11. Little Miami Railroad, *Annual Report,* 1845, 28–29.
12. *Ibid.*
13. Ohio Local Laws for March 1, 1845 (XLIII, 146) and January 17, 1846 (XLIV, 27) quoted in *The Charter and Laws Relating to the Mad River and Lake Erie Rail-Road Company* (Sandusky City, 1847), 25–26.
14. J. P. Cushing, Stocks and Bonds Railroad Accounts, Cushing MSS., Vol. 2, Baker Library.
15. *"Our First Men,"* 33, 41.
16. Mad River and Lake Erie Railroad, *Annual Report,* 1847, opposite 1.
17. Henshaw to Chamberlain, May 18, 1849. Mad River and Lake Erie MSS., Baker Library.
18. *American Railroad Journal,* XXII (July 7, 1849), 426.
19. *Ibid.,* XXI (September 30, 1848), 626.
20. *Ibid.,* XXIV (January 25, 1851), 56.
21. See Black, *Little Miami,* map opposite 90.
22. *Bankers' Magazine,* III (November, 1848), 324.
23. J. M. Forbes to P. S. Forbes, May 18, 1858. Forbes MSS. Typescript, Baker Library.
24. See Black, *Little Miami,* map opposite 90.
25. See Walter J. Hansen, "State Aid to Railroads in Michigan during the Early Statehood Period." Unpublished Ph.D. dissertation, University of Michigan, 1941, 60–62, 80, 81, 192–193.
26. Reginald C. McGrane, *Foreign Bondholders and American State Debts* (New York, 1935), 162–163.
27. Quoted in Hansen, "State Aid to Railroads in Michigan," 247–248.
28. Charles Francis Adams, Jr., "The Canal and Railroad Enterprise of Boston," in *The Memorial History of Boston,* Justin Winsor, ed. (4 vols., Boston, 1883), IV, 144. Thomas C. Cochran, *Railroad Leaders, 1845–1890; The Business Mind in Action* (Cambridge, Massachusetts, 1953), 37.
29. James F. Joy, "Railroad History of Michigan," Michigan Pioneer and Historical Society, *Collections,* XXII (1894), 301.
30. Irene D. Neu, *Erastus Corning: Merchant and Financier, 1794–1872* (Ithaca, New York, 1960), 74.
31. Joy, "Railroad History of Michigan," 301.
32. "Charter of the Michigan Central Railroad Company," in John W. Brooks, *Report Upon the Merit of the Michigan Central Railroad . . .* (New York, 1846).
33. Neu, *Erastus Corning,* 75.
34. James F. Joy, "Railroad History of Michigan," 301.
35. Quoted in Hansen, "State Aid to Railroads in Michigan," 260.
36. *Ibid.,* 262.
37. Circular, John M. Forbes to subscribers to Michigan Central stock, September 14, 1846. Although the Michigan Central apparently exchanged stock for Michigan state bonds at 70 per cent and turned them over to the state at par, the charter seemed to call for a far different rate of exchange on a majority of the internal improvement bonds (i.e. each $1,000 bond as of January 1, 1846, was to be valued at $403.88, including principal and interest).
38. *Charter of the Michigan Central Rail-Road Company,* section 15.
39. The Forbes brothers had the first steamer to operate in Chinese waters. For the *Iron Witch* episode, see Robert Bennet Forbes, *Personal Reminiscences* (Boston, 2d ed., rev., 1882), 216–217.
40. John M. Forbes to Paul S. Forbes, September 30, 1846, quoted in Cochran, *Railroad Leaders.*
41. Gross earnings for the year ended May 31, 1846, were $277,478 (Michigan Central *Annual Report,* June 1848, 10). Earnings for preceding years were $202,746 (1845), $211,170 (1844), $149,989 (1843). *Hunt's Merchants' Magazine,* XIV (February, 1846), 179. Brooks estimated a 7 per cent return on investment for a rejuvenated road in

Report Upon the Merits of the Michigan Central Rail-Road as an Investment for Eastern Capitalists (1846), 22.

42. Sarah F. Hughes, ed., *Letters and Recollections of John Murray Forbes* (2 vols.; Boston, 1900), I, 116–117.

43. Swift to Ward, February 14, 1852. Baring MSS., cited by McGrane, *Foreign Bondholders*, 273.

44. John M. Forbes to P. S. Forbes, November 30, 1845. Forbes MSS. typescript. See also Henry V. Poor, *History of the Railroads and Canals of the United States . . .* (New York, 1860), 201.

45. John M. Forbes to Paul S. Forbes, October 31, 1846. Forbes MSS. typescript.

46. *Charter of Michigan Central Rail-Road Company,* section 22.

47. George F. Porter to William Dwight, August 3, 1846. Pepperell MSS., case 3, Baker Library. On the Dwights' bank investments, see Harry N. Scheiber, "The Commercial Bank of Lake Erie, 1831–1843," *Business History Review* (Spring 1966), 47–65.

48. Neu, *Erastus Corning,* 77; McGrane, *Foreign Bondholders,* 160–162.

49. Hughes, ed., *Letters and Recollections,* I, 119; Neu, *Erastus Corning,* 78, citing Edith P. Cunningham, ed., *Charles Eliot Perkins and Edith F. Perkins, Family Letters, 1861–1869* (Boston, 1949), 27–28.

50. Joy and Porter to William Dwight, August 18, 1846. Pepperell MSS., case 3.

51. Edmund Dwight to William Dwight, August 20, 1846. *Ibid.* The Dwights apparently held securities issued by the city of Detroit. (Joy and Porter to William Dwight, October 13, 1846. *Ibid.*). They were also important in the Bank of Michigan.

52. Porter to William Dwight, August 28, 1846. *Ibid.*

53. *Ibid.;* John M. Forbes to Joseph Grinnell, September 1, 1846, quoted in Cochran, *Railroad Leaders,* 326.

54. Neal Journal, September 24, 1846. Neal MSS., vol. 8. Baker Library.

55. Porter to William Dwight, September 4, 1846. Pepperell MSS., case 3.

56. Porter to William Dwight, September 5, 1846. *Ibid.*

57. *Ibid.*

58. John M. Forbes to Joseph Grinnell, September 1, 1846, quoted in Cochran, *Railroad Leaders,* 326.

59. Porter to William Dwight, September 7, 1846; D. D. Williamson to William Dwight, September 9, 1846. Pepperell MSS., case 3.

60. Porter to William Dwight, September 10, 1846. *Ibid.*

61. Quoted in Hughes, ed., *Letters and Recollections,* I, 119.

62. John M. Forbes to Joseph Grinnell, September 1, 1846, quoted in Cochran, *Railroad Leaders,* 326.

63. Hughes, ed., *Letters and Recollections,* I, 119.

64. Michigan Central Railroad, circular of September 14, 1846, signed by J. M. Forbes as president.

65. *Ibid.,* circular of September 12, 1846, signed by J. M. Forbes as president.

66. Michigan Central Railroad, *Annual Report,* 1848, 8.

67. Quoted in Henry G. Pearson, *An American Railroad Builder, John Murray Forbes* (Boston, 1911), 29–30.

68. See John M. Forbes to William Dwight, October 15, October 28, 1846. Pepperell MSS., case 3.

69. Brooks to Corning, December 25, 1846, quoted in Cochran, *Railroad Leaders,* 268.

70. Corning to Brooks, January 12, 1847, quoted *ibid.,* 303.

71. Neu, *Erastus Corning,* 77–79.

72. Michigan Central, *Annual Report,* 1848, 5, 8.

73. John M. Forbes to Brooks, September 10, 1847, quoted in Cochran, *Railroad Leaders,* 99.

74. Corning to Brooks, September 3, 1847, quoted by M. C. McConkey, "James F. Joy," (MSS. biography, Michigan Historical Collections, University of Michigan), III, 268–269.

75. *Bankers' Magazine,* II (February 1848), 511.

76. *Ibid.* (April 1848), 640.

77. Michigan Central, *Annual Report,* 1848, 5–6.

78. John M. Forbes to Paul S. Forbes, June 30, 1847. Forbes MSS. typescript.

79. *Ibid.,* October 31, 1847.

80. *Ibid.,* September 5, 1848.

81. See *supra,* p. 98.

82. John M. Forbes to Paul S. Forbes, September 5, 1848. Forbes MSS. typescript.

83. *Ibid.,* November 28, 1848. Paul S. Forbes apparently loaned money to the road on the same basis. (See *ibid.,* December 5, 1850.)

84. See Neal Journal, October 14 and December 9, 1848. Neal MSS., vol. 8.

85. Michigan Central, *Annual Report,* 1849, 3.

86. John M. Forbes to Paul S. Forbes, October 29, 1849. Forbes MSS., typescript.

87. See Neal Journal, February 14, July 31, August 8, August 12, September 2, and December 31, 1848. Neal MSS., vol. 8.

88. Neal Journal, December 31, 1850. *Ibid.*

Chapter 6

Emerging Investment Patterns: The Forbes Group, 1850–1860

1. John M. Forbes to J. W. Brooks, August 18, 1849. Norcross papers, Massachusetts Historical Society, Boston, Massachusetts.

2. Quoted in Henry G. Pearson, *An American Railroad Builder, John Murray Forbes* (Boston, 1911), 98.

3. Michigan Central Railroad, *Annual Report,* 1848, 23.

4. *Ibid.,* 1849, 14–15.

5. *Ibid.,* 7. For a discussion of the advantage of choosing New Buffalo over St. Joseph, see *American Railroad Journal,* XXI (April 29, 1848), 277–279.

6. *Hunt's Merchants' Magazine,* XX (March 1849), 281.

7. John M. Forbes to Brooks, August 18, 1848. Norcross Papers.

8. Michigan Central, *Annual Report,* 1850, 6.

9. *Ibid.,* 23.

10. *Ibid.,* 5.

11. *Ibid.,* 1851, 5.

12. James F. Joy, "Railroad History of Michigan," Michigan Pioneer and Historical Society, *Collections,* XXII (1894), 303.

13. William E. Hayes, *Iron Road to Empire* (New York, 1953), 9, 13–16, 19.

14. Frank F. Hargrave, *A Pioneer Indiana Railroad: The Origin and Development of the Monon* (Indianapolis, 1932), 106–107; Joy, "Railroad History of Michigan," 303–304.

15. *American Railroad Journal,* XXIV (July 12, 1851), 437.

16. Hargrave, *Pioneer Indiana Railroad,* 107–108.

17. Michigan Central, *Annual Report,* 1852, 6.

18. A copy of this agreement may be found in "Statements and Replies in Reference to the Compensation for the Use of the Road of the Illinois Central R. R. Company, from Calumet to Chicago, by the Michigan Central R.R. Company," (Boston, 1860), 86–92. Illinois Central Railroad, Primary Miscellaneous Material, vol. III, Corporation Records Division, Baker Library, Harvard University Graduate School of Business Administration.

19. Pearson, *An American Railroad Builder,* 47–49.

20. Richard C. Overton, *Burlington West, a Colonization History of the Burlington Railroad* (Cambridge, Massachusetts, 1941), 30.

21. *Statements and Replies . . . ,* 159, 166.

22. *Ibid.,* 93–94.

23. Overton, *Burlington West,* 30–31; Hayes, *Iron Road to Empire,* 19. The Michigan Southern had an alternate method of entering Chicago by utilizing the charter of a plank-road company with railroad privileges. (Overton, *Burlington West,* 28–29.)

24. Pearson, *An American Railroad Builder,* 50.

25. *Ibid.,* 51.

26. Michigan Central, *Annual Report,* 1855, 8.

27. *Statements and Replies . . . ,* 199.

28. *Ibid.,* 244.

29. Ralph W. Hidy, *The House of Baring in American Trade and Finance: English Merchant Bankers at Work, 1763–1861* (Cambridge, Massachusetts, 1949), 603, n. 13.

30. W. M. Spriggs, "Great Western Railway of Canada," Railway and Locomotive Historical Society, *Bulletin,* LI (February 1940), 7.

31. *Report Upon the Merits of the Great Western Railroad Canada West: by a Committee of its American Friends* (Boston, 1851), 4. Other members included President Wilkinson of the Syracuse & Utica and President Gibson of the Syracuse & Rochester.

32. *American Railroad Journal,* XXIV (June 21, 1851), 391.

33. *Ibid.* (September 20, 1851), 595.

34. Michigan Central, *Annual Report,* 1851, 6–7.

35. Irene D. Neu, *Erastus Corning: Merchant and Financier, 1794–1872* (Ithaca, New York, 1960), 81–82.

36. *American Railroad Journal,* XXIV (November 1, 1851), 689; Neu, *Erastus Corning,* 81.

37. William Sturgis to J. N. L. Pruyn, November 7, 1851. Bryant & Sturgis MSS., vol. 11. Baker Library.

38. Postscript to letter, Sturgis to John Wilkinson, November 7, 1851, *ibid.:* Sturgis to Henry B. Gibson, November 8, 1851, *ibid.*

39. Neu, *Erastus Corning,* 81–82.

40. Michigan Central, *Annual Report,* 1854, 4.

41. Spriggs, "Great Western Railway," 9–10.

42. Directors' Minutes, Boston and Worcester Railroad, May 10, 1864, Boston and Worcester MSS., vol. 8. Baker Library.

43. Spriggs, "Great Western Railway," 19.

44. Michigan Central, *Annual Report,* 1856, 16.

45. Neu, *Erastus Corning,* 82.

46. Michigan Central, *Annual Report,* 1853, 5.

47. See, for example, *ibid.,* 1850, 4; 1853, 4.

48. *Ibid.,* 1852, 4.

49. *Ibid.*

50. Neu, *Erastus Corning,* 48.

51. John M. Forbes to Paul S. Forbes, November 29, 1847; January 27, 1848. Forbes MSS., typescript. Baker Library.

52. *Ibid.,* December 21, 1859.

53. Irene D. Neu, "The Building of the Sault Canal, 1852–1855," *Mississippi Valley Historical Review,* XL (June 1953), 28–33, 38.

54. *Ibid.,* 35.

55. *Ibid.,* 36–37.

56. *Ibid.,* 44.

57. St. Mary's Falls Ship Canal Company, *Catalogue of 525,000 Acres of Pine Timber Lands . . . 1863,* X.

58. St. Mary's Falls Ship Canal Company, *Annual Report,* 1858, 20, 31.

59. *Ibid.,* 1859, 9; 1860, 3.

60. Larry Gara, *Westernized Yankee: The Story of Cyrus Woodman* (Madison, Wisconsin, 1956), 153–156.

61. *Ibid.,* 156–157.

62. *Ibid.,* 157.

63. *Ibid.*, 158–159, 172.
64. Neu, *Erastus Corning*, 153–154.

CHAPTER 7
EMERGING INVESTMENT PATTERNS: BOSTONIANS AND THE ILLINOIS CENTRAL, 1850–1860

1. *American Railroad Journal*, XXV (August 7, 1852), 506.
2. David A. Neal, *The Illinois Central Railroad: Its Position and Prospects* (July 1, 1851), 8. See *American Railroad Journal*, XXIV (August 9, 1851), 497–498, for a summary of Neal's pamphlet.
3. See Paul W. Gates, *The Illinois Central Railroad and Its Colonization Work* (Cambridge, Massachusetts, 1934), 27–41.
4. See the data in *ibid.*, 38–39.
5. For Billings and his activities, see the letters preserved in the Illinois Land Agency MSS., vol. 19. Baker Library, Harvard University Graduate School of Business Administration; and Gates, *Illinois Central*, 50 ff.
6. See, for example, Billings' letters of June 19 and 27, 1850, Illinois Land Agency MSS., vol. 19.
7. Gates, *Illinois Central*, 55–56.
8. *Communication from the President to the Directors of the Illinois Central, August 10, 1853* (New York, 1853), 4. Charter expenses prior to organization were reported as $51,299.
9. Biographical data are taken chiefly from William K. Ackerman, *Historical Sketch of the Illinois Central Railroad, together with a Brief Biographical Record . . .* (Chicago, 1890), 42–46, 51–53, 58, 73.
10. Neal, *Illinois Central*, 9.
11. Robert Bennet Forbes, *Personal Reminiscences* (Boston, 2d ed. rev., 1882), 367.
12. Alsop to Heard, June 4, 1851, and April 3, 1852, Heard MSS., vol. BQ-24, Illinois Central folder. Baker Library.
13. Robert Rantoul, Jr., *Letter to Robert Schuyler, Esq., President of the Illinois Central Railroad, on the Value of the Public Lands of Illinois* (Boston, 1851), 46.
14. Neal, *Illinois Central*, 13–14, 22.
15. Neal Ledger, 1846–1855, March 10, 22, 24, April 28, 1851; December 31, 1852. Neal MSS., vol. 12 and ledger. Baker Library.
16. *American Railroad Journal*, XXIV (December 13, 1851), 792.
17. *Ibid.*, XXV (January 10, 1852), 26.
18. Gates, *Illinois Central*, 70–72.
19. *Ibid.*, 72.
20. *American Railroad Journal*, XXV (February 21, 1852), 114.
21. *Ibid.*
22. Schuyler to Loring, October 29, 1852, Illinois Land Agency MSS., vol. 19.
23. Gates, *Illinois Central*, 73.
24. Neal Journal, 1846–1855, December 31, 1853. Neal MSS. Baker Library.
25. *Communication from the President to the Directors . . . August 10, 1853*, 6; *Report to the Board of Directors . . . by a Committee . . . November 10, 1853*, 13.
26. Expenditures have been derived from W. H. Osborn's communications to Robert Benson and Company in Judge Lane's *Report on the Illinois Central*, November 14, 1857, 10. Mileage figures are from Howard G. Brownson, *History of the Illinois Central Railroad to 1870* (Urbana, Illinois, 1915), 61 n.
27. U.S. Bureau of the Census, *Historical Statistics of the United States, Colonial Times to 1957* (Washington, D.C., 1960), 115, 121.
28. Brownson, *Illinois Central*, 124.
29. Gates, *Illinois Central*, 76. According to one study, the index for railroad stocks generally rose from the late 1840's to 1853. Thenceforth, with the 1853 average as 100,

they averaged 95 during the first half of 1854, then declined steadily to 67 in December of that year. (Walter B. Smith and Arthur H. Cole, *Fluctuations in American Business, 1790 to 1860* [Cambridge, Massachusetts, 1935], 184.)

30. *Hunt's Merchants' Magazine,* XXXI (July 1854), 81.

31. John M. Forbes to Paul S. Forbes, December 14, 1854, Forbes MSS., typescript. Baker Library.

32. Illinois Central Railroad Company, *Report and Statement of the Fnancial Condition of the Company,* January 11, 1855.

33. Illinois Central letter to the stockholders, October 1, 1855.

34. Lane, *Report,* 6–7.

35. Illinois Central, *Report and Accounts,* March 18, 1857, 1; Lane, *Report,* 7.

36. For stock prices see the weekly issues of the *American Railroad Journal*; for the taking-up of shares, see Lane, *Report,* 7; and Illinois Central, *Report to the Shareholders,* March 17, 1858, 5.

37. *American Railroad Journal,* XXX (September 5, 1857), 567–568.

38. Illinois Central, *Report to the Shareholders,* March 17, 1858, 1.

39. *American Railroad Journal,* XXX (October 17, 1857), 667; (October 31, 1857), 690.

40. See *ibid.* (December 5, 1857), 776–777.

41. *Ibid.,* XXXI (October 9, 1858), 651; Brownson, *Illinois Central,* 128.

42. *American Railroad Journal,* XXXI (July 3, 1858), 427; *Annual Report,* February 4, 1861. By the end of 1864, all shares issued (211,081) had been paid in full. (*Annual Report* for 1864.)

43. London *Times,* July 23, 1858, quoted in *American Railroad Journal,* XXXI (August 7, 1858), 508.

44. Quoted in Brownson, *Illinois Central,* 117.

45. President's Report to the Directors, September 12, 1851, in *Documents Relating to the Organization of the Illinois Central Railroad Company* (New York, 2nd ed., 1852), 57.

46. David A. Neal, Autobiography, 87. Neal MSS. Baker Library.

47. *Ibid.,* 82, 84.

48. In Illinois Central Railroad, *Annual Report,* March 15, 1854, 23–30.

49. Gates, *Illinois Central,* 158.

50. Ibid., 160.

51. Illinois Central, *Annual Report,* 1855, 7. In addition, more than 102,000 acres of preempted land had been sold for $255,694.

52. See reports to the directors of November and December 21, 1855 (the latter by W. P. Burrall) in the company's records at the Newberry Library. Twenty-seven depots were involved: twelve on and fifteen immediately adjacent to Neal's lands.

53. See Gates, *Illinois Central,* 163–168.

54. *Ibid.,* 166–167; *American Railroad Journal,* XXVIII (March 29, 1856), 201.

55. See Gates, *Illinois Central,* 169–302.

56. Neal, Autobiography, 85. Neal MSS. Baker Library.

57. Report to Board of Directors (November 1855), Newberry Library.

58. Gates, *Illinois Central,* 123–124.

59. Neal Journal, December 31, 1853; December 31, 1855. Neal MSS. Baker Library.

60. *Ibid.,* December 30, 1852; December 31, 1855.

61. For these holdings, see *ibid.,* December 31, 1853; August 9; December 31, 1855. Memorandum of Agreement, July 9, 1856, Illinois Land Agency MSS., vol. 20. Baker Library.

62. Gates, *Illinois Central,* 124.

63. T. A. Neal to Proprietors of "Associate Lands," June 27, 1860. Illinois Land Agency MSS., vol. 3. Baker Library.

64. *Ibid.,* vol. 17.

65. Journal entry, July 1, 1858. Illinois Land Agency MSS., vol. 1. Baker Library.

66. Gates, *Illinois Central,* 127.

67. Illinois Land Agency MSS., vol. 4, May 27, 1861. Baker Library. The stockhold-

ers were Jonathan Sturges, Executors of George Griswold, Morris Ketchum, Edward Bement, Jason Rogers, J. D. Rogers, C. B. Rogers, T. Rogers, Maria Gray, M. E. Frelinghuysen, Cornelia W. Haven, Sarah H. Green, J. N. A. Griswold, J. W. Haven, Guardian, D. A. Neal, and T. A. Neal.

68. T. A. Neal to Edward Bement, March 13, October 10, 1860; T. A. Neal to Jonathan Sturges, December 24, 1861. Illinois Land Agency MSS., vols. 3 and 4. Baker Library.

69. Neal, Autobiography, 91–92, Neal MSS. Baker Library.

70. *Ibid.*, 85.

71. William Sturgis to Henry Martin, February 10, 1849. Bryant & Sturgis MSS., vol. 11. Baker Library.

Chapter 8

Prewar Strategic Investment: The Genesis and Expansion of the C. B. & Q.

1. Table 17–2 in Lance E. Davis *et al., American Economic History, The Development of a National Economy* (Homewood, Illinois, 1961), 305.

2. Marvin W. Towne and Wayne D. Rasmussen, "Farm Gross Product and Gross Investment in the Nineteenth Century," National Bureau of Economic Research, *Trends in the American Economy in the Nineteenth Century* (Princeton, 1960), 261.

3. Quoted in Henry G. Pearson, *An American Railroad Builder, John Murray Forbes* (Boston, 1911), 45.

4. A. W. Newton, "The Chicago and Aurora Railroad," Part II, Railway and Locomotive Historical Society, *Bulletin*, No. 76 (March 1949), 7.

5. Brooks to Corning, April 14, 1852, quoted in Thomas C. Cochran, *Railroad Leaders, 1845–1890, The Business Mind in Action* (Cambridge Massachusetts, 1953), 268.

6. Quoted in Richard C. Overton, *Burlington West: a Colonization History of the Burlington Railroad* (Cambridge, Massachusetts, 1941), 37.

7. Overton, *Burlington West*, 37–38; Newton, "The Chicago and Aurora Railroad," 7, 9.

8. Quoted in Pearson, *An American Railroad Builder*, 75.

9. Newton, "The Chicago and Aurora Railroad," 8.

10. *Ibid.*, 9, 11.

11. Brooks to Nelson Robinson, March 7, 1853, quoted in Cochran, *Railroad Leaders*, 269.

12. Irene D. Neu, *Erastus Corning: Merchant and Financier, 1794–1872* (Ithaca, New York, 1960), 84–85.

13. Newton, "The Chicago and Aurora Railroad," 11.

14. Overton, *Burlington West*, 38–39; Neu, *Erastus Corning*, 84.

15. Ralph W. Hidy, *The House of Baring in American Trade and Finance . . . 1763–1861* (Cambridge, Massachusetts, 1949), 603, n. 13.

16. Overton, *Burlington West*, 39–43; *American Railroad Journal*, XXX (July 18, 1857), 453.

17. Pearson, *An American Railroad Builder*, 77.

18. *Ibid.*, 78.

19. Overton, *Burlington West*, 58. For the early history of the road and steps leading to the land grant, see Hannibal and St. Joseph Railroad, *Annual Report*, 1854, 6–16.

20. John M. Forbes to Charles Sumner, February 14, 1853, quoted in Pearson, *An American Railroad Builder*, 187–191.

21. Hannibal and St. Joseph, *Annual Report*, 1854, 13–14. See also, State of Missouri, Act to Expedite the Pacific Railroad and Hannibal and St. Joseph Railroad, approved February 22, 1851.

22. Hannibal and St. Joseph, *Annual Report*, 1854, title page.

23. *Ibid.*, 21, 24.

24. John M. Forbes to Paul S. Forbes, October 13, 1854, Forbes MSS., typescript. Baker Library.

25. *Ibid.*

26. For a discussion of recent reinterpretations of the role of railroads in American economic growth, see Chapter I.

27. John M. Forbes to Paul S. Forbes, October 13, 1854. Forbes MSS., typescript.

28. Hannibal and St. Joseph, *Annual Report*, 1850, 40.

29. John M. Forbes to Paul S. Forbes, February 25, 1855. Forbes MSS., typescript.

30. Hannibal and St. Joseph, *Annual Report*, 1855, 6.

31. *Ibid.*, 11.

32. John M. Forbes to Paul S. Forbes, December 2, 1855. Forbes MSS., typescript.

33. *Ibid.*

34. *Ibid.*, postscript dated December 4, 1855.

35. *Ibid.*, January 21, 1856.

36. Hidy, *House of Baring*, 426–427.

37. *American Railroad Journal*, XXIX (December 20, 1856), 805. Subscribers included John C. Green, David Leavitt, S. Austin, T. B. Curtis, McCalmont Brother & Company, von Hoffman & Company, Schuchardt & Gebhardt, "and others in New York on German account." (Hidy, *House of Baring*, 604.)

38. *American Railroad Journal*, XXX (February 21, 1857), 121.

39. Quoted in *ibid.*, XXX (October 3, 1857), 636.

40. Pearson, *An American Railroad Builder*, 90; John M. Forbes to Paul S. Forbes, June 20, 1858. Forbes MSS., typescript. The difficulties with the contractor are described in John M. Forbes to W. H. Swift, June 17, 1858, Forbes MSS., typescript, and in Hannibal and St. Joseph, *Annual Report*, 1859, 3–4.

41. John M. Forbes to Paul S. Forbes, December 22, 1857. Forbes MSS., typescript.

42. *Ibid.*, June 20, 1858.

43. John M. Forbes to William H. Swift, June 17, 1858. Forbes MSS., typescript.

44. *Ibid.* This correspondence was "inspired" by Samuel G. Ward, the Barings' Boston agent.

45. John M. Forbes to Paul S. Forbes, July 2, 1858. Forbes MSS., typescript.

46. *Ibid.*, August 2, 1858.

47. *Ibid.*

48. *Ibid.*, August 10, 1858.

49. *Ibid.*, September 21, 1858.

50. Hannibal and St. Joseph, *Annual Report*, 1859, 4, 19. After a struggle in which at least one man was killed, the Hannibal succeeded in ousting Duff & Company from the construction work. (See John M. Forbes to Paul S. Forbes, December 5, 1858. Forbes MSS., typescript.) For a statistical comparison of Hannibal finances with those of other Missouri roads in 1859, see *American Railroad Journal*, XXXII (February 19, 1859), 123–124. Discounts, commissions, and exchange accounts absorbed close to $2,400,000 out of a total of $8,445,000 represented by land, state and company bonds issued for the Hannibal. (*Ibid.*, 216.)

51. Hannibal and St. Joseph, *Annual Report*, 1859, 25.

52. William E. Hayes, *Iron Road to Empire* (New York, 1953), 23–25.

53. Overton, *Burlington West*, 55–62.

54. *Ibid.*, 65–66.

55. *Ibid.*, 68, 71.

56. *Ibid.*, 73.

57. Overton, *Burlington West*, 98.

58. John M. Forbes to Erastus Corning, May 11, 1857, quoted in Pearson, *An American Railroad Builder*, 86.

59. Pearson, *An American Railroad Builder*, 87.

60. John M. Forbes to Paul S. Forbes, March 17, 1857. Forbes MSS., typescript.

61. Overton, *Burlington West*, 99.

62. *American Railroad Journal,* XXX (April 25, 1857), 258.

63. *Ibid.,* 259. The circular may be found in Baker Library.

64. Pearson, *An American Railroad Builder,* 87; Burlington and Missouri River Railroad, *Annual Report,* 1858, 3.

65. Burlington and Missouri River, *Annual Report,* 1858, 2.

66. A copy of the 1858 trust mortgage may be found in the miscellaneous records of the Burlington and Missouri River Railroad, Corporation Records Division, Baker Library.

67. Cochran, *Railroad Leaders,* 40.

68. John M. Forbes to James F. Joy, January 1, 1858, quoted in Cochran, *Railroad Leaders,* 331.

69. John M. Forbes to Paul S. Forbes, September 21, 1858. Forbes MSS., typescript.

70. *Ibid.,* March 19, 1861.

71. Overton, *Burlington West,* 231

72. *Ibid.,* 108–111.

73. Edward W. Emerson, *Life and Letters of Charles Russell Lowell* (Boston and New York, 1907), 176.

74. Quoted in Overton, *Burlington West,* 112.

75. See Richard C. Overton, "Charles Elliott Perkins," *Business History Review,* XXXI (Autumn 1957), 292–309.

76. Quoted in Pearson, *An American Railroad Builder,* 102.

77. Pearson, *An American Railroad Builder,* 59.

78. Quoted in Sarah F. Hughes, ed., *Letters and Recollections of John Murray Forbes* (2 vols.; Boston, 1900), I, 167. The Michigan Southern was torn with strife, and at the end of August the unpaid balance of its floating debt was revealed to be larger than the whole debt was popularly supposed to be. (*American Railroad Journal,* XXX [August 29, 1857], 552.)

79. Pearson, *An American Railroad Builder,* 61. Brooks's anguish is reflected in a letter to R. N. Rice, October 7, 1857, in which he says: "I have not time to think of anything but *money money money* to pay our daily maturing debt with . . . A floating debt is the greatest curse man is heir to and for a corporation it is infinitely worse." (Quoted in Cochran, *Railroad Leaders,* 271.)

80. Pearson, *An American Railroad Builder,* 61.

81. *Ibid.,* 62.

82. *Ibid.,* 63.

83. *American Railroad Journal,* XXX (October 10, 1857), 641–642. See *ibid.,* 654, for the circular advertising this loan.

84. Michigan Central, *Annual Report,* 1859, 16.

85. John M. Forbes to Paul S. Forbes, October 16, 1857. Forbes MSS., typescript.

86. Hidy, *House of Baring,* 426–429.

87. *Ibid.,* 462–463.

88. *Ibid.,* 464. According to the *American Railroad Journal,* however, a sinking fund had been set up for the 1857 bonds before Forbes departed for England. (*American Railroad Journal,* XXX [October 10, 1857], 654.)

89. John M. Forbes to Paul S. Forbes, November 8, 1857. Forbes MSS., typescript.

90. *Ibid.,* November 21, 1857.

91. *American Railroad Journal,* XXX (October 17, 1857), 667. For the terms of the bids to be opened November 10, see *ibid.* (October 10, 1857), 654.

92. John M. Forbes to Paul S. Forbes, November 8, December 7, 1857. Forbes MSS., typescript.

93. Michigan Central, *Annual Report,* 1858, 9. The full terms of agreement reached by the Central with the Southern's new board may be found in *American Railroad Journal,* XXX (November 14, 1857), 730.

94. John M. Forbes to Paul S. Forbes, December 22, 1857. Forbes MSS., typescript.

95. *Ibid.,* November 8, 1857.

96. *American Railroad Journal,* XXX (December 26, 1857), 817–818.

97. John M. Forbes to Paul S. Forbes, December 22, 1857. Forbes MSS., typescript.
98. *American Railroad Journal,* XXXI (January 9, 1858), 24.
99. John M. Forbes to Paul S. Forbes, November 8, 1857. Forbes MSS., typescript.

CHAPTER 9
PREWAR RAILROAD INVESTORS: A BRIEF APPRAISAL

1. David A. Neal, Autobiography, Neal MSS., vol. 14, Baker Library, Harvard University Graduate School of Business Administration.
2. John M. Forbes to Paul S. Forbes, January 13, 1857. Forbes MSS., typescript, Baker Library. Forbes would not buy Illinois Central shares in September 1858, because he did "not know eno. about it to feel sure of it." (*Ibid.,* September 6, 1858.)
3. *Ibid.,* March 10, 1857.

CHAPTER 10
BOSTONIANS AND THE UNION PACIFIC RAILROAD, 1862–1873
CONSTRUCTION AND CONFLICT

1. Henry V. Poor, *The Pacific Railroad, The Relations Existing between It and the Government of the United States* (New York, 1871), 21–22. (Quoting Congressman Morrill's speech from the *Congressional Globe,* Part II, 2d session, 37th Congress, 1708).
2. *Ibid.,* 22. (Quoting Congressman Pike's speech from the *Congressional Globe, ibid.,* 1707).
3. *Ibid.,* 24. (Quoting Congressman Phelps's speech from the *Congressional Globe, ibid.,* 1590).
4. *Ibid.,* 27. (Quoting Senator Wilson's speech from the *Congressional Globe,* 3d vol., 2d Session, 37th Congress, 2257).
5. United States Pacific Railway Commission, *Testimony* (50th Congress, 1st Session, Senate Ex. Doc. 51, Washington, 1887), II, 875–877. Hereinafter cited as Pacific Railway Commission.
6. Thomas C. Durant testimony, in U.S. Congress, House, Select Committee (No. 2) on the Credit Mobilier, *Report* (42d Congress, 3d Session, House Report No. 78, February 20, 1873. Washington, 1873), 515. Hereinafter cited as Wilson Report.
7. Wilson Report, 597–598.
8. Oliver Ames testimony, *ibid.,* 256.
9. The Hoxie contract may be found in Wilson Report, Part II, 2–3, or in U.S. Congress, House, Select Committee to Investigate the Alleged Credit Mobilier Bribery, *Report* (42d Congress, 3d Session, House Report No. 77, February 18, 1873. Washington, 1873), 60–61. Hereinafter cited as Poland Report.
10. Poland Report, 61, 62.
11. *Ibid.,* 60–61.
12. Wilson Report, iv-v.
13. *Ibid.,* Part II, 4–5.
14. Durant testimony, *ibid.,* 64.
15. J. B. Crawford, *The Credit Mobilier of America* (Boston, 1880), 17–22.
16. Oliver Ames testimony, Wilson Report, 250.
17. J. M. S. Williams testimony, *ibid.,* 164.
18. Benjamin F. Ham testimony, *ibid.,* 20.
19. Robert W. Fogel, *The Union Pacific Railroad, A Case in Premature Enterprise* (Baltimore, 1960), 58.
20. Pondir testimony, Pacific Railway Commission, I, 438.
21. Durant testimony, Wilson Report, 88–89.
22. *Ibid.*
23. Subscription list to the Credit Mobilier, *ibid.,* 159–160.

24. Correspondence relating to this enterprise, in which Ames had invested $325,000, may be found in the Manuscripts Division, Baker Library, Harvard University Graduate School of Business Administration.

25. Alley testimony, Poland Report, 77; Wilson Report, 323.

26. Alley testimony, Poland Report, 77–78; Oakes Ames testimony, Wilson Report, 29, 724.

27. Helen A. Claflin, *A New England Family* (Belmont, Massachusetts, privately printed), 55–59.

28. Atkins testimony, Wilson Report, 303. Atkins dated his first purchase from January 1865, but his name is not listed in the stockholders of March 1865. *Ibid.*, 160.

29. List of stockholders of Credit Mobilier, *ibid.*, 155.

30. Edwin L. Sabin, *Building the Pacific Railway* (Philadelphia, 1919), 130.

31. Oakes Ames testimony, Wilson Report, 29.

32. Written statement by Oakes Ames, Poland Report, 16.

33. Fogel, *Union Pacific*, 76.

34. Oliver Ames testimony, Wilson Report, 252.

35. Nelson Trottman, *History of the Union Pacific, A Financial and Economic Survey* (New York, 1923), 32.

36. Fogel, *Union Pacific*, 63–64.

37. Henry K. White, *History of the Union Pacific Railway* (Chicago, 1895), 24.

38. John P. Davis, *The Union Pacific Railway, A Study in Railway Politics, History, and Economics* (Chicago, 1894), 164, 167.

39. Durant testimony, Wilson Report, 66–67; the Boomer contract may be found in *ibid.*, Part 2, Addenda, 7–8.

40. Durant testimony, *ibid.*, 66–69. See also *ibid.*, viii–ix.

41. Bushnell testimony, *ibid.*, 40–41.

42. Rowland Hazard, *The Credit Mobilier of America* (Providence, 1881), 20; Bushnell testimony, Wilson Report, 40–41; Poland Report, 179.

43. Bushnell testimony, Wilson Report, 40–41.

44. Durant testimony, Poland Report, 171.

45. Durant testimony, Wilson Report, 70–71.

46. For the proposals, see *ibid.*, 70, 162–163.

47. Bushnell, *ibid.*, 41.

48. *Ibid.*

49. *Ibid.*, 42. Advertisements appeared in the Boston *Advertiser* as early as April, 1867.

50. Bushnell testimony, Wilson Report, 42.

51. Durant testimony, Poland Report, 367.

52. The trusteeship agreement may be found in Wilson Report, Part II, Addenda, 13–16.

53. The Ames contract may be found in *ibid.*, Part II, 10–12.

54. Ham testimony, *ibid.*, 13.

55. Durant testimony, Poland Report, 372.

56. Bushnell testimony, Wilson Report, 42.

57. Bushnell testimony, *ibid.*, 41–42.

58. *McComb vs. The Credit Mobilier of America*, given in Poland Report, 56. Credit Mobilier declared a dividend of 12 per cent in 1867, covering both 1866 and 1867. Durant testimony, Wilson Report, 91–92.

59. Crane testimony, Wilson Report, 630.

60. Oliver Ames testimony, *ibid.*, 256.

61. Oakes Ames testimony, *ibid.*, 28.

62. See Fogel, *Union Pacific*, Appendix B, 117–119.

63. Poland Report, ii.

64. Trottman, *History of the Union Pacific*, 47.

65. Oliver Ames testimony, Wilson Report, 295; Alley testimony, *ibid.*, 317.

66. Trottman, *History of the Union Pacific*, 48.

67. *Ibid.*, 48–49.

68. Resolution of the U. P. directors, June 12, 1872, may be found in Wilson Report, 614–615. See also Fogel, *Union Pacific*, 111.

69. Oliver Ames to editors of New York *Evening Post*, January 14, 1871.

70. The circular may be found in Wilson Report, 358.

71. The circular may be found in *ibid.*, 359.

72. See Fogel, *Union Pacific*, 112–113, for a discussion of whether the difference of $1,168,000 is properly considered a profit.

73. The lists of stockholders may be found in Wilson Report, 155–160. Apparently Hooper took the full amount of increased stock plus U. P. bonds involved in the increased capitalization of Credit Mobilier. *In re Grimes*, see *ibid.*, 29.

74. Oakes Ames testimony, Poland Report, 20.

75. Letters quoted in Crawford, *Credit Mobilier*, 104–107.

76. Clark testimony, Wilson Report, 404.

77. Oakes Ames testimony, *ibid.*, 29.

78. Alley testimony, *ibid.*, 559. Although Alley gave the name as Wells, internal evidence indicates that he meant Weld.

79. Writing to J. B. Sanborn in June, 1878, Forbes declared: "It was a hard job Oakes Ames had to do in those times & I did not hanker after joining him in the undertaking when he would have given me as good terms as he did his Congressional partners." Quoted in Thomas C. Cochran, *Railroad Leaders, 1845–1890: The Business Mind in Action* (Cambridge, Massachusetts, 1953), 336.

80. Wilson Report, xx.

81. See Fogel's analysis of public response to U. P. securities, *Union Pacific*, 79–80.

82. Durant testified that the road cost approximately $20,000 per mile; while under the Ames contract the U. P. paid $42,000 and $45,000 per mile for this section. See Durant testimony, Wilson Report, 67.

83. John Duff testimony, *ibid.*, 493.

84. Durant testimony, *ibid.*, 116, 119.

85. Oakes Ames testimony, *ibid.*, 28.

86. *Ibid.*, xv.

87. Crawford, *Credit Mobilier*, 71–72.

88. Fogel, *Union Pacific*, 70–71.

CHAPTER 11

THE C. B. & Q., 1865–1873: CONFLICTING STRATEGIES OF EXPANSION

1. Richard C. Overton, *Burlington West: A Colonization History of the Burlington Railroad* (Cambridge, Massachusetts, 1941), letter, September 6, 1858, Appendix B, 493–504.

2. Burlington and Missouri River Railroad (Iowa), Circular, n.d. Corporation Records Division, Baker Library, Harvard University Graduate School of Business Administration.

3. B. and M. R., Circular by Edward L. Baker, President, to bondholders, September 20, 1861. Corporation Records, Baker Library.

4. B. and M. R., Circular to bondholders, October 7, 1863. Corporation Records, Baker Library.

5. Perkins to Forbes, March 27, 1865, quoted in Overton, *Burlington West*, 172.

6. B. and M. R., *Annual Report*, 1865, 5.

7. *Ibid.*, 4.

8. *Ibid.*

9. Edith P. Cunningham, ed., *Charles Elliott Perkins and Edith Forbes Perkins, Family Letters, 1861–1869* (Boston, 1949), 290.

10. Theodore S. Case, *History of Kansas City, Missouri* (Syracuse, New York, 1888), 142–143. For the early history of Kansas City, see Charles N. Glaab, "Business Patterns

in the Growth of a Midwestern City . . . ," *Business History Review,* XXXIII (Summer 1959), 156–174.

11. Charles N. Glaab, *Kansas City and the Railroads* (Madison, Wisconsin, 1962), 146–150.

12. *Ibid.,* 152–153.

13. Overton, *Burlington West,* 180.

14. *Ibid.;* Cunningham, *Family Letters,* 290, 293.

15. Case, *History of Kansas City,* 142–143.

16. See Circular dated January 25, 1867, by committees of the directors of the C. B. & Q. and Hannibal and St. Joseph to stockholders. Hannibal and St. Joseph file, Corporation Records, Baker Library.

17. Chicago, Burlington & Quincy Railroad, *Documentary History* (3 vols.; Chicago, 1928), I, 634.

18. Quoted in Thomas C. Cochran, *Railroad Leaders, 1845–1890: The Business Mind in Action* (Cambridge, Massachusetts, 1953), 333. (Deletions as in Cochran.)

19. Several Thayer account books were found in 1961 among the records of Kidder, Peabody & Company, successors to the Thayer firm. At the time of the preparation of this book, these records were on loan to Harvard University Graduate School of Business Administration. All references to Thayer's holdings are taken from these account books.

20. C. E. Perkins to his wife, September 7, 1886, in Cunningham, *Family Letters,* 319, n. 1.

21. Quoted in Overton, *Burlington West,* 180–181, n. 63.

22. C. B. & Q., *Documentary History,* II, 980.

23. Overton, *Burlington West,* 222.

24. Quoted in Overton, *Burlington West,* 221.

25. C. B. & Q., *Annual Report,* 1867, 29–30.

26. Denison to John M. Forbes, August 9, 1867, quoted in Overton, *Burlington West,* 220–221.

27. Robert E. Riegel, *The Story of the Western Railroads* (New York, 1926), 97–98.

28. Circular to C. B. & Q. stockholders, September 18, 1867. Corporation Records, Baker Library.

29. C. B. & Q., *Annual Report,* 1868, 16.

30. C. B. & Q., *Annual Report,* 1869, 13. Italics supplied.

31. Circular to C. B. & Q. stockholders, February 20, 1868. Corporation Records, Baker Library.

32. C. B. & Q., *Annual Report,* 1869, 12.

33. Brooks to John M. Forbes, April 2, 1868, quoted in Overton, *Burlington West,* 227.

34. Quoted in Cunningham, *Family Letters,* 320–321.

35. *A Letter to the Stockholders . . . of the Hannibal and St. Joseph Railroad Company . . .* (New York, 1870), 47. Corporation Records, Baker Library.

36. H. and St. J., Circular to stockholders, January 24, 1870, 3, 8. Corporation Records, Baker Library.

37. H. and St. J., *Annual Report,* 1872, 7.

38. See Missouri River, Fort Scott & Gulf Railroad Company, *Annual Report,* June, 1871, Appendix D, "An Act granting Lands to the State of Kansas . . . ," 50, 54.

39. Paul W. Gates, *Fifty Million Acres: Conflicts over Kansas Land Policy 1854–1890* (Ithaca, New York, 1954), 161–162.

40. Gates, *Fifty Million Acres,* 163.

41. *Ibid.,* 164.

42. *Ibid.,* 164–169.

43. *Poor's Manual of the Railroads of the United States,* 1870–1871, 406.

44. See C. B. & Q., *Documentary History,* II, 986–987.

45. K. C., St. J., C. B., *Annual Report,* 1871, 11–12.

46. *Ibid.,* 8.

47. *Ibid.*, 1872–1873, 6–7.
48. *Ibid.*, 8.
49. *Ibid.*, 1878, 17.
50. Julius Grodinsky, *Jay Gould, His Business Career, 1867–1892* (Philadelphia, 1957), 234; *Poor's Manual of Railroads*, 1880, 872.

CHAPTER 12
THE UNION PACIFIC RAILROAD, 1873–1890: CONSOLIDATION AND CONFLICT

1. Julius Grodinsky, *Jay Gould: His Business Career, 1867–1892* (Philadelphia, 1957), 117–118.
2. Gould testimony, U.S. Pacific Railway Commission, *Report* (10 vols.; U.S. Cong. Senate. 50th Cong., 1st Sess. Ex. Doc. 51. Washington, 1887), I, 446–447. Hereafter cited as Pacific Railway Commission. Dexter testimony, *ibid.*, II, 713.
3. Grodinsky, *Jay Gould*, 134–136.
4. *Ibid.*, 137, 139–141.
5. Gould testimony, Pacific Railway Commission, I, 451.
6. *The Railroad Gazette*, XI (February 21, 1879), 106.
7. F. L. Ames testimony, Pacific Railway Commission, II, 645–646.
8. Oliver Ames 2d, testimony, *ibid.*, II, 804, 813–814.
9. F. L. Ames testimony, *ibid.*, II, 646, 649–654.
10. *Ibid.*, II, 657, 660–662.
11. Gould testimony, *ibid.*, I, 505, 509.
12. F. L. Ames testimony, *ibid.*, II, 663.
13. *Ibid.*, II, 685–689.
14. Dexter testimony, *ibid.*, II, 704–705.
15. *Ibid.*, II, 703–704.
16. Oliver Ames testimony, *ibid.*, II, 818.
17. *Ibid.*, II, 809.
18. Oliver Ames testimony, *ibid.*, 805.
19. *Ibid.*, 806.
20. *Ibid.*, II, 807, 810.
21. *Ibid.*, II, 818.
22. From 1874 to 1880 there was no time when the Kansas Pacific was not in default on some interest charges. (Reports of Accountants, *ibid.*, VIII, 4975.) On the other hand, the K. P. was less heavily capitalized than the U. P. and was located in a fast-growing country. See Henry K. White, *History of the Union Pacific Railway* (Chicago, 1895), 56–57.
23. Nelson Trottman, *History of the Union Pacific: A Financial and Economic Survey* (New York, 1923), 164, 167.
24. Pacific Railway Commission, I, 558.
25. Trottman, *History of the Union Pacific*, 174. Gould and Russell Sage resigned as directors in 1885.
26. Pacific Railway Commission, II, 688, 730.
27. Atkins testimony, *ibid.*, II, 774.
28. *Ibid.*, II, 779, 781.
29. Adams testimony, *ibid.*, II, 972–973.
30. Arthur Pound and Samuel T. Moore, eds., *More They Told Barron* (New York, 1931), 117.
31. Quoted in White, *History of the Union Pacific*, 63–64, footnote.
32. *Ibid.*, 64, footnote.
33. *Charles Francis Adams, 1835–1915: An Autobiography . . .* (Boston, 1916), 191–192.
34. John P. Davis, *The Union Pacific Railway: A Study in Railway Politics, History, and Economics* (Chicago, 1894), 216–217.

35. Union Pacific Railroad Company *v.* United States, 99 U.S. 402–434.
36. *Ibid.*
37. Trottman, *History of the Union Pacific,* 209.
38. *Ibid.,* 213–214.
39. Charles Francis Adams, Jr., before the Committee on the Pacific Railroads, February 24, 1886, *The Case of the Union Pacific Railway Company,* Statement.
40. *Ibid.,* 4.
41. *Ibid.,* 6.
42. Charles F. Adams, Jr. to Colgate Hoyt, n.d., in Union Pacific Railway, *Annual Report,* 1884, 170–172.
43. Charles F. Adams, Jr., *Case of the Union Pacific,* 3–4.
44. Charles F. Adams, Jr. to Senator George F. Hoar, February 9, 1885, in U. P. *Annual Report,* 1884, 173–175.
45. Charles F. Adams, Jr., *Case of the Union Pacific,* 10.
46. Trottman, *History of the Union Pacific,* 230.
47. U.S. Pacific Railway Commission, *Report of the Commission and of the Minority Commissioner* (*Report,* vol. 10), as summarized in Trottman, *History of the Union Pacific,* 233–234.
48. Trottman, *History of the Union Pacific,* 234–235.
49. Quoted in U. P. *Annual Report,* 1888, 7–8.
50. *Ibid.,* 1889, 9.
51. Charles F. Adams, Jr., *Case of the Union Pacific,* 7.
52. U. P., *Annual Report,* 1889, 11.
53. Grodinsky, *Jay Gould,* 577–578.
54. *Commercial and Financial Chronicle,* II (November 15, 1890), 681.
55. Pound and Moore, eds., *More They Told Barron,* 114–117.
56. *Ibid.,* 121.
57. *Ibid.,* 114.
58. White, *History of the Union Pacific,* 90, 116–117, 119, 121.
59. Robert W. Fogel, *The Union Pacific Railroad, A Case in Premature Enterprise* (Baltimore, 1960), 98–102.

Chapter 13

The C. B. & Q., 1874–1890: Completion of the System

1. Joy to Newell, March 27, 1871, quoted in Thomas C. Cochran, *Railroad Leaders, 1845–1890: The Business Mind in Action* (Cambridge, Massachusetts, 1953), 368.
2. See the statement of this policy in C. B. & Q. *Annual Report,* 1870, 14.
3. Joy to Nathaniel Thayer, September 10, 1875, quoted in Cochran, *Railroad Leaders,* 113.
4. See *Commercial & Financial Chronicle,* XX, (February 20, 1875), 184–185.
5. See Thomas C. Cochran, "The Legend of the Robber Barons," *The Pennsylvania Magazine of History and Biography,* LXXIV (July 1950), 316–318.
6. Cochran, *Railroad Leaders,* 114.
7. Quoted, *ibid.,* 113–114.
8. Quoted, *ibid.,* 114.
9. John M. Forbes to Green, June 16, 1873, *ibid.,* 334.
10. July 13, 1873, quoted in Henry G. Pearson, *An American Railroad Builder, John Murray Forbes* (Boston, 1911), 163.
11. Quoted, *ibid.,* 167.
12. *Ibid.,* 173; see *Commercial & Financial Chronicle,* XX (February 20, 1875), 184–185.
13. Sarah Forbes Hughes, ed., *Letters and Recollections of John Murray Forbes* (2 vols.; Boston, 1900), II, 215.
14. Forbes to Joy, May 14, 1875, as quoted in Cochran, *Railroad Leaders,* 114.

15. See Pearson, *An American Railroad Builder,* 174–178, for Forbes's account of the maneuvers. See also New York *Tribune* for the month of February 1876.

16. John M. Forbes to Griswold, February 14, 1875, quoted in Cochran, *Railroad Leaders,* 334.

17. *Commercial & Financial Chronicle,* XX (February 20, 1875), 185. Eventually the directors who were involved in the River Roads, and who remained on the C. B. & Q. board, repaid the company for their coupons. (C. G. & Q. *Annual Report,* 1878, 25.) For details of subsequent controversy between Forbes and Joy, see Statement of the Case of John A. Burnham, J. N. Denison, and James H. Blake, Trustees, *vs.* The Chicago, Burlington and Quincy R. R. Co., for Wm. G. Russel, Arbitrator. Corporation Records Division, Baker Library, Harvard University Graduate School of Business Administration.

18. *Poor's Manual of Railroads,* 1875–1876, 504. Joy continued as president of the Michigan Central until 1877. Burnham continued as a director of the B. and M. R. in Nebraska.

19. *Ibid.,* 1876–1877, 290.

20. Richard C. Overton, *Burlington West, a Colonization History of the Burlington Railroad* (Cambridge, Massachusetts, 1941), 397.

21. Julius Grodinsky, *Jay Gould, His Business Career, 1867–1892* (Philadelphia, 1957), 226.

22. C. B. & Q. *Annual Report,* 1876, 3.

23. *Ibid.,* 19–20.

24. See map of the C. B. & Q. in 1877 in the *Annual Report* for that year.

25. C. B. & Q. *Annual Report,* 1878, 18.

26. Perkins to Tyson, December 27, 1879, quoted in Overton, *Burlington West,* 401.

27. John M. Forbes to Perkins, July 12, 1879, quoted in Cochran, *Railroad Leaders,* 337.

28. Perkins to John M. Forbes, November 22, 1879, quoted in Cochran, *Railroad Leaders,* 433.

29. Perkins to John M. Forbes, November 24, 1879, *ibid.* (Deletions as in Cochran.)

30. John M. Forbes to Lucius Tuckerman, February 14, 1880, *ibid.,* 338.

31. C. B. & Q., *Annual Report,* 1880, 18.

32. *Poor's Manual of Railroads,* 1881, 623.

33. Hughes, ed., *Letters and Recollections,* II, 216–217.

34. John M. Forbes to F. L. Ames, September 8, 1880, quoted in Cochran, *Railroad Leaders,* 339.

35. Perkins to John M. Forbes, September 26, 1880, quoted in *ibid.,* 434.

36. For details of Perkins-Gould maneuvering, see Grodinsky, *Jay Gould,* 238–248.

37. C. B. & Q., *Annual Report,* 1881, 18–19.

38. C. B. & Q., *Annual Report,* 1882, 17.

39. *Commercial & Financial Chronicle,* XXXI (September 1880), 259.

40. C. B. & Q., *Annual Report,* 1883, 17.

41. *Poor's Manual of Railroads,* 1881, 623; *ibid.,* 1891, 650, 656.

42. C. B. & Q., *Annual Report,* 1890, 22.

43. *The Railway Review,* XXX (September 27, 1890), 565, quoting *Wall Street News* (n.d.).

44. For example, see C. B. & Q., letter to stockholders from J. N. Denison, February 13, 1873, concerning the B. and M. R. A dividend was frequently involved, as in the case of the B. and M. R. in Nebraska when it was merged in 1880.

45. See *Commercial & Financial Chronicle,* XXVII (December 21, 1878), 651.

46. C. B. & Q., *Annual Report,* 1878, 16.

47. *Commercial & Financial Chronicle,* XXVII (December 21, 1878), 651.

48. C. B. & Q., *Annual Report,* 1879, 18–19.

49. *The Railroad Gazette,* XI (December 5, 1879), 652.

50. C. B. & Q., *Annual Report,* 1879, 21.

51. *Ibid.,* 1871, 18.

52. *Ibid.*, 1879, 19.
53. Cochran, *Railroad Leaders*, 72–73.
54. See C. B. & Q., letter to stockholders, October 12, 1863; C. B. & Q., *Annual Report*, 1869, 21.
55. C. B. & Q., letter to stockholders, August 15, 1871.
56. John M. Forbes to William Endicott, Jr., April 27, 1881, quoted in Cochran, *Railroad Leaders*, 72.
57. *Commercial & Financial Chronicle*, XXXI (December 4, 1880), 588.
58. John M. Forbes to J. N. A. Griswold, May 12, 1880, quoted in Cochran, *Railroad Leaders*, 338.
59. John M. Forbes to George B. Roberts, November (n.d.) 1880, quoted in *ibid.*, 339.
60. John M. Forbes to N. M. Beckwith, March 30, 1881, *ibid.*
61. *Commercial & Financial Chronicle*, XXXIV (June 17, 1882), 687. Power to increase the stock was granted to the directors at a meeting of the company March 24, 1880.
62. C. B. & Q., Circular of September 15, 1881.
63. *Commercial & Financial Chronicle*, XXXIV (March 25, 1882), 343.
64. C. B. & Q., *Annual Report*, 1888, 19–20.
65. *Ibid.*, 624. Compare with somewhat different figures in *Poor's Manual of Railroads*, 1891, 655.
66. U.S. Cong. Senate. Committee on Finance. *Wholesale Prices, Wages, and Transportation* (Washington, 1893), Pt. I, 617.
67. Pamphlet reprinted from Boston *Daily Advertiser*, January 25, 1889, 2, 3, 10, 13.
68. *Commercial & Financial Chronicle*, XLIV (April 2, 1887), 415–416.
69. *Poor's Manual of Railroads*, 1891, 655. A detailed comparison of significant financial data for 1873–1890 can be found on page 656.
70. C. B. & Q., *Annual Report*, 1890, 19, 21–22, *passim.*
71. *Railroad Gazette*, V (April 12, 1873), 148.
72. John M. Forbes to Charles E. Perkins, December 29, 1888, as quoted in Cochran, *Railroad Leaders*, 138–139.
73. October 3, 1883, quoted by Ralph Budd, president of the C. B. & Q., in an address before the American Newcomen Society, *The Burlington Railroad's Boston Background* (Boston, April 22, 1949), 12.
74. Quoted, *ibid.*, 16.
75. Michigan Central, *Annual Report*, 1848, 23.
76. U.S. Census. *Abstract of the Eleventh Census; 1890*, 12; Overton, *Burlington West*, 536.

Chapter 14
The Atchison, Topeka & Santa Fe, 1870–1883: A New Response to the Transcontinental Challenge

1. Atchison, Topeka & Santa Fe Railroad, Manuscript list of stockholders . . . October 11, 1883. Corporation Records, Baker Library, Harvard University School of Business Administration; section on the Atchison in [Clarence W. Barron], *The Boston Stock Exchange* . . . (Boston, 1893), unpaginated.
2. Two standard works on the railroad, which have been drawn on for much of the general material here, are: Glenn D. Bradley, *The Story of the Santa Fe* (Boston, 1920) and Lawrence L. Waters, *Steel Trails to Santa Fe* (Lawrence, Kansas, 1950).
3. *Zarah, Its Present and Future* (a promotional pamphlet, 1871), 4.
4. Interstate Commerce Commission, 127 *Val. Rpt.* 1 [Valuation Docket 625, "Atchison, Topeka & Santa Fe"], 361.
5. *Ibid.* A discount of $22,000 (20 per cent) was mentioned, although evidence exists that within two months the Boston firm was offering bonds at 85, plus a 5 per cent

stock bonus (Kidder, Peabody & Company, Circular, November 1, 1870). Henry Keyes, Thomas Nickerson, and Oliver W. Peabody were trustees for the bonds.

6. *Documents Relating to the Atchison, Topeka & Santa Fe Railroad* (1890), I, 61–2. In addition, 1,500 shares were substituted for $150,000 of county bonds which did not materialize. If we include the exchange of stock for county bonds, the transactions with the Associates and Kidder, Peabody, and other security transactions, by the end of 1873 the following outstanding liabilities were in existence (according to the *Annual Report* for the year ending March 31, 1873): $8,615,000 capital stock; $7,041,000 first-mortgage bonds; $3,455,500 land-mortgage bonds; $1,600,000 consolidated mortgage bonds; and $530,000 long-term notes.

7. Julius Grodinsky, *Transcontinental Railway Strategy, 1869–1893* (Philadelphia, 1962), 41. For Nickerson, see the obituary in the *Railroad Gazette* (July 29, 1892), 569; Henry Hall, ed., *America's Successful Men of Affairs* (New York, 1896), II, 593–594.

8. A. T. & S. F., Manuscript list of stockholders . . . 1883.

9. See Charles Francis Adams, "The Canal and Railroad Enterprise of Boston," in Justin Winsor, ed., *The Memorial History of Boston* (4 vols., Boston, 1883), IV, 147.

10. A. T. & S. F., *Annual Report*, 1873, 25. Also see the descriptive brochure: *The Atchison, Topeka & Santa Fe Railroad* (Boston, 1871), 11.

11. Julian D. Morgan, *Some Controlling Factors in Kansas Population Movements* (Lawrence, Kansas, 1953), 31.

12. A. T. & S. F., *Annual Report*, 1875, 27–28.

13. Calculated from *Annual Reports.*

14. Paul W. Gates, *Fifty Million Acres: Conflicts over Kansas Land Policy, 1854–1890* (Ithaca, New York, 1954), 269–272.

15. For details, see Waters, *Steel Trails*, 223–234, 238, 242–245.

16. A. T. & S. F., *Annual Report*, 1874, 25.

17. *Ibid.*, 1875, 27.

18. *Ibid.*, 1879, 42. The experimental stations were described in *ibid.*, 1874, 42–43.

19. Quoted in Waters, *Steel Trails*, 241.

20. U.S. Bureau of Statistics, *Report on . . . Internal Commerce . . . 1889*, 192, 208.

21. *Ibid.*, 193. For data on yields and acreage of grains, see *ibid.*, 219–222, 235. The same source (238) gives the following figures for the number of livestock packed in the state:

Dates	Cattle	Hogs
1868:	4,200	13,000
1870:	21,000	36,000
1880:	30,992	530,097
1885:	78,903	1,529,415
1888:	361,252	1,578,240

22. Adams, "Canal and Railroad Enterprise," 147.

23. Waters, *Steel Trails*, 76.

24. Grodinsky, *Transcontinental Railway Strategy*, 115–116.

25. *Ibid.*, 165–166.

26. *Ibid.*, 64–66.

27. *Commercial & Financial Chronicle*, XXXIV (March 4, 1882), 243–244.

28. Published letter to Kidder, Peabody & Co., and Lee, Higginson & Co., April 15, 1882.

29. Gates, *Fifty Million Acres*, 170–179.

30. *Ibid.*, 197–200, 203–206, 210.

31. A. T. & S. F., *Annual Report*, 1880, 6.

32. Julius Grodinsky, *Jay Gould, His Business Career, 1867–1892* (Philadelphia, 1957), 234–236.

33. *Commercial & Financial Chronicle*, XXXI (October 9, 1880), 381.

34. *Ibid.*, XXXII (April 23, 1881), 432.

35. Rendig Fels, *American Business Cycles, 1865–1897* (Chapel Hill, North Carolina, 1959), 121.

36. Fred A. Shannon, *The Farmer's Last Frontier: Agriculture, 1860–1897* (New York, 1945), 417.

37. A. T. & S. F., *Annual Report,* 1882, 19.

38. Financial data from Coolidge ledgers. Manuscript Division, Baker Library.

39. *Commercial & Financial Chronicle,* XXX (May 22, 1880), 533.

40. Perkins Letters, 1880–1901, in Cunningham-Overton Collection of Perkins' Papers, University of Western Ontario.

41. Charles E. Perkins to John M. Forbes, November 4, 1880, in *ibid.*

42. T. Jefferson Coolidge, *Autobiography . . . , 1831–1920* (Boston, 1923), 88.

43. *Documents Relating to the A. T. & S. F.,* 62–64.

44. Clarence H. Venner & Company, *Facts for Investors Concerning the Atchison, Topeka and Santa Fe R. R. Company* (Boston, March, 1883).

45. *Commercial & Financial Chronicle,* XXXIV (April 29, 1882), 475; A. T. & S. F., *Annual Reports,* 1875, 1882.

46. A. T. & S. F., *Annual Report,* 1883, 6, 9.

47. *Ibid.,* 11.

48. Grodinsky, *Transcontinental Railway Strategy,* 220–222.

49. Waters, *Steel Trails,* 130.

50. Letters from Kidder, Peabody & Co., George B. Wilbur, Lucius G. Pratt, B. P. Cheney, Thomas Nickerson, and A. B. Lawrie to Stock and Bondholders of the California Southern Railroad, October 25, 1884. Corporation Records, Baker Library.

51. A. T. & S. F., *Annual Report,* 1885, 22.

52. Quoted in *ibid.,* 1886, 22.

53. *Ibid.,* 27.

54. Charles E. Perkins to Henry L. Higginson, October 20, 1886, Charles E. Perkins Letters, 1880–1901, in Cunningham-Overton Collection of Perkins' Papers, University of Western Ontario.

55. Charles E. Perkins to John M. Forbes, October 21, 1886, *ibid.*

56. Quoted in Grodinsky, *Transcontinental Railway Strategy,* 281.

57. Waters, *Steel Trails,* 85.

Chapter 15

The Atchison, Topeka & Santa Fe, 1880–1890: Financial Aspects of Expansion

1. Boston *Herald,* November 16, 1880.

2. *Commercial & Financial Chronicle,* XXXI (December 18, 1880), 638–639.

3. Atchison, Topeka & Santa Fe Railroad, Manuscript list of stockholders . . . October 11, 1883. Corporation Records, Baker Library, Harvard University Graduate School of Business Administration.

4. F. H. Peabody to George Magoun, May 7, 1888, Kidder, Peabody & Company, Confidential Letter Book, 1887–1895, 31.

5. The following letters are examples: Oliver W. Peabody to Jesse Seligman, February 18, 1885; Peabody to Benjamin P. Cheney, March 4, 1885; Peabody to Cheney, July 10, 1885. *Ibid.,* 1883–1887.

6. Oliver W. Peabody to Francis H. Peabody, in London, September 20, 1886. *Ibid.,* 46–47.

7. Letter to finance committee of the A. T. & S. F., July 30, 1888. *Ibid.,* 1887–1895, 59–60.

8. A .T. & S. F., *Annual Report,* 1888, 10–11.

9. *Ibid.,* 16.

10. *Ibid.,* 16–17.

11. *Ibid.,* 17.

12. Kidder, Peabody, Confidential Letter Book, 1887–1895, 69½.
13. Letter to William B. Strong, October 16, 1888, *ibid.*, 70.
14. Francis H. Peabody to J. J. McCook, October 20, 1888, *ibid.*, 72.
15. *Commercial & Financial Chronicle,* XLVIII (April 9, 1889), 462.
16. *Ibid.* (May 11, 1889), 610, 632–633.
17. *Ibid.*, XLIX (August 31, 1889), 262, 268; *ibid.* (September 7, 1889), 300.
18. *Ibid.* (October 19, 1889), 483.
19. For the reorganization plan, see *ibid.;* A. T. & S. F., *Annual Report,* 1890, 16–32.
20. *Commercial & Financial Chronicle,* XLIX (December 21, 1889), 804.
21. Letter to Edwin H. Abbott, October 23, 1889, Kidder, Peabody, Confidential Letter Book, 1887–1895, 100.
22. Letter, December 12, 1889, *ibid.*, 106.
23. *Commercial & Financial Chronicle,* L (May 10, 1890), 661.
24. A. T. & S. F., *Annual Report,* 1890, 13.
25. *Ibid.* See also *Commercial & Financial Chronicle,* XLIX (December 21, 1889), 804–805.
26. See Lawrence L. Waters, *Steel Trails to Santa Fe* (Lawrence, Kansas, 1950), 205 ff.

Index

HARVARD STUDIES IN BUSINESS HISTORY

1. JOHN JACOB ASTOR, BUSINESS MAN, by Kenneth Wiggins Porter
2. JAY COOKE, PRIVATE BANKER, by Henrietta M. Larson
3. THE JACKSONS AND THE LEES: TWO GENERATIONS OF MASSACHUSETTS MERCHANTS, 1765–1844, by Kenneth Wiggins Porter
4. THE MASSACHUSETTS–FIRST NATIONAL BANK OF BOSTON, 1784–1934, by N. S. B. Gras
5. THE HISTORY OF AN ADVERTISING AGENCY: N. W. AYER & SON AT WORK, 1869–1949, revised edition, by Ralph M. Hower
6. MARKETING LIFE INSURANCE: ITS HISTORY IN AMERICA, by J. Owen Stalson
7. HISTORY OF MACY'S OF NEW YORK, 1858–1919: CHAPTERS IN THE EVOLUTION OF THE DEPARTMENT STORE, by Ralph M. Hower
8. THE WHITESMITHS OF TAUNTON: A HISTORY OF REED & BARTON, 1824–1943, by George Sweet Gibb
9. DEVELOPMENT OF TWO BANK GROUPS IN THE CENTRAL NORTHWEST: A STUDY IN BANK POLICY AND ORGANIZATION, by Charles Sterling Popple
10. THE HOUSE OF HANCOCK: BUSINESS IN BOSTON, 1724–1775, by W. T. Baxter
11. TIMING A CENTURY: HISTORY OF THE WALTHAM WATCH COMPANY, by C. W. Moore
12. GUIDE TO BUSINESS HISTORY: MATERIALS FOR THE STUDY OF AMERICAN BUSINESS AND SUGGESTIONS FOR THEIR USE, by Henrietta M. Larson
13. PEPPERELL'S PROGRESS: HISTORY OF A COTTON TEXTILE COMPANY, 1844–1945, by Evelyn H. Knowlton
14. THE HOUSE OF BARING IN AMERICAN TRADE AND FINANCE: ENGLISH MERCHANT BANKERS AT WORK, 1763–1861, by Ralph W. Hidy
15. THE WHITIN MACHINE WORKS SINCE 1831: A TEXTILE MACHINERY COMPANY IN AN INDUSTRIAL VILLAGE, by Thomas R. Navin
16. THE SACO–LOWELL SHOPS: TEXTILE MACHINERY BUILDING IN NEW ENGLAND, 1813–1949, by George Sweet Gibb
17. BROADLOOMS AND BUSINESSMEN: A HISTORY OF THE BIGELOW–SANFORD CARPET COMPANY, 1825–1953, by John S. Ewing and Nancy P. Norton
18. NATHAN TROTTER: PHILADELPHIA MERCHANT, 1787–1853, by Elva Tooker
19. A HISTORY OF THE MASSACHUSETTS HOSPITAL LIFE INSURANCE COMPANY, by Gerald T. White
20. THE CHARLES ILFELD COMPANY: A STUDY OF THE RISE AND DECLINE OF MERCANTILE CAPITALISM IN NEW MEXICO, by William J. Parish

21. THE RISE AND DECLINE OF THE MEDICI BANK, 1397–1494, by Raymond de Roover

22. ISAAC HICKS: NEW YORK MERCHANT AND QUAKER, 1767–1820, by Robert A. Davison

23. BOSTON CAPITALISTS AND WESTERN RAILROADS: A STUDY IN THE NINETEENTH-CENTURY RAILROAD INVESTMENT PROCESS, by Arthur M. Johnson and Barry E. Supple